A GOLDEN AGE

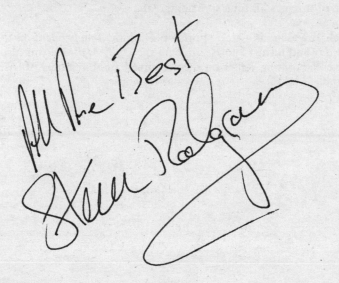

Born in Marlow in Buckinghamshire, Steve Redgrave was 13 years old when he began rowing at Great Marlow School. Now a five-times Olympic gold medal winner, Steve is undeniably one of Britain's all-time sporting greats.

Nick Townsend is a staff sportswriter on the *Independent on Sunday* and former sportswriter on the *Daily Mail*. He was also the collaborating writer on the acclaimed autobiography of Irish gambler and racehorse trainer, Barney Curley.

A GOLDEN AGE

Steve Redgrave: The Autobiography
with Nick Townsend

BBC
BOOKS

Published by BBC Books, BBC Worldwide Limited,
Woodlands, 80 Wood Lane, London W12 0TT

First published 2000
Reprinted 2000 (three times)
First published in paperback 2001
Reprinted 2001 (twice)
Reprinted 2002
This edition first published 2004

ISBN: 0563 52203 8

Printed and bound in Great Britain by Mackays of Chatham
Colour separations by Radstock Reproductions Ltd
Colour section printed by Lawrence-Allen Ltd, Weston-super-Mare
Cover printed by Belmont Press Ltd, Northampton

CHAPTER 1

LURE OF SYDNEY
IS TOO STRONG

I t was 10.30 on the morning of 23 September 2000. The water of Penrith Lakes, scene of the Sydney Olympics regatta course, was, thankfully, relatively calm, barely stirred by a slight head-wind, as I made my final preparations for the last day of my major international rowing life. Behind me lay a 24-year rowing career; before me lay a little over six minutes in which the product of four years of labours would, if all went to plan, be a fifth consecutive Olympic gold medal.

If successful, I was aware that many were ready to acclaim the fact it would immortalize my name in the annals of Olympic history. But no such thoughts were in my mind then. They never had been, even when I had decided four years earlier that there was another Olympics in me. It was just another race and, if we won, I would be the recipient of a gold medal at Sydney – the one I hadn't got. That's the way I had to regard it. I had come through too much frustration, worry and pain in the intervening period, indeed we all had – Matthew Pinsent, Tim Foster and James Cracknell – to jeopardize things now by thinking beyond the next 360 seconds. More than once during those four years I had seriously considered my future as I was struck by chronic illness and self-doubt about my ability to stay the course.

Yet, here I was, ready to respond to the green light with a sus-tained burst of energy-sapping strokes. We knew our sheer power would propel us clear of the field after just a few strokes. Could we maintain it until the finish, 2000 metres away? I looked around. Conditions were excellent. I couldn't have felt more pleased. Our warm-up had gone well. Everything felt good. So good, that in a strange kind of way I didn't even want it to start. I was enjoying the occasion too much. But then the starter went through the roll-call of six finalists in the Olympic coxless fours: ourselves, Italy, the USA, New Zealand, Austria and Slovenia. As he did so, the thought went through my mind: 'We're going to win this. We're going to win this by quite a long way.'

As thousands of British supporters at the Olympic regatta course and many millions more back home watching on television were to discover, that's not quite how it turned out. But nothing about the previous four years had exactly gone smoothly. That final was no exception. Indeed, considering what I had said after winning my fourth Olympic gold at Atlanta, there were those who doubted whether I would be at Sydney at all.

•

I have never been allowed to forget the declaration I made one sweltering July morning at Lake Lanier, outside Atlanta, Georgia. I had just won my fourth consecutive Olympic gold medal, making me one of only six men ever to achieve that feat. Together with my partner in the coxless pairs event, Matthew Pinsent, who was celebrating his second Olympic gold, I was still recovering from the exertion and in a state combining euphoria with fatigue. We had paddled slowly back to the pontoon, from where we would make our way to the medal podium to accept the only gold medals presented to Britons in any sport at those Games, but were intercepted by Dan Topolski. He is a former international oarsman, Oxford Boat Race coach, and writer, then working at the Games for BBC Television. At such moments, the last thing you want is a microphone thrust into your face. However, instant reaction is what TV demands these days. Dan crouched down to conduct an interview as I sat in the boat, the adrenaline still rushing through me with the force of a newly drilled oil-well after the 240 strokes of our blades in 380 seconds that had repelled the runners-up, Australia, by just under a second.

I cannot recall Dan's first question, and have absolutely no memory of my reply, but apparently I blurted out the words, as I attempted to catch my breath: 'If anybody sees me near a boat again, they have my permission to shoot me. I've had enough.' To my eternal embarrassment, the strange fact is that the only thing I do remember about those few seconds is swearing. Dan had gestured towards Matthew and asked me, 'What do you think about this fellow?'

Without thinking, I gushed: 'This guy's a f****** powerhouse.' True, but not the way I'd articulate it in a more reflective condition.

This was live television, and I immediately realized with abject horror exactly what I'd said. It was bizarre, because I'm not normally one who curses, at least not in normal conversation. Certainly not on TV. I thought to myself, 'Don't make an issue out of it. Just carry on. Pretend nothing's happened.' I believe it was cut in subsequent transmissions. At least, I hope so.

I heard those first words seemingly nearly every day of my life in the following four years. They became a media catchphrase. Even the Queen mentioned it when Matthew and I attended a lunch at Buckingham Palace later that same year. 'Ah, yes,' she said, with a knowing smile, 'you're the person who's *never* going to get in a boat again.' If that statement constantly reminded people of what I'd achieved, I wasn't going to complain – even if, as the sporting world was soon to discover, there was no truth in it. Sportsmen are about as reliable as the late Frank Sinatra when it comes to making a final curtain call. Yet anybody who heard that announcement may, rightly, be wondering why that same man committed one of the greatest U-turns in Olympic history and, four years later, was back there, seated in that Great Britain coxless fours boat, awaiting the start at Sydney 2000.

What nobody at the time – not even my family, although my wife Ann undoubtedly had her suspicions – realized is that there was never any real chance that I would have quit. In fact, you would have had to shoot me to keep me out of that boat in Australia.

To explain just why I uttered that now-famous quote, it is necessary to go back to the summer of the previous year, 1995. It was following the World Championships in Tampere, Finland, that I began to tell people that I was going to retire after Atlanta. Matthew, my close friend as well as my crew-mate for the past six years, had been interviewed, also by Dan Topolski, for the BBC at those championships. At the end of the interview, Dan had said light-heartedly, 'Oh, Steve's not going to give up, is he?'

According to Dan, Matthew got quite shirty about the suggestion and replied with words to the effect, 'Of course he is. Don't be stupid!' After Dan relayed this to me, I thought to myself, 'Either we've got to sit down and discuss this or I've got to take the heat out of the situation.' I decided on the latter.

At Sydney, Matthew would be challenging for his third Olympic gold (assuming that all went well for us at Atlanta), and there's only been a handful of people in British Olympic history who have ever done that. Yet that feat would always be overshadowed if he occupied the same boat as someone bidding for his fifth.

He had done his apprenticeship and earned his first Olympic gold at Barcelona in 1992, then repeated it with me at Atlanta. I suspected that Matthew felt it was his turn to be king in British rowing, without his glory deflected by one of the most successful Olympians of all time. I could fully understand that.

I honestly hadn't given the matter a lot of thought until that moment. But then it began to concern me. Matthew was mentally prepared for me to stop. The message was clear that this was potentially a source of friction. That's the last thing you need in a pair when preparing for an Olympic Games. I didn't want to disturb the equilibrium. I was pretty sure, although not 100 per cent, that I was going to carry on, but I felt that it wasn't worth having a conversation to explain that and for it, possibly, to end in conflict. So I took the easier option and just went along with the general perception among fellow-oarsmen and journalists that I was going to retire. Nobody really makes a decision like that in a split second after a race, nor do they do so in the months leading up to it.

My life has always involved the constant search for new challenges. If I needed an incentive, it was that the celebrated British rower Guy Nickalls, from my own Henley-based club Leander, came out of retirement to win an Olympic gold medal at the age of 42. Admittedly, that was back in 1908!

Matthew himself claimed during the lead-up to Sydney that he was not sure if he was going to continue if we won the gold. Until it's all over you're never 100 per cent certain how you feel.

Only one man knew my true feelings. When we were out at a training camp in Australia prior to Atlanta, I went off on my own with our coach, Jurgen Grobler, one afternoon to discuss a few matters. Matthew had stayed behind to rest. During our talk, Jurgen put the question to me directly. 'Are you going to give up at the end of the year?'

'I don't think I am,' I replied. 'I'm going to carry on for another four years, for Sydney.'

'I thought that was the case,' Jurgen said. And that was how we left it.

That was in January 1996, and was the only conversation Jurgen and I ever had on the subject.

Yet the more I confirmed that I was going to retire, initially to keep the peace, the more I convinced myself that I would never row again afterwards. By the time we were six weeks away from the Atlanta Games and seriously into the build-up, I was beginning to feel a heavy pressure of expectation, from my family and friends and the media. The hours before the final at Atlanta were the worst. But then they always were. There have been times when you'd almost have had to press-gang me into the boat before a race.

That's the horrible part about racing, the two or three hours beforehand. People don't realize the sheer hell of waiting around when you are favourites to claim the gold. It's far worse than the pain you endure in the race. It's the sitting around, the waiting and imagining how much it's going to hurt, and going over in your head whether you are going to win. All kinds of thoughts wing their way into your head so that your mind is like a cave full of bats. Your stomach turns. The toilet seat seems a better bet than the one in the boat. The bigger the event, the worse it gets.

I don't know how many times I've gone off to be by myself at a World Championships or an Olympic Games with the minutes ticking down ever so slowly, with thousands of thoughts in my mind. 'What the *f**** am I doing here? *Why* am I doing it? I don't want to be here. It's absolutely *horrible*.' At Atlanta, I was just walking around saying to myself: 'The pressure's too much. I just can't do this at all.' If somebody had given me any sort of excuse to pull out, I'd have happily done so. But then you have mentally to give yourself a slap and say, 'Steve, if you keep thinking like this you're not going to get the best out of yourself. You're not going to win.'

You have to pull yourself together and tell yourself, 'Right, you've done all this training. If you don't go out there and race now, if you don't go out and do yourself justice just because you don't fancy it, what a waste it all will have been.'

What I did was to visualize the race, picture ourselves, and alongside us the Australian pair, whom we knew would be our principal rivals. Then I said to myself, 'What are you going to do about it?' The answer was, of course, 'There's no way I'm going to let them beat me.' I just kept picturing myself in that situation.

Then I said: 'Right, I'm going to go out there and give it my best shot, but that's it. I'm never going to do it again. You've kidded yourself in the past, but this really is going to be the final one. You won't have to go through all this again.' That's how I motivated myself and that's probably the origin of my statement to Dan after Atlanta.

Despite all those promises to myself, I have kept coming back, of course. In the same way that a recidivist keeps burgling homes.

Some months after that Olympics or World Championships, I could be sitting there following a particularly hard training session or be rowing upstream against a high flood stream with the wind howling against me, and suddenly I would remember that vow I made and think to myself, 'I said I was never going to do this again. Why am I back here? Why am I doing this?' You realize that what you have told yourself at the Olympics is just to get you through that situation at that particular time, to ensure that mentally you don't lose it in that last run-in.

Matthew always gave me space on those occasions just before a big race. He knew what I was going through. There was nothing he could say except to reassure me that we were going to win. Once you're on the water in the environment that's so familiar, doing your warm-up, those worries just melt away. Yes, the nerves are still there, but that's a force for good. The important thing is that you're in control. Your destiny is in your own hands.

When we parted after Atlanta, when all the revelry following the receipt of our medals had ceased, it was, according to Matthew's recollection, with 'just a stare and a firm, silent handshake'. His clear assumption was that, although our friendship would endure, the boating partnership had ended.

Two days after our Atlanta triumph, I took Ann and the two children we had then, Natalie and Sophie, down to Orlando. As a treat, having seen very little of them during the previous eleven weeks when I was preparing for and participating in the Games, I'd promised to take them to Disney World's Magic Kingdom. We spent the first two days on rides like the 'Splash Mountain' and the 'Runaway Train'. I rode on an open-topped fire engine with the girls and even donned a pair of Mickey Mouse ears. Rowing was given a back seat, although it was impossible to escape completely as I was recognized by British tourists and given a cheer. The following day we sat round the pool of our hotel. It was there that I cast my mind forward four years and the notion began to nag at me incessantly: 'I think the Sydney Games are going to be good. Very good indeed.'

I knew that if I stopped, I would have suffered from a persistent ache in my stomach, originating from an unsated hunger for a challenge. I would have been watching it all, like a child with his face pressed up against the sweet-shop window. I would have been saying to myself, 'I could do that. I could have still been here, competing.' I would have observed gold medals being placed around winners' necks and thought, 'That should have been mine'.

I couldn't face that feeling. I couldn't have watched it on TV from back home in Britain. Even being involved around the British team wouldn't have helped. In fact, it would have made it worse. But then the logical side of your nature tells you: 'Come on, Steve, be realistic. You've just won. This is all just a natural reaction to your victory.' Eventually, I accepted that there was only one way to overcome that huge dilemma: go and do it all again.

I decided not to tell anybody that I was definitely going to row again, not even Ann, but vowed that I would give myself a mental cooling-down period for as long as I possibly could, just to be totally certain. I'd allow myself until formal training started again on 1 November, and only if I still felt the same then would I publicly declare my intentions. I didn't want to get half-way down the line, say two years into the next four, and think, 'I made a mistake. I don't really want to do this.' I had to be sure.

Just in case I did retire, I'd enquired about a coaching job out in Australia. The day after the Atlanta win I was talking to John Boultbee, an Australian whom I've known for years. He used to be the general secretary of FISA, the international organizing body of rowing, and was head of the Australian Institute of Sport. He is now in charge of the Sports Academy in Canberra. John spoke to Ann later in the day and asked, 'Is he serious about retiring?' She replied, 'Yes, I think he is,' though probably more in hope than expectation. Ann was well aware that Australia is the only place in the world, apart from Britain, where I'd live. The climate, the outdoor life and the sporting culture all appeal to me. The Aussies like to party hard, but are also very keen on fitness and sport. Altogether, it's a wonderful lifestyle.

When you think that in Britain there's about one month in the year when you can sit out late in the garden, Australia appears a very attractive alternative. I thought it would be at least a four-year move, which would require me taking the family out there. Ann would have been quite keen to go. She would certainly have preferred that to me carrying on rowing. The children would also have loved it.

In fact, I was subsequently asked to coach at Sydney Rowing Club. Ann, an orthopaedic physician, who is the British rowing team doctor, was also offered a job with the Australian Sports Institute. But by then it was too late, my future for the next four years was set in stone, and I turned down the opportunity. I had already decided to answer the siren's call from the water, as some sceptics were to interpret my decision. Not to my mind. I was intent on a destination of sporting distinction, not one of destruction.

It was not until his first day back in training in November 1996 that Matthew had any idea that I hadn't retired as he'd assumed. As far as he was concerned, I would accept a coaching post, although to judge by his comments, he wasn't totally convinced that I had the personality for it, suggesting in one newspaper interview that I would need 'to lose the competitive sharpness that makes him so aggressive and single-minded – which is why he can be stand-offish and arrogant'.

Matthew never asked me about my plans, although we'd got together for several promotional events after the Olympics. Some people may find it really odd that I never discussed my future with a guy I had rowed with for six years. However, I believe that the individual in those circumstances has to make his own decision. It is a very personal thing. Frankly, it didn't really matter to me what Matthew's views were. I had to come to my own conclusions; so, indeed, did he about his own future. Nobody wants to see a once-great sportsman decline into an apology for one; but there's a tendency in this country to enter sportsmen into the history books far too early. Even when I came back from the Seoul Olympics in 1988, people were saying to me, 'You've got two Olympic gold medals. Are you sure you want to go for another?' with the inevitable rider, 'You wouldn't want to go and not do very well.'

When I was younger I saw people approaching retirement after a really successful career and I'd think, 'Why are they giving up *now*?' I believe you should carry on until you're ready to retire. It's not always a question of quitting right at the top. If you enjoy it, carry on. Fortunately, I rarely follow other people's advice. I prefer to follow my own instincts. As someone once wrote, when discussing whether I would retire after Atlanta, 'The usual rules do not apply to Redgrave.'

If I'd heeded the advice given after Seoul, I would have missed out on seven more World Championships and two Olympic golds. But I ignored it and, as I approached Sydney in the year 2000, could claim that I'd achieved just about everything to which any sportsman could aspire and more. That was four Olympic golds, nine World Championship golds, and I'd carried the Union Jack at two opening ceremonies. I'd been awarded two honours, an MBE and CBE. And all that, I might add, from a man who, in his early twenties, struggled for success at the highest level as a single sculler; one who had begun to fear that he'd never realize the goals he'd set himself as a 10-year-old, who'd sat wide-eyed in front of the television, enthralled by the American swimmer Mark Spitz; and one who, in later years, defied two chronic medical conditions to succeed.

There are probably some who imagine that continuing my Olympic odyssey to Sydney was merely the obsession of a man who had nothing better to do. Indeed, at the press conference in November 1996 when I announced that my next four years would be on water, one journalist was heard saying, 'He simply doesn't know what to do with the rest of his life.' That's simply not true.

It is said that the Olympic Games is not about winning but taking part. Perhaps it is for some. I prefer another maxim – the one that someone used before Atlanta: 'If you're not here to win, you're a tourist.'

What I would stress, however, is that the decision had nothing to do with potentially securing a fifth gold in consecutive Olympics – unprecedented though that would be for an endurance sport. I can honestly say that didn't enter into it.

I never set out to be a prospector of Olympic golds. It was never my intention to boast a particular record at the end of my career. Each Olympiad – every four-year cycle – has represented a separate challenge. That remained the case up to 2000. The four medals I won up to 1996 were not even at my Marlow home for me to look at and provide me with fond reminiscences of those Games. They were on display in the River and Rowing Museum across the Thames at Henley from where I trained at the Leander Club.

I have always tried to put my previous successes out of my mind. As I advise business and sports people, when giving motivational talks, 'You never win with last year's performance.' Even less so with your last Olympic performance.

Which is why, as the 2000 Games approached, it was as if those previous four Olympic victories had never happened. The fact that my Olympic record, if successful at Sydney, would be inferior only to that of the Hungarian fencer Aladar Gerevich, who won six consecutive golds between 1932 and 1960, would be for others to discuss.

As I approached Sydney, I was in the fray, with my three fellow crew members – Matthew Pinsent, Tim Foster and James Cracknell – determined to achieve something for the first time. I had to regard the Sydney challenge as though I'd been selected by my country for the first and only time – like the vast majority of athletes who get the chance of going to one or, if they're lucky, two Olympics and, if they're at the right time and right place in their sport, could have a chance of success.

Something inside my mind kept telling me: 'Don't get carried away with all this hype, Steve.' Achieving a possible record mustn't assume more importance than competing in the event itself. That would lead to complacency and should be avoided at all costs. That is why, as I prepared for Sydney, a fifth medal didn't mean anything to me whatsoever. Only afterwards, if I succeeded in it, would it achieve the significance it deserved.

Back in 1996 the result of all my inner deliberations was that I came down to the Leander Club the day before we were due back in training to tell Jurgen, 'I definitely want to come back, but I'm not quite ready. I need another two or three weeks.' It meant that I missed the first autumn event, in early November, the Fullers Head of the River Fours, between Mortlake and Putney, the reverse of the Boat Race course. But I needed to relax because I'd been chasing around, doing lots of publicity and promotional work, giving motivational talks at company lunches, making celebrity appearances and doing all manner of strange television programmes as Matthew and I capitalized on our Atlanta gold. I had stood next to Bob Monkhouse on the Daihatsu stand at the Motor Show, attended an 'Investors in People' dinner, promoted everything from apples to an Australian wine, and was involved in a book called *Dad's Fishy Favourites for Kids*. We also participated in 'The Lord Mayor's Show Welcomes Britain's Olympic Heroes'. It wasn't the longest procession London has ever witnessed. Probably the most embarrassing moment was kitting ourselves out in aprons, alongside Nanette Newman, to make presentations to prizewinners in a national washing-up competition, entitled, 'Are you as fast as new Fairy Liquid?'

I'd thrown myself into all that because, to be candid, it's really well paid and doesn't take up all your time. And money and time were useful as we'd just moved house. If I didn't continue rowing, promotional work might have been my future and I might have found it exciting. I might even have preferred it to rowing, but I quickly decided I didn't. I wanted to be back on the water. It meant another four years of seven-days-a-week training. On some days I'd feel like hell, but there were worse ways of making a living. To me, the real madness is being stuck on the M4 in the rush hour.

And what did Jurgen say? He regarded me solemnly and replied, 'If you're not back on 1 December, don't bother coming back at all.' It gave me four weeks. But that was important because I knew that once I returned it would be a four-year stretch. Once back in a boat of whatever size, I knew that there would be no escape. Jurgen told Matthew the following day, with the words, 'Steve's coming back to the water.' By all accounts, he was absolutely astonished and thrilled. His thinking was probably different by then; in the cold light of day, being out of competition and with another medal round his neck, I think his feeling was, 'Well, yes, I wouldn't mind carrying on in a boat with Steve.'

Once I had decided how my future was mapped out, I had to convince my family. Ann knows me far too well and was never convinced when I said that I was going to stop, although I know that in her heart she hoped I would. She never tried to dissuade me, though. That's not her way. She did not put her foot down because she knows how important rowing is to me. She has always been my number one supporter. Her main concern was that I should finish at the top. That is what I intended to do. I remember the first time I went away on a training camp after being diagnosed with diabetes in 1997. It was out in South Africa. I was struggling with all the work. They were dark days. I phoned Ann and discussed my medical problems. That would have been her moment, if any, to say that nature had given me its verdict. Part of me expected her to say, 'Tough. You've got yourself into this. You wanted to carry on.' Instead she said, 'We're in this together. We'll find a way of getting through. And if you can't carry on, we'll find something you can do.' She made everything so much brighter. In all honesty, I hadn't expected that support from somebody who'd made it very clear what she thought.

There was no formal discussion with the family. I made something of a joke about it at the ensuing press conference where the official announcement was made at the Leander Club on a frosty November morning, four months after Atlanta. I told how there had been a vote and how I had bribed the children with lollipops to ensure that it went 3 to 1 in my favour. But that was just a nice story for the benefit of the assembled media. In fact, I just told the children and they were very supportive. The first day I returned to the water, as I prepared to leave the house, Natalie said, 'I want you to go training, Dad, because I want you to win in Sydney.' It brought a lump to my throat. I thought, 'I'm not just doing this for myself after all. This is important for other people. I'm doing it for my family. And, hopefully, for the pride of the entire British nation.'

So that is how I came to be seated at the start of the coxless fours final at Sydney on that most memorable day of a career that began when I was a 14-year-old schoolboy. But perhaps I should start at the beginning.

CHAPTER 2

SCHOOLBOY WITH AN OLYMPIC DREAM

For over two decades I have had a mistress. I find her charms irresistible and few weeks pass by each year when I don't have a liaison with her. The River Thames has been the 'other woman' in my life and, perhaps as well as any waterman, I understand the river's secrets, her moods and her idiosyncrasies. Also, as I will recount later, I have the utmost respect for her.

Perhaps it all comes down to the fact that I am apparently descended from a Viking called Eric the Red – hence my surname. At least that is according to my elder sister, Christine, who is interested in genealogy and has traced our family tree. She has discovered that our family originally came from Norfolk, where there were a lot of Redgraves and where the Vikings are said to have landed in large numbers. I wouldn't object to that heritage. Certainly, it would be rather apt that, as an oarsman, I should have such forefathers.

It was almost pre-destined that I should take to the water. My first school, at the age of five, was St Peter's in Marlow, the Thames-side Buckinghamshire town where I have lived virtually all my life. The school was only a hundred yards from the river. Interestingly, it was in this same street that the writer Jerome K. Jerome often stayed at an establishment called the Fisherman's Retreat. He, of course, was responsible for that much-loved humorous study of life on the River Thames, *Three Men in a Boat*. I'd like to think that were he alive today, he'd adapt it to my circumstances, *Four Men in a Boat*.

We refer to Marlow Bottom locally as 'The Valley'. Although it is part of an area of Buckinghamshire which also contains Marlow town centre and Bisham – home of the National Sports Centre where the England football team trains – it is very much its own separate, small community. I am a real homing pigeon. Apart from renting a place in London for a time in my early twenties,

I have lived in Marlow Bottom since I was born Steven Geoffrey Redgrave on 23 March 1962, the youngest child of Geoff and Sheila. I arrived weighing 8lb 6oz, length 21in – not enormous for a baby, but I soon began growing. As I write this, I'm 16 stone 7lb, and 6ft 5in tall. I have two sisters, Christine and Jane, who are nine and five years older than me respectively.

We are actually related to the distinguished thespian family of Redgraves. Sir Michael Redgrave and my grandfather were cousins. Coincidentally, one of Sir Michael's daughters, Lynn Redgrave, did quite a lot of fundraising for the British Olympic team out in Atlanta. She may never have realized that a relative of hers won a gold medal at those Games.

My father served in the Merchant Navy. It allowed him to indulge his love of travelling, a fascination shared by his elder brother Bill. But once my father returned home, he was always successfully self-employed. My earliest recollections are of him being a builder and running a firm in which he had a partnership at that time. I was always around building sites with him, doing foolish things like climbing up scaffolding.

In fact, my father built our first house in Hill Farm Road, in which my younger sister, Jane, now lives. Our next-door neighbour at that time, Joan Pritchard, came out of her back door one day to find Redgrave junior, then not even old enough to speak properly, standing on the roof of the half-built house, with no one else in sight, shouting: 'Hello, 'oan,' as I used to call her. It really caused quite a panic.

My father's attitude rubbed off on me. I never assumed that I'd go down the avenue of working nine to five for somebody else. When I was in my teens, my father started up his own garden centre. At the same time, I began my own landscape gardening company by distributing leaflets door to door, and also got work through his business. I did everything, from mowing lawns and building rockeries, to cleaning out swimming pools. I always harboured an interest in designing things and doing physical work. I also excelled at woodwork, and at one stage was tempted to go into boat-building.

My mother hailed originally from Birmingham, where her father, Harold, worked on the buses most of his life. When he retired the company presented him with an engraved watch. He gave it to me, and I still treasure that. I had a great regard and fondness for my grandparents, Harold and Ada, on my mother's side. My grandfather, on the Redgrave side, was a very hard man, and very strict. He was a carpenter, like his own father, and used to make propellers for Spitfires in the Second World War.

The Redgraves have lived around Marlow ever since my great grandfather moved into the area. Marlow is adjacent to High Wycombe, once a great furniture-building centre of England, where he could employ his skills. At that time Marlow Bottom was just a collection of farmhouses linked by gravel tracks. It was not until the Second World War that the area started to be inhabited on any scale. At first it was more of a shanty town, with lots of wooden shacks, some of which still existed when I was a child. It had a proper road, but absolutely no street lighting. In the winter, I'd go off to Cubs, and by the time I returned I had to do so in the pitch black.

My father's brother Bill is now in his eighties, but was a great adventurer and used to go away on world tours. He once cycled his way around Africa. Bill ended up in America with hardly a dollar to his name, but now has a family out there. I think he's regarded as something of an English eccentric. Bill started a plant-growing business just outside Tampa, Florida, an enterprise that was quite successful. It's where my father got his idea of opening a garden centre. I also have an Aunt Doris, who is in her seventies and over 6ft tall. I come from a very tall family – both Doris and Bill are like beanpoles – and I have inherited that trait, along with the physique of my father, who's altogether more solid and physically very agile.

My mother was always heavily involved in the local community. She was secretary of The Barn Club, a social venue, in Marlow Bottom. My sister Jane lived there for a while as stewardess and ran the club. Before she and her husband took over, I used to go and stock the shelves in the mornings before we went training.

My mother also started the Marlow Bottom Youth Club at the village hall, which provided everything from table tennis to a record player, and ran it during my early and teenage years. I was a regular, and although some youngsters might have been embarrassed about having their mum around, it never bothered me. She was like an institution in the area and had always been associated with the club. Anyway, there was little alternative. The social scene was not exactly like the West End.

Everybody knew my mother. In fact, there was hardly anybody in the valley who didn't know my family, which meant that if I ever got into trouble they soon got to hear about it. I was only allowed to play in the immediate area, and not allowed to go into Marlow town centre, which was about two miles away. When I occasion-ally ignored that ruling, my mother would find out. If I ever got into a fight, she knew about it before I got home.

Probably the biggest surprise I ever had was the prizegiving the year after I'd left senior school, in 1978. There is an annual prize presented by the Marlow Rotary Club. It's called the 'Best Potential Citizen' award and normally goes to the head boy or girl, or somebody who has excelled academically. For reasons best known to others, I won it. As I went up for the presentation, I couldn't help thinking, 'Why have I got this?' It puzzled me for years. It wasn't until quite a while later, probably in the late 1980s, that I looked back and thought to myself, 'Well, somebody obviously had the foresight to see something within me.' While no one knew at that stage that I would go on to achieve what I have within sport, by that time the Great Marlow School crew, of which I was a member, had been remarkably successful. Somehow those judges were prophetic enough to believe that I was going to make something of myself, even though it probably wasn't going to be through the normal route of further education, followed by moving on to one of the professions. Whenever I go back, I can't resist searching for my name up there on the roll of honour. Even after having won so many rowing medals over the years, that makes me feel humble.

To appreciate quite what it meant, it must be understood that, academically, I was never going to rival my classmates. I was about 10 when it was discovered I had dyslexia, or what used to be known as 'word blindness'. I was then at Burford School in Marlow Bottom, only a minute or two from where I live now, and the headmistress, Mrs Cloak, used to give me extra reading lessons in her office. There are many different types of dyslexia and it's very difficult for people who can read to understand how frus-trating a condition it is. In my case, I see letters upside-down or back-to-front, though not all the time. To give an example, there's a story involving my eldest daughter. When Natalie went to Montessori nursery, before moving on to infant school, the chil-dren were given wooden boards with letters of the alphabet made out of sandpaper so that they could trace them with their fingers and feel their shapes. She brought them home. Natalie's very smart and at three knew her alphabet, and on this particular day I asked her, 'What's this letter?' pointing to an A, and she replied, 'I don't know.' I said, 'I *know* you do know,' holding it out to her, but then Ann walked past and said, 'But you've got it upside-down.'

The strange aspect of dyslexia is that sometimes I can look at an A and it appears perfectly normal, or what I think is normal. But sometimes, say, if I've got to write it down, I might do so the correct way, or I might do it back-to-front.

Apparently, the condition was identified over 100 years ago by a Dr W. Pringle Morgan, who was treating a boy who could not read, yet who could recite the whole alphabet fluently. He was also bright and intelligent. That is what many people do not understand about dyslexia. It doesn't mean that those who suffer from it lack intellect. In fact, often to the contrary. Famous dyslexics include Agatha Christie, Tom Cruise and Leonardo da Vinci.

I've never been formally diagnosed or had any specialized treatment for my dyslexia. When I was a schoolboy in the 1960s and 1970s, there wasn't a lot known about it, and they were only just starting to help people deal with the problem. As far as my schooling went, I did the same subjects as everyone else, but found it harder to keep up and do my work. In fact, it can take a sufferer two hours to read what takes everyone else 30 minutes. Some children become so frustrated that they develop temper tantrums. Taunts by their schoolmates exacerbate the problem.

Since having my own children, I've developed into a better reader than I used to be. As might be imagined, my 'job' doesn't require too much reading and writing. Just the occasional bit of 'rithmetic'. So you get into the situation of just not bothering. But when you have children, you want to make sure that they can read and write, so you spend a lot of time reading to them. You're almost starting out again yourself by reading children's books and that's easy. My reading ability has improved a lot.

However, I have to confess that I don't read much. I do look at the newspapers, mostly the sports sections, and the odd book, but certainly nothing like as much as Matthew, who can get through three or four books while we're away at training camp. I started reading Nelson Mandela's autobiography when I was training for Atlanta, but I haven't finished it. I'd like to do so when I have more time on my hands.

Given my dyslexia, I always knew that I wasn't going to pass my Eleven Plus. It didn't concern me greatly at the time. Several of my classmates went with me to the local comprehensive, Great Marlow School, where I was taken out of French lessons to do extra English. Children can be cruel in those circumstances, when they find out that you are somehow 'different', but in my case the other pupils didn't make much of it. I'm sure that was partly because of my size. Even then, I was so much bigger than everybody else that nobody really picked on me. In fact, the complete opposite. A lot of people actually used to help me.

When we had dictation, I used to cheat and copy off the person next to me. Even that was tricky because I'm also short-sighted, and I refused to wear glasses. I always had problems with my homework. Whatever I'd written down looked all jumbled up, and I couldn't understand my writing. I used to phone one of my friends and say, 'What is the homework? What am I supposed to be doing?' From an educational point of view, my first two years at Great Marlow were not particularly happy. It was hard work and I was always bottom in English, although I wasn't too bad at maths. One asset I did have, though, was a really good memory, so I'd develop that to overcome my problems. It was only in the last couple of years at school, when I was a senior pupil and could choose my own subjects, that I really enjoyed school work.

There was never any chance that I'd excel at exams because they are pressure situations. That's when the chemistry in the body has a power surge and makes the dyslexia even worse. You might have something relatively easy to do, some fairly simple questions, but then panic sets in and you start thinking, 'I can't do it.' I did CSEs instead of 'O' and 'A' levels, and got a Grade One in woodwork, but even that meant completing some written work. I was surprised I actually got through it, though I must admit the woodwork paper had multiple-choice answers that suited me. I was good at anything practical but writing essays was a waste of time because I couldn't spell. No one could understand what I'd written.

The one thing I loved about school was sport. I played cricket, football and rugby. When I was in the Cubs I was the fastest sprinter in the district. I wasn't so keen at cross-country running, and still have grim memories of running up the hill towards the Handycross roundabout, which spans the M40 motorway, round the Three Horseshoes pub, down the lane and back to the school. I used to try to skive out of that or, if I had to take part, cut corners. But football was the big one. Everyone was mad keen on that.

There had been a period when I attended Burford School when there was a fashion for non-competitive sport. For a time it was seen as politically correct, and we went for about two years without any real competition between schools, or even between ourselves. I regained my competitive edge at Great Marlow and was still fastest sprinter in the school, but people that I used to beat were up there with me and some could out-sprint me at times.

It scarcely needs asking what my view is on that policy of non-competitive sport, which, thankfully, has now gone out of vogue. It's completely crazy. Sport is, by definition, about competition. According to my dictionary, it is: 'A game, activity; for pleasure, competition, exercise.' Life itself is about competition, from the day you're born to the day you die. There's an element of survival in nearly everything we do.

Fortunately, some of our parents didn't think that policy was correct and used to organize football games for us. We couldn't play against other schools, so we used to take on the boys from an American Air Force base in High Wycombe.

Competitive sport in schools remains a controversial issue. People often say to me when I'm doing a question-and-answer session after a public-speaking engagement, 'Do you think it's wrong to put kids through competitive events?' My reply is that it is impossible to avoid an element of competition at school, not just in sport but in everything. I say: 'When you think about it, school takes competition to extremes.'

The question that critics of competitive sport put forward is: 'Should children be under a competitive edge at such a young age?' My response is that they're under a competitive edge whatever they do. If you stop competition in sport, then presumably you should stop exams in academic subjects for the same reason. Nobody was ever too concerned at how it affected those who came bottom all the time in subjects like English, at which I was hopeless.

Those who argue against competitive sport suggest that children can be mentally scarred for life because they are made to do something they don't like and aren't good at. Well, I'm scarred for life, in a sense, because I had to do English. Those of us at the lower end of academia were also forced to do things we didn't like. That was tough; you had to do it. People forget about the ribbing that goes on when everyone else in your class can read fluently and you can't. That's much worse than going out on the playing field and finding that you're not very good at a physical activity.

Schools should have sports departments that can offer all pupils a sport they can enjoy and perform well. I used to love rugby, but I accept that you shouldn't be forced out on to the rugby field to have loads of people fall on top of you as you all chase after a ball if you really don't enjoy it.

In cross-country, there is often a large child who can't run very well because he is carrying a bit too much weight. In that situation, it is understandable that he will hate sport. But maybe he will excel at throwing the discus, or at shot-put, and that's what should be concentrated on, so he gets something out of competing in a sporting environment.

Every parent wants their child to do well at school. The academic side is a competitive environment at its most extreme. In my view the testing of the three Rs within a class is much more potentially scarring than whether you can kick or run with a ball competently. That's why you tend to find that boys and girls who are not good at the three Rs end up as the principal trouble-makers in school. It's a show of their frustration. I don't think I fell into that category, but I certainly saw evidence of it around me. I did get into the odd scrape, but I was quite intelligent, and I was clever enough not to get caught. I was cheeky rather than seriously bad. For instance, we used to play football every break. We split into two teams and inevitably the ball got kicked on to the flat roof of a building. Convention dictated that whoever kicked it had to get it, although it was against school rules. I was once on top getting the ball, and the teachers heard that someone was on the roof and waited. I was crafty, however. I climbed down the other side, rather precariously I must say, ran round unseen and stood next to the teacher, saying, 'I wonder who's up there?'

Generally, though, I was well disciplined, if for no other reason than self-preservation. I remember a science master who was excellent, but he was always threatening us with corporal punishment. He used to wield a great long stick with a nail in it. He never ever used it, of course, but I wouldn't have tested his patience. I got hit by him only once, and then across the hand with a short stick. Another teacher was Francis Smith, head of English, who later introduced me to rowing. He used to get trouble-makers to kneel down and hold out in front of them those big, long, stools that you find in science rooms. It was impossible to do it for more than a couple of minutes, and was very humiliating.

As a teenager, I loved cars and became very keen on car maintenance. We had a piece of spare land at home where I worked on an old Ford Prefect. I could drive long before I was old enough to go out on the roads. I had also driven a Caterpillar digger on building sites where my father worked. Later, he bought me an old wreck of a green Mini that I took to the school workshop, stripping the engine completely and putting it back together. To my amazement, it performed beautifully. I just had to drive it there and then, so the three of us who had worked on the car drove straight out of the workshop on to the playing field, churning up the grass. As it was my car, I was called in to see the head, who demanded to know who had been driving. I told him that I was holding the steering wheel, somebody else controlled the handbrake, and the third boy was sitting where the bonnet should have been, pulling the accelerator cable. 'Take your choice!'

Like many boys who live near a river, I used to go fishing. My father would take me, though they were slightly bizarre occasions. I recently discovered that he used to hate it, and as I wasn't too bothered either, it was all a big waste of time. However, he was convinced that this was what father and son were meant to do, being part of the bonding process. We'd go down to the Thames, just below the lock at Marlow, where he would carefully set up a rod, reel and line for me, but I'd just rush off and play in a field. He eventually persuaded me to take it more seriously. I was always lucky, even at fishing. I remember climbing up to get a good position with the rod in my hand and, as I did so, the line must have accidentally dipped into the water. When I pulled it out there was a fish! If I ever caught anything, Dad would have to come and get it off the line. I hated fish – both catching them and eating them – and still do, although I do occasionally indulge in smoked salmon and shellfish.

But sport was my abiding interest. While I can't claim that I woke up one day and decided that my whole life would be guided by a desire to be a gold medallist, I will admit that the event which had the most significant effect on me was the 1972 Munich Olympics. I was 10 at the time and watched it on TV. I remember thinking, 'Yeah, I'd like to win a gold medal at something. That's got to be brilliant.' I could imagine myself being like the Russian Valeri Borzov, winner of both the 100 and 200 metres, because sprinting was what I was best at in those days. But the vivid memory from that Games was Mark Spitz. 'Spitz for Six' was the big headline on the back of the *Daily Mirror*. In fact, he won seven in the pool, which was quite amazing.

Newspapers and magazines carried boxes for you to fill in results and how far the athletes were progressing. I did that avidly during those 1972 Games when four medals were won for Great Britain, including Mary Peters' for the pentathlon. Obviously, in later life the full horror of the shooting of eleven Israeli athletes by the Arab terrorist group Black September made an impact on me, but I only vaguely remember that outrage; I was more entranced by sporting success. I also watched the FA Cup and wanted to play football for England at Wembley and rugby at Twickenham. Everything about sport fascinated me, and I wanted to be part of it. But even then I wanted to be a winner, not just a participant.

Somehow, even at that age, I felt that my path was laid out for me. I knew in my heart which direction my life would take. People often assume that I would not have pursued the life I did if I had excelled academically. But I believe I would still have done so, whatever my educational progress. I'd always loved sport, even before I knew that I would face problems at school because of my dyslexia.

There were a lot of factors involved in my eventual decision to immerse my life in rowing, but the most crucial one was my parents' encouragement of that interest and, in a way, the age gap between me and my sisters.

Because I was significantly younger than my sisters, by the time I was in my teens they had their own lives and it meant that my mother had considerably more time on her hands to devote to my future. My parents saw me performing well at rowing and wanted me to pursue that interest as far as I could.

I hate class systems, but if you twisted my arm, I'd say that I'm from a working-class family, whose parents worked themselves up to become middle class. It was expected that my sisters would study, then go out to work before getting married, settling down and having children. As the sole male child, I was regarded slightly differently by my parents, however.

I was also fortunate that my parents had the finance and time to help me follow that route. Their attitude was always 'Let's see how far you can go' without actually saying it. When I eventually left school, I didn't have any pressures from them saying, 'You can carry on rowing but you've got to find yourself a job.' For that I will be eternally thankful. Without it, I might not have flourished as I have done.

As a child, seeing my sisters preparing to go out to pubs with friends in the evenings and bringing home boyfriends made them appear very mature and adult. I remember thinking one of Christine's boyfriends was great because he gave me his Action Man, which I kept and still have now. By the time I went to secondary school, Christine had already got married, at the age of 19. Jane followed her down the aisle, at the same age.

If I spent time with anyone, it tended to be with my parents and their friends, so I grew up quickly. As a child, I was never very intense about anything; I was carefree and easy-going. However, I tended to be rather shy and slightly introverted and would talk to myself quite a lot, probably because I didn't have any brothers or sisters of a similar age. I used to spend quite a lot of time on my own, by my own preference. Of course, I developed friendships at school, but I have never been one for big groups. I have always preferred to socialize with just one or two others.

I don't want to give the wrong impression about my sisters. They were always there for me if I needed them, but in a rather distant way. Christine was particularly protective of me as a young boy. I remember her taking me to the fair which is always held at Marlow Regatta time, and we went in a dodgem car together. She seemed to know everybody. She would tell all her friends: 'Don't bump into us; I'm looking after my younger brother.'

After leaving school, Christine went to college, studied to become a beautician and is still in the business now. She is divorced, has no children and lives near us in Marlow.

We're very close. When I went off to Los Angeles in 1984 to secure what turned out to be my first Olympic gold, the day I left she came up to say her goodbyes, wished me good luck and shed a tear or two. I was very surprised about that because I never thought of her as being the emotional type. But then, travelling was still quite new to our family and it's hardly every day that your kid brother goes off to an Olympics.

Jane was always more overtly emotional and I was probably closer to her, purely because there was not so much of an age gap. When Jane was at college, her boyfriends were always coming round on motor-bikes. They gave me a ride now and again, which used to irritate my mother intensely as she hated the machines.

At the time Jane left school, I was starting at Great Marlow, which we all attended at different times. Jane went to Wycombe College, but dropped out, and her first job was on the accounts side of the Chiltern Newspaper Group, which published the local newspapers and was then based in Marlow.

She worked there for some time, and when I left school one of my first jobs, through Jane, was to act as a courier for Chiltern Newspapers. I collected the advertising copy from garages and estate agents and delivered it to their Marlow office. Then I'd take it on to the printers in Oxford. It was only two and a half days of work a week, but very useful money at the time.

Jane's now married, with twins, who are also pupils at Great Marlow. She achieved her own bit of celebrity status as the first woman in the country to have a known egg donor of her test-tube babies. Until that time, donors had always been anonymous. But she conceived with the eggs of a colleague at work who already had children of her own, and gave birth to the twins at the Wellington Hospital in London.

It was about the same time that Ann and I were getting married, and although we never had any problems of our own on that score, we were aware of what Jane and her husband were going through. It did get quite a bit of publicity at the time, but it has not been known before now that we were related. I'm godfather to one of the twins, named Ben.

My best friend at junior school was Craig Gibbons. We attended Burford School together, then moved on to Great Marlow, but were in different classes and we slowly drifted apart. His family moved to the house in which Jane lives now, the one I was brought up in. A boy called Robert Hayley moved near him and they became pals. I was left on the fringes initially, but soon Robert and I became great friends. By then I had discovered girls and I had my first 'love affair', if you can call it that, during my early teens. I met Caroline when I was with Craig Gibbons on an adventure holiday in Cornwall where we stayed in a camp and went sailing, windsurfing and abseiling, among other activities. Caroline also came from Marlow and I immediately fell in love with her, as you do at that age. When we returned home, we went out two or three times but eventually she said she didn't want to carry on because we were too young and she didn't want a long-term relationship. That absolutely devastated me and I was completely taken aback. Next time I saw her, she was going out with a guy a couple of years older and they went out for years.

I met my next girlfriend, Julie, at a fund-raising disco for the school boat club. All the parents had got together to help buy us a new boat (a four) and equipment, and various events were organized, including a sponsored row and disco. Julie and I went out together for about eighteen months. I must admit we made a bizarre sight because I was about 6ft 3in even then, and she was around 4ft 7in. At discos, she danced with her head level with my chest! Julie moved into our area and went to school at Great Marlow before going to Wycombe High School. She used to help me a lot with my school work and did the odd essay for me, which I'd copy out.

There was one date in June that we all looked forward to – Marlow Regatta. It used to be the biggest one-day rowing regatta in the world. To everybody I knew, it really meant just one thing. The fair was coming to town for three days. Although I was aware of rowing events taking place, that side of it never interested me at all.

It certainly never crossed my mind that I might actually, one day, be out there participating.

That was all to change one February day as I approached my fourteenth birthday. Francis Smith, head of the English department at my school, whom I referred to earlier as the teacher with the interesting line in punishments, was very sports orientated. He helped out with sports days and took the rugby side. One day, completely out of the blue, he came up to me and said: 'Steven, do you fancy trying rowing?'

'During games?' I thought to myself. 'Going out on the river during school time?'

That sounded like a really good skive.

CHAPTER 3

AT THE CENTRE OF A
BOATING BATTLEGROUND

F rancis thought I had the ideal physique for rowing, according to his fairly crude, yet effective selection procedure. He would go round and look at pupils' hands and feet. If they were bigger than average, he'd ask them to row because the chances were that they would grow into tall, powerful specimens. Mine certainly came into that category.

I remember my first time on the water very clearly. I really enjoyed it. It was an odd sensation initially, because clambering into a not particularly stable boat and then thrashing it along the river was not something any of us had experienced before. Whether I was good, bad or indifferent on that occasion I'll never know; it just seemed a good idea. According to Francis, I was uncoordinated initially, but I was also quite good at adapting to any sport. I was certainly a better rower than the others. Immediately there was a sense of excitement and expectation. About 10 of us drove down to Marlow Rowing Club with Francis that first time. Within two weeks, we had been whittled down to four and that was it, the school crew.

The four were Robert Hayley, whom I have already mentioned, Stuart Painter, Clive Pope and myself. The cox, who joined us later, was Nicholas Baatz. We became the school crew because there was nobody who rowed in the year above us. Some boys in the top year rowed, but they were very much coming to the end of their school life. From the start, it was hard work, but unlike cross-country, nobody was hiding. Nobody was skiving.

Not that much was expected from a comprehensive with no tradition in rowing. This was no public school like Eton or Shrewsbury. At that time the school had only one boat, but if you joined the school boat club, you were immediately attached to Marlow Rowing Club and then you could use their boats.

When we started there was a device attached to the side of the bank so you could practise your rowing technique with the blade in the water, but without actually moving. Then, after a time, we went out in pairs in wide, skiff-like boats, before ending up in a clinker-built four, which is a very stable craft, although not the quickest in the water. The first couple of weeks, we just went down to the river in games sessions. Francis sensed that we were keen and asked us if we wanted to practise after school. We soon got into the routine of cycling the mile or so down to the rowing club straight after lessons had finished. We learnt fast and impressed him with our enthusiasm. It was only a few weeks later that Francis asked, 'Do you fancy rowing in a regatta?' We looked at each other and replied in unison, 'Sure.' We still all thought of it as just a bit of a laugh. It would be great to go away with your mates during the weekend. We never thought to ourselves, 'Oh, yes. We're going to win this.'

So, on a Saturday in May at Avon County Schools Regatta, just east of Bristol, we made our debut in the coxed fours. It was a brilliant day. It didn't enter my head that we had a chance of success; it was just good fun to be part of the whole occasion. Apart from anything else, we were still virtual novices. We rowed in four races. The first we won quite comfortably, beating Monkton Coombe, and we then beat Strode's College by three-quarters of a length in the final over 1000 metres. If we hadn't won that first regatta, I don't honestly believe it would have made any difference. We didn't expect anything. It was just all new, fresh, exciting; just a great adventure in which four friends were doing something different and enjoying new experiences. But once you start winning, then you want to keep going. And win we did on all types of water, from the Thames Tideway to the Thames at Marlow or Reading, to the Ouse, the Avon, and canals and lakes.

My sister Christine began keeping records of our races in an album and stuck a gold star next to our victories. By the end of that first season we had six of them – from Avon County, Hereford City, Reading Town Centenary, St Neots and Trentham Regattas, and Monmouth Small Boats Head of the River – and we remained undefeated. After three years, that album positively glittered with stars.

In those early days, we raced in what is called a restricted four. The boat is slightly wider than the shell four that we use now, and has a keel to make it more stable. Francis decided early on that I should take the stroke position (at the rear of the boat), probably because I was potentially the best rower. I was also the biggest, strongest and quite dynamic. There's a picture at Marlow Rowing

Club from that time, in which I dwarf everyone, although there wasn't much difference in weight. Robert was the smallest. He went into the bow seat. Stuart was quite big, but not very dynamic, and he went to number three, also on bowside. Clive joined me on strokeside.

Whenever anyone starts rowing, the coach begins by telling them whether they are going to row strokeside or bowside. Looking towards the stern, as you always are, apart from the cox (if there is one), strokeside is on the right, and bowside the left. It's got nothing to do with being right- or left-handed. In a four or eight, the best athlete tends to be allocated the stroke seat; the bigger, stronger men are placed in the middle, and the smaller guys tend to be put in the bows.

Once they've settled into a particular side, it's rare for people to swap. There are exceptions and I have been one of them, which I will return to later. To use a simple analogy, switching sides in rowing is rather like having to handle a foreign car, and adjusting to the gear lever and handbrake being on the 'wrong' side. For a while, it just doesn't feel right.

The stroke, in theory, is the person who sets the pace and the rhythm that will get the best out of his or her crew and which everybody else follows. He's the one who drives the crew on. That's why it's usually the most explosive athlete who is selected, although not necessarily the strongest. In small boats, up to fours, that's quite a good philosophy. In eights, it's not quite so important. There you want your strongest athletes in the middle. In an eight, you've got the powerhouse through the middle four, the more dynamic at seven, then technical people, who are not the strongest but who won't slow the boat down, as the bow pair. Similarly, if you've got four big guys, you're not going to put all of them strokeside, and the smallest bowside. It would unbalance the boat. You place two either side.

From the moment I began competing in regattas, my parents accompanied me to virtually every one. Admittedly, once you arrived there, you didn't really want your mother and father following you about, so they were dispatched to the riverbank while you spent the whole day rowing and generally messing about with your mates. Later, you met up with them and went home. I always appreciated having my parents there supporting me. Wherever you are in the world, having familiar faces around can be a great source of inspiration. That's why I liked to have my three children with me as well. My parents tended to look after them during the competition period, but they were always there if I wanted to see them before and after a race. Invariably after I had won a medal, they were photographed clustered around Dad.

For the Great Marlow four, the tankards, medals and other trophies began to accumulate. It was possibly the worst thing that could have happened to us. We were so successful we began to think we were God's gift to rowing. Our initial attitude was, 'What an easy sport this is.' It was not until much later that I realized we were as good as we were because we used to train more than anybody else. We were basically stronger than all our rivals. However, we used to row appallingly and our technique, frankly, was so poor that we soon became the butt of other crews' jokes.

There were times when other schools' coaches used to laugh at us as they saw us paddle to the start, then be absolutely stunned when we came back down and were metres out in front of their boys. But the reaction of those people didn't annoy us; we just went out with the intention of enjoying ourselves.

Francis had rowed only at a very modest level, but that didn't matter: his enthusiasm was infectious. Often he would meet us by his car, drive us to the rowing club and take us home. If it hadn't been for him, I wouldn't have got in a rowing boat. It's as simple as that. Without his patience and enthusiasm, my future would have been different. If there is one person – other than my parents – I have to thank for planting that original seed of interest and then proceeding to encourage my burgeoning talent, it is him.

At about the same time that he got us started he became captain of Marlow Rowing Club, a position he held for about 10 years. He was a quiet man, but could be amusing, with a dry sense of humour. He was just a very genuine, honest guy, who retired from the school during the mid-nineties. The amount of time and effort he put in was incredible. That's something that we're losing from our schools because of the curriculum set-up. Such are the demands on teachers these days that people like him just don't have the time after school for sports or clubs.

About the time I began rowing, Craig Gibbons moved to Banbury, which left Robert and myself. He was a very expressive type of character and always had something to say, with strong opinions on many subjects, even at that relatively tender age. Even then, in our mid-teens, Robert was a bit of a ladies' man. What we had in common was determination, and the fact that we both excelled at sports; he was a very good footballer and I was probably better at rugby. After leaving school, we both played for Great

Marlow Old Boys rugby team. It was pretty tough stuff. I remember our opening game. In the first 10 minutes I was knocked unconscious, then five minutes before half-time I got a large gash on my calf from a kick.

Francis ran that team, too, although rowing was always his first love. We were quite successful. The few games we had we used to win quite easily. There were actually only about six or seven of us who really enjoyed playing rugby, but we were joined by members of the football team if we had a game. It didn't last for much more than a year, though. Rumour had it that the side ran out of fixtures because potential opponents didn't want to play us.

Robert was the next best oarsman in the school crew: talented, strong and gutsy, though a little bit on the small side. He'd have made a brilliant lightweight oarsman if he'd lived into his twenties and thirties because he was naturally light and didn't have to diet. But he never got the chance. Of the two other crew members, Stuart Painter didn't stay the course, mainly, I think, because he didn't relish the training and routine. He did not enjoy it as much as the rest of us, and dropped out. I remember him saying with a wry smile, 'I think I've won enough.'

Stuart was replaced by Peter McConnell, who was a year younger than us. He lived with his parents at a local RAF base. He joined us in 1978 and stayed with us until the National Championships of 1979, when we failed to qualify for selection to the World Junior Championships in Moscow. However, Clive was to go on to compete in the World Junior Championships in the coxed four the following year. Today, they all still live quite locally to me and we get together occasionally.

We trained enthusiastically and regularly, but Francis made it so convenient, so easy. We used to be out virtually every day except Saturday, and in summer that was normally race day. Even in winter, there were occasional long-distance races on Saturdays. Obviously, it was nothing like as sophisticated as the training provided by rowing clubs and schools now. For a start, there were no rowing machines, otherwise known as ergometers (or ergos for short); it was not until the early 1980s that they appeared.

We rowed up and down the river, doing three 'laps' of the Marlow stretch. Francis would time us from Marlow Rowing Club, which is just upstream of the bridge. We'd row up to Temple Lock and back. It was not until later that we discovered our rivals' training routine used to involve only about three or four sessions a week, while we were rowing six or seven. No wonder we were so much fitter and stronger. Even before I rowed, I liked to try to keep myself fit. I pleaded with my parents for a stopwatch, and once it arrived one birthday, I timed myself running from home to the end of Marlow Bottom and back. As I had no one to run against, I competed against myself. That fiercely competitive edge was evident, even then.

Right at the beginning, under Francis, I'd describe it as fun rather than serious training. There was no real pressure on us, and Francis did not keep records of what we achieved. However, the following season, as 15-year-olds, we started doing weights twice a week. The next year, by which time we were competing in the junior under-16s, we began to approach the whole thing more seriously. Francis would bring a few weights up to school for us to use in the gym at lunchtime. It was so well organized that you'd never think, 'Oh God, we've got to do this again.' However, he always insisted that we did a reasonable amount of running. Francis was quite crafty. He'd take us out in his car, drop us off and make us run back to base. You couldn't cheat.

After Pete joined us, we didn't train so hard that winter. It was not nearly as intensive as when we started. We thought we were so good, we didn't have to try so hard. In our second season, we competed in 15 events and won eight. We were defeated by crews from places such as Sutton School, whom we had beaten easily before. That annoyed us because we knew that we were a better crew. Losing, though, gave us the jolt we needed. The following winter, we trained exceptionally hard for the junior under-16 year and improved immeasurably, though it may also have been that Pete had developed and caught up with us. We won everything in our own category and did well against crews who were much older.

Our buccaneering foursome competed at a very high level and ended up taking part in the National Championships at the end of the 1979 season. We were bronze medallists in the junior event, and gold medallists in the junior under-16 event. We were also selected for the Home Countries International at Llandedfedd, just outside Cardiff, and won that as well. Overall, our technique had improved with time. It became, at the very least, adequate. The comments of the other coaches soon stopped. From the moment we won the Abingdon Head of the River in late February, beating King's College School by over 10 seconds, there was no stopping us. At Bedford Fours and Sculls Head of the River, we were eleventh equal of 231 competitors. The crew we shared eleventh place with was Nottingham Britannia senior coxed four.

During this period, I developed a desire to do the single scull. Just to clarify, rowing involves each member of the crew having one oar, whereas sculling involves having an oar in each hand, one on either side of the boat. Single sculling is the most demanding of all rowing disciplines because, as they say, 'there is nowhere to hide'. My parents bought me a sculling boat when I was 16; a George Sims Racing Boat, bought second-hand from Lady Margaret Hall, Oxford, from the Olympic oarsman D. P. Sturge. I started doing some single sculls events and won my first such race, appropriately enough, at Marlow Junior Regatta in May 1978.

The single sculls gave me the opportunity to display my individual skills but under no circumstances would I have deserted the Great Marlow coxed four. Our junior under-16 year in 1978 was the best by a long way. At the main Marlow Regatta, we won the junior coxed fours and were presented with our trophies by the late John Snagg, who commentated for many years on the Boat Race. Our next year was our first at fully fledged junior level. We had come a long way in a short time since those first faltering strokes in 1976. We all decided, after that successful year of junior under-16s, that we would stay together, whatever, and try to get selected for the Moscow Junior Championships in 1979. But soon it all went sour.

Marlow Rowing Club had many ex-internationals, oarsmen who had achieved much in the sport and knew what it takes to get to the top and what qualities you had to have to succeed. They were all people whose views I respected. They were men such as Nigel Read, who had won lightweight gold medals in World Championships, and John Pilgrim-Morris, who never really made it as an international rower but was always a borderline contender for international crews. It was already starting to be suggested to me that I could become a future world champion. I remember John saying to me when I was 15, 'Potentially, you can become a world champion in the singles,' although he actually advised me rather differently when I was sculling and he became chairman of selectors! Another character at Marlow was the former international coach Mike Spracklen, who also had great faith in me. When I first came across him, he was rowing with the veterans' four at the Club. Mike later became my coach.

I was pleased that all these excellent judges had faith in me, of course, but I said to myself, 'Why world champion? I want to be Olympic champion.' Also, while it was good to know that other people thought I could achieve something, at the same time it was counter-productive. I began to expect things to happen automatically.

During the summer of 1978, we were assessed for the British junior team for Moscow. I came out quite high in gymnastic tests. My excellent record on the water had also obviously been noted, and following the National Championships in which our Great Marlow four won a bronze, I was asked to take part in the World Junior Championships being staged that year in Belgrade. The junior selector at that time was David Tanner who, in Sydney 2000, was Britain's international manager. It was unusual to be selected at my age, but it does happen now and then.

Unfortunately, not for the first time in my career, the opportunity was snatched away. The event was the coxed four, the lowest ranked of the rowing boats, and the proposed boat included two boys from Abingdon School. Apparently they objected, claiming, 'We don't want to row with somebody that young. There's no point.' So it didn't happen. I've often wondered what went through their minds later. Somewhere, there are a couple of chaps, a bit older than me, who must be saying to themselves, 'Why on earth did we say that?' Fortunately, I didn't find out until later what had happened. At the time I wasn't that stressed about it.

Increasingly, it became evident that the selectors were determined to entice me out of the Great Marlow four and into a boat that they thought would have a realistic chance at Moscow the following year. What particularly irked the selectors was that Great Marlow was not what they considered to be a rowing school.

Junior rowing has changed now, but it was then principally run by rowing teachers from public schools. You had to be invited into their own special club, which they called the 'Kitchen Society', and Francis, as a teacher from a small comprehensive school, was certainly not any part of that. It was almost Masonic in its exclusivity, which meant that there was absolutely nobody to fight our case.

The junior rowing hierarchy didn't like us doing as well as we had in the last two or three years, particularly as the public schools were then going through a bad patch and not producing that many good athletes. I was probably perceived as pig-headed, but the fact was I wanted to remain part of the Great Marlow junior four. It was not as though that was anything out of the ordinary. Unlike now, many crews at that time came from the same club or school, and my overriding inclination was loyalty to my friends in the crew. I've proved throughout my career that once I've decided to do something, I'll give it my best shot. And one of my rules has always been that you don't ditch your mates.

What annoyed me was that, because of these behind-the-scenes politics, our four was ignored, despite some excellent results. David Tanner, who headed the three-man junior selection panel at the time, was also coaching a senior four. That meant we never saw him assessing us at the races because he was always away with his four. He received the details over the telephone. We felt that we never got any support from the Great Britain junior set-up at all. Their principal aim was to separate me from the rest of the crew, and their attitude was, 'We won't be dictated to by you.'

Despite still being a junior, I entered open, long-distance sculling races, Head of the River events as they are called, in which competitors set off at regular intervals against the clock. I suddenly found it all much more daunting. In the juniors, I had been used to overtaking five, maybe 10 boats in a 15-minute race. Now it was different. I remember at Wallingford Head of the River, in October 1979, one of the other competitors was Eric Sims from Maidenhead Rowing Club. We always got on well, and remain good friends to this day. Eric had competed in the past two World Championships. He had been in the 1978 British quadruple scull coached by Mike Spracklen and the British eight in that year's World Championships. I was able to gauge my progress through him.

In the 1979 race he beat me by 14 seconds, which is a huge margin. I found that really difficult to cope with, even though I finished fourth behind the Olympic and world silver medallist in the double sculls, Chris Baillieu. I was expecting too much of myself too soon. The following year, when I was the best young sculler in the country, I got my own back on Eric. I won the Wallingford Head over 4 km and beat him by 37 seconds.

By 1979, it was evident to everyone that I was one of the country's top young oarsmen. On an individual basis, I was probably better than everyone in that year. I was coming out so much higher than the other young rowers in performance testing levels. According to the *Daily Telegraph*, before the junior rowing championships at Nottingham's Holme Pierrepont course, 'He looks to be in a class of his own as a junior sculler.' But the fact that my ability shone through increasingly created difficulties as I became the subject of a tug-of-war between the loyalties to my own crew and those of the Great Britain team selectors.

British team officials were intent on dismantling our crew just to get me out to row in another boat. They wanted to break us up in mid-season and for me to row in one of the squad boats, probably the eight, which was considered to have an excellent chance of a medal at Moscow.

The British selectors didn't really encourage me to scull either because we're essentially a rowing nation, and most of our best results have come in rowing boats. At both senior and junior level, our scullers had been absolutely hammered by the opposition. They wanted the best people in rowing boats.

Yet, come what may, we were determined to try and get our junior four selected for those World Championships. But that 1979 season turned out to be a bitter disappointment. That was partly because everywhere we raced the selectors would split Britain's strongest junior boat, the eight, into two fours to race us. One crew would always beat us. We would defeat the other four.

Decision time came at the National Championships at Holme Pierrepont one Saturday in May. The eight would stick to their own event and not be split on this occasion, which gave us a good chance – until we found that the British 'squad' four, an amalgam of the country's best club and school rowers, against whom we'd never raced, would also be in the line-up. To make things worse, we were told that even if we won, we'd have to stay up there until the Monday and take part in another trial against the 'squad' four.

From my own point of view, there was also the possibility that if I did well at Nottingham in the single sculls I could make the Moscow championships on my own account in that event.

On the Friday, I had to race in a sculls first round and semifinal, followed by a coxed fours heat over 1500 metres, all between two and five o'clock. I won my events, and our four won their heat, which qualified us for the final.

The fours final the following day was our worst nightmare. Clive's seat broke and we finished last. The selectors said that was it. The squad coxed four, who we'd never actually raced all season, won the trial and had their selection confirmed. We would not be going to Moscow. It scarcely mattered to me that I still had a chance of making it in the single sculls.

I was desperately upset because it appeared that everything had conspired against us; but immediately after that fours race, I was driven to the start and George Turner, who had been in the British junior quadruple sculls (usually known as a 'quad') crew the year before and rowed for Marlow, had my sculling boat ready for me.

I was very emotional, in fact close to tears because of the failure of the four. George had walked away, but as I was getting into my boat, he came sprinting back and said, 'I've just been sitting in the car with the selectors, and if you can win this by a long way, they might select you for the single.' I didn't care about that. When the race started I was still shedding tears. It didn't stop me winning; in fact, the sense of injustice might have driven me on to even greater efforts than normal. But I had no idea by how much I'd won and, to be honest, I didn't care. I collected my medal and returned, very down, to find that I had been selected as a single sculler to go to the Moscow Junior Championships and was also named spare man, who could deputize in case of injury or illness in one of the crew boats. I accepted and went.

It was not until around four years later that I discovered the truth of that sculling display, when a guy called Jonathan Spencer Jones, known as 'Joff', joined the senior sculling team I was then involved in at Marlow. 'Did you know,' he said as we greeted each other, 'that as a 16-year-old, I came second to you in the Junior National Championships?' It turned out I'd won by 17 seconds which is a massive margin over 1500 metres.

There was less than a month between those National Championships in July and the Moscow championships in August for me to prepare to venture into unknown territory. I'd been rowing for the majority of the season, and while I'd climbed into a sculling boat now and again and performed very well against seniors, I'd never done anything like an international regatta.

Francis knew he was out of his league, and he was not really a sculling coach anyway. Fortunately, Mike Spracklen offered to help me and I went out on the water with him a few times before going to the championships. It was to prove invaluable experience. But before I departed for the Soviet Union, something occurred which was to have a traumatic impact on my life.

CHAPTER 4

MISERY IN MOSCOW

At school, Robert Hayley and I didn't attend the same classes but we spent a lot of time together. Even after we left school and I began working as a landscape gardener and he went to Buckinghamshire College of Education in High Wycombe, we rowed together virtually daily. And that meant even within the closeness of that four, there were two separate groups. Once training was over, we'd go off and leave the others. Robert and I had a very close relationship: we were like brothers, except that we never fought. He would come round to my house and treat it like his own; I did the same at his place. There was hardly a day when we weren't together, even on holidays. He was a larger-than-life, irreverent character. There were many stories about him, and one was absolutely typical. We were racing a blind crew, obviously with a sighted cox, from a college in Worcester at Birmingham Regatta. We were juniors rowing in a seniors event held at Edgbaston reservoir.

Now when you race, you can hear what other crews are saying, and we could hear their cox bellowing out encouragement. At one stage he shouted, 'You're doing well. You're coming back on the Marlow crew.' Straight away 'Bill' responded off the top of his head, like he was in a pantomime audience, 'Oh, no you're no-o-o-t!' It was a bit cruel, but that summed him up. He was very sharp in certain situations.

It was one day during the holidays, in August 1979, that Robert, Nicola – my girlfriend at that time – and I were lounging around at my parents' house in the afternoon after our normal training, watching a movie on television. For some reason, I remember it was the Tony Hancock film, *The Rebel*.

Suddenly, Robert said to me, 'Can I have an apple?' which struck me as strange because he'd normally just get up and pick one without asking. I said, 'Of course,' and as he got to his feet and went to reach for one, he collapsed on the floor. Fortunately, my sister Jane was in the house as well. She had completed Red Cross first aid courses and knew how to react. A doctor and ambulance were called immediately.

Everything was happening very fast but to me it seemed to be in slow motion. Robert's mother, Joan, and stepfather, Colin, were playing golf at Henley Golf Club that afternoon. I was given the job of phoning to tell them to come over but without worrying them too much because we had no idea then how serious it was, although it really didn't look good. Somehow, I had an ominous feeling that Robert wasn't going to survive, but I refused to admit it to myself.

I had to do something. I couldn't just sit there. So I walked out of the house and met Joan at the end of Marlow Bottom. As I walked down Marlow Bottom Road I was in tears, absolutely overcome with emotion. I was thinking of all the things I wanted to say to Robert and all the things we discussed about what we wanted to do in our lives. I always knew I was going to carry on rowing; he was already training to be a graphic artist and planned to continue rowing as well. My mind was a maelstrom of thoughts.

I forced myself to think about the possibility that I'd never see him again. Part of my future would be ripped away, even though I recognized that we would probably follow different avenues after that year when we left school. It's different when it's your parents; you know they're going to die at some stage, and probably before you. When they pass away, it will be a shock, but you're prepared to cope with it. It's expected.

When it's somebody who's just 17, and for whom life is in some respects just beginning, it's difficult to accept that he's been taken away. At that age, you're setting up relationships that in some cases can last a lifetime. There was certainly a very strong bond between us. Wherever we'd ended up in the world, we'd have retained strong links. That's the way we used to talk. To lose all that would leave a huge gap in my life.

Joan and I went to Wycombe hospital, where Robert had been taken, and were immediately told that he was dead. It was as stark and final as that. Joan went to see him in the room where he had been taken, but I walked about outside trying to come to terms with the news.

Robert had been going out with a nurse, Alison, at the time. She worked at the hospital and at that very moment she walked past the casualty department. I told her what had happened and she was obviously distraught.

It was the first time I'd encountered death at close quarters. It seemed so horribly unfair. He was, to all outward appearances, a very fit young man. Only the weekend before we had won a senior coxed four event at the Bedford Regatta. The previous weekend we had taken part in the Marlow Rag Regatta and gone to a disco on Saturday night. According to the subsequent post mortem, he had died from 'natural causes'. The explanation given to me afterwards was that his heart had stopped after not following its normal beat. That happens to everyone's occasionally, but his had stopped and wouldn't start again.

The funeral was held at Amersham crematorium. The crew, including our cox, Nicky Baatz, carried his coffin. Robert's ashes were interred in the graveyard of All Saints' Church, next to Marlow Bridge. It is directly on the Thames waterfront. I know a few of our contemporaries – Clive for one – who still go down there to visit his grave and pay their respects. It might sound strange, but Robert's remains being placed in a small square box and buried in a hole meant nothing to me at all.

I prefer to retain my memories of how we were before, and what we were doing. Once the crematorium part of the service was over, the physical presence of Robert ended for me. I can't remember the last time I went to the grave; it was probably when I was at the church for some other reason, like a wedding. I've never gone out of my way to visit the grave. I just can't relate what he was then to where he is now.

I still think about him a lot, and Ann and I are still very close to Joan. She's godmother to Natalie, and our son Zak's middle name is Robert. Robert's younger sister, Andrea, who was 15 at the time, found it very hard to accept his death and it hit her badly a year later. She lives in Spain now and has a son called Roberto. Joan and Colin also went to Spain, to live with Andrea and her husband, and it was there that Colin died, but Joan is now back and remarried. I was one of the witnesses at the wedding. I used to play golf with them at Henley Golf Club, and keep in close contact with Joan and her new husband, Ray.

A lot of people feel that when they have suffered the death of a family member or close friend, there's no point in carrying on. That wasn't an issue for me, but I must confess that, for a while, I did not find it easy to continue with my preparations for Moscow. It was Mike Spracklen who did more than anyone to focus my mind once again on those championships. Not long after Robert had died, I went to talk to Mike at his house on the Thames at

Marlow. He told me it was inevitable that I would suffer from the trauma of my best friend dying, but that life had to go on. 'I think that you can be an outstanding athlete,' he told me, and encouraged me not to be sidetracked and not to give up on going to the Junior Championships, a matter of weeks away.

For years afterwards, not a day went past when I didn't think of Robert, although it's not something I've ever really spoken about in detail to other people, even Ann. There was a night in 1986 when Ann and I, together with Clive, went down to Leicester Square to see the film *Top Gun*, which had just been released. There's a very emotional scene in the film where the best friend of the character played by Tom Cruise dies. It brought Robert's death back and affected me very badly. By the time we left the cinema, I was in floods of tears. I just couldn't stop myself. It was only then that I told Ann the whole story.

Even now, more than 20 years on, his death has an important place in my memory. In moments of pressure, I still draw strength from the idea that Robert's there somewhere, guiding me. I know that's not actually the case, but in my mind it helps.

When Robert died, I'd been going out with Nicola for about 18 months and we were coming to the end of our relationship. The tragedy of Robert's death brought us closer, and helped keep us together for another year before we did eventually go our separate ways. She came to the Moscow Junior Championships with me and my parents. It was good to have her there because nobody else would talk to me, even the coaches. Thinking back, it was abhorrent behaviour from supposedly responsible adults. The only person who did speak to me was Richard Wait, the newly appointed coach of the junior eight, and that was exceedingly brief and to the point. He hadn't spoken to me during the whole season, and the only time he did was when the championships had finished!

The eight eventually won a bronze, an excellent result, but when it was all over – and presumably irritated by the fact that I had not helped it to an even greater prize – he said testily, 'I hope you don't waste your time next year.' The implication was that I should have ditched my fellow crew members, and should do so when I returned. I didn't think I was wasting my time at all. It was something I wanted to do. I saw nothing wrong in being loyal to my friends and remaining an integral part of the Great Marlow four. That was where my heart lay. We may have failed in what we wanted to do, but I still felt it was the right path to follow.

A clash was inevitable. While we were participating purely for the joy of the sport and to derive whatever pleasure we could out of it on an individual or crew basis, the coaches were attempting to turn it overnight into their version of a squad system.

There wasn't a precedence of that in this country. It was very much a total transformation from 'You're the fastest crew in the country and you're selected' to a total squad system, 'You're the best athlete around; you're going in this or that boat and we'll see how it goes.'

The effect on the Great Marlow four was that instead of giving us support or help, the coaches tried to destroy us. It's the wrong way of doing things. I found it very schoolmasterish and petty. But that, unfortunately, was how the sport was run at that stage. They just regarded us as malleable youngsters who would do their bidding without question. The carrot, of course, was a place in the Junior World Championship squad. To be frank, during that junior year nobody even discussed with me the possibility of rowing in the eight, or whatever crew they had in mind. Probably it was all done through Francis, with whom I had become very friendly. We spoke on Christian-name terms out of school. I have no idea what conversations he had had or how stubbornly he might have resisted the notion. However, I don't think it would have made any difference even if the coaches had spoken to me, or if there had been a meeting with myself and Francis, or even with the whole four. We had made our decision at junior under-16 level to go to Moscow and nothing was going to destroy that trust and agreement.

I'm quite a civil person and we could easily have sat down and tried to work out a compromise, but there was no way I was going to be dictated to. As it worked out, we couldn't have raced as a four in the Junior World Championships anyway because of the death of Robert. If I had been in charge of the junior set-up and wanted to bring in a new crew member, I'd have gone out of my way to talk to them. But that was never, ever done. Even the team manager, Geoff Brook, who wasn't one of the coaches but someone independent, never came up to me and gave me any assistance when we were out in Moscow.

Fortunately, the sport at junior level was slowly changing for the better. Whether the selectors liked it or not, the sport was widening its appeal beyond the public schools. Traditionally, virtually every boy at Eton, Radley and Shrewsbury will row at some stage, even though they don't necessarily enjoy it. It was all very much a hit-or-miss procedure and they weren't producing really high-quality rowers. At my school you had to be picked out, and time was invested in those who possessed the natural attributes to be successful.

The team for Moscow included rowers from the Forest School in east London, and the double sculls were from Hollingworth Lake, just outside Rochdale. They included a fellow named Adam Clift, who was later to partner me. There were also representatives from Nottingham. It was a real mixed group and certainly not dominated by the public schools. Fortunately, since those days when I was involved in the juniors, rowing has become a sport in which anyone who is potentially talented could end up representing his country.

At most, a dozen pupils rowed at Great Marlow in the years that I was there. Of those 12, from four different years of students, three of us progressed through to the 1988 Olympic Games and came fourth or better, winning two fourth places, a bronze and a gold.

That's a phenomenal record for a small comprehensive school, with no sort of rowing tradition at all. It just proves to me that we have so many potential world and Olympic champions walking round the streets who haven't found a sport at all, or haven't been encouraged to find one at which they could succeed.

Now many more young people go on to higher education. Universities and colleges tend to be in or near major cities. They are usually located on rivers, which often have rowing clubs, so there is every opportunity for those with an interest in rowing and sculling to develop their potential.

Back in Moscow in the summer of 1979, I didn't feel that at all. I just felt that I was being excluded from an élitist club. Crew members of the British eight were not exactly antagonistic, but most were decidedly off-hand because they felt I should have been in the boat as well. I was left to my own devices to organize myself, sort out my tactics and get myself to races on time. Yet I had no international experience at all. In those days at international regattas the officials were French and they spoke to you in French. I could hardly speak a word of it. Fortunately, the British boat-trailer driver felt sorry for me and helped me get on to the water. Before my first event, an elimination heat, I was so concerned that I was going to miss the race that I didn't go to the warm-up area, which they provided at Moscow. Instead, I went straight to the start and waited nervously until the other competitors arrived. I started well in that first heat – in which only the winner qualified automatically for the semi-final – and was leading, but then got my blade caught underneath a buoy and that destroyed my rhythm.

Obviously, I lost a lot of speed and I eventually finished fourth of five. I knew I wasn't going to win it. I actually passed one boat in my initial attempt to repair the damage and I remained in front of him, but there was no point in catching anybody else. I thought to myself, 'What's the point in going flat out and coming third?' I decided to reserve my energy for the repechage, where the losers of the heats get another opportunity to qualify.

There were three heats of the repechage, with two to qualify for the semi-final from each one. Unfortunately, I was drawn in the toughest heat, which included the West German sculler, whom I knew I'd have trouble beating. In fact, once the race had begun, he disappeared down the course and I never saw him again – well, not until after the final when he was standing on the podium being presented with a silver medal. The Czechoslovakian competitor also beat me narrowly and, as only two qualified for the semi-final, I was eliminated. The irony was that, had I actually finished last in the first race, I would have been in one of the other two heats and almost certainly would have qualified. Apparently, half-way through my repechage everybody in the stands was saying, 'That's OK, Steve's got a good finish, he'll blast through and qualify.' The trouble was that I always went through a lazy spell in the middle of a race, conserving energy to do just that, but this time I had nothing left. The frustrating thing was that I did a really fast time, and I would have won any of the other repechages.

When I came off the water, I was pulled out for my first random drugs test. I thought that was bizarre as I was out of the competition. Why test somebody who hadn't made the top 12? If I'd taken a performance-enhancing substance, it hadn't been too effective. I went to the room with the team doctor, a guy named Noel O'Brien, a real character who was coming to the end of his team stint.

Bearing in mind you would probably be dehydrated after competing, to help provide the urine sample required you had the choice of water, a soft drink or a Polish beer. These days, the latter has been taken off the list, perhaps understandably, although it doesn't actually affect the test for drugs. Anyway, I went on the beer after coming straight off the water and not having eaten much beforehand. Unlike my practice these days, I hadn't drunk much liquid before the race either.

It took me two and a half hours before I produced a urine sample. By then, I was totally out of my head on the beer. There was a whole crate of it, and we just sat there and drank. The doctor had more than matched what I had downed. By the time we came out, the whole place was deserted and we were the only people left, stuck on the outskirts of Moscow.

Eventually, we phoned for a taxi to get us back to the team hotel. When we returned, we went to the doctor's room and carried on drinking. Eventually, I made it back to my room, but as I got into a lift to get there, some of the other British rowers were getting out, and I virtually fell in among them. I must have looked in one hell of a state. It was not my finest moment.

That experience taught me a lot. Until then, it had just been a matter of going to school, getting in the car, going training, going home, doing your homework. Even after I had left school and started work, there was a lot of routine to my life, but I got to the stage where I knew things had to change. I would have to make things happen.

The natural talent I had for rowing put me head and shoulders above everyone else of my own age in this country. But internationally I was struggling. What I was beginning to realize was that my rivals were used to a far more competitive environment. They were used to fighting for their place, whereas for me it was too easy. I had been used to races where I'd explode off the start, establish a healthy lead and take it relatively easy in the middle, before putting in a burst at the end.

I was always known, when I raced in the singles, as someone who had an incredible finish. In fact, it was only because I had conserved energy mid-way through a race that I was able to do that. This tactic worked in races at home, but failed against top young internationals in Moscow. Fortunately, the next development in my life gave me every opportunity to improve matters.

CHAPTER 5

THATCHER THWARTS
MY FIRST OLYMPIC BID

When I returned from that dismal sojourn in Moscow, I was more certain than ever that sculling was my real forte. It had provoked a fierce desire in me to prove myself at world level. Robert's death and my selection for the Moscow junior team obviously meant the demise of the Great Marlow four. It was sad but inevitable. I could never see myself returning to a rowing boat.

In all honesty, there was no recent British tradition of success to follow in either discipline, apart from Chris Baillieu in sculling. His best performance was a World Championship gold with Mike Hart at Basbaan, near Amsterdam, in 1977, and an Olympic silver medal in the double sculls with the same partner in Montreal the year before. However, on the rowing front, you had to be of a certain age to remember when Britain last won gold. That was at the 1948 Olympics.

I wanted an Olympic gold in the single scull, perhaps because Chris Baillieu had shown it could be done with consistently fine results in the double sculls. And he'd been coached by Mike Spracklen, who was already becoming my mentor. Had Britain then been successful at rowing, as we recently have, with my own and others' achievements, I would probably have been drawn towards that. In fact, today it's very difficult to get anybody to scull because everybody wants to be in the rowing team. If you're in the top rowing boat, the chances are you'll win; even if you're in the second boat, there's a very good chance of a medal.

If the best chance of a medal was in the quadruple scull, for example, all the best athletes would be out there sculling, and the sculling trials, just before Christmas at Boston, Lincolnshire, would be a major attraction, not the non-event they are now.

It is always easier to follow than to break new ground. The motivation is much greater if there's something to aim at which somebody has done before, if you can say, 'If they've done that, why can't I do it?'

I was guided in everything I did by Mike Spracklen, who had been away from the international side of things for a couple of years, but possessed the experience and ability to coach at the highest level. He coached Chris Baillieu and Mike Hart to a silver at the 1976 Olympics and then both to a gold at the following year's World Championships. There could be no better man to steer you through to the top. I sat down with him and formulated a plan that appeared realistic, at least on paper.

Everything was to be geared up to prepare me as a single sculler for the 1988 Olympics, capable of winning gold. That was our ultimate goal; if I could get to the Moscow Games in 1980 it would be an excellent start, but more for valuable experience than with any great expectation. Mike was very confident that I could achieve that.

To start with, I would join the sculling group that he was in the process of forming. As I entered my twenties, I hoped to attain as high a position as possible, but not necessarily win medals. In 1983, I'd move to the double sculls, with the aim of pushing myself into the medals at the 1984 Olympics, or at the very least into a very good final place. The following year I'd go for the World Championships in the double once again, then in 1986 move into the singles, with my final goal a victory in the 1988 Olympics.

That was the plan and I believed it was attainable. I was supremely confident and told my family and friends that I was going to three Olympics, at Moscow, Los Angeles and Seoul, with the ultimate aim of a gold in the single scull at the last.

Mike had been asked to set up his sculling group by the British team management. His brief was to start a young development scheme to build for the future, not just the 1980 Olympics, although the plan was to form a quadruple sculls boat to compete at Moscow. The group was based at his Thames-side home in Marlow. Mike and I had much in common already, having links through Marlow Rowing Club and both living in the town. Everybody else trained at their own rowing clubs, but I used Mike's house as my training venue and kept my boat there. It was a real rowing household. He had a few weights in the garage and liked building boats there, too. When you train at someone's house, you get to know the family well. His sons – Chris, who was two years younger than me, and Adrian, four years my junior – both attended Great Marlow and were both rowing under Francis Smith. Mike's wife

Ann was involved in the school boat fund. Our paths often crossed off the water, too. It became a very close relationship and Mike and I quickly became good friends.

Being quite a small man, it was unfortunate for Mike that, in his prime, there were no lightweight boats, in which he could have excelled. In fact, when lightweight crews were first formed, he coached them, though in truth he was good enough to be in the crew. As an oarsman Mike had won the Empire Games (which became the Commonwealth Games) in 1958 with a fellow named Geoff Baker, who also rowed at Marlow, and who still does a bit of coaching at Leander. They beat the Australian double sculls at that Empire Games, a boat that included an incredible, larger-than-life character called Stuart Mackenzie.

Mackenzie had never won an Olympics, always finding the great Russian sculler Vyasheslav Ivanov too good for him, but he always did well at Henley Royal Regatta. He used to try to beat the opposition by the greatest possible distance, cross the line, then back the boat down and sit on the wooden booms which mark out the course below the finish. His opponent would assume he'd hit the booms and crashed, and would row triumphantly past thinking that he'd won, only to discover the truth. At other times, Stuart would try to get back to the boathouse, change into his jacket and tie, and emerge to shake the vanquished sculler's hand as he came off the water.

Stuart pulled some amazing stunts, things that I'd never do. In fact I've always gone out of my way to avoid upsetting people on the water; yet somehow that's easily done, however honourable your intentions, particularly in the early rounds at Henley. If you row just in front of inexperienced or moderate opposition and win by, say, half a length, then you're accused of taking the mickey out of them. If you row quite hard and win by a long margin, then you're just showing off and being arrogant. But what can you do? You have to try to beat them, but by an 'acceptable' margin, such as two lengths.

But to return to Mike Spracklen...he was an outstanding sculler and once won the Scullers' Head, a gruelling event that takes place over the Boat Race course, so everyone respected him greatly. Mike, who was in charge of the women's team at Sydney, is a fanatic, a perfectionist. Maybe I also had an affinity with him because he's always been his own boss. He's got a family building business and a decorating concern in Marlow, but his real love is rowing, and particularly coaching.

In the summer we often trained at Thorpe Park in Surrey. Mike would drive us there and on the way we'd discuss many issues. He was very determined and single-minded and nothing would distract him from what he wanted to achieve and what he wanted you to achieve. He was self-taught; the skills he developed were from his own experiences, in contrast to the East German system, where you're trained to be a coach. Our relationship changed over the years from master–pupil to equals, who'd break new ground together. By 1986, after six years with Mike, I had learnt all he could teach me, and from then on it was new for both of us. Andy Holmes, with whom I won two Olympic golds, sometimes found that closeness between us difficult. He became the outsider of the group, when normally it's the coach who's the outsider. Apart from Jurgen Grobler, who arrived in 1991 from East Germany, I had only one other coach, Pat Sweeney, who was also our cox at one time. He coached Matthew Pinsent and myself during our first year.

Mike's sculling group contained senior, more experienced oarsmen who had been to international events to give the group a bit of depth, but the members were generally young. I was the youngest, together with another teenager Adam Clift, with whom I'd clashed blades before. He'd also been a member of the British team in Moscow, where he and his partner, both from Hollingworth Lake Rowing Club, had performed excellently to finish sixth in the double sculls. Adam had moved south from Hollingworth Lake, near Rochdale, where he had been at college. Initially he lived with his uncle in Haslemere, but later came to stay at my parents' house, and was soon followed by Julian Scrivener. It became something of a young rowers' academy. Besides competing in the double scull, Adam had also been selected to go to the Junior Championships in the quadruple scull the year before in Belgrade. We'd raced each other a number of times and I'd generally beaten him, but he was my closest rival. Technically, we were still juniors. Then there was Ian Gold, who had done the junior singles a couple of years before, and two older athletes. Andrew Justice had competed in the quadruple scull in the 1976 Montreal Olympics, and also rowed at Marlow, so I knew him quite well. And Mark Hayter had been in the 1975 World Championship quad and the 1976 Olympics. His brother James was my GP in Marlow. They had both retired but came back to the group, tempted by the Moscow Olympics.

I used to row quite a lot with Andrew Justice in a double, and learnt a lot from him. He was very consistent and solid, but did not produce good enough performances when we trained in singles to get a top four position that would get him into Mike Spracklen's quad. However, Andrew was a very good crew member, capable of making crew boats go fast. Those who rowed with Mark, who was coming to the end of his career, and Andrew, gave them a lot of respect. Other members included Gordon Jacks and Julian Scrivener, both former junior internationals. Eric Sims, who came into the group later, had been in Mike's sculling groups in the past.

Other oarsmen joined us at weekends, but there was a core group of about eight of us. Adam and myself, as the two youngsters, were looked on as the basis of the group for the future. We were given as much chance as we needed to prove that we had what it takes.

Looking back, there was never any evidence of great confidence in the individuals themselves that, yes, one day they were going to be Olympic champions. I got the distinct impression that it was more about people trying to get into the senior team for the Olympic Games; that was an end in itself. They didn't appear to share my sense of urgency about winning medals. It was talked about, but without real serious intent. Frankly, that didn't bother me unduly because my long-term aim was to shape my own destiny as a single sculler.

The disappointment suffered in the Moscow Junior Championships had made me determined to do really well in the junior singles the following year. But there was also the possibility of going to the 1980 Moscow Olympics in the quadruple sculls boat that Mike was putting together.

Chris Baillieu and Mike Hart had gone their separate ways after the 1978 World Championships when Mike retired. Chris Baillieu formed another double with Jim Clark. Hugh Mattheson became the single sculler. Where sculling was concerned, the seats in the quad were the only ones still empty. The lure of the Olympics was much greater than anything else, but Adam and I vowed that if we did not make the Games, we would do a double scull in the Junior World Championships a couple of weeks later.

Through that first winter of 1979–80, I was in the middle of the sculling group where general training was concerned, but when it came to set pieces of work, I found myself towards the top. I was able to raise my game when necessary. However, it was very tough going and very intense compared with what I had been familiar with as a junior. It was like constantly going out to race rather than just to train. We got together on Saturdays and Sundays for two sessions each day and we also trained in our own time. Then we'd go out as a group on Tuesday and Thursday nights, even if it was dark, which it was in winter.

Everybody had a job of some sort, except me, in the early stages. That's the way it was with most Olympic sports at that time, when amateurism was still a virtue. Eric was an electrician, Julian was at art college in Guildford. Ian Gold, who was a member of Polar and Blackwell District Rowing Club, used to come over from the East End. His father would drive him in a mini-van in which Ian would sleep *en route*. He would do his training and then get driven back. You had to have an income of some sort, though, and by the time I had turned 18, I was working for myself as a landscape gardener and helping my father out with building work. It still allowed me to dedicate as much time as I needed to training. My parents were tremendously supportive throughout. I don't know if they really believed I'd reach the heights that I eventually did. They knew I had ability, but one of the thrills for them was seeing how far I could go. They never said to me, 'Oh, we always knew you'd be Olympic champion.' Their prime objective was to let me achieve what I could.

Sometimes that first winter I'd be absolutely shattered by the training regime. We normally trained in single sculls and, with the flood streams coming down at that time of the year, you'd get swept to the bottom of the stretch quite quickly without doing very much, and have to slog all the way back. Inwardly, you would be screaming, 'God, I can't manage this; this is just too hard work.'

So you'd find yourself slacking off and not doing the training properly in your own individual sessions. You were aware that when you got to the weekends it would all be so competitive in the single sculls and you knew that your performance was being ranked. It could make the difference of being in the top four or not.

Now the training is all geared up to the Olympic Games, not your performance next Saturday. That always seemed a very short-sighted view at the time. It made the training very intense on those set days and very difficult to put the right effort in the rest of the time. As years went by, I coped with the training much better and developed stamina and endurance, which had been my weaknesses.

My great asset within a boat has always been my explosive power and ability to create sheer speed from the start. I was by far the physically strongest of Mike Spracklen's group. But in my earlier years, I lacked that vital quality – endurance. To improve that, I had no alternative but to go out on my own and build up my stamina steadily over a period of time. It was always something that I needed to work on more than my basic strength. Eventually, that factor was to make the difference between me being the best athlete in the UK and one of the top performers in the world.

Eric Sims, with whom I won my first Henley medal, was the complete opposite. He never possessed the acceleration levels that I had, but his endurance levels were incredible. He could row at a high level for a long period. In fact, I found it quite hard training with him; he was always there, like a snappy dog biting at your ankles, determined to be the best in the group. But you knew if you could hang on for a spurt at the end, you'd win.

Despite the tough training that winter, Adam and I showed enough potential to demonstrate that we should have a place in the British quadruple sculls crew bound for Moscow. When Eric joined, he slotted into that top four crew as well. Mark Hayter was initially in that group, but age was against him. Julian Scrivener was around the bottom end of the group all winter, but as soon as the boat did not perform as had been expected, Julian was in and Mark out. And that was the crew under Mike's direction. Some weekends we got together with the rowing group. We used to train against Martin Cross and his coxless four, who had been World Championship bronze medallists the previous two years. We should have been faster because the quad is a much quicker boat. (In terms of speed, the eight is the fastest, followed by the quad, the coxless four, coxed four, double scull, coxless pair, single, and the slowest – the coxed pair.) Martin's crew was at the top of the coxless fours, and we were at the middle to bottom of the quads, so it was quite competitive.

Gradually, I began to push myself to the top of the sculling group. There were very few that I felt were of my calibre, so I couldn't see it being a highly successful boat, winning medals. The talent wasn't there. It might be considered arrogant, but at that stage I was so much faster than anyone else in a single. And on the few occasions that I did revert to rowing, I did very well. But the brutal truth was that if I hadn't hit the standard yet to do well in world events, as Moscow had led me to believe, then nobody else in this country was anywhere near the right level either.

I should say a little about Great Britain team selection. Traditionally, going back a decade or more, Olympic places were given to the club producing the fastest eight, or any other crew, that particular season. It was a fallible system because it didn't guarantee that the best people were chosen. On the contrary, good oarsmen were often left behind.

Although we had changed by the early 1980s to what was called a 'squad system', in reality crews were more like private armies under a squad banner. For instance, at that time the British coxless four, coached by David Tanner, was a club-based crew from the London Rowing Club. (Coincidentally, it included Martin Cross at stroke. He was to be a member of the boat in which I won my first Olympic gold.)

Under David, this crew won the junior silver in 1975, got selected as a four for the World Championships in 1977, when they came tenth, and then at Moscow in 1980 claimed an Olympic bronze. As our tally of Olympic medals then was about as numerous as Richard Branson's successfully completed balloon flights, a bronze was ranked very highly.

However, in no way could that be considered a squad system. The four had been kept together since competing as juniors and their seats had not been challenged from one year to the next. By contrast, Mike Spracklen's sculling group was based more on a pure squad system. Where everyone trains in single sculls, as we did, you can establish a genuine ranking of crew members.

In 1980, our first season together, the quadruple sculls boat performed well enough at international regattas in Essen, Mannheim and Copenhagen, finishing third at the last, to be optimistic about Olympic selection. We then won the Nottinghamshire International Regatta, where Adam and I, who had formed a successful partnership in the double sculls, were also victorious in our event.

In July, we returned to Nottingham for the National Championships, from where I departed with three gold medals all won on the same day – in the junior and open double sculls with Adam, and in the open quad sculls in a crew that comprised Adam, Eric Sims, Julian Scrivener and myself.

However, away from sport, events had been taking place across Europe that had a dramatic effect on our hopes of an Olympic place. When we started the international season in May, there were already political noises in the West that there might be a boycott of the Moscow Games because of the Russian invasion of Afghanistan.

Under pressure from President Jimmy Carter, the America Olympic Association – the equivalent of our British Olympic

Association (BOA) – barred their athletes from competing in the forthcoming Olympic Games, as did West Germany and Kenya. Here in Britain, the government left the decision to the BOA, which in turn left it to the individual sporting associations. Most remained committed to sending teams. Each sport was asked, 'Should we boycott the Olympics?'

In rowing, we were committed to competing – I certainly was – although some individuals were not happy. Mike Spracklen, for one, believed that the Games should be held at an alternative venue, or postponed.

However, the issue was far more complicated than that because of Margaret Thatcher's stance. The Prime Minister had made it abundantly clear that her government was totally opposed to Britain competing. She was quoted as saying, 'British athletes have the same rights and the same responsibilities towards freedom and its maintenance as every citizen of the UK...for British athletes to take part in the Games in Moscow...would be for them to seem to condone an international crime.'

The government does not give money directly to send a team to the Olympics. Funds come from the BOA, which privately fund-raises through sponsors. The only money rowing receives from the government is from the Sports Council (now Sport England), but that is to administrate our sport, not send an Olympic team. But once a government comes out with the statement that a country should not send an Olympic team, what are sponsors going to do?

The BOA carried on its fund-raising efforts as normal, but it was much harder to find sponsorship for the Olympic team that year because of the political situation. Many companies got cold feet. In particular, a lot of money would have come from American companies based in the UK, but they couldn't be seen to be acting in a manner contrary to their own government's policy.

The outcome was that the BOA wasn't able to raise the necessary money to send the numbers of athletes that it originally intended. Only a skeleton team was sent and the lesser-ranked athletes in all sports were left behind. That, we soon discovered, included us.

The BOA worked everything out in percentage terms, with sports being given a quota of the numbers they were allowed to send. At that time, there was no formal qualification for the Olympics. If your country wanted to send you, you went. Now, in rowing and most other sports, you have to pre-qualify to demonstrate that you are of a certain standard to gain selection for an Olympic Games.

In 1980, the yardstick was that if you could reach ninth place world-wide within your discipline, you were good enough to gain selection. We were at that sort of level, about ninth.

Normally, there would have been 14 Olympic boat categories, but the quota meant that only seven of the eight men's boats and five of the six women's crews would be sent to compete. Although Britain did not win gold medals, it did produce a lot of finalists. The women's eight, for example, would almost certainly be in the final because there'd be only six boats competing. That meant they were ranked above us, although there might be anything up to 20 boats in our event.

It was understandable that boats with better chances should go. We were a borderline case. But at least we had produced some reasonable results, unlike the British eight, which was performing badly.

I felt that the British team officials were anxious for the eight to go rather than us. We heard comments on the grapevine, such as, 'Oh, they're the youngest group. Eric's the oldest – and he's 21. Their time will come. Anyway, two of them are still juniors [Adam and me]: we can't take them to the Olympics and allow them to miss out on the opportunity of doing well at the Junior Championships.'

In the event, there was a reshuffle of the eights group, and that crew then produced two outstanding performances during their last two races. That pushed them above us in the rankings, and we dropped off the bottom.

When we were told that we were the only men's crew not going to the Moscow Olympics, I was extremely bitter. We'd put in a lot of dedicated training to try and get there. If there had never been any realistic chance, I would have accepted it. But here I had been teased with the opportunity, then seen it snatched away from me.

Even though I knew I wasn't going to be an Olympic champion at that time, it was something I had set my sights on when I had sat at home and watched the Munich Games as a young boy. Based on a normal year's performances, we'd done enough to be selected as part of the British team, even though we would undoubtedly have done poorly once we were there. Our quadruple sculls boat wouldn't have won, or come anywhere close. There is no disputing that. We were at the bottom end of the standard required. I harboured no romantic notions that if we had been there we would have won. However, that wasn't the point.

Although it was left to individual sports, it was effectively Margaret Thatcher's stance that denied us the chance. Understandably, it provoked an extreme anti-Thatcher feeling among many of us. For her, it was just a matter of political expediency. She and her government were anxious to follow America's lead. Although she could not actually prevent the team from travelling, the position she took had a significant effect.

I've always taken the view that sport and politics should never be mixed. Unfortunately, it's the easiest thing for a government to make a political statement by using sport. It doesn't cost them anything. If you wish to persuade the Soviet Union to pull out of Afghanistan, what do you do if you are American politicians? Stop your Olympic team going to the Moscow Games, or stop selling grain to Moscow? Obviously, the latter, because that's going to punish the Soviets much more in real terms, potentially threatening their survival. But the fact is that stopping grain exports would have hurt the Americans financially. Denying the Olympic athletes their chance of glory wouldn't.

It's the same with the question of apartheid in South Africa. We wouldn't play them at sport for many years. But what good did it do? Did we stop trading with South Africa? No. We traded near enough right the way through, and it wasn't until quite late on when it was obvious that the sports boycott was not having any real effect at all that we actually stopped trading. We had continued to import South African gold, still bought their diamonds, and a lot of our banking was South Africa-based. But stopping that would have had financial implications, and however great the principle is, people are not going to throw away money.

Yet, media-wise, they can get a quick fix through sport. The Olympics is the ideal platform for that. I'm not saying that a sports boycott is necessarily right or wrong. If it has an effect, maybe there's an argument for it; but the reality is that it doesn't change anything in itself. If you're going to boycott a country, you go the whole way. You stop trading with them on a sporting and a business basis. You totally blackball them. You don't go half-way and use amateur athletes who have trained for years.

I know Americans who had prepared for years for the Moscow Olympics and, unlike myself, actually had first-rate chances of a medal, but weren't allowed to go because their association is government-funded. It was the same with the West Germans. They were all told they could not go.

In the UK, you might have had athletes who had put six, maybe 12 years, of their life into preparing for an Olympics and the possibility of winning a gold medal, then literally three or four months before they were due to depart, some politician says, 'Oh, I'm awfully sorry, but you can't go.' Then he adds: 'Because of the Russians going into Afghanistan, we want to make a statement on this. Sorry and all that, old chap. Oh, and we're still going to trade with the country and carry on other contacts, but sporting-wise we want to use you to make a point.' It simply wasn't right.

If you feel strongly about the situation in Afghanistan as an individual and want to make your own statement, that's acceptable. If there was someone within my crew saying 'This isn't right,' fine. I could have accepted that. But someone outside, not involved, who most of the time didn't give a damn about what happened in sport? I couldn't accept that at all. That bitterness stayed with me for a very long time.

What difference did it actually make to that situation? Twelve months later where were the Soviets? Still in Afghanistan. It took them three and a half years before they withdrew. Why did they? Because the Afghan people were such good rebel fighters. They were killing a lot of the Russian forces and they had to make a tactical retreat. So the political statement that people made at the Moscow Olympics made absolutely no difference at all. It was just a good media bandwagon to be on at the time.

The only consolation I can take is that I can look back at every Olympic Games I've been to with the knowledge that I've won a gold medal, which I wouldn't have done if I'd gone to Moscow. I've always achieved my best performances in Olympic Games and that has given me great confidence going into the next one. I can just about put up with that Moscow disappointment now.

At least it meant that, as I prepared for Sydney 2000, I had never lost in an Olympics. As I will discuss later, the psychological battle is extremely important. Your rivals might have been able to say, 'Well, he didn't win at his first Olympics at Moscow – perhaps he won't win at his last in Sydney.'

Those are the kind of areas where you're always looking to score mentally. In the build-up, every rower in the coxless fours at Sydney will have been thinking, 'How am I going to beat this person?' If you are convinced that somebody is beatable, you've got more chance of defeating them.

The importance of psychology in sport is far greater than many people believe. If you look in percentage terms at the difference in abilities, it's very small. It's the belief in that person that they can win, and probably, more importantly, the belief that their opposition are not invincible.

If that was to have been the only Olympics I ever had the chance of being selected for, or if, by the nature of my sport, I was at the top for only a short period of time and that was the Olympics I was going to win a gold medal in, yes, I'd feel even more angry about the whole affair.

Fortunately, at that time Adam and I had another challenge to meet, one which, on paper, gave us a definite chance of gold in 1980.

CHAPTER 6

LOSING MY COOL

Once it was announced that the quad was not going to Moscow, it looked like I'd join the Olympic eight. They were coached by Graeme Hall, who often consulted Mike Spracklen because of his fine reputation as a coach. Despite some solid performances leading up to the Games, which meant that the eight were going and not us, Graeme was having problems with one of the crew, Alan Whitwell. He had been in Mike's sculling groups in the past and rowed with Eric Sims in the 1978 quad that went to New Zealand, but he was regarded as an awkward individual. Although a decent athlete, Alan always knew a better way of doing things. Everything had to be done his way or it was not good enough. It was a very destructive attitude and Graham did not want him in his group. The idea was to bring me in to replace him.

In fact, I was not selected because it was decided that Adam and I should go to the Junior World Championships where everyone hoped that we'd get a gold medal.

At that time, none of us were to know that the eight would go on to win a silver medal at the Olympics. That crew, incidentally, included the man who was later to become the Conservative Government's Sports Minister, Colin Moynihan, as cox. In the final, Moynihan's rudder strings broke and he had to steer the last part of the course with his hands behind his back.

Obviously, I would still have liked to go to Moscow, and the course of events irritated me. I knew I was as good as if not better than some members of the eight. Indeed, on physical testing, I was better than most of them.

If they had picked me in that eight, could it have won gold? I don't believe so. East Germany won by a convincing three seconds. Nevertheless, it was disappointing to find the door half opening for me, and then closing again. But I forced myself to be philosophical about it. I was still only 18, and there had only been a year between thinking that I might make the Olympics and then discovering I wouldn't. Other people can take five, six years to find that out. So it was not a huge blow.

When I had performed so poorly in the Junior World Championships the year before in Moscow, my initial aim had been to put that right the following year and do well in the single sculls. Because I had been crew sculling there was no way I could compete at the level I'd have liked to, even in the junior singles. It's just not possible to make that transition. The option, with Adam, was to go to the Junior Championships in the double, although we were by no means well prepared for it.

Mentally, Adam and I, while trying to be selected for the Olympics, had blocked out any thought of going to the Junior Championships, or if we did go, it would just be very much of secondary importance. Because we'd been used to racing seniors, Adam and I thought we'd have no problem taking on our peers again. Anyway, the course was shorter, at 1500 metres, and the opposition obviously weaker. We should win easily. That was our attitude as Adam and I, who were now rowing under Marlow Rowing Club colours, travelled out to Hazewinkel in Belgium for the championships.

It was during our preparations for that event that Adam and I came to blows. It would not be the only occasion during our time together. It happened after training at Marlow when Mike had not been out with us on the water. As Adam was bow of the double, in theory it was his responsibility to steer the boat. It's easier to steer in the bow position than any other. I became increasingly annoyed with him because we'd not only hit the bank several times, but on the opposite side to the one we should have been on.

Steering upstream, when the stream is fast, is not easy. The idea is to get as close to the bank as possible because you're out of the current. But there are also a lot of hazards such as overhanging trees. You've got to know exactly where you are. The more you do it, the better you become.

In 1980 when Adam and I were in the quad, I got the job by default. It meant that I was used to steering on that stretch of the river. I was aware of all the hazards and rarely got caught by trees. I would be annoyed with myself if I did, but tried to see how quickly I could get out of that situation and get going again. Adam, however, just lost his temper.

Anyway, when I complained, he swore back at me and an argument ensued with several threats issued. Adam's final shot, in his strong Lancastrian accent, was: 'When we get back I'm going to give you a real leathering.' I can't say I was too worried. Although he was tall, like me, he was not so heavy and because we trained with each other I knew I was much stronger.

We finished the session and returned in silence. Mike came out of his house. We put the boat away, went back for the blades and put them away. We were on opposite sides of the garden and appeared to be totally calm. Spontaneously we looked up and flew at each other like a couple of tom cats. Mike rushed over and jumped on my back. He said it was like being on the back of a camel as Adam and I set into each other. He was completely taken aback, and he never allowed us out on our own again. He just didn't trust us. We calmed down eventually but there was friction between Adam and me for a time. It was probably caused by us living out of each other's pockets. Not only was Adam was living in the same house as me, but we were also rowing and socializing together. It was too intense, too claustrophobic, and familiarity was breeding contempt.

I'm not normally one to lose my rag. When I do, I'm as volatile as anyone, but I take a long time to get there. There could be weeks of being slowly wound up and the fuse burning before the explosion will detonate. That incident probably didn't do us any harm. It allowed us to let off a bit of steam.

As a character, Adam was always very honest and up front, which I liked in a rowing partner. He has always said exactly what he thought, didn't call a spade a digging implement, and you knew where you stood with him. I've always rated him very highly.

Adam was in the difficult situation of coming down from the north, having had an unusually disciplined upbringing. That's no reflection on his family, whom I know very well and with whom I have remained great friends. His father was in the Guards and then joined the police force and that way of life rubbed off on Adam. I always thought that if he hadn't become a rower, and then a coach, he would have gone into the forces like his father.

We were intense rivals as well as fellow crew members. We were both very headstrong at the time and felt we were better than each other. In that situation, it can be difficult to be friends on and off the water. Adam used to come up to me and say, in his domineering way: 'I'm going to thrash you this time.' Never once did he actually do so in any race. But he would never accept that.

Yet, the friction between us was not just caused by us being over-competitive on the water. When he first came down south it was very soon after my great friend Robert had died. My mother was worried that I did not appear to have any close friends, and Adam and I were pushed together.

Other friends I'd been rowing with had gone off to university. My relationship with Nicola, the girl I had been going out with when Robert died, was coming to its natural conclusion. I was always something of a loner, as I've already mentioned, and in my mother's eyes that was unhealthy and it concerned her.

Yet my friendship with Adam endured and, once we went off on our separate rowing ways, we've always got on with each other. In fact, his wife Melanie, who represented Britain in the junior and senior eight and lightweight four in the early eighties, now works as my personal assistant. Adam oversees the rowing lake at Eton, which opened in 2000.

People often ask whether training on the Thames, particularly when it's fast-flowing, can be a hindrance or a help. After all, apart from Henley Royal Regatta, virtually all the international races are on lakes without currents. In fact, it does help in a way. It gives you more awareness of what's around you. During winter you're struggling with the stream, and in summer the hazard is holiday cruisers. And at least we do train in winter; in a lot of European countries training is held up because the rivers freeze up. We plough on regardless.

Sometimes the cruisers do, too. There was an incident back in 1981 when Eric Sims, Julian Scrivener, Adam Clift and myself were doing some work in a quad between Marlow and Cookham. We came round a corner at Bourne End and a cruiser suddenly appeared from nowhere, smashing into our blades. We were shocked. The cruiser was in completely the wrong position on the river. We were really going to give them a mouthful. Then the boat circled round and a sweet little old lady appeared. She called out cheerily in that typically British way, 'Would you like a cup of tea, boys?' That deflated us completely. We didn't have the heart to berate her.

Otherwise I have escaped major incidents, although Simon Berrisford, who was to partner me in the pairs for a time in 1989, and I once smashed head-on into a narrow boat that had been moored up near Leander with its stern sticking out into the river. That crumpled the bows of our boat. The pair of us also collided with the barge that is used for placing the pylons in the river bed which hold the booms during Henley Royal Regatta. That time, we took on water, but emerged unscathed.

Occasionally, there can be collisions off the water too. That happened to our coach Mike Spracklen as Adam and I prepared at Hazewinkel for those 1980 Junior World Championships. We had cruised through our heat and it was the same with the semi-finals, but then things started to go awry. Adam and I were doing a piece of work and Mike was taking the times, cycling along the bank, looking across the water.

Unfortunately, the French team manager was doing the same with his crew, but coming the other way, and they collided at full pelt. Mike was knocked unconscious and was in hospital for three days. His absence at that crucial period was a major setback. In the final we discovered that we'd all underestimated the East German double. We didn't know much about them because we'd never come across them before. Obviously any competitor from that nation was likely to be a threat, but Adam and I thought we'd beat them anyway.

We shot into the lead, then really struggled through the middle 500 metres. I looked across and, to my mind, the East Germans had gone for home. They were well in front, leaving us neck and neck with the West Germans and Russians. I remember thinking, 'Shit, we're not even going to win a medal. What's gone wrong?' Suddenly, we kicked into a different gear and the boat flew. I looked across at the Russians during the last few strokes, gritted my teeth and put everything into a final effort which I thought might get us the bronze. We actually got the silver. It was not until four or five hours afterwards that I plucked up the courage to look at the time sheets and saw we'd failed to reach the East Germans by less than one second. Afterwards, we took the boat off the water and went off in different directions. We were bitterly disappointed. If we'd have raced the East Germans 10 times, we'd have beaten them nine times. It was one of the few times in my life when I felt that a boat I was in was capable of winning, but failed.

In a strange way, we both felt that we'd let each other down. What we could not have known was that the East German boat had a character called Thomas Langer, only 16 at the time. He later won two Olympic gold medals and five World Championships. He also won three junior golds, aged 16, 17 and 18, before moving straight into his nation's senior team and becoming world champion. The first time he lost was in 1990 at the World Championships in Tasmania, although he came back and won the Olympics in 1992. Despite poor preparation for the event, we had lost to one of the most outstanding scullers the world has ever seen, and his partner, by the narrowest margin. However, there was little doubt that we'd approached those championships far too light-heartedly. We felt we were superior beings because we had been regularly racing the 'big boys' distance, and because we were then way ahead of the rest of the British juniors. Once we had come to terms with that defeat, at least we could console ourselves with the knowledge that winning a junior medal told the world something. By achieving that, we had proved we were up there with the best. We had no doubt that we would continue into the seniors.

Shortly afterwards, I started going out with Belinda Holmes, who was in the British junior women's team. It was a relationship that lasted six years in total, although initially it was not easy as Belinda was at college in London and training at Hammersmith while I was out in Marlow. In 1982 and 1983, she was in her last year at university and I moved into London. We rented a flat in Kew. When she finished college a year later we moved back to Marlow Bottom.

Belinda rowed in the 1984 Olympics in the eight which was the best women's boat for most of the years I knew her. One of her fellow crew members was Ann Callaway, who would later become Mrs Ann Redgrave. At the time, Ann's boyfriend was Martin Cross, who would row with me at the Los Angeles Olympics. And they were not the only cross-boat partnerships. Belinda's younger sister Melanie was a year younger than Adam and me. She joined the women's junior team in 1980 and went straight into the senior squad. Inevitably, we all saw a lot of each other in that period and Adam had his sights on Melanie for a long time. They eventually followed Ann and me down the aisle. The river was a very romantic place in those days!

On the water, the events of 1980 had a significant effect on me. They fuelled my determination to go to an Olympic Games but my aim remained the same, to get there in a single scull. My early results in 1981 showed that I was making excellent progress. I won the Elite Sculls at the Delft International in Holland over a 6km canal, and then, significantly, came second in the Head of the River Race for Scullers. Out of 433 competitors I was beaten only by the country's number one at the time, Chris Baillieu, who won the event for a record sixth time. He also knocked two seconds off the record time. Alan Whitwell and Eric Sims were just behind me.

At the time, I partnered Eric in the double sculls and our victories included the Double Sculls Challenge Cup at Henley Royal

Regatta, the first of my many successes there. It was an overdue first victory at Henley in 100 years for a member of Marlow Rowing Club. Meanwhile, our quad was beginning to emerge as a potent force. Eric and I joined Adam and Malcolm Carmichael at Henley in the inaugural Queen Mother Challenge Cup. We lost in the final to a German crew.

A couple of weeks later, Eric and I celebrated victory in the open double sculls at the National Championships at Holme Pierrepont and a crew of Julian Scrivener, Eric, Adam and myself won the open quadruple sculls event. That earned the quad a place in the World Championships at Munich.

We enjoyed a mixed few days in Germany, and for the first time I had the experience of criticism in the press. Although we gave it absolutely everything in our heat and were spent when we came to the finish, we did not qualify for the semi-final automatically.

We got a slating in the media. However, we compensated for it somewhat by winning our repechage, so we got into the semi-final by that route. Unfortunately, we failed to make it into the last six, and had to take part in what is usually referred to as the 'small final' (from the French '*petite finale*'), where we could record a position of seventh to twelfth place.

We were so disappointed that we did not have the enthusiasm for it. We went out half-heartedly, and in the middle of the race we were last, but started overtaking boats and eventually realized we were in with a shout of seventh place overall. We finished with a powerful burst and secured second spot, which gave us a final finishing position of eighth. The press reports the following day said that we had shown a gutsy performance.

It wasn't, by any stretch of the imagination. It was just deceptive to those in the stands. When the rowing correspondents sit there at the finish, they only view the latter stages of a six-minute race – or did before TV coverage became more comprehensive – but tend to judge a crew on that 45 seconds' glimpse. If we should have been taken to task, it was because of our attitude in the small final. We'd gone out there with the wrong attitude and the way we approached the race was totally wrong. Because it looked good in those last 45 seconds, we were applauded in the newspapers. That frustrated me. Since then, I have stopped reading regatta reports.

I was disappointed not to have at least made the final at my first senior World Championships. But we always knew the real aim was the 1984 and 1988 Olympics. It was pleasing to find that the sport's annual bible, the *British Rowing Almanack*, suggested that

'If the crew stays together and improves its middle 1,000 metres it can only be time before it realizes its undoubted potential.' I was not quite so convinced, though. As I have already said, in my own mind I saw our progress merely as a stepping stone for my personal ambitions. I believed myself to be considerably better than the rest of the quad, but had to serve my apprenticeship before moving on to bigger and better things. However, things were about to change on the administration and political front that were to break the sculling group apart.

In the autumn I continued to do well in single sculls events, beating Adam into third place at the Weybridge Silver Sculls, but still found Chris Baillieu too good when finishing second to him in the Marlow Long Distance Sculls. It was also the year when I won my first award, Wycombe District Sports Personality of the Year. Meanwhile the quad continued to perform with the dominance expected of the nation's top boat in that discipline in long-distance events. We won the Head of the Rivers Fours Race and the Tiffin Scullers Head, from Kingston to Hampton Court.

It was at the beginning of 1982 that Martin Cross joined the group. He had been a bronze medallist in the coxless fours at Moscow, and that boat had also finished third at each of the two preceding World Championships. None of his boat were outstanding athletes but they had been moulded into a fine combination, under the coaching of David Tanner.

At that time, a controversial figure named Penny Chuter was in charge of the whole team and her specific role was to coach the eight. Martin didn't want to be part of that, or be involved with her in any way. He did not respect her because of the way that she had run groups in the past, an issue I will return to later. Martin had not sculled before and was not the smoothest of oarsmen, but he was very determined.

We had all kinds of assessments that winter, during which Mike was out in India for a time, coaching. Training continued to be very intense and times were taken. Martin scored quite well on one of the tests. For some strange reason, all the records when Mike was away were lost apart from that one. Martin made sure Mike saw the finishing order when he got back. I found that quite amusing, but as I got to know him better I realized it was typical of Martin, who in all senses of the word was, and still is, very much a political animal. In the end, Martin made it into the quad that year. We switched the order around. In the previous two years, I'd been stroking the crew, but that seat was now given to Martin and

I moved back into the three seat. To my mind, the sculling group was progressing well and I thought I was making a significant contribution. But suddenly, for the first time in my career, I was told that my attitude was not good enough. It happened at the first regatta of the year in Vichy, France. While we were out there Mike Spracklen took me to one side and accused me of being destructive with some of my comments about the quad in crew discussions. He said I should buck my ideas up, and added that I should make my mind up 'whether you want to be part of the crew. Otherwise you'd better go off and do your own thing.'

I was taken aback. Mike had never spoken to me like that before. In the past he had always tried to build me up. Now he was tearing into me. But it did make me think. In truth, there has always been a negative side of me, by which I mean that I was rarely satisfied with a performance of a boat I was in and, perhaps too often, voiced that feeling. In Mike's view it destroyed the harmony that should exist within a boat. My response was to work hard to change that attitude. But over the years it remained a characteristic of mine. Of the Sydney 2000 crew, I'd say James Cracknell was the most negative, in the sense of rarely being satisfied, followed by me. Matthew was probably the best balanced, while Tim Foster always looked for the best in everything.

Returning to 1982, that chastisement from Mike did me no harm. Adam and I continued our success in the double sculls. After victory at Marlow, we won the double sculls at Henley, the first occasion that a Marlow crew had won the trophy outright for our club. We then joined with Eric and Martin to establish a record-breaking win in the quads event, the Queen Mother Cup, albeit that the previous record had been set the year before, the inaugural year of the event! Before the World Championships in Lucerne we raced at Duisberg, in West Germany, and performed reasonably well. We did not leave immediately afterwards on the Sunday night; instead everybody went out drinking and socializing. It might appear by now that I was a thoroughly abstemious sort in my youth, but I have to confess I had my nights. Generally, though, I was only a moderate drinker. There was no alternative if you considered yourself an elite athlete, as I did.

I remember that night particularly well because a few of us were in a bar drinking from a large glass boot. Once you lifted it up and downed the beer, the top became an air lock. Unless you had perfected the technique, the forces of physics suddenly came into play and the drink was propelled all over you, rather than going down your throat, much to everyone's merriment. I left relatively early to go back to the hotel room which I was sharing with Adam. I then got to hear that some of the team had been arrested.

Apparently, they had come out of the bar and were walking over the tops of cars on the way back. Some members of the lightweight eight had also been playing a game of 'How many lightweight rowers can you squeeze into a telephone box?' when the police arrived.

Surprisingly, it seemed that Martin had been involved and got arrested, although that was totally out of character. They all spent the night in jail. The upshot was that our crew was banned from going to the Amsterdam Regatta, the top international regatta that year, prior to the World Championships. David Tanner, who was coaching a lightweight four that year, was very friendly with Martin because of all the years they'd been involved in that successful four together. He put up a really strong political fight because it transpired that Martin hadn't been involved in any trouble; he had just happened to be there when the police were hauling people in. We had our ban lifted, but decided not to race anyway. Nevertheless, the whole affair was embarrassing for the British team.

During that period Alan Whitwell replaced Eric, who had been ousted from the crew by Mike Spracklen. Alan strengthened the boat for the World Championships, though he must have wondered what he'd walked into when he witnessed two of his fellow crew members, Adam and myself, take yet another swing at each other. We were at a training camp at Varese in Italy, just before the 1982 World Championships. Tension had been building up again between Adam and me, and this time we got into a ridiculous argument about rowing. We had been doing some timed pieces and they hadn't gone as well as expected. At the end, as we sat in the boat, we all had our say, which is quite normal. I pitched in with, 'Well, I wasn't really pulling, anyway.' It wasn't true. I just felt in a bolshie mood and wanted to be argumentative. But Adam, who was sitting next to me, said, 'Yes, I know.'

That set me off and the shouting turned into a fight. Or it would have, had we been able to make serious contact with each other. In a rowing boat, that's not easy, take it from me. You're on sliding seats and your feet are attached to the boat! He'd take a swipe at me and I'd slide back out of the way. I'd then try punching him, but couldn't reach. I just about succeeded in hitting his legs because they were the only things in range. Then Alan, at bow, joined in. 'I've come to row this boat to win a World Championship,' he bellowed, 'and you're blowing my chances.' The rest looked on in astonishment. It was quite juvenile.

Eventually, it abated as quickly as it had blown up. We paddled back to the landing stage, where Adam and I both disappeared in opposite directions until we'd calmed down. In fact neither of us had been doing ourselves justice in training and that incident did clear the air, focusing our minds on the task. I can honestly say that those spats with Adam were the only times that I've really got into a fight, on or off the water. As a rule, rowers are far more composed and disciplined than sportsmen involved in contact sports. You have to be when you're sitting in a precarious conveyance no wider than a briefcase. But there are stories of characters like the Olympic gold medallist Searle brothers, Jonny and Greg, actually plunging into the water and swimming to the bank to settle their differences.

At the Lucerne World Championships of 1982, our quad consisted of Martin Cross, Adam, Alan Whitwell and myself. Despite his unpopularity with the eight in the lead-up to Moscow, Alan had slotted into our boat quite smoothly in the short period that he had been with us. Alan had won an Olympic silver medal and, after the 1980 Games, had attempted to move into the single scull, but had not quite made it, having been beaten by Chris Baillieu, who was the sculler in the British team at that time. Nevertheless, Alan was ranked very highly. He was an excellent athlete, proven at top international level. He was considered to be one of the best scullers around and it was a definite asset having him in the crew. I remember him finishing second, eight seconds behind winner Chris Baillieu in the Head of the River race for scullers that April. I was a further 26 seconds adrift in third.

Certainly, compared to Adam and myself, who ended up fighting, he had matured over the years. By then, Alan was married and his wife actually gave birth to their first child while those World Championships were taking place. He fitted in really well, and added good technique to the boat, as well as banter.

The World Championships amid the scenic splendour of Lake Rotsee were not a conspicuous success, for us or the British team; in fact, it was 'catastrophic' according to the *Daily Telegraph*. From five British finalists, only two escaped last place. The eight had their worst result since 1968. We progressed to the final via the repechage. We knew we were slowest or maybe fifth fastest of the six finalists, but I felt that if we rowed a tactically adept race we had a good chance of fifth. Instead, because Martin and Alan were successful athletes in the boat, both having won championship medals before, the decision was, 'Now we're in the finals, anything can happen. Let's give it a go and see.'

It was a ridiculous policy. We tried to compete with the speed of top boats like the East and West Germans', but it didn't come off. We died quickly because of our initial efforts, and eventually came home a dispirited last by a long way. We were 13 seconds behind the victorious East German crew. That was a very low moment and, after my two first World Championships, an Olympic gold medal appeared as elusive as the Holy Grail. I can recall us approaching the stands and hearing the roar of the crowd, which you do at Lucerne. There's always a lot of cheering from the spectators. Then, I heard the beeps as the winners crossed the line, followed by four more. Then the crowd went silent again and we were still rowing. That's how far behind we were. Even fifth-placed France beat us by seven seconds. A few expletives quietly passed my lips. I hadn't been impressed by the way Martin stroked the crew, or the approach to that race.

I remember vowing to myself at that moment that I would never row with him again. Our technique had broken down completely; it had become more of a rushed rhythm and a desperate scramble rather than trying to apply the power smoothly, which would have been far more effective. We had started off putting everything into it, and moving very quickly, but the boat just wasn't responding to that. Now I've been successful myself, I know that if I'd have had the same target I'd have gone about the task in a completely different manner. It was far too gung-ho. We should have accepted that we weren't going to win and gone for a medal instead. In other words, we should have rowed from start to finish as fast as we were capable, and if that was good enough to win, fair enough. If we had come sixth, fair enough. But we never gave ourselves a chance.

CHAPTER 7

'DO AS YOU'RE TOLD – OR YOU WON'T GO TO THE OLYMPICS'

My irritation with Martin tended to obscure the broader picture. In time I appreciated that it was a massive step forward for a sculling crew to reach the final of a World Championships, and finish sixth overall while performing badly. It was thought if we could stay together, having reached the final, we could go a long way. We were up there with the top countries.

Mike Spracklen's group was really beginning to fulfil its aim, which was to produce finalists, and hopefully medals, by 1984 and beyond. But at a team meeting before those Championships, Mike, who was going to India to coach their national squad for the Asian Games, had given us an ominous warning. He said that while he was away there would be a lot of pressure from the rowing hierarchy to disband us and lure the best scullers into the rowing set-up.

What he feared was exactly what happened. We got tarred with the same brush as the rowing contingent following that dismal summer of 1982. Everything that happened at that time could be traced back to one basic problem: the British team had done so poorly at the 1980 Olympics where our total haul had been one silver and two bronze. That was followed by a silver and one bronze in the 1981 World Championships. And now this latest 'catastrophe'; British rowing was regressing and not improving. Because the rowers had performed so wretchedly, it was considered a case of scrapping the whole thing and starting again. The emphasis was placed on the rowing group, because that's where it was considered the future of the sport, and medals, lay. Increasingly, I was being pressurized to abandon sculling and switch to rowing.

For the past couple of years, I'd had the question of the eight rammed down my throat. After that superb silver the eight won at Moscow, followed by another at the Munich World Championships in 1981, I was constantly being reminded of what the boat could have achieved if I'd been in the crew. However, I continued to insist that I wanted to scull and had no interest in rowing.

Those 1982 World Championships provoked much discussion and there was a lot of political back-biting behind the scenes. Many people in the sport were asking how we had done so badly and the knives were out for the Director of Coaching, Penny Chuter, who had been in charge of the whole team.

Penny has dedicated her life to rowing. In her younger years she had won a silver medal in the European Championships in the single. A very large, robust lady, she had been brought up by the river and, since her earliest years, had been a natural competitor on the water, whether racing punts, skiffs or boats.

Penny studied to become a teacher, and then became involved in coaching. She coached the junior men's eight the year before I joined the team, then made the step up from the juniors to the seniors, so although I knew of her reputation I did not have any contact with her until 1982. Her experience and enthusiasm should have made her a natural coach. Instead, Penny's manner and style of coaching and management had created many enemies.

The fall-out over Britain's failure led to Penny losing her job at the start of 1983. Her replacement was Bob Janousek, a Czechoslovakian by birth, whose real first name was Bohumil. He had arrived in Britain during the time of the Russian invasion and had coached the British eight to a world silver medal in 1977. Bob had departed the international scene by the time I came on it and had been concentrating on his boat manufacturing business at Shepperton Marina.

Before then, most rowing boats had been constructed from wood. He made craft similar to our Aylings boats now, under the trade name Carbocrafts, based on the same technology, using plastic and carbon fibre. The same material is used for the interior of Concorde, with a honeycomb sandwich between two layers of plastic. His slogan, referring to the manufacturing process of his boats, was: 'We don't build them – we cook them!'

Unfortunately, Bob quickly got the nickname 'Pay-Czech', because he was taking his money from the Amateur Rowing Association, but appeared to be more interested in boat-building than he was in being chief coach. He seemed little more than a caretaker coach, his heart not really in it.

However, that period proved to be the end for our sculling group. Martin Cross had grown up as a junior under Janousek and the romanticism of rowing drew him back into that side of the sport. Penny had gone, so there was no conflict there. Adam Clift was asked directly if he would switch to the rowing group. He thought that was a fantastic opportunity, and did so. He saw it as promotion because scullers tended to be dismissed as second-class citizens. Alan Whitwell returned to the eight, and then moved on to the lightweight sculls, winning a gold in the World Championships in 1986. Those defections meant that the sculling group was reduced to four or five doughty souls.

The British team management found I wasn't nearly so compliant. Admittedly, I'd had enough of rowing in quads. I felt I would get better results in a double, which was the boat closest to the single which had been my aim for Seoul, 1988, but I was damned if I was going to join a rowing crew just to please the powers that be. I rebelled and in early 1983 decided to go it alone in the singles. In truth, my hand had been forced. I wouldn't go into a rowing group, there was no one else to scull with, and therefore my only option was the single scull. I always thought this was too early because I didn't think I'd improved enough, or could reach the required level for the 1984 Olympics. Seoul in 1988 seemed a long way away at that stage. Things got resolved when I had a meeting with Bob and he agreed I could carry on sculling, and needn't get involved in rowing. We must have parted on amicable terms because I came away with one of the sculling boats made by his company, which he loaned to me!

My decision drew the battle-lines between the outstanding international sculler Chris Baillieu and myself. For several years previously, he would have been a formidable obstacle to those aspirations. But Chris had finished only sixth at Lucerne in 1982 and appeared to be coming to the end of his career.

I was enthusiastic about single sculling because I wanted it to be my show, and mine alone. The plan I had worked out with Mike Spracklen was still in my mind. There didn't seem any point forming a crew with anyone if it didn't benefit my career. In an ideal crew situation, you want to be the weakest link, not the best. It always appeared that concentrating on the single sculls was the right course for me. In domestic competition, at least, sculling presented few problems. I had taken up the sport as a rower, but as soon as I got into a sculling boat I immediately adapted and found that I was faster than anyone else in my age group. Adam Clift, for example, had always been a sculler and had competed in Junior Championships, but when we raced I used to beat him, no matter how badly I sculled.

When Mike returned to England in early 1983 there was just him and myself left, and two younger members, one being Jonathan Spencer-Jones, or 'Joff', the sculler I had beaten so far in the National Junior Championships back in 1979. As things materialized, Chris Baillieu decided not to do the single but form a double with 'Joff' instead. I put in some good performances at Nottingham, Copenhagen and Henley Royal Regatta – at the latter winning the Diamond Sculls – which ultimately tipped the balance. It was touch and go, but I impressed the selectors sufficiently to scrape through. I had done just about enough for them to name me in the team for the World Championships. At Copenhagen Regatta, as a prelude to the World Championships, I won on consecutive days. On the first I beat my rivals convincingly, but on the second day struggled to beat an unknown Polish oarsman, a shortish, fat guy who stood out because he always wore red braces when he was competing. I was not deceived. None of the top scullers were there.

So to the 1983 World Championships in Duisberg, which proved to be a critical moment in my sculling career. In my heat I was fourth, nearly 17 seconds behind the multi-world champion Peter Michael Kolbe. I took part in the repechage, but people whom I should have beaten were defeating me, even that tubby Pole. I remembered him – probably because of his garb – and thought, 'Ah, there's somebody I know I can beat.' He ended up coming third and I was eliminated. I didn't even make the top 12 overall. It was totally frustrating. I was just not performing. People that I knew I could beat, like the Pole, had suddenly seemed to develop extra velocity – or I was going much slower.

By the Wednesday of the week it was all over for me. Chris Baillieu and 'Joff' Spencer-Jones were eliminated, too. That appeared to be the final act of a great career for 33-year-old Chris. 'Sad end to career of a great warrior,' read the headline in The Times.

The coxless pair, which included my former partner, Julian Scrivener, followed suit. So, the whole group of us was knocked out within about 45 minutes.

I enjoyed the second half of the week. There was water skiing nearby and 'Joff' and I spent a lot of time learning that once we got knocked out, though it wasn't exactly what we had come to Copenhagen to do.

The British team, as a whole, managed to produce just one finalist. That was the coxed four, which included Martin Cross and

Richard Budgett. It was a poor year, and it was perceived, by all concerned, that bringing Bob back hadn't been the correct thing to do. So Penny Chuter was back in charge again.

In a strange way, being eliminated was the best thing that could have happened. It forced me to make major changes in the way I approached racing, training and preparation. From the age of 15 people had been saying to me that I would be world champion and I had remained confident that it would happen, despite the way my career had meandered from moments of glory to occasional ones of ignominy. Having been told that I was going to be world champion one year, I thought, 'What year is this going to be? When's it going to happen?' Since those early days, I had assumed that my name was already engraved on the trophy and I just had to wait for the right year to come along. If I'd have come somewhere between ninth and seventh at those World Championships, I'd have said, 'OK, that's another step forward. Next year I'll get into the final.' I'd have justified it to myself that everything was progressing as I'd plotted with Mike Spracklen. Because I'd failed so manifestly, it dawned on me that it wasn't going to happen. I was not going to be world, or Olympic champion.

People around me now, like Melanie, Belinda's sister, say I was exceptionally self-assured at the time. Undoubtedly, that's how I appeared – on the surface. Underneath, it was all rather different. At the age of 21, I was worried that it all seemed to be slipping away from me.

In 1983, I realized Olympic and World Championship success wasn't going to materialize like manna from heaven. So Mike and I looked at other sports to see how other people trained round the world. That changed the way we prepared. The most important factor was that I had already begun to train full-time, despite the financial hardship. I felt that there was a lack of professionalism in the sport and that most people rowing and sculling simply weren't capable of becoming world or Olympic champions while we did everything on a part-time basis. By that stage, I had given up my part-time work. As I was unemployed, I could claim the unemployment benefit while devoting all my energies to rowing. There was always the problem, of course, that I might actually be offered a job. But in the early eighties there was such massive unemployment that it was unlikely in the case of someone like me, with virtually no qualifications or skills. On the claim form it said: 'Are you available for full-time work?' I wrote 'No' because I was training professionally and felt I should be honest. Instead, I wrote that

I was looking for part-time employment, if it was available. When I turned up at the employment centre in High Wycombe, the chap behind the desk said: 'You've ticked part-time work? If you do that, you won't receive any benefit.' I told him, 'Yes. I'm training for the Olympic Games. That's my only aim.' He said, 'I think you should re-complete the form, saying you're looking for full-time work. You're never going to get a job anyway – and good luck to you.'

So I continued signing on every fortnight and received around £35 a week. Although I didn't feel that I was really sponging off the system, I never felt comfortable about it at all; but I knew there were no other options open if I was to train in the way I wanted to do. If that benefit clerk was satisfied with it, then why should I worry? What I couldn't understand was that the people who were at college were entitled to sign on and receive dole money between terms. I thought that was appalling. That made me feel better about the claims I made.

It enabled me to make a contribution of £15 a week for food and board to my parents. To supplement the family income and help finance my rowing, it was around this time that my mother decided to become a driving instructor. My mother had taught my sisters and me to drive, and enjoyed doing it. She felt it was something she could do well. My father had always been self-employed, and she believed there was no reason why she shouldn't run her own small business too. It lasted four or five years and it's amazing the number of people who come up to me today and tell me that they know somebody whom my mother taught to drive. That was her way of helping me get as far as I could in the sport without having to worry about where the cost of the next regatta was coming from. She also used to lodge, for very little money, some of the guys I rowed with then. My parents both got pleasure from seeing how much I could achieve. Without their backing, it's quite possible that I would never have reached the zenith of my sport.

My only other income in those early years was from the Sports Aid Foundation. In 1984, the year that I won my first Olympic gold, my grant for the year was £300 or £5.76 a week. It was performance related. If I had been successful like Martin Cross and Richard Budgett in the World Championships the year before, I'd have been awarded a bit more money.

In the 1970s, you did not have to pay to represent your country. But by the early eighties the sport couldn't afford to subsidize all the travelling and other costs and you actually had to pay £20 to go on weekend trips. That amount increased every year until

Atlanta, 1996, when the expense of attending all the regattas and training camps for that year cost the athlete more than £6000. The bigger the grant you received, the more the Amateur Rowing Association took a chunk back off you. The reality for me was that I just ran up more and more debts. That was the case for many years. Even coming back from Atlanta in 1996, I was grossly overdrawn.

Overall, 1983 was not a memorable year for me, at least not by the standards I'd set. The problem was not beating other people in this country – I could do that with almost consummate ease: I simply went out and eclipsed all my rivals from the start. It was when I went abroad that I suddenly found I was in a much different, more competitive league. There'd be people absolutely dominating me and I realized that at home I was in a pack of average scullers. Mentally that was quite tough to cope with because you can fall into a slough of despondency and a belief that you will never overcome your rivals. There was such a gap between us and the top sculling nations. It's still the same. Nothing has changed.

My early background as a rower partially explains the gap in ability because I was competing against people who had been sculling from the day they got into a boat. Single sculling is a very different discipline from crew sculling and crew rowing. I felt I was always technically disadvantaged. In hindsight, I was never really in harmony with the singles. The world's top scullers tend to be attached to that discipline from the first moment they pick up their oars. It is very unusual for scullers to come from rowing, and that is one of the problems we have always faced in this country. Traditionally, this is a rowing nation. Schools all concentrate on rowing, and not sculling. At Henley Royal Regatta, the top schoolboy event is the eights and that's what the schools aim for, the pinnacle. Trying to change that, and compete against, say, the Germans, many of whom have been in sculling boats ever since they started, is very difficult.

Mike and I recognized that we'd have to do something radical and reviewed my training schedule. The traditional British way of doing things was short and sharp but we'd heard about the Eastern Bloc doing low rates of striking for long periods of time.

Rates of striking are the number of times the oars move through the water each minute. It's our equivalent of revolutions per minute, which Grand Prix drivers use rather than miles per hour. Generally speaking, we will start a race at around a rate of mid-40s, decrease to around 36 in the middle of the race, and then go back to 40 or more at the finish, but much depends on other factors, like water conditions, and how your rivals are faring. A high rate doesn't necessarily equate with speed. Our Sydney 2000 coxless four tended to have a lower striking rate than anybody we raced because of our power in the stroke.

Back in 1983, Mike and I looked at swimmers and observed how many lengths they practised in order to compete in a race lasting just a couple of minutes. We ended up doing lot more endurance training. Instead of one or two sessions a day, we changed to two or three. I would get up in the morning and run down to Mike's house, which would take about 25 minutes. There I'd do a long endurance session on the water, but cut out weights. What was the point of practising weights, we both came to the conclusion, when I actually wanted to be good at sculling?

During that winter, the sculling schedule we agreed for me was 100 miles one week, 150 miles the next, 200 the next, then back down again. I'd complete most of the work on my own and I must admit I'd try to clock up as many miles as possible early in the week, because I knew I'd be so fatigued by the end.

It was very different from what I'd done before, when sessions had been intense and short. Intensity of training was decreased, with the accent now on stamina.

Off the water, there was a sustained political attack from the likes of Penny Chuter and the selectors. Their attitude was, 'You're never going to make it as a single sculler. You've got to get into a rowing boat. That's your future.' I disagreed. I refused to train or even consider racing in a boat with other people. By doing that, I was making life very difficult for myself. Single sculling is physically and mentally the toughest of all disciplines. There's nobody to take the pressure off you. Yes, you may have a coach, but when you're out on the water you're on your own. I felt under even more pressure than most doing single sculls. When I was not producing good results in international events people would be saying, 'Why is he wasting his time doing that? He could be doing something else – and doing better at it.' In a crew boat, even if it's you that's not performing, you can delude yourself that it's the unit that's not going well and that you can work together and overcome it. With single sculling, your performance can plummet more quickly than in any other boat. At that time perhaps I didn't have the character to hold my head above water and keep the performances going.

But through that winter of 1983 I became more consistent in everything I did. Consistency was the key with everything. I was learning that it wasn't about occasional great performances, but maintaining a standard day in, day out, at a very high level.

By this time, Mike had been brought back into the Great Britain set-up and was asked to coach a group of a coxed four and a coxed pair. I trained with them, although I continued to do the single scull, under Mike's supervision. I did very well in the trials over the winter, helped by my new training regime. In the single scull I was much faster than anybody else – even the coxless pair. It made me increasingly arrogant and my attitude was: 'Why should I row with people who don't show the same commitment as me?'

Mike's rowing group consisted of six besides myself – Martin Cross, Andy Holmes, Richard Budgett, Tom Cadoux-Hudson, John Beattie and Paul Wensley, whom I'd known from the juniors. Within the group, there were cliques. Richard and Tom had won a bronze medal in the coxed pair a couple of years before. That was a combination that had potential for winning a medal at the 1984 Olympics and they wanted to stay together. Martin always preferred to row with John Beattie.

Andy Holmes was something of an odd man out. He competed in his first senior World Championships in 1981 when he was in the coxed four that led the world to 1000 metres, a length up on the East Germans, before they eventually weakened to finish fifth. Andy had this reputation of being very strong, but also being incapable of lasting the distance. Martin was once quoted as saying that he'd never row with him, and that seemed to be the general view. Nobody would give Andy the time of day because of his previous performances. But under Mike's training and tutelage, he started progressing well. As a character, Andy didn't make that much impact on me initially, but he always came across as very determined and single-minded. He always made it very clear that he wanted to win an Olympic Games.

By early in the year Penny Chuter, who had returned to take charge of the team for the 1984 Olympics, was making her presence felt. At a training camp in Italy in the spring she ruled the group with a rod of iron. There was no discussing anything. It was clear that you did what she said or you were out. I was the only one who seemed to be getting my own way and deciding my own destiny. I raced in the single at the small regatta that went on around that camp, and won both days, though not against world beaters. Meanwhile, there was still no one who had much respect for Andy, and Mike cajoled him, 'Nobody really wants to row with you. You've got to prove them wrong.' He was given Paul Wensley, the weakest of the group, to row with as a partner against Martin and John, and Tom and Richard. Andy and Paul went out and beat them. It wasn't down to Paul; it was Andy who was driving the boat on. That did his river credibility a lot of good.

The first international regatta of the season was in Mannheim in May. I'd face two legendary figures, the then two-times Olympic champion Pertti Karppinen, the so-called 'Floating Finn', and Peter Michael Kolbe, the former world champion. But before that, in February, the tug-of-wills between Penny and me finally came to a head at her office at the ARA in London. It was a time when Margaret Thatcher reigned supreme and Penny clearly saw her as a role model. As I've stressed, Penny has always been blessed with an incredible knowledge of the sport, in fact she's lived her life through it ever since she was able to walk, scull and row. Unfortunately her communication skills didn't seem quite as good. And that's where Mike Spracklen excelled.

He always made sense. He'd normally get the Oxford Boat Race crew for two or three weeks at the beginning of January. I'd be there too and sometimes take the second boat. He'd be given a training format, but after seeing them for two or three minutes he'd stop them and take the whole thing apart. He'd say, 'I can't watch this, it's awful.' Then he'd explain what he wanted. Most coaches put rowers out on the water and then try to blend different styles together. He wouldn't do that. He had very fixed ideas about how to row and the correct body position, and how to apply yourself. He had tremendous respect from athletes. In contrast, Penny's methods were far more forceful. It seemed she could never accept that there could be any opinion but hers. That created a definite problem between us because I thought she was wrong. And I was obstinate enough to make that clear.

There were no pleasantries at that meeting. Penny was very hard-faced and her message to me was blunt as she sought my agreement that I would row in the coxless four. 'If you don't do as I say, if you don't row, then you're out. You won't go to the Olympics,' she snapped. There was no hint of diplomacy. However, even if she had put it to me in her best manner, I still wouldn't have accepted it. Not then. In such circumstances, I'm a man of few words. 'I won't go then,' I declared, and walked out. I officially left the group. It was only Mike who found a way through the impasse and got me back in. Apparently, he told Penny: 'You're crazy; you're losing one of the top guys in the team here. He's pig-headed enough to stick by what he's saying.'

My target remained the long term: Seoul 1988, not Los Angeles that year. I couldn't see myself winning an Olympic gold in 1984 in the single sculls, not with Karppinen and Kolbe around, but I was being threatened to do something that was against my nature, and I'm not the kind to capitulate under such demands.

As far as I was concerned, that was it. I thought instead that I'd aim for the under-23 championships, which weren't ranked very highly, but where there'd be competitors that I would be able to beat. Coming back as under-23 champion would be much better than returning vanquished from the Olympics.

Fortunately, Mike negotiated a compromise. He got me back into the group on the basis that I'd row *and* scull. We had an agreement that I would scull at Mannheim on the first day, the Saturday, and row in the coxed four on the Sunday.

I had no problem with rowing in the four at an international regatta, but the single was my priority and I'd know from my own performance on Saturday against world-class opposition if the new training schedule had paid off, and I'd made the anticipated advances.

The British coxed four at Mannheim on the Saturday was Martin Cross at stroke, John Beattie at bow, with Richard Budgett at two, and Andy Holmes at three. Adrian Ellison was cox. The following day, they would switch round, and I would come in as stroke. In my heat, I missed Kolbe but was drawn against Karppinen. Two would qualify for the final and it was neck and neck between us in the second half of the race, with just him in front. We'd both dropped the pace at that time, certain to qualify, but I thought, 'You don't get this opportunity very often,' and decided to turn it up and see what happened. He didn't really respond and let me win. By the line I was nine seconds ahead of him. My time was also 15 seconds better than Kolbe's in his heat. I always thought that if you beat Karppinen you'd made it, but I wasn't fooling myself.

In the final Kolbe won, Karppinen was second and I came third, more than nine seconds behind the winner. But I was a competitive third when before I'd been out of it. I was improving. I felt that justified the way I now trained; I'd broken through an invisible barrier. I could compete with the best in the world even though, at that stage, I couldn't see myself beating the top two. I was quite realistic about that. What I had done was install myself in the group just behind them, fighting for the bronze. It was something for my doubters to think about.

The coxed four had also won on the Saturday, producing a strong finish to defeat the West Germans who'd been fourth at the last World Championships. I was pretty satisfied all round.

We were staying at the army barracks in Mannheim and I bumped into Andy Holmes who always seemed to be on his own. The other three were quite cliquey off the water. 'We had a fantastic row today,' he said. 'We did really well. I can't see us doing any better than that tomorrow with you in the boat.' Well, frankly, I didn't care anyway because I was so pleased with my own achievement, and was determined to devote my energies to the single scull.

I had agreed a deal, though, and I had to go ahead. I came straight into the stroke seat of the coxed four, Martin took the bow seat, and John was ousted. We competed against the same crews as they'd raced the previous day and, instead of being behind the Germans and rowing them down, we won by eight seconds. We dominated the race from start to finish. The victory had to be put into perspective. The West Germans were the only top crew there and beating them so emphatically didn't mean that we were suddenly world beaters. Despite that victory, people still expected me to say, 'Sorry, I'm going to carry on in the single. That fours result doesn't affect anything.' However, another factor entered my calculations.

About that time, it became clear that there would be a retaliatory boycott by the Eastern bloc countries as a response to what had occurred in 1980. They would not be going to the Olympics, and in rowing, with the East Germans so strong, that was a crucial decision. It was then I suddenly realized that the direction my heart wanted to take me might have to give way to hard-headed pragmatism. In the single sculls, I had to take into account the fact that Kolbe and Karppinen were from countries not involved in the boycott; they'd be going whatever. At best I could visualize myself going for bronze. But if the Russians and East Germans, the two top rowing nations, were not entering the fours (disciplines in which they were particularly strong) there was a genuine possibility of a gold for our boat.

Yes, it was a selfish attitude, but the way I saw it a gold for me in the four would help my bid for sponsorship as I prepared for the single in 1988. I was shrewd enough to work out that if I could win gold in the four, it could make my quest for gold at Seoul a more realistic, achievable aim. That was important because I could not see myself continuing for the next four years without financial support. It wasn't a major setback in terms of the singles. This would just be a stepping stone to my ultimate goal. It was agreed that we'd persevere with me stroking the coxed four.

Lucerne regatta took place about six weeks before the Olympics and would be a really important test. We believed that the Eastern Bloc countries would use the event as a show of force. They wouldn't be going to the Olympics, so they'd try to dominate Lucerne instead.

Our coxed four qualified for the final, where we met the East Germans, who boasted some fine oarsmen. They included the stroke Harald Jahrling, whom, coincidentally, Jurgen Grobler used to coach. We led from start to finish and beat the East Germans by about half a length. In doing so, we broke the world record for the course. We clocked just under 6 minutes 8 seconds, helped by excellent conditions. As we came off the water, people were acclaiming a wonderful performance, and remarking how our record would last for years. It was that display which provided me with conclusive evidence that I had made the right decision to carry on in the four.

We decided with Mike that we wouldn't race again on the Sunday – there were two separate regattas – as we had proved our point that we were the better crew. Conditions were even better on the Sunday, and all the other boats that we had raced took part. Everybody went quicker than the previous day, and the East Germans won, in a time of just over 6 minutes 5 seconds. My first world record was held for less than 24 hours!

When I met Harald Jarhling in the nineties he insisted that their motivation was lacking because of the knowledge that they would not be going to the Olympics. Who knows? However, I still believed that if they had gone to Los Angeles we'd have beaten them anyway. Martin apart, we were young and inexperienced, but raw determination would have got us through.

Harald, now a leading coach in Australia, had already won two Olympic golds and would have been bidding for his third in Los Angeles. The fact that he never got the chance because of political reasons was far harder on him than it had been for me when I was prevented from going to Moscow. It was Russia telling East Germany they couldn't go. It wasn't even his own country. He is very resentful about that. Also, I was going for my first gold at Los Angeles, when he would have been going for his third in the same event, so in a way it affected the status of both of us.

But to return to Penny Chuter's role in the direction of my career. She has always claimed that it was only because she insisted that I rowed in the coxed four that I won a gold in 1984. I will always maintain it was my decision, based on my own judgement. I don't think her motivation was entirely positive; in fact my impression is that her feelings were quite long lasting. When my wife Ann was rowing she was one of the top performers in the women's group at a time when we weren't that strong. She was in the eyes of Penny, who was then coaching them, the golden girl. But Ann had to take a year off to complete her medical studies. She was still training but didn't compete. When Ann returned she struggled to get back in the team. She found Penny very difficult to work with, and I've always wondered whether she lost Penny's respect because of missing that year, or whether Ann's place in the team was affected by the animosity between Penny and me. Penny's now on Sport England as its development officer. Despite all the problems I've had with her over the years, I still have tremendous respect for her knowledge and what she did for women's rowing and the sport generally.

If it had just been a question of my own suitability, I probably wouldn't have taken such a hard line. But it wasn't. It was the whole British approach to the sport which aggravated me. I thought I'd seen the light of how we, as a country, should be doing things, how we should be training. I'd looked at all those other sports which, like us, were amateur, but unlike us, trained professionally.

I used to think to myself: 'How do these people think they've got a chance of winning an Olympic medal when they don't train full-time, yet would be competing against rowers and scullers from the Eastern bloc and even other Western countries who are doing nothing other than preparing to race at the highest level?' Here, most athletes were holding down full-time jobs, so training sessions had to be short and sharp. There was an increasing gulf between us and other countries. We were getting left behind. If everybody else was training full-time, that had to be the way forward. For me, it was the only way.

CHAPTER 8

TRIUMPH OF
THE UNLIKELY LADS

O ur 1984 Olympic coxed four was a motley crew. Richard Burnell of the Bushnell–Burnell pair, our last rowing gold medallists at the 1948 London Olympic Games in the double scull, described us in the *Sunday Times* as 'a job lot' and 'the unlikely lads'. We were certainly an extremely diverse group who did not mix socially. Mike Spracklen conceded afterwards that he was concerned that we wouldn't adapt to each other's strengths and weaknesses on the water either. It was a testimony to him as much as anything that we did, though he later admitted, 'When I first got hold of them, they simply didn't want to know. But as soon as they showed some improvement and started winning there was no stopping their enthusiasm for success.'

Dr Richard Budgett, then recently qualified at St Mary's Hospital, Paddington, was at number two. He had been at Cambridge and failed to get a Blue but within a year of moving to London University had got noticed by finishing third in the world coxed pairs in 1981. Andy, at number three, was then a hod-carrier, having been a student. He had been in the 1983 eights group but refused to row in it. I was at stroke, an unemployed rower who wanted to be a single sculler, while Martin Cross, a teacher, was at bow. He was vastly experienced, having won the Henley Visitors' Cup in 1975 as a schoolboy before winning bronze medals in the coxless fours at two World Championships and an Olympics. Adrian Ellison, the cox, was a radiographer at Charing Cross Hospital. He had steered the coxed pairs to a bronze in the 1981 World Championships.

Martin was the senior man, at 27, in years as well as experience. He would manipulate any situation to his benefit. He was very political, in both senses, and a very social animal. Martin wanted to win and was very determined, to the point of being aggressive. But more than the rest of us, he loved the social side. We used to call him 'Mr Have-a-chat'. At regattas, we'd be rigging the boat and he'd be off talking and gossiping to people from all different countries. His attitude contrasted with mine. Where I have always been concerned, rowing means racing. I have many friends in the sport throughout the world. But, to me, rowing had one dimension. I was doing it to win, and nothing was going to distract me from that.

Immediately I got into the boat you sensed friction. Martin took great pride in his achievements, understandably, and you always sensed that he felt he should have had more media exposure. He disliked the fact that the moment I got in it became the 'Redgrave Four'. He had a point. Purely in terms of results he was by far the better athlete. He'd won an Olympic bronze and three World Championship bronze medals but he was aware of the type of athlete I was and what I was capable of doing. Martin knew that potentially I had more to offer the boat than he did.

As a character, Martin has always been a 'doer', always wanting to be involved. He's only just stepped down from the role of chairman of the athletes' commission on FISA – the equivalent of the rowers' shop steward – and has always tried to improve the sport in general. When the sport was in turmoil, with the ARA both internationally and domestically being very poorly managed at one stage, he was in the forefront of trying to get things changed. He pushed for athletes to have more say in what was going on. Several of us have been awarded honours for services to rowing, but he's probably done more than any of us.

His involvement as the athletes' representative was in line with his politics. He is a die-hard socialist. In theory that's fine, with everybody sharing everything, getting equal opportunities. Unfortunately, it's not an ideal world and the reality is that socialism, certainly as we used to know it, doesn't work. Martin tried to get elected as MP for Richmond but that's not the best place for Labour to win! Today, he is still a schoolteacher, head of the sixth form at Hampton School, and covers rowing for BBC radio and television. You either loved or hated him, but you always got on with him. He is a very easy-going character with a deceptively forceful way of doing things.

To return to our Olympic build-up, even though we had broken the world record, albeit for only 24 hours, and had defeated the mighty East Germans, it was not a foregone conclusion that we'd win gold. New Zealand, the reigning world champions, had not been there, but we felt ourselves favourites, and the rest of the rowing world appeared to believe that, too.

To the general public within Britain we were still something of an unknown quantity. Rowing did not receive much TV and newspaper coverage then, and there was little recognition that we had the potential of winning a gold. It was probably only my local paper, the *Bucks Free Press*, which announced that I could make history by becoming the youngest ever rower to win an Olympic gold medal. In some respects the lack of media hype did us no harm. We were, it must be remembered, a pretty inexperienced crew.

We raced at Henley, winning convincingly, having no real competition, before going to a pre-Olympics training camp in America. We arrived at our base in San Diego three weeks before the Games. Here we stayed at a naval college and trained 45 minutes away inland at Lake Otay. It was basically just a fishing lake with a few wooden huts and a trailer park, but we had special permission to use it. There were no landing stages and we just paddled from the bank. It was exceptionally nice water and we had a really good camp as we geared up for the regatta. For your first Olympic experience, to have training facilities like that was fantastic.

To avoid the athletes suffering from the smog and unbearable heat synonymous with Los Angeles in summer, the Olympic regatta started each day at 7 a.m. The coxed fours was the first event on the men's race days which were Monday, Thursday and Sunday. We changed our whole routine to make sure we were fresh and awake first thing in the morning. The theory is that you're supposed to perform better in your second session of the day so, each morning, we decided to get up at 3.45 a.m., drive to our lake, do two training stints, a warm-up session and work session, and be back in San Diego by midday. In between, we rested in the trailer.

The Olympic rowing venue was Lake Casitas, which was nearer Santa Barbara than Los Angeles. We moved up to Santa Barbara a few days before racing started and stayed in our own Olympic 'village'. It was normally a college, and was only used by the rowers and the canoeists during the Games. That helped us. The main Olympics venue is such a massive event and a media circus. Being involved with all the other sports, you can get swamped by the whole scale of the thing. Here, we had our own identity. We kept to that 3.45 a.m. routine but most countries did not do that. They came down at 8 a.m. for their normal training session, and trained again later in the day. That was the traditional way of preparing for a World Championships or Olympics when the finals are in the afternoon. Crews only got up early on days when they raced. We felt strongly then that it gave us an advantage, though in hindsight I'm not so convinced.

A few of the British rowing squad went to the opening ceremony on the Friday evening, but we decided that because our first race was on the opening Sunday, we wouldn't do that. Travelling 90 minutes into Los Angeles and returning through all the crowds was a bit too much. Also, at the time, we were going to bed at 7.30 p.m. because we were getting up so early. However, we watched the event on television. The whole razzmatazz of the occasion was exactly what we expected from the home of Hollywood.

Getting up early was strange. It was dark and you're not at your best at that time, even though you've been sleeping since 7.30 p.m. Between the training sessions you'd sit around, relaxing. There was nothing else to do. At San Diego, because of that early start, we had finished our work in time to return for lunch and then went down to the beach. At the village they laid on rock and roll bands in the afternoons and there was a games arcade. I remember the day we arrived because we went for a stroll on the beach and met a naval officer who invited us aboard an American nuclear submarine. It sounded weird, but we turned up a few days later and were given a tour.

Overall, it was a perfect, relaxing prelude to the business of justifying ourselves as pre-race favourites for Britain's first rowing Olympic gold since 1948. It was the best build-up to a Games I've ever experienced. Apart from being able to do our work on the water in such splendid isolation, the laid-back atmosphere of the village was crucial. There was one moment, though, when I did fear that I would miss yet another Olympics. I came back from training one day to Santa Barbara, a couple of days before we started racing, and thought, 'Bloody hell, my wrists are getting quite sore. What's going on here?' I planned to see the physiotherapist and get some treatment as soon as possible. It was extremely worrying. There is a common rowing injury to the wrist called tenosynovitis, which is inflammation of the inner lining of the tendon sheath. It is caused by over-use. Apart from the soreness, you know you've got it because it makes a sound like a barn-door creaking as the tendon moves through the sheath which has become too tight. It is actually the wrist's own protection mechanism to ensure that you don't over-use it, although it's almost inevitable in rowing because of the constant gripping and bending of the wrist.

As I was returning to my room in the village, I passed the arcade where there were all sorts of electronic games the athletes could play for free. There was an extremely popular game that year called 'The Olympics'. Each competitor had a little figure and the quicker you tapped your button, the faster he'd go. If you did a fast enough time in the 100 metres you'd go on to the hurdles, then other sports. I played it quite a lot. Ignoring the wrist problem briefly, I thought I'd just stop off to play it. When I started striking the button, the pain seared through my wrist again. I realized it wasn't the rowing at all that was affecting me. It was that damned arcade game! I banned myself from using it until the Games were all over and the problem had cleared up.

There were only eight entries in our event, which meant that if we won our heat we'd go straight through to the final and not race again for another seven days. We drew the Americans and New Zealand, two crews that we feared, but got an excellent start, and forged into the lead. The Americans closed us down and drew back level, but then we pulled away and won by three-quarters of a length. The worst thing was waiting for the final. The pressure really started building then, and those seven days were like an eternity as the nerves became frayed. The Italians won the other heat, but all the other crews had to go into the repechage.

That included the Americans, who kicked up a rumpus because they felt we'd jumped the start. They insisted we must have been cheating, because there was no way a crew could get that much of a lead on them. Obviously you aim for a quick start, but you can't cheat, because there are video cameras and judges to ensure that you don't move before the flag is dropped.

Because of the momentum of putting the power on the foot-stretcher, the boat naturally moves backwards slightly, so if you can actually predict the flag and start squeezing a split second earlier you can get a good start. If you get it wrong, however, the boat gets called back and the umpire awards you a false start. Two of those and you're eliminated.

The tension reached a peak on repechage day. Apart from us and the Italian boat, all the others, including the USA and New Zealand, had to go out and race again. The final line-up was Canada, USA, New Zealand, Italy, West Germany and Great Britain.

The day of the final at last arrived. I felt excited, yet apprehensive. That particular morning there had been no need for an alarm to pierce my dreams. I was already awake and just lying there. Normally, I struggle to get out of bed when I wake up, but not on this occasion. Usually, again, my appetite is very good at breakfast time. I always think it's one of the best meals of the day. But on this day I struggled to eat anything. I pushed things round the plate. Finally, I drank a glass of orange juice; that was about it. I couldn't really face anything else.

Normally, school buses conveyed the rowers to the lake. But that morning, we drove down in a car. As we arrived at the course there was a deathly silence, the kind you only experience at the time of day the world wakes from its slumbers. There are a lot of finger-like tributaries to Lake Casitas and they'd built plastic pontoons across them to allow us to reach the landing stage. As we walked across them, carrying our boat, all you could hear was just a gentle plip-plop of the water underneath. The five of us hardly exchanged a word. We went through our warm-up routine that we had been through many times before, first at our training camp in San Diego and then, here, at Lake Casitas. We were well-drilled and the warm-up went quite well. At these sessions, you do little bursts of work, and this morning it felt good.

The sun was beginning to peer over the horizon and, as it did so, I became aware that over in one of the far corners of the lake a huge bank of mist was forming. It was an eerie backdrop. As we completed our preparations, it was clear that the mist was going to engulf the course. We went to the rest tent and waited for our race, but even as we did so, we were all harbouring the same doubt: 'They surely can't row an Olympic final in these conditions? It's got to be delayed.'

I must confess that I thought to myself, 'Thank God for that.' We had been waiting weeks and weeks for this day to arrive. Now it had, and yet here I was pleading with that Great Umpire Above to postpone proceedings: 'God, why has it got to be today?' I asked Him. 'I wish it was tomorrow. I wish it was next week.' My mind was playing the most terrible, mischievous games on me.

Although I was pretty certain the morning's events would be postponed, we had to go through our normal schedule. We did our immediate pre-race warm-up and it was still quite misty. But then I saw the umpire boats chugging up to the start and I thought to myself, 'Shit, it is going to happen now.' Once I realized that this was it, I became more positive.

At the start, a multitude of thoughts went through my mind. Things like: 'We're favourites to win this. We should win this.' But then I looked across at the opposition and thought: 'Is today, the 5th of August, going to be our day? Can we stand on the winners' rostrum in a few minutes' time and be Olympic champions? Have we got what it takes? Can we row this 2000 metres faster than anybody else? We think we can. But can we do it on this particular day, this one day in every four years on which the Olympics comes around?'

I looked across at Canada on the one side of us, and all the other crews as the umpire went through the roll-call of each country. The adrenaline was surging through me. My nerves saw to that. Again, we got a good start and burst straight out into the lead but, with about 250 metres gone, the Americans started coming back at us. Then they moved level with us. They moved in front of us. I remember straining every sinew, just pulling as hard as I possibly could through the 1000 metres in the middle of that race, just to stay with them.

The brain tends to go into an almost suspended state at these times. But I recall thinking: 'What's happening? Why are they out in front? We should be out in front.' Coming into the last 500 metres, we were pushing our legs as hard as we could. Martin, in the bow seat, gave a shout: 'Let's go.' Something just sort of clicked in. Our cruising speed wasn't quite up to scratch, but we had a tremendous burst of power when we needed it. That's why we got out of the blocks well. We were on full throttle and slowly, agonizingly slowly, we edged back again at the USA. As we drew up to the line we just got our bow back in front again. We finished just under half a length in front. The gold was ours.

You would imagine that, after winning an Olympic final, the excitement would be overwhelming. It would be sheer elation. All I felt was relief; a sense of blessed relief that what I believed we could do, what the crew believed, and the coaches believed, we'd actually achieved. I leaned back in the boat and we all congratulated each other. I was lying on Andy's legs and feet, utterly exhausted. We had to turn the boat, paddle back to the 250 metre mark and wait for the next race to finish, before arriving at the landing stage and the medal rostrum in front of the grandstand.

My stomach muscles were completely shot. I couldn't sit back up again. Andy had to push me back up straight. I was absolutely shattered, and worse, I felt really ill. As we paddled back up, I was physically sick over the side of the boat. It was the first time that had happened to me. The orange juice, all that I had been able to get down in the morning, came back up.

The procedure was that you climbed on to a pontoon directly in front of the main grandstand, shook hands with the opposition, and waited for the medal ceremony. I just felt so sick, so out of it completely. Rarely have the demands of a race taken such a toll on me. Slowly, normality returned. We stood forward, one by one, and received our medals, then turned to one side as the national anthem was played and the national flags raised. It was a very emotional, very special moment. Something I'll never forget. I was fighting the tears, without success.

Then we returned to the boat, paddled back over to the landing stage. We embraced Mike Spracklen, our coach; everybody in the British team congratulated us. Belinda had rowed in her women's eights final the previous day – they had come fifth – and she was there, too, along with my parents who been staying in a hired camper-van.

I remember in particular that Richard Stanhope, who'd won a silver medal in the eight at the previous Olympics, was roaring, 'Well done, well done,' and patting us all on the back as we carried our boat back. Penny Chuter had appeared with a bottle of wine, which is the last thing you'd want to drink at that moment. I remember refusing it.

I was selected for the random drugs test and went off to provide a urine sample. I met Pertti Karppinen in the testing room. He was my all-time rowing hero, who'd just won his third Olympic singles sculls title. I could speak no Finnish; he could speak no English. But somehow we managed to congratulate each other. That moment is vivid, even now.

We did numerous interviews in the press tent. Suddenly, everybody wanted to know all about us. Richard Burnell, the only Briton around who understood what emotions we were going through, came up to me and said, 'You're world champion for one year; you're Olympic champion for life.' That summed it up for me. World Championships come and go, but the Olympics are only every four years and you have to get it right on that one day.

Because the race was so early, it was strange going back to the village with nothing to do. You get used to World Championships, which generally finish at four or five, where afterwards everyone goes back to the hotel and the partying begins. But we were back in the village at one o'clock and I had so much time to contemplate what had just occurred. I was in a curiously mercurial mood.

One minute, I was thinking, 'Yes!', I'm Olympic champion!' and then the next, 'Yes, but so what? What's the big deal?' And then, 'Hang on, I've won the Olympics. That's what I've always wanted to do.' You go through so many highs and lows.

All kinds of emotions pass through your mind. You've been building up to this day for so long and now it's over. Suddenly, you've got this enormous void. The question you start asking your-self is: 'I've done it now; what do I do next?' It was a really odd experience. You'd think you'd be dancing around, getting drunk, but it was actually a very sobering moment. That's something that's hit me a few times throughout my career.

That was the turning point for me. Even when I had been sitting in the boat at the start, I was asking myself whether we could actually do this. It was the most anxious I've ever been. Now, I had conquered those doubts.

Everything before and immediately after the race seems so crystal clear; everything after that seems so vague. Belinda and I went off with my mother and father up to San Francisco, where we did a bit of sightseeing. We returned for the end of the Games, managing to get beds in the main Olympic village, and caught the athletics finals, which was a great thrill. It was Carl Lewis's year, the remarkable American winning the 100 metres and 200 metres, the long jump and 100 metres relay.

On the home front, Seb Coe claimed another Olympic gold in the 1500 metres, as did Tessa Sanderson in the javelin and, of course, Daley Thompson in the decathlon.

I really enjoyed the closing ceremony, walking around with an Olympic gold medal slung around my neck. We had to don British tracksuits for the occasion, but I wore it underneath and positively glowed with pride. I thought of all the British champions who had gone before – and how I'd joined this exclusive club. They all seemed to be household names: Seb Coe, Steve Ovett, Daley Thompson, men like that, who you'd watched on television and were now as big celebrities as pop and film stars.

Suddenly you're a member of this elite yourself. You start saying to yourself: 'What's going to happen when we get home? Trying to find sponsorship is going to be so easy. People are going to be falling over themselves to offer me deals. It's going to be wonderful'.

Belinda and I stayed out in America for a while, went across to Florida, spent a while with my uncle Bill and then returned home. My family were at the airport – but nobody else. I couldn't under-stand that. I'd seen Olympic stars getting a hero's welcome, but there was nothing. I'd returned as anonymously to most of the general public as I'd departed.

With hindsight, I'd built it all up in my mind too much. I'd thought I'd be right up there with the rest of them on a pedestal. It was inevitable that everything would be a complete anti-climax. I'd thought that I wouldn't be able to walk down Marlow High Street because I was Olympic champion. I'd be mobbed. I'd be famous.

But it's not like that at all. You're still the same person, going back to your home town, and it's exactly the same as it was when you left. There's no real difference as to how people look upon you. They've seen you grow up. They're pleased that you've achieved something, but you're no different from what you were before. I found that a very good leveller. It's kept my feet very firmly on the ground.

Of course there were some celebrations. The bunting was out when we got home, the flags, banners and flowers put up by my parents, my grandmother Ada and the neighbours. Then, a week after our return, Marlow laid on a civic reception for the five members of our crew. It began with an open-topped bus ride from Marlow Bottom to Marlow town centre. The Mayor walked in front of the bus down a packed high street and the *Chariots of Fire* soundtrack blasted out. At Marlow Council's Court Garden there were speeches. I didn't have one prepared in my pocket. I was still only 22, and absolutely terrified I might have to speak. The mayor presented me with a glass engraving, but there was no opportunity for me to say anything, for which I was grateful. He then turned to Mike to make a presentation to him, too. I thought, 'Thank God, I don't have to speak. I've got away with it.' I was able to relax. Then the mayor said, 'I think Steve wants to say a few words.' I gulped, but actually it was very easy. I just thanked the big gathering of my old school teachers, people I'd known at school, local councillors and friends generally for their support, and for making the day so special. It is something I've had to learn to do over the years. Now I don't find public speaking too bad at all.

There was champagne for everyone and The Compleat Angler had made a massive cake, three and a half feet across, containing 60 eggs and three pounds of sugar. The icing was in the design of an Olympic medal. Coming back to the community where I had been born and bred, and had lived all my life, the place where I had trained for the Olympics, I really did feel very close to the people and the town. Marlow has always remained very special to me.

Once things had settled down I still imagined that all kinds of sponsorship deals would flood in. But nothing. There was some media interest and just one really interesting spin-off. I was invited on BBC's *Superstars* programme with judo's 1984 Olympic silver medallist Neil Adams. There had been five gold medallists that year, including ourselves: Malcolm Cooper, the shooter; Tessa

Sanderson; Seb Coe and Daley Thompson. All really big names already, except Malcolm. Our crew basically got overlooked, as all the media attention centred on the track and field athletes. We also suffered from the implication that we'd only won because the Eastern bloc countries weren't there, even though we'd beaten everybody beforehand anyway and were favourites to win.

Attracting sponsorship deals proved exceptionally difficult. The local butcher offered to supply me with meat, but the only serious offer I received was from DAF Trucks in Marlow through a family connection. I was introduced to Chris Thorneycroft-Smith, the company's marketing director. He lived in Marlow and was very enthusiastic and knowledgeable about sport. Chris bought me a boat, some weights and clothing. He also wrote to companies like Adidas suggesting they sponsor me, and was very supportive. Adidas said they were not into rowing but would give us a discount on their products. That's how my sponsorship began. Before, I had only benefited from the British team sponsorship at the Olympics by the NatWest Bank and the £300 Sports Aid Foundation grant.

Each year, DAF Trucks increased their sponsorship and the company certainly got value for money, considering what they put in. It was a really friendly relationship. Later, they were bought out and became Leyland DAF, and sponsored Andy Holmes and myself as a pair when we got together in 1986. It was essentially my sponsorship but he benefited, too. At the time there were many political problems over the issue with the Amateur Rowing Association (ARA), but I simply had to go out and find my own sponsors because the ARA couldn't raise any money themselves.

Then TSB Trustcard came in. They wanted to sponsor the team as a whole, and there then ensued a major battle between TSB and Leyland DAF. The ARA attempted to force Andy and me to end our involvement with DAF and be part of the TSB sponsorship. Fortunately, the precedent had been set and we were allowed to continue. At that time the MI group took over the TSB contract with the ARA and they agreed to a trial year's contract with the team, on condition they took over my contract with Leyland DAF.

In practical terms the MI group's sponsorship of the team lasted about three months, though they continued as our sponsors for the next four years. In my opinion it was never a smooth relationship. Unfortunately, our hands had been tied because of the deal that the ARA had signed.

It was only after 1988 that rowers were allowed to receive cash. Before that, it all had to be done through trust funds. One was set up for me after Peter Coni, a lawyer, who was then in charge of the ARA and chairman of Henley Regatta, as well as being an influential member of the international committee of FISA, had looked at other sports. But although the deeds were set up, I never earned enough to use the trust fund. You needed £25,000 to make it worthwhile, and at that time, it was never the case.

As far as my immediate future was concerned, various family fund-raising activities were held to help finance my next campaign which would end at Seoul, including a 'Scull for Gold '88' disco in a Marlow restaurant. It made £300.

What happens now is that any money earned through the sport as sponsorship – in our case that is principally the four-year deal that Matthew and I have with Lombard – goes to the ARA, and is then sent back out to you. The ARA likes to know what is going on, which is understandable. I'm happy with that.

After a month or so basking in the euphoria of Los Angeles, it was time to get back on the water and start training again. That success had been a bonus to my plans. The quest for a gold in 1988, which had been my principal target since I was 16, remained. It was marvellous to luxuriate in the feeling of being Olympic champion, which had arrived earlier than expected. So important was that triumph to me that the house in which Ann and I now live is called Casitas, after the name of the 1984 Olympic regatta lake.

But all that had to be put to the back of my mind. My ambitions now were directed towards the Korean capital of Seoul, where I was determined to win gold for Britain again, but this time as a single sculler.

CHAPTER 9

PUSH COMES TO SHOVE

That victorious Olympic coxed four broke apart quicker than it had been put together. Richard Budgett was always going to retire from international rowing to concentrate on his medical career. Andy Holmes intended to give up, get married and capitalize on his gold medal. That left Martin Cross and me, but we rowed on the same side of the boat. Anyway, I intended to return to single sculling, which I much preferred to rowing in a crew boat. Martin got together with Adam Clift to form a pair, in which they would go on to win a silver medal at the 1985 World Championships.

When the celebrations had died down, I returned to single scull training at Marlow, preparing for the 1988 Olympics. I felt more confident than I'd been in 1983 when I first did the single, and though Chris Baillieu, now 35, had threatened to make a comeback, I knew that I was much better than him.

However, an incident during the World Championships at Hazewinkel in Belgium, when I realized one of oarsmen's worst fears, proved to be a critical point in my career. In the semi-final, my back seized up completely and I was unable to complete the race. I couldn't even get out of the boat and had to be carried out and taken to the medical area. I remember how Wendy Green, our physiotherapist, applied an ice-pack on the affected area. It had come straight out of the freezer and stuck to my skin. She pulled it off and the skin came with it.

The back is a perennial trouble spot for any rower, but previously I'd only had few niggles. I'd seen an osteopath when I rowed at school and had been troubled now and again, but this was a major problem. Penny Chuter was in charge of the team. She was quoted as saying, 'He's only saying he's got a back problem because he wasn't doing very well. That's why he stopped in the race.' She was right. I was not doing very well, but I don't think that was the reason I came to a halt. Yet, her comment was to nag away at the back of my mind. Maybe I had been imagining I had a back problem and was using it as an excuse?

Wendy advised me that there was no reason why I couldn't race in the 'small' final. I was still in a lot of pain, and thought, 'There's no way I can go out and do this,' but I must have forced myself. I toiled desperately before coming home sixth. I couldn't put any pressure on at all. It was a dispirited Redgrave party that travelled home. Belinda, my girlfriend, who had been in the coxless pairs with Fiona Johnston, could only finish ninth overall in her event.

I arrived home very despondent, still convinced in myself that there was a problem with my back. My brother-in-law Philip, who worked for Saab, was in contact with an osteopath called Terry Moule. Terry had done some work with Saab on the design of their seats and was well known for treating sportsmen. Philip asked him to have a look at me.

I told Terry the whole story, he took some notes and said, 'Let's have a look and I'll see if there's anything I can do.' I lay down on the couch, and before he'd even touched me, he said, 'Ah, I can see where your problem is. It's just here.' And he put his hand on the area which was troubling me.

More than anything else, I was relieved that he'd found something. I had been quite worried about going to see him. What would have happened if he had told me there was nothing wrong with my back, that it was psychosomatic and Penny Chuter had been right all along?

It was curvature of the spine and a slipped disc. It gave me great confidence in Terry and I saw him twice a week. He gave me exercise programmes to build up my back and regain the strength in it. While I did so, I dwelt on where my career was going. I was really frustrated with my performance in the single. It just wasn't happening. It wasn't just the injury at the World Championships. Even earlier in the season, I hadn't been getting the sort of results to satisfy myself. I was so low that I actually contemplated giving up the sport I loved. My mood was not helped by the fact that, during this period, my relationship with Belinda had deteriorated. The relationship had been quite serious, certainly on my side, and quite soon I felt it might lead to something permanent. When you're with somebody for as long as we were that assumption gets even stronger. I was heart-broken when she left me in the autumn of 1985. I had never considered formalizing it, but when I realized that we were in danger of splitting up because our relationship had become stagnant, I did think to myself: 'Should I take the plunge and get married to bring it back to life?' We talked about it, but things had gone beyond that. That tends to happen. You muddle through for a long time, but when you try to put things right, it's all too late. Maybe if I'd tried harder earlier it would have been different.

Belinda was determined, very intelligent and sensitive, but in the past I had always been the better athlete and got more recognition that she had. I was the dominant partner in the relationship, but by 1985 all that had changed.

I was at a very low ebb both in terms of my rowing and life in general. Belinda was the opposite; her rowing was going well and she was supremely confident. She had also found a job. Suddenly our roles completely altered and neither of us could handle it. She found it difficult to give me the type of support that I'd given her and, worse, I found it difficult to receive support. Our lives flipped and turned upside down. It drove us apart. We went in different directions, and eventually moved apart too far to salvage things. Later she wanted to get back together but by that time I'd moved on. It was always difficult to socialize with Belinda because she was training before and after college, while I was training and doing part-time work. We'd occasionally go out to parties together, but not often.

My inability to sustain a relationship until I got together with Ann later in my career was undoubtedly a result of my fixation on rowing. It was all-consuming. Up to 1984, I was very intense in the way that I looked upon my sport. It was totally at the forefront of my focus, with the rest of life just a background blur. Not until the nineties would I be able to step back and survey a broader picture.

It was very much part of the Mike Spracklen approach to participation in sport. His philosophy was that, if you're going to perform well, absolutely nothing should distract you. There was no room for free-thinking and socializing outside that, although of course I continued to occasionally get together with my close friends, whom I still see now. In the early eighties, I used to train at Maidenhead Rowing Club quite often and I would stay behind and have a drink afterwards, usually with Eric Sims. We still keep in touch.

But that was about the limit to my social excesses at that time. I was very blinkered, completely single-minded. Belinda probably suffered because of that. Whatever I did, my thought was: 'How is this going to affect my rowing? If I go out tonight, I'll be tired tomorrow.' With Mike, I'd come out of school and, relatively quickly, I'd won an Olympics. So, he must be right. Mustn't he? If you weren't like that, then you wouldn't win. It was that simple. I now know rather differently.

I was probably at my wildest, if you can call it that, in the late seventies, when I'd go out with friends to listen to a few bands. It was the end of the punk rock era. I recall going to see XTC and The Pretenders. I had the chance to go and see an unknown group called The Police who were performing at Aylesbury, just a few miles down the road, but didn't bother. Within a few weeks, they were the biggest thing around.

During the early years, I had enjoyed the considerable benefit of living at home with my parents. I did not move away until I was 21, when Belinda and I shared a flat in London. Until then, all I had to do was find part-time jobs so that I was able to put petrol in the car.

One of my parents' homes in Marlow Bottom came with eight acres of land. My father later sold the property with one acre and built a garden centre on the remainder. The family lived in the flat above it and that's where I was based until I moved out to Kew. We also had a large three-car garage and store above it a couple of hundred yards away. We converted the upstairs of that into a flat. I lived there when I came back from London, until the end of 1986.

I moved away originally because I always felt a little bit claustrophobic living with my parents in their house. We always had a good relationship, but I just felt it was time to make the break. I always felt quite a lot of pressure, especially from my mother, because they'd put so much time, effort and finance into helping me aim for the top in rowing.

When I went through that bad patch in 1985, and actually considered packing it all in, I remember every foot of the 200 yards that I walked from my flat to the family home, having plucked up the courage to tell my parents I was going to quit. I felt I owed it to them to carry on because of all their commitment. When I told them, the response I received from my mother, who had always been the talker in the family, was totally different from what I expected.

She said, 'Well, we think you're mad. You obviously enjoy what you're doing and even though it's gone badly this year, you won the Olympics the year before, but if that's your decision we'll go with it.' That really shocked me, because it wasn't what I was expecting at all. It gave me a lot more respect for my parents than I had already.

I let my hair down a bit once Belinda and I had parted. I had a few girlfriends after that. I went off the rails somewhat, and was generally determined to have a good time; yet never at any stage did I stint on my training. However, that was probably when my absolute commitment to rowing, to the exclusion of all other interests, began to weaken. I found that I still performed quite well when I was not being quite so focused and dedicated.

During that lull in my career, following the back injury, a fellow named Larry Tracey, who often helped me with financial advice and sponsorship, took me for lunch at The Compleat Angler.

Larry had started up an electronics company which became very successful; he floated it and made a tidy sum of money. He rowed at Weybridge Rowing Club and tried to win a place in the lightweight team in the 1970s but never quite made it. He's a close family friend, and is godfather to my son Zak. In 1984, he had approached Mike Spracklen who had been coaching the lightweight team that Larry had been trying to get into. Larry said that he'd like to sponsor the team because he'd heard that they were short of money to take them to the next World Championships. Mike retorted: 'What do you want to sponsor them for? You want to sponsor Steve. He's successful and he's won an Olympic gold medal.' So Larry came in and helped me with sponsorship instead.

We sat down to lunch and discussed many subjects, although not much about rowing. Just before we were about to leave, he said casually: 'Oh, I'm off to the British Bobsleigh Championships next week. Do you want to come and be my pusher?'

What do you say to that kind of offer? I replied: 'Yes, that sounds great,' presuming that he'd been bobsleighing for years and was really experienced. At that moment, the winter of 1985, my love affair with rowing was on the rocks and some time spent on the ice sounded just what I needed. I'd seen bobsleighing on TV and thought it looked really exciting.

We arrived at the British Championships, held in Winterberg in Germany. They were split over two weeks. The first few days was 'novice week' for beginners who were taught the basics. At the end of it you could compete with the best in the National Championships, after which the British team was named for the internationals. The whole affair was dominated by the forces, particularly the Army and RAF, and there were a few civilians.

The first bobsleigh club was founded at St Moritz in 1897. Initially it was just fun for the rich and famous and it wasn't until the 1950s that serious athletes from other sports began to get involved. It attracted anyone with the physique to push hard at the start. In many ways I had the physical requirements to be the perfect pusher. My strength was my explosive power. The two-man bob has a brakeman or 'pusher' and a pilot; with two extra crewmen-pushers in the four-man bob. From a standing start, you push in unison for up to 50 metres (165 ft), which usually takes around six seconds, and speeds of around 65 kph (40 mph) are reached before the crew even get into the sled. You wear shoes with really fine spikes, about 200 of them, and as brakeman you have to place your feet either side of the driver as you leap in. Frequently, you manage to stab him as you do so. A fast start is critical, and an initial lead of a tenth of a second can increase to three-tenths by the end. Speeds of more than 135 kph (83 mph) can be reached, and crews are subjected to four times the force of gravity. Most tracks consist of a concrete base topped by artificial ice. Winterberg is 1325 metres (nearly 4350 ft) long, with a drop of 110 metres (360 ft). Parts of the decline are as steep as 15 per cent.

It was hugely enjoyable. I loved it. That was even after we arrived and I discovered that Larry had only gone down a bobsleigh run twice, both times at St Moritz, with his partner from work. He was just about a complete novice.

We started off on the diamond start, which is three or four bends down from the normal start. It means you can learn there, without picking up too much speed. The first time, we'd had no practice. Larry and I both sat in there and were pushed down gently. You still travel at a reasonably fast speed and you can do yourself some damage if you get it wrong. That is what happened on the second day when we turned over and went down sideways.

We had gone into a bend, when you have to steer up and then off, but Larry hadn't done so early enough. We had run out of bend, gravity had taken control and we had turned straight over on our side. The bob had slid down, pinning us up against a wall.

It was something I had been dreading. When we had arrived everybody had been watching wipe-outs on video. Some were pretty horrific. A lot of people hadn't walked away from their smashes. I remember a Chinese crew had crashed and one had been stretchered away. Somebody cracked a joke about a Chinese takeaway, but it hardly got a laugh. The atmosphere was very subdued because when something goes wrong in bobsleighing it normally goes wrong in a bad way. You get fatalities. There was one at Cortina d'Ampezzo in Italy. It was one of only a few tracks made of naturally-packed snow. The covering had been insufficient in the finishing straight and there were wooden posts, normally covered with ice and snow, that on this occasion were exposed. An American four-man bob had come round the last bend, on its side, and two had died as the posts virtually tore their heads off.

My thoughts as we turned over can be imagined. 'This is going to be nasty,' said a voice inside my head. Or an expression similar to that. Fortunately, in a two-man bob, you're tucked well inside, bent over forwards and as we slid to a rest I found, to my relief, that I was in one piece. The experience was not nearly as bad as I feared. I climbed out, pushed the bob away with my feet and said: 'Are you OK, Larry?' Not a sound. I repeated my question. 'Oh, shit,' I said to myself.

When, finally, he mumbled that he was, indeed, OK, I was greatly relieved. But that was not the end of it. He sat up and starting yelling: 'I'm bleeding, I'm bleeding. Get my helmet off.' I started to do so, although it was not easy because of the cold. What had happened was that his head hadn't been fully inside the sled, and it had been being dragged along outside. The crash helmet had no visor. You just wear goggles underneath. The ice had scraped off and had packed in really tight in his helmet. What he could feel trickling down his face was not blood, but melting ice.

It shook Larry up, and he lost a bit of confidence after that. But we persevered, rattling along, hitting all the sides. It was really quite a rough ride, so rickety that it felt like the sled was going to fall apart because there was much vibration, even when travelling at 80 kph (50 mph) at the finish instead of 130 kph (80 mph), when you go off the top. To me, it was exciting and great fun, even having watched all that blood and gore on video. You knew it was a risky business. But because of my disaffection with rowing, I thought: 'Well, I have won an Olympics. It's time to try something else and move on. This looks really enjoyable. I'll try this for a week, go back, and see what happens from there.'

I enjoyed being brakeman; it's a crucial but limited role. In fact brakeman is a misnomer because there's no braking until you actually cross the finishing line, and the distance you push for is restricted by the speed at which the sled is going. What you have got to be good at is jumping on.

The Canadian team was over on a training camp, being coached by Gomer Lloyd. He was Britain's best driver at the 1984 Olympics, but had then retired and had gone into coaching. He wanted to prove that he was still the best British driver, and needed someone to push him to show that he still had what it took.

Larry, who was a good talker, convinced him that I was that man. I was rather apprehensive. I'd been involved in a crash the night before, and had been bobsleighing for all of two days. Yet, here I was pushing one of the best British drivers off the top of a bobsleigh run, as fast as I possibly could. I was determined to give it my best shot. But I must confess I was really worried. I had no idea what was really going to happen. 'This is scary,' I thought. 'On top of everything else, I've got to stop this bloody thing once we get round the finishing bend and make sure we don't disappear off into the trees.' However, Gomer said reassuringly: 'Don't worry about anything. Give it as hard a push as you can. When we get into the braking straight, I'll tell you when to brake.'

I pushed as hard as I could, jumped in, and held my breath. There was nothing to do other than brace myself, and wait for the moment to brake. 'God, what's going to happen next?' I said to myself. I gave him a pretty good push and it turned out to be so smooth. It was a real thrill, even though it lasted just a minute. We didn't hit any sides, or any corners and, relatively speaking, we floated down, compared to what I'd experienced with Larry.

Then we came round into the finishing straight. The only other job I had was to stop the damn thing. He shouted out, 'Brakes! brakes!' and I threw my head back and put all my weight on the brake handles, while mouthing the words, 'Please stop!' Then Gomer yelled: 'Stop the brakes, then.' I'd more or less stopped the bob dead and they had to push it to the finish.

We were second fastest, but only fractionally behind Nick Phipps, the top Briton at the time. Gomer was pleased. He'd done what he'd set out to do: prove he was still up there, even with a novice pusher. Then Larry and I went off the top, too, but he'd lost his bottle a bit by then. We still finished 15th out of 22 in the British Championships.

I'd quickly learnt that the real skill is in the driving required to steer the bob on to the bends and, more importantly, steering it off. If you go in too late the G-forces will keep you up there and it's really difficult to steer it off. If you steer off violently, it goes the other way and hits the opposite side and starts rattling down. If you stay on it too long, the bend has gone and you're still on your side, gravity takes over and you drop down sideways...as I'd soon discovered.

After that fortnight I walked away from bobsleighing thinking: 'I really enjoyed that. But what a stupid thing to do. I'm not going to make it in bobsleighing, but at least I got away without being injured. Thank you very much. I'll never do that again.' I would return to my first love of rowing, where I didn't expect to lose a limb every time I went out on the water. I was also, as I reminded myself, pretty good at rowing.

With bobsleighing, I was just one of many.

A year later Larry set up the Irish bobsleigh team, and drafted me in to help with the push-starts. Sophisticated it was not. Larry had a house on the other side of Marlow with quite a long flat drive. We took the runners off the bob and put on wheels and pushed the Irish lads down his drive. We also went to Thorpe Park, where the national bobsleigh centre was based, and practised push-starts. In fact the centre was basically a hut next to a concrete run with rail tracks. The 'bob' was a flat contraption with push handles and no cowling. It was there that Peter Brugnani, who was the Irish team coach, said to me, 'Do you fancy pushing me at the British Bobsleigh Championships?' It was getting to become a habit. This was in the winter of 1987. Perhaps foolishly, I agreed. But that old desire for a challenge resurfaced. I thought that we had a chance of making the British team. I thought it would be really something to go for the winter and summer Olympics.

The two top drivers were Nick Phipps and Mark Tout. They had been pre-selected as Britain representatives for the Winter Olympics, and these championships would determine who would be the third member of the team. Tom Delehunte was the other driver around at the time, and our main rival, although his face didn't really fit because he was RAF and the others were all Army.

The championships were held again at Winterberg, and due to the melting of the track the runs were cut from the usual four to three. On the first run, Pete and I were fastest by a reasonable margin, but on the second we made a steering error on the second bend. We shot up and came back down again. If you make mistakes at the top end of the course when the bob is travelling slowly, you lose a lot of time.

Down the far end, you've got more chance of turning over, but you don't lose quite so much time. We lost our lead and slipped back to second. Tom Delehunte sneaked in front of us. On the third run, we were the fastest again, but couldn't make up on the time that we'd lost on the previous leg. One mistake cost us the championship, and we had to content ourselves with a silver medal.

Tom Delehunte went to the Olympics, where he was the best British driver. I was upset that we had not got the chance of competing against Nick and Mark. I've always thought, 'I could have been there,' although I'd realized that I'd never be able to take part in the Winter Olympics *and* prepare for the summer equivalent at Seoul. I walked away vowing that I'd never do it again.

The following year, 1989, Tom Delehunte phoned, asking me if I'd push him at the British Bobsleigh Championships. I find it extraordinarily difficult to say no and so off I went to Winterberg as brakeman and I became British champion in the four-man bob. That gold medal will always rate highly amongst everything I've achieved. On the back of that performance I was asked to join the British squad for a series of World Cup events. I agreed but stressed that I couldn't go to the first because of rowing commitments, but would go to the second at Sarajevo. I went home to do some training while my bobsleigh colleagues departed for that first World Cup event in East Germany. A team of Romanians crashed and one man died, which reinforced my thinking that 'this *is* a dangerous sport'. I joined them the following week in Sarajevo, a really tight bumpy course, to be asked to race in a four-man, driven by Mark Tout. I was the powerhouse of that bob but they didn't want me in the brakeman's position because I wasn't fast enough. The other two pushers were pretty good sprinters and normally the slowest man gets in behind the driver. The problem is you're packed in so tight in a four-man. At certain corners, you travel round quite sharply and your head would glance off the ice. When the bob hits the wall, you're protected by only thin fibreglass, which whacks against your shoulders. The remainder of the four had red marks from the paint of the bob on their helmets after the race. I was getting paint on my shoulders, which received a hell of a battering. I had to have special padding to reduce the bruising. Also, the aerodynamics are not very good when someone sticks out, and – from a personal point of view – if it did turn over I'd have nowhere to hide. I didn't fancy that at all, although in truth, despite all the videos you see of people losing their sleds and falling over the sides, serious accidents are relatively rare.

Perhaps most crucially, you haven't got much time before the first bend and I was useless at clambering in over the sides. I remember climbing in over the side behind the driver and not getting my leg in, and going round the first bend with my leg stuck in the air. It must have looked hilarious. Then the guy behind, Lenny Paul, grabbed my leg and pulled it in after the second bend, spiking Mark's back as he did so. After that, it was decided that they would put up with me not being the fastest. I would be the brakeman and would jump on when I felt I had run myself out. The other guys, with more sprinting ability, would take two or three strides more, then jump in over the side. It worked quite well.

In the competition we were seventh after the first three runs. I thought we could move up another couple of places, which wouldn't be bad going in world terms. Unfortunately, Mark didn't steer very well at all. He succeeded in smashing us into one of the bends and nearly knocked Lenny Paul out completely, we lost a few places and finished 11th. I thought to myself as the bob came to a rest, 'You're crazy, you're absolutely crazy. Why are you doing this? You're good at one sport. Why are you playing about at another which, relatively, we're not very good at as a country? You may get to an Olympics one day, but you're never going to win anything. You're wasting your time. Just stick to your rowing, and what you're good at.'

That was the last time I bobsleighed. I had got married by then, and Ann might, rightly, have had something to say if I had carried on. However, I've always thought that, maybe, I'd go back and do some driving one day...

A couple of years later, while I was at Boston, USA, competing in the world ergo championships, news came through from the Winter Olympics that the British bob, containing Mark and Lenny, was leading. It was quite a thrill that I'd been with those guys. I thought, 'Shit, why did I give it up? I could have been there.'

But then Mark did his usual thing, and blew it on the second day with bad driving. They ended up coming fourth. Still, I was really pleased to learn that at the last Winter Olympics, in Nagano, Japan, the four-man bob – Sean Olsson, Dean Ward, Courtney Rumbolt and Paul Attwood – won the bronze medal. I was really pleased for them.

The phone went quiet. There were no more requests for my help as a pusher, though I did have one call from Mark Tout in about 1990. I thought he would be asking me to be his brakeman. But no. It was to tell me that after the next Winter Olympics he wanted to compete in the summer Olympics and out of all the sports he thought he could succeed in rowing. That was on the basis of trying out my ergo at Sarajevo and declaring that it was 'easy'. I thought, 'Oh, yes...'

To a certain extent, if you were prepared to put your time and effort into it and to build up your endurance levels, there would be an outside chance that you could make it into an eight if you were strong enough. If you're technically inept, you can get away with a lot more in an eight. An American crew won the 1997 World Championships with a man who was so strong, so fit, that he had to be in the boat, but couldn't row to save his life. At the finish of a stroke he'd be in all sorts of problems with his oar in the gate, so they arranged for his oar to be fixed in place. He was worth having in the boat purely because of his strength.

Mark had apparently done a 2000 metres ergo test and asked me, 'How does that compare?' I replied, matter of factly, 'Not too bad. That puts you in the bottom end of the women's team.' It shocked him. He didn't like that. I said, 'If you can get your times down to below six minutes for a 2 km test, you've got a chance.' To help him I sent him a copy of my technical book for rowers, *Steven Redgrave's Complete Book of Rowing*. I haven't heard from him since.

CHAPTER 10

ANDY NO HANDICAP

I returned for the 1986 rowing season with my enthusiasm restored, and my back in better shape. After that winter's bob-sleighing I easily slotted back into the rowing schedules. I'd just turn up and win long-distance trials very comfortably. I also won the Scullers' Head of the River race.

It was in 1986 that Andy Holmes came back on the team again, having not rowed at all in 1985. He had a very clear idea in his mind. He wanted to win gold in the Commonwealth Games and the World Championships, so that he could claim to be a Commonwealth, Olympic and world champion simultaneously. The notion really appealed to him. Very few people had achieved that before, if any. He believed it made sense to form a pair. As Andy, who was particularly concerned with the commercial implications of any decision, put it, 'Four names don't fit into a headline. Two do.'

Andy had a high opinion of himself. Although Martin Cross had got together in a pair with Adam Clift and won that silver at the 1985 World Championships, Andy still considered himself better than both of them. He had already started rowing again with John Beattie – a member of the coxed four before I replaced him in our Olympic year – who was also Martin's best friend.

As I have related, I had been out of the rowing world, disillusioned, following that back problem. I didn't know what to concentrate on when I returned, although the Commonwealth Games appeared a logical target.

It was Mike Spracklen who suggested I *scull* at the Commonwealth Games and *row* at the World Championships. Mike, then chief coach of the team, was the go-between with Andy. Mike knew Andy had been training with John, but it was rather a hit-and-miss arrangement; they didn't do a great deal of work and just went out now and again.

Andy and I met in a pizza parlour next to Hampton Court Bridge, where he explained that he was determined to do the Commonwealth Games. I said I had planned to do the single sculls in them and also at Henley Regatta. The agreement we came to was that I'd carry on single sculling as originally planned and take part in the Commonwealth Games. Together, we'd row in a pair. Our first target would be the Commonwealth Games, where we'd compete in the coxless pairs. That was assuming that we beat off the challenge of Martin Cross and Adam Clift for the right to do so, but I knew we were faster than them. In the World Championships, to be held at Nottingham a couple of weeks after the Commonwealth Games, Andy and I would do the coxed pairs. The ultimate plan was to continue through to the Seoul Olympics. That's how our partnership began, one that was to intrigue people and attract much media attention.

Many observers have suggested that we did not have much obviously in common, apart from self-belief in our capabilities. That was not true. In fact, Andy and I were quite similar in some respects, not least our family backgrounds. Although he had attended a public school and then gone on to college, his family were middle to working class. If I had to classify my parents, I'd put them in the same category.

Our characters weren't dissimilar either. I was quite quiet, introverted and never made a song and dance about things. I just got on with them. That's how I saw him. Admittedly, I've come out of my shell now because of the motivational talks and after-dinner speeches I've done, and nobody can shut me up once I start.

Andy, whose father ran a one-man boat-repair business, had taken up rowing at Latymer School, Hammersmith, where it was on the sporting curriculum. He went on to take a French degree at college, where he met Pam, who would become his wife.

They'd got married during 1985 and, after Seoul, had a daughter, Amee. Pam is an artist and art therapist, who enjoys long-distance walking. She did not take that much interest in rowing.

During our days in the coxed four, Andy had not made that much of an impression on me. He was never much of a conversationalist. That was the domain of Martin Cross and John Beattie. They always had the stories to tell and everything had to revolve around them. Andy never got involved with other people in the group and just concentrated on the training in his own quiet way.

Prior to the 1984 Olympics, Andy and I roomed together. We generally kept ourselves to ourselves. There was never any friction between us, except one time when we were playing football in 1983 and it turned nasty. It was just over-enthusiasm, really. We were playing in a gym and the ball got caught in a corner. Andy was shielding it and I was hacking away at his legs, my usual tactics. That nearly turned into a fight, but the others broke it up before we got carried away.

Andy had arrived in our coxed four with a worrying reputation. He had originally been in the eight. Before he had joined them the eight had won two World Championship silver medals. When he became a crew member, they ended up last. The belief was that Andy would always blow up, and lacked endurance.

As I have already touched on, Mike Spracklen went so far as to tell Andy, when he joined our four, that nobody wanted to row with him. It didn't actually seem to bother him; he never seemed to care what people thought about him, but it all contributed to his poor image, a man to be avoided.

They may as well have slung a notice around his neck, proclaiming: 'Beware. This is Andy Holmes. He makes boats go slow.' But it was his attitude that caused even more concern. You'd hear stories about him being scheduled to go away on a training camp, or regattas abroad, and just not appear. When he did arrive, he just wasn't motivated.

In 1983, when he was in the eight, the top British boats were the coxed and coxless fours. When the eight had a camp somewhere, he'd decide: 'I'm wasting my time here' and not turn up. Not only that, but he wouldn't bother to tell anybody. Many people had all sorts of problems with Andy.

But that's not the Andy I knew at all. If it had been, our relationship wouldn't have lasted as long as it did. In all the years I rowed with him, Andy very rarely missed a training session, and, if he did, there was always a valid reason. He rarely complained, and just got stuck into the work. Though it may surprise those who believed all the stories written about us before, during and after Seoul, I could not fault him on the water. He was a great oarsman to row with.

Yes, he was sometimes a difficult, enigmatic character, but once he was committed to doing something his dedication to that cause was second to none. The rumours that I'd heard about him didn't seem to fit in with the guy that I knew.

The strange thing was that, after Seoul, he apparently reverted to type and lived down to his earlier reputation. In 1989, after we had split up, Andy decided to carry on. I believe his prime motivation was to prove that he could beat me, which was fair enough. He was unsuccessful in the pairs trials, but got into a four. They went to Duisberg Regatta and performed really well, finishing third one day and winning the next. But he just walked away, saying, 'I'm wasting my time. I'm not going to do this.' Yet he had done a whole winter's training and the international season had just started.

Early in our first season together, we went on a training camp to Saboudia in Italy, then raced at Piediluco, which is the rowing base for the Italian squad. Andy and I did some sessions against Adam and Martin and, both in endurance work and short bursts, proved ourselves to be faster than them.

While we were away, we formalized the selection process for the coxless pairs place at the Commonwealth Games. The first international regatta was to be at Mannheim, where we would compete in the pairs against each other. Whichever pair lost that race could decide whether they wanted to continue the trial to a best of three. Whatever that decision, we decided that we'd all get together in a four and race on the second day with a view to competing in the coxed four in the Commonwealth Games. That would mean that I would enter, possibly, three events; whoever was in the coxless pair would do at least two. The pair which did not win selection at least had a chance of taking part in the Commonwealth Games in the four.

Also at Piediluco were the legendary Abbagnale brothers, Carmine and Giuseppe, the reigning Olympic and world champions. They had hardly been beaten since their first season together in 1980, when they won the under-23 championships and went to the Moscow Olympics. They were the dominant force in the coxed pairs, having been beaten on only one or two occasions and not by very much. Andy and I raced them on the first day, the Saturday, and beat them by nine seconds. They were from Naples and never appeared to be appreciated very much by the rest of Italy. Piediluco was nearer to Rome. As we both rowed past the grandstand there was absolute silence. The great Abbagnales had not just been beaten but been humbled. Now we knew that our coxed pair could dominate the event. Adam and Martin did a coxless pair on the same day and then we swapped on the Sunday. They beat the Abbagnales, too, but only just. Nevertheless, the Italians had been beaten twice in one weekend, and that was a major shock.

We prepared through the spring for the first international regatta, and the first leg of the challenge at Mannheim. The course there is in a dock, and is just under 1800 metres long, so you do not row the full championship distance. On the first day, Andy and I beat Martin and Adam very comfortably. The margin of 17 seconds was significant. Adam wanted to take the challenge further, principally because the two of us had always been avowed rivals right from the beginning of our sculling and rowing careers. Martin advised him not to be daft. He knew that the chances were that they would get beaten by just as far the following day, even with a 10 per cent improvement. So it was agreed that Andy and I would do the coxless pairs at the Commonwealth Games.

After Mannheim, we all combined at Nottingham International Regatta to do the coxed four. We met the Abbagnales again in one of two Italian fours competing. We expected them to do well, but they didn't. The Abbagnales were performing poorly in every boat they got into. We weren't deceived. They had made a habit of that – unless the boat was the coxed pair, which always seemed to go exceptionally well.

Following Mannheim and Nottingham, Andy and I went to Henley Royal Regatta, to contest the Silver Goblets. I was also in good heart for the singles event, the Diamond Sculls. But the final of that turned out to be one of the most humiliating defeats of my career, when I was beaten by the lightweight world champion, a Dane called Bjarne Eltang, who weighed 20 kg (44lb) less than me.

At Henley, where you always compete against only one other boat, it's not like normal international racing where you would have up to six crews spread across the water. It is also a slightly longer course than the usual 2000 metres, and upstream. That means races can take at least a minute more to complete than a race on a lake or canal. With only one boat in opposition, if you get a big lead, their heads drop and the race is over. Events very rarely go the whole distance. By the end of Temple Island, less than a minute into the race, I was a length clear.

My thoughts at the island were: 'If I push on now, I can break him.' By the barrier, which is just over two minutes into an eight-and-a-half minute race, I was three lengths clear – an enormous margin. Yet, remarkably, the Dane gradually edged back at me all the way up. He got level and started rowing away from me. By the time I got to Remenham, which is roughly half-way, I had conceded the race and actually stopped.

It was not one of my proudest moments, and it hurt badly. Afterwards I felt thoroughly ashamed. I shouldn't have stopped, of course, but I just felt embarrassed rowing past the enclosure packed with people who had expected to see me win.

Predictably, Eltang had plenty to say for himself. The 1983 and 1984 world champion gold medallist quipped, 'I thought of saying "a nice little paddle, Steve", but I didn't because this race is for gentlemen, not for monkeys.' That was in response to reports that Andy Holmes had stopped rowing to remove his sweat shirt during our semi-final defeat of Robin King and Ian Stevens in the Silver Goblets the previous day. More pertinently, as far as our race was concerned, was Eltang's observation that 'You cannot do everything by muscles; you have to use your brain.'

Chris Baillieu, who'd retired from international competition after 1984 when not selected for the Olympics, spoke to me afterwards and said that Eltang was known for not being that fast off the start, but stressed, 'One thing he's got is staying power and guts. He'll keep going whatever.' I thought, 'Well, if I'd known that I'd have taken the length lead that I got from my fast start and sat on it.' I was sure I could have won. I should have known about Eltang's tactics but I'd never watched him race. I knew he was a world champion, but I just didn't know how he'd achieved that. Normally if you're leading at 500 metres you're likely to be leading at half-way, and leading at the end. That's true 90 per cent of the time.

It was very naive of me, and also of my coach Mike Spracklen. We should have known better. I probably deserved headlines like that in the *Guardian*, 'Diminutive Dane makes a monkey out of Redgrave'. I was also privately seething about Chris Baillieu's lack of assistance. Having done the single for a number of years, he knew that information and could have said something beforehand. Because of the rivalry that had previously existed between us he was probably quite pleased by the result.

In one way, however, defeat by Eltang taught me a lot. It added significantly to the realization that I would never come up to the standards I had set myself in the single scull. I was becoming very disillusioned by it all. My only consolation was going out later with Andy to win the Silver Goblets easily, beating the previous year's holders, Ewan Pearson and Dave Riches.

The last international regatta before the Commonwealth Games and World Championships was Lucerne. Again we faced the Abbagnales, but this time beat them only by six seconds. However, Andy and I also beat the world record, which was to stand until 1994 and the Indianapolis World Championships.

I remember doing the warm-up. There was one race between the coxless pairs, in which Adam and Martin were competing, and our coxed pairs event. I heard on the water that Adam and Martin had won. I was pleased, of course, but I thought, 'Bloody hell, if they've won, we've definitely got to win.'

Not only did we break the world record, we were only two seconds behind Adam's and Martin's time, when the difference between a coxed pair and a coxless pair should be around 15 seconds. To put it in perspective, we'd have been in the medals, even with the 50 kg (110 lb) load of coxswain in the form of Adrian Ellison who was doing the steering for us at that time.

The 1986 Commonwealth Games were held at Strathclyde Country Park. Despite being July, it was bitterly cold. We didn't feel it. Those Games provided ample compensation for some of those dark days of the last two years, and particularly, for me, that defeat at Henley.

The way that the competition was organized, some events took place on the first three days, including the single scull; the remainder, including the coxed pairs and coxless pairs, on the second three days. Following my experience at Henley, I planned to go out as hard as I normally did from the start in my singles races, but then switch to a lower pace, and if the opposition came back at me not to worry unduly, but to increase my rate significantly in the second half of the race.

It worked to perfection. They were the best series of sculling races I had managed up until that point. My victory in the final was easily the best of them all. It was the first final of the rowing regatta and it was a stirring moment to see the Cross of St George fluttering on top of the flagpole. (Having said that, I don't regard myself as English. I'm British. I believe we should all come under the same banner as one nation, just as we do at the Olympics.)

I'd made a breakthrough. I'd paced myself so much better. The silver medallist, Australian Peter Powell, whom I'd beaten by more than four seconds, was no mug. Neither was the bronze medallist, the New Zealander Eric Verdonk. Yet, the sheer irony was that it was to be the last major sculling race I ever competed in. It was the finest performance that I had ever produced, two years before the 1988 Games that had always been my target, and yet I was never to row as an international sculler again.

I had, reluctantly, come to the conclusion that there remained a void between me and the elite internationals. It would be something that I'd probably never overcome. For too long I had deluded myself because I was so superior to anyone else in this country. By top international standards, I just couldn't stay the pace. I needed my fast start just to be up there with the best of them. Then I'd struggle to stay with them, and be too far out of it to come back towards the finish. I had to accept that they were a little bit quicker than me between 250 metres and 1000 metres. I'd try to turn the screw during the third 500 metres and that seemed to work. But by then it was all too late.

During the second three days we did the pair and the four. Andy and I cruised to victory in the coxless pairs. In the coxed four, there was a little bit of needle between the New Zealand crew and ourselves. The New Zealand boat comprised half of the eight, and they clearly believed themselves to be a really strong unit. We shattered their illusions, winning in very tricky conditions – a very strong tail wind – with New Zealand and Australia second and third respectively.

They were excellent results, and I was especially pleased with myself, having won three golds at one championships, which really produced some unprecedented media interest. Matthew Pinsent likes to tease me and describes it all as 'a pot-hunt', but I think the Commonwealth Games are splendid, and I'd like to see rowing re-introduced as one of the sports. At least I can claim that I'm still reigning champion as that was the last regatta at a Commonwealth Games.

Before the World Championships, there was one outstanding issue to resolve. I knew it was of particular concern to Andy because he had brought it up at Lucerne: the question of replacing our coxswain, Adrian Ellison. He had coxed the four at Los Angeles and had steered us whenever we had contested a coxed pair. His departure was subsequently described by Penny Chuter, then national coach, 'as a clash of personalities' between Adrian and us. That was to put it mildly. Andy said that he could not get on with Adrian and didn't want him in the boat. Andy's words were to the effect that 'this time he doesn't deserve to be world champion. He is Olympic champion already, and will be Commonwealth champion in a couple of weeks' time. He just doesn't deserve three titles.'

I didn't take such a forceful view but I knew what he meant. Adrian always had the attitude that he was the Formula One driver and we were just his engine. Frankly, his condescending manner got people's backs up and that's not a good situation in a boat when you all have to be in harmony with each other.

I was never a great fan of Adrian, and the way that he issued commands. One of his nicknames was 'Microchip'. He'd have every gadget going, and any information you received seemed to be computerized.

I never had a great love of coxes anyway. Most boats I'd been in were coxless. My attitude was always, 'If it's possible to have a coxless boat, why have a coxed boat? What's the point?' The fact that you have to carry an extra 50kg is probably the best reason to avoid it!

In fairness the coxed four is a very traditional boat and I've got a soft spot for it. However, it was developed in days when most racing and training was on rivers and you needed someone to steer you round the bends. But international events now all take place on straight courses, on lakes or canals, apart from Henley.

The coxless pair has always had more prestige than the coxed. The coxed pairs, together with the coxed fours, has now been removed from the Olympic programme. The top coxed pairs standard was very good, but it tailed off quickly, and all the time I competed in that discipline, there were less than 12 entries. It devalued the event. The only time there were more than 12 entries was at the 1988 Olympics. I wish there had been less then; it would have helped our cause!

The coxed four has always been more of a class event, but it, too, struggled on numbers internationally. However, the tradition has always been in this country that, if you learn to row, it's in a coxed four – apart from in the bigger schools and colleges, where the trend is to put newcomers in eights. A club boat is a coxed four. It was disappointing when that discipline was discontinued in the Olympics.

I accept that where the interest is less than it should be in an event it is quite right to remove it from the schedule. But to lose quality boats like them and to introduce restricted weight categories does not get my approval at all. (In a lightweight boat, oarsmen must be no more on average than 72.5kg, and women 59kg.) Now, we turn up at the Olympics with two double sculls – one heavyweight and one lightweight – and two coxless fours. That can't be right. The argument is that it encourages nations who have smaller-framed people, like Asians and Africans, into rowing, but it doesn't work like that. Which are the countries that win? The same Western countries that have always done so. There is no evidence to suggest that there are more third-world countries trying to get into the sport because lightweights have been introduced into the Olympics. The argument doesn't stand up at all. The world champions are still from the same countries, and the successful heavyweight nations are mirrored at lightweight. If you look at the Danish lightweights, who are Olympic and world champions, they were also very competitive in the open class. Their four would have been pushing for medals against us.

But to return to the subject of Adrian. The outcome of the discussion at Lucerne between Mike Spracklen, Andy and myself was that we would look for somebody else to cox. It was no raw youth that we went for. We phoned Pat Sweeney who was coaching at Berkeley University in San Franciso to see if he'd come over. Mike knew him well and Andy and I were acquaintances because Pat did some work with the women's eight before the 1984 Olympics. In fact, Penny Chuter phoned him. Pat apparently answered the phone sounding slightly distracted because he was watching a gridiron game, with a beer in one hand and hamburger in the other. She asked him to come over and steer the coxed pair. He said, 'Sure, delighted.'

Pat arrived when we were at a training camp in Amsterdam. One of the team coaches was Jim Clark who had been in the 1976 Olympic eight that Pat had coxed to a silver. When Pat turned up we'd been there training for days, going out with a 50kg tool box in the cox's seat. We had steered the boat ourselves. Jim shouted out to him, 'You lucky bastard. You're going to be a world champion.' Pat, being away from the British scene, had no idea. He said, 'What are you guys talking about?' Jim retorted, 'This crew have just stamped on everything this year. They're firm favourites to win the World Championships.' Pat, who had been on a crash diet because he was a little bit heavy, knew we were quite good, but not that we had taken the Abbagnales apart every time we raced them.

His immediate thought, he told us later, was 'Oh, *shit.*' We went out for a first training session and stayed in our lane – well, just: we weaved all the way up the course. Pat hadn't been in a boat for ages. Andy and I turned to each other and said, 'What have we done? We're favourites to win, but we've got some joker in the cox's seat who can't steer straight.' Fortunately, Pat quickly sorted himself out.

He had to, because only days later the World Championships at Nottingham were due to start. Not surprisingly, they attracted a large, enthusiastic crowd. But we gave them something to cheer about in our final, which turned out to be the most gruelling race of my career up to that point. The East Germans, Thomas Greiner and Olaf Foerster, blasted out into lead, while we were narrowly in front of the Abbagnales. It took an eternity for us to reel in the East Germans, with Pat becoming increasingly anxious.

'You've got to go now,' he shouted at the three-quarter mark. We pulled ahead with 200 metres to go and, even then, we were chased hard to the line by the fast-finishing Italian brothers. The East Germans, who came third behind us and the Abbagnales, had put so much into their effort that one of them couldn't even make it to the medal rostrum afterwards.

Overall, it was the culmination of a highly satisfactory year as a pair, if not for my aspirations to become the world's leading single sculler. Andy and I had achieved everything that we had set out to do. Now we had Seoul in our sights.

I needed a long break and, after those 1986 World Championships I went off to Australia, eventually spending seven weeks out there. Belinda came out to join me, because before we'd split up we'd originally planned to travel together. In the event, we went separately and met up out there.

We spent quite a lot of time touring around together, but then had a couple of rows and split up again before we eventually both ended up in Fremantle, where one of my best friends, Paul Rushent, was on the crew of *Crusader*, the British yacht which was attempting to qualify for the forthcoming Americas Cup. Paul used to row at Maidenhead Rowing Club and we raced against each other quite often. He was best man at my wedding. I was best man at his. He claimed a crew he was in once beat me in a four at Walton Regatta when we were about 16, though that seems to have faded in my memory. He gave me a tankard at my wedding, inscribed with my name and 'Runner-up, Walton Regatta', which gave everyone a laugh.

While I was in Fremantle, I used to help bring in the sails of *Crusader*. Because of my strength and fitness, I would have been perfect at winding in or letting out the sails. In fact, I was actually asked to be first reserve for the crew, ready to step in if any of them was injured or ill. I was never actually required, but it did strike me as surreal that, having never done a day's sailing in my life, here I was being asked to get involved with those Rolls-Royces of the yachting world. Like the bobsleighing, it had certainly been tempting to get involved. But with Seoul less than two years away I had a rather more important challenge on which to focus my mind.

CHAPTER 11

WILD WATER AT HENLEY

The following year began well, too, with my award of an MBE in the New Year's Honours List. I was inundated with congratulatory letters, including a message from Francis Smith, who had been responsible for starting my career a decade before. That particularly pleased me.

The only person who didn't figure among the most obvious well-wishers was Andy. He was normally so placid about things. But on this occasion, there was no doubting his annoyance the morning we rowed together on New Year's Day when he had just found out about my award. He was very upset about it, partly because he didn't get one and also because I'd hadn't said anything to him in advance.

The procedure is that you get a letter through the post – mine actually arrived while I was away on holiday in Australia in late 1986 – asking whether, if you were given an award, you would accept it. It also says there is no guarantee of you receiving one, and that you are not to say anything to anyone. Then you don't hear anything else until the names are released on embargo to the media, just before New Year's Eve.

I kept my mouth shut. That's the kind of person I am. If I was told to do something like that, I'd do so. Andy and I were never really very talkative on the water, or off it, anyway. I'd be the one to give the rowing commands, and between sessions we only talked about rowing. There was no time to waste on idle chit-chat. We also trained a fair bit by ourselves.

The other fact was that I had honestly been convinced that Andy would get an honour as well. I competed in the single at the Commonwealth Games that year, but otherwise what we'd achieved at the Olympics and since then, we'd done together. It was very strange. Similarly, there was surprise that not one of us in the coxed four had received an honour after Los Angeles. As Martin Cross pointed out to me there were few Olympic gold medallists who had not received an honour of some sort on their return. The coxed four seemed to have been forgotten. It is not as though this country wins Olympic golds by the sackful. But on past experience, when the modern pentathlete team won gold in 1976, Jim Fox was given an OBE on behalf of the team. When, in 1988, the Great Britain hockey team won the competition, the striker Sean Kerly and captain Richard Dodds both received honours. You wouldn't have expected all 16 members of that hockey squad to receive an award, but at least they got some recognition. For us rowers, the postman never called.

Maybe because of the Eastern bloc boycott it was perceived that our success had been diminished. But I believe that the real explanation was that Margaret Thatcher, who was then Prime Minister, had to approve all honours. It seemed as if sport was never very high on her agenda unless she wanted to use it as a political weapon.

Since her demise, when John Major – a genuine sports enthusiast – took over, governments have become much more responsive to sporting accolades. Today, anyone who achieves a certain level of success receives something. Andy eventually received his award in 1988 after winning a second gold with me, although the other two oarsmen, Martin and Richard Budgett, have still not got an honour. I'm sure both will receive recognition at some stage for service to sport. They deserve to. Martin is on all manner of committees, while Richard Budgett is medical director of the BOA.

There is frequently criticism of the whole honours system. But I support it; I like the tradition of it. Cynics might comment that 'I would say that, wouldn't I?' as I've now received a knighthood, as well as an MBE and a CBE. However, I'd like to see a bit more fairness about the system. The present Government is trying to formalize it more, and ensure that it's not just down to the whim of the particular Prime Minister of the day.

I believe that if you achieve a certain level, there should be an award that the country bestows on you for doing that, regardless of the personal preferences of Prime Ministers. Honours are especially important as a testimony to the commitment that people put into amateur sport. The recognition that they receive for their efforts is, on the whole, very small.

There are many countries, including France, Australia and Italy, where, if you win a medal, you are paid for that achievement. I don't really approve of that system. An honour is far more appropriate than a cheque.

People often used to say to me, even before Sydney, 'You should be knighted for what you've done.' But my view was that knighthoods tended to be given to people who were not only successful, but had contributed something in more than one field, whether it was charity or work for the national good, like Sir Bobby Charlton. He was not just a fine footballer and member of a World Cup-winning team, but is an ambassador for British sport, and has done a lot of charity work. So, you can imagine what an honour it was for me when I joined those distinguished ranks.

Andy's irritation about my honour could not detract from the fact that we had made continued progress on the water. Since we had got together again in December 1985 everything we had touched as a pair had turned to gold. We were so much better than anyone else in this country, and those championships convinced us that there was nobody who could touch us in the world. It contrasted greatly with my sculling fortunes. It made the training really enjoyable to do.

The training was part of the secret. I believe that we were so successful because of our consistent and demanding routines. The two-hour round trip to do two sessions a day in the winter at Hammersmith, and in the summer at Molesey, from our respective homes was frustrating, but we were both so single-minded that it became a minor inconvenience.

We chose those two Thames training centres because they were roughly equidistant between our homes at Thornton Heath and Marlow. We did two sessions every morning, very consistently, very hard. Overall, it was relatively good fun, though it didn't necessarily come across that way to outsiders.

Originally, Andy and I had decided to compete in the Seoul Olympics as a coxless pair, the event in which we had won the Commonwealth Games. But, as fortune would have it, the programme had been changed after 1986 for the forthcoming World Championships and Olympics. The finals of the women's events used to be on the Saturday, and the men's on the Sunday. But FISA decided that, because not many spectators were turning out for the women's finals compared with the men's, it would change the programme to half and half each day to attract more spectators on both days.

Madmen like Andy and myself immediately rubbed our hands in anticipation and thought, 'Right, if the coxless pairs are on the first day and coxed pairs are on the second, why don't we do both? They've actually geared up the programme for us.'

Competing in two finals on the same day was impossible. To do two on successive days was still pretty difficult, but at least it was feasible. That's what we decided to do. The 1987 World Championships were the first using the new format.

The rationale was simple; we always felt that we were good enough to win either. If we just entered one, we could not envisage ourselves being beaten. It was far more of a challenge to see if we could succeed in two. It was sheer arrogance, really, that we were intending to make a hard task even tougher. The problem would be the lack of a recovery period. We realized that we might have to race eight times in seven days at Seoul.

We knew that we'd have to approach the events differently. The one which came first was the event that we had to be certain we'd win – the banker, if you like. We'd try to win that by conserving as much energy as we could. The second event we would attack with a more gung-ho attitude, and see what happened. In hindsight, it probably wasn't the best way to go about it.

It was a challenge I wanted to attempt later when Matthew joined me in a pair, too. If we had done both events, I believed, we could have probably won both, but our coach Jurgen and Matthew himself were set against it.

Before preparing for the 1987 World Championships at Copenhagen, Andy and I had an important date at Henley Royal Regatta. It promised to be a titanic confrontation between the reigning world champions in the coxless pairs and the coxed pairs when Andy and I would take on the Soviet Pimenov brothers, Yuri and Nikolai. Instead, it will always be remembered for turning into sheer farce.

The Pimenovs were always known as very fast starters. As we got up to the Barrier, which is just over two minutes into the race, we had expected to be down at that stage, but in fact we were level. It was looking good because we knew that we'd be stronger in the second half. Suddenly, Peter Coni, the chairman of the Regatta, who was umpiring our race, shouted a warning. It was too late. A Canadian wooden canoe had been pushed out in front of us. Two girls were in it, but they had no paddles. Fortunately, they jumped out of it just as we hit the canoe amidships.

It turned over, and came to a stop just underneath my rigger. I was so furious that I punched a few holes in the bottom of the canoe with my fist. I was pretty hyped up for the race, we were performing well, and suddenly it had been stopped. Sometimes, you react without thinking. We discovered later that the girls had actually been pushed out by a group of drunk young lads, who thought it was just a bit of fun. Later, the owners of the boat wrote me a letter, apologizing.

Peter asked me if my hand was all right. I said that I thought so, although it hurt like hell, but that we'd do a burst to make sure. The Soviets thought it was a re-start, claiming they couldn't understand English, and started off again with us, just to confuse matters further. Eventually, we did re-run the race. This time, we were down by a length and a half at the same stage, which annoyed me as I thought we'd get beaten, but what had happened was that the Pimenovs obviously thought that they hadn't gone off hard enough the first time, so they really went for it on the second start. We paced it really well, and two or three minutes further on, it was clear that they were weakening. We just rowed past them and the Pimenovs came to a stop, before paddling home.

Henley is rigorous in its insistence on standards, and the post-script to the affair was that Peter Coni criticized Andy and me to the media for waving to the crowds in the enclosure as we rowed past. Earlier in the week, he had complained about the 'McEnroe Syndrome' creeping into the Regatta.

However, that canoe incident illustrated just how much pressure rowers are under, and how, when pushed, we are just as susceptible to the same emotions that affect other sportsmen. So much for ice-cool Steve Redgrave. I have often been accused of being unemotional. That's not true. Inside, there can be a volcano threatening to erupt. Sometimes, it does flow over the brim.

There was also another occasion when I must confess I lost my composure. It was in 1994, when our Leander crew had been asked to do some timed training pieces with Cambridge before the Boat Race. It was the year that the Light Blues had probably their best-ever crew. We had previously always trained with Oxford because Mike Spracklen used to do some pre-Boat Race work with them, and I did some coaching too. When Mike stopped coaching us in 1989 and went off to Canada, it broke that association.

I felt that the Cambridge crew were arrogant and unpleasant, their whole approach unsavoury, and that one of their coaches who did the umpiring seemed so biased that I suspected we were probably going to lose. That didn't bother me in itself. With Oxford, our eight mostly won, understandably, but occasionally they would beat us.

No, it was the manner in which Cambridge conducted themselves which infuriated me. During one of the pieces they were leading us by a length when one of the Cambridge crew shouted something dismissive at us. That really wound me up, and riled everybody else in my crew, too. It was the worst thing they could have done.

We changed up a couple of gears and surged back at them. We came alongside them so close that the blades were clashing like eight sabres, and all that was going through my mind was that I wanted to smash my oar through the side of their boat. I wasn't even trying to put my blade in the water. I was just aiming to put a hole in their hull. Fortunately, the fury abated.

If you're beating your opponents, you don't have to shout out. You don't have to make a statement. You win, or you lose. End of story. You walk away from it. The more you win, the less you need to say anything. Cambridge asked us again for our help, when Robin Williams took over as coach, but I just told them that I didn't want anything to do with them.

In view of those examples it's probably fortunate that mine is a non-contact sport. Once you are involved in a contact sport, you don't know how you'll react. I'm sure that, in certain circumstances, I'd respond and lash out exactly like some of our footballers who are so wrongly condemned in the media. Who's to say that I wouldn't?

David Beckham handles all the attention he gets extremely well. That kick out at the Argentinian player Diego Simeone in the 1998 World Cup was stupid; you shouldn't do things like that, but they happen. Players like him are bound to have passion, and that leads to temperament. It's what Sir Alex Ferguson wants. In our sport, the flair is taken away; it's ground down by the way that we train.

Returning to the Pimenov brothers, having lost by default because they had not rowed out their race against us at Henley they had the chance to exact revenge against Andy and me at Lucerne five days later, but went down almost as ignominiously.

Their coach Anatoliy Balenkov bravely tried to suggest that the Pimenovs 'have only one real race in them a year', that being the World Championships, where we planned to double up in both pairs races, just as we intended to a year later at Seoul.

Penny Chuter, who was in charge, had decreed that we should 'concentrate on winning the coxless pairs first' and we duly did so. On Lake Bagsvaerd, Copenhagen, we again showed the Soviets no mercy in the coxless pairs, not only claiming their crown, but even relegating them to third. We then attempted to record a double, with Pat Sweeney increasing the load, on the second day, but the Abbagnale brothers proved too strong and we had to settle for silver.

In the build-up to Seoul, Andy and I became, for the first time in our respective careers, the subject of intense media interest. Before, it had been confined mostly to local newspapers and the regular rowing media. Now, major articles were being prepared on us. You could understand the fascination. Here were two men who were planning to win two golds at Seoul, which had never been achieved before. And they had a serious chance of doing it, too. But there was an added ingredient to the story. We had come to be regarded as the 'Odd Couple'.

At the beginning of that Olympic year we agreed to allow Peter Gillman, a writer with the *Sunday Times Magazine*, to spend three months with us. In hindsight, we were slightly naive and it was probably a mistake.

He had access to us virtually every day. There were several interesting things which could have been written about. One was how we lost our first international regatta and how we'd re-rigged the boat. The set-up was completely different and no-one had rowed like that before. There had been traumas, too, with Andy sustaining a bad rib injury just before the Games. I was expecting a really professional, in-depth article.

I saw a copy of the newspaper with the feature in it just before the Games at Seoul. I decided not to show it to Andy because, a week before our first race, the timing was just all wrong. There was nothing in the article I had expected at all. It merely concentrated on the negative aspects. How we were totally different characters. How the writer thought it was amazing that we rowed together, these two people from different walks of life (although this was not actually the case). How our habits were totally different. It was a bizarre piece.

Following on from that, the *Sun* pitched in with '20 rowlocking things you never knew about our splashing oarsmen' and how much antagonism there was. Yet it just wasn't true. The only time we came close to falling out was the occasion when we clashed playing football, and that was not only before we rowed together as a pair, but before we were even in the four.

The *Sunday Times* writer was of the opinion that two rowers should work in absolute harmony, like shadows. In our case, he suggested: 'Harmony is sometimes lacking.' Sometimes, he wrote, we gave the impression that we didn't like each other.

And, so it continued. He said that Andy and I both felt we should be training harder, 'but admit that they do not enjoy rowing with each other enough to do so.' Mike Spracklen was quoted as saying that we were 'unhappy 80 per cent of the time'.

The piece referred to 'antagonism' growing as training progressed. It suggested that I was irritated that Andy made clear that

ll dressed up for the family album. Me with my sisters, Jane (left) and Christine.

LEFT Almost cherubic. A photograph taken at junior school.

BELOW Symbols of success. The cups, trophies and medals won by the Great Marlow School coxed four 1976–8. I'm second from the right; the other members of the crew are (from left) Clive Pope, Pete McConnell, Nicky Baatz and Robert Hayley, my great friend who died in 1979.

ABOVE RIGHT Feeling the strain. That's me (right) with my partner Adam Clift in the Double Sculls Challenge Trophy at Henley in July, 1980. Adam's wife Melanie is my personal assistant.

BELOW RIGHT Have boat, will travel. Setting off for an event in one of my early cars.

ABOVE LEFT The first of many championship medals. I am presented with a gold after the Great Marlow School crew won the junior under-16 coxed four at the national championship, held at Holme Pierrepont in 1978. Our cox Nicholas Baatz is in the foreground. Behind me are Robert Hayley (bow), Clive Pope (2) and Pete McConnell.

BELOW LEFT Victory at Henley. I lead the way in front of the packed enclosures at the Royal Regatta in 1983. I beat Tim Crooks in the Diamond Sculls.

ABOVE Disappointment this time. Adam Clift and I could only manage a silver at the 1980 World Junior Championships at Hazewinkel, Belgium.

ABOVE My first Olympic gold. The triumphant Great Britain coxed four crew at Los Angeles in 1984.

The 1986 Commonwealth Games at the Strathclyde Regatta Park were filled with success for me: (right) preparing for the final of the coxless pairs with Andy Holmes, when I won my second gold, and (above) celebrating my third gold in the coxed four.

Moment of pride. I show off my first Olympic gold medal after the 1984 Los Angeles Games.

rowing was not the 'sole imperative of his life'. He had apparently once said: 'The whole thing is pretty pointless anyway.'

The item added that Andy actually preferred music. When he was 17 a coach had, by his account, asked him, 'Oars or drums?' His response to the *Sunday Times* man was: 'Like an idiot I stayed with the sport.' He now wished he had gone into music. According to the piece, I had pondered whether I should have stuck with sculling after that Commonwealth Games gold, saying: 'I feel that I have wasted the last couple of years.'

There was more. In our 1988 preparations, for instance, we had been beaten at Essen by a young Romanian crew in the coxless pairs, although we won the coxed event. Andy had just recovered from flu, and also we had not yet reached our peak. The Romanians had probably reached theirs already. Andy, the article related, was not happy. He felt that guts and determination could have won it. My response was that it was 'no good just hacking and bashing along'.

Andy's injury occurred only three days before Henley Royal Regatta. It was diagnosed as a sprung rib. We rowed in a heat at Henley and won that easily, although Andy was working at only 60 per cent. I was quoted as saying: 'The thing about Andy is that you never know how much he's worrying, and how much it really hurts.'

We withdrew, and also from Lucerne the following week, which meant that we were unable to row against the Romanians and the Abbagnales. It turned out that the Romanians won the coxless pairs and the Abbagnales the coxed pair. Mike felt the Abbagnales lacked power and the Romanians were benefiting from their training programme but 'didn't row very well'. However, in the final build-up all went well for us, and in practice we came close to beating the British coxless four.

That is a precis of the first half of the 1988 season, if you had read that *Sunday Times* feature. As I have learnt since, most journalists arrive with a certain theme in mind when they come to interview you. It's easy for them to pick out odd remarks, mostly made when you're feeling low, to support the tenor of an article. That writer had really gone to town with them. These days, I can see it coming from some distance. But at that time we were perhaps too willing to voice every frustration. The end result was that it all gave the wrong impression about Andy and me.

That article, and ones that followed, made us look at ourselves and we probably started reading more into our relationship than actually existed. In reality, there wasn't the gulf between us that the piece had made out. The whole thing was blown out of proportion. People were not just reading between the lines about our relationship, but three pages deep. There was nothing there. If we had a fault it was simply that Andy and I very rarely spoke to each other. We used to make assumptions about what the other person was thinking.

I'd been with Andy, on and off, for four years when that article was published and it started to make me think: 'Yes, we are very different in some respects.' But it wasn't true. At our sponsors Leyland DAF, there was a girl on the press relations side called Sandy Law. She was once asked about how these totally different people could be such successful partners. Sandy replied: 'There are people that you work with in an office, or factory, whatever you are doing, that you get on really well with, and work really well with, but whom you don't really socialize with after work hours.' That was how she perceived Andy and me. It summed up our relationship extremely well.

In fact, Andy and I did have the odd night out. I remember going out to Henley with a group of his old schoolfriends. But when you're living two hours' drive from each other's house, an hour to where you meet to train, and you are training together for four, five hours a day, seven days a week, then driving an hour back, it's not likely that you are going to say afterwards, 'Oh, I think I'll go out this evening. I'll just give Andy a ring, and we'll pop down the pub.' It wasn't practical at all from the point of view of our training environment and where we were living. It wasn't even a thought that came into our minds. If we had lived just round the corner from each other we would have got together more. However, the fact was that, as Olympic athletes, you don't socialize that much anyway. That still applied right up to Sydney. In a sense, we got together for set goals and in between went our separate ways.

Only in later years was there was some sniping from Andy about my perceived flaws. But, at the time, there was never a cross word between us, principally because we were so professional. The desire for what we were trying to achieve was far greater than anything else.

The whole time that I rowed with Andy, we never had an argument about rowing, what we were doing or the way we were going about it. Yet people reading the article that went out in the *Sunday Times Magazine*, or saw the item in the *Sun*, and all the spin-offs from that, which have really carried on right up to the present day, say: 'You and Andy really hated each other, didn't you?' It wasn't true at all, certainly on my side. I hope I've got enough belief in the character of the person that I was rowing with to be able to read that it wasn't true on his side either.

CHAPTER 12

SEOUL, AND THE POWER OF POSITIVE THINKING

I travelled out to Seoul a married man. Around a year after I had split up with Belinda, Ann got in touch with me. She had been going out with Martin Cross, but their relationship ended after the 1986 World Championships. Ann and I had spoken quite a bit that summer, and we got on very well with each other, but I had no idea that it would eventually blossom into romance.

Ann and I started going out during the winter of 1986 and very quickly I realized that this was the person I wanted to marry. However, because of the turmoil I had gone through with Belinda, I was determined that I wasn't just going to jump into anything. I decided to wait a year, and if I still felt that way in a year's time I'd ask Ann to marry me.

That's what I did at the end of 1987. I decided to take Ann to The Compleat Angler to propose, but when we arrived they were fully booked. I'm not very good at planning things. Instead we went to The Cavaliers, as it used to be called. I think it's now a pizza parlour, but in those days it was quite a nice Marlow restaurant. I proposed to Ann during the meal. It was all very romantic. She replied: 'I think you know what the answer is.' Fortunately, it was yes.

Ann and I had decided that we'd have our wedding well before the Games, on 12 March 1988. It was two weeks before the Eights Head of the River, which I didn't enter that year, and the same weekend as the Women's Head of the River. Ann was considering racing in that and getting married immediately afterwards, but her mother put her foot down and said that wasn't on.

The wedding didn't really affect my routine unduly. Being the male part of a marriage, you can get away with doing very little on the organization side.

I had an excellent stag night at Marlow Rowing Club, according to everybody who was there! There were some people present who

I did not even realize had turned up, so large were the numbers. The bar-takings on that particular night must be a record.

The service was held in the crypt of St Paul's Cathedral. One of the privileges of being an MBE is that you're allowed to be married at St Paul's, as well as have christenings there, which is what we have done with all three of our children. You can even arrange for your funeral to take place there. There were about 150 guests at our wedding ceremony, including Mike Spracklen, who was one of the guard of honour. It turned out to be a great day and really good fun.

Ann, who has two brothers and two sisters, was born in Crawley, but brought up in Wargrave, Berkshire. When she went to London University, her parents moved to Box, near Bath. She felt that she didn't really have a church in a real family base. I had strong family ties with Marlow, and we asked the vicar at Marlow to conduct the service for us. He had performed the marriage ceremony for both my sisters at Marlow. If Ann had lived in Wargrave all her life, we would probably have got married there. But we decided to take advantage of my being an MBE, as I was at the time, and got married at St Paul's.

Ann's parents have separated, and her father lives in Cyprus. She was very upset with him for a long time because he just upped and left her mother and she found that difficult to take. Her father came to the wedding, but she refused to have him give her away. Instead it was a long-term family friend that she chose for the role.

That particular location, grand though it is, does have its drawbacks because the wedding ceremony has to take place to an audience of coachloads of tourists. I had my picture taken with several Japanese visitors, who probably had no idea who I was, but assumed I must be terribly important. At least, as the groom, you can get away with a certain amount of anonymity, clad in topper and tails, but it was worse for Ann, wearing a long, flowing wedding dress. All the foreign tourists were staring at her, and clearly thinking: 'She's got to be somebody really famous.'

We went away for a week afterwards on honeymoon to St Vincent, in the West Indies, and then I just continued with my normal routine. I wasn't entirely happy that the honeymoon would interfere with my training schedule, but you have to make exceptions on such occasions. It was a relaxing week, apart from one incident. I'd never done any wind-surfing before, and I discovered it was possible to do that between the mainland and the island we were staying on.

Ann easily switches off, and is quite content to lie in the sun, while I get bored with that after 10 minutes. I found a guy who taught me how to wind-surf, and he got me to go back and forth between the seashore and a boat moored out in the bay. Nothing too ambitious. I thought that was easy enough and I tried to see how close I could get to the boat, and felt I was pretty skilful at it. He busied himself with somebody else.

Unfortunately, the strong current round the island is liable to sweep you off into the Atlantic if you get caught in it. I started to get swept away. Whatever I did, I didn't have the technique to bring the board back. A coxless pair on a lake was one thing; this was something completely different. Eventually, I thought I was going to disappear and never be seen again. I'd have to jump off and swim for it. I tried to swim with the board back to the shore, but found it pretty nigh impossible. To my relief, I found that on tiptoe I could just touch the bottom, which consisted of coral and was extremely sharp.

Fortunately, the chap in charge of the boards saw I was in trouble and swam out. He said, 'You swim back to the shore.' He then jumped up, sat on the board, picked up the sail and paddled back without any problems. I felt extremely embarrassed with myself, and not a little relieved. I trudged back to Ann and said, 'Did you see that?' She was totally unconcerned. 'Oh, yes, you were really brilliant,' she replied. I said, 'No, you don't understand. I was just swept out to sea. I could have drowned and you were just lying there.' To this day, she probably imagines I was exaggerating the whole incident, but it was a nasty moment while it lasted.

The year 1988 was, in general, an excellent one for us. All that soured it was that fact that Ann had been bidding for a place in the women's eight at Seoul. She had taken a year's sabbatical from her work to prepare for it. Then the ARA decided not to send an eight as such, but instead to make up the crew from some of the competitors in the smaller boats. Both Ann and I were extremely upset.

Before the Olympics, Andy and I travelled out to a place in Korea called Chuncheon City. It had a training camp at a lake just outside town where we stayed for about 18 days. The biggest worry for us was the food. As finely tuned athletes, we could take no chances with our diet, or the way our meals were prepared. So we took over a small hotel and flew in a Forces chef, a fellow who was based out in Hong Kong. He oversaw everything and ensured that our food was prepared in a western way. The meals were excellent, and so, too, was the camp.

The regatta itself was held on the Han River Basin, an amazing setting amid green mountains which, as someone said, was reminiscent of a scene from the film *M*A*S*H*. In Los Angeles we had been in a separate village from the track and field athletes at Santa Barbara, and the whole thing was geared up to us. This time we were all together, and the rowing venue was 20 minutes away from the village.

When I say village, that gives the wrong impression. There was nothing charming or oriental about it. The place was actually a concrete jungle of four- or five-storey buildings, with just a few trees dotted about. It was also very noisy. Apartments were designed for about eight people each and intended to be re-sold afterwards.

In fact, it was quite stimulating to be involved with all the other sports and being able to appreciate the sheer magnitude of it all. A total of 1300 athletes were there, with their coaches. However, the top British athletes tended to stay out in hotels, and very rarely came into the village, people like Steve Cram, Linford Christie and Daley Thompson.

Andy's older brother, Simon, who was a doctor with a special interest in sports psychology and also a hypnotherapist, had travelled out with us. He had done some work with us previously at the 1987 World Championships, and Andy had successfully lobbied to get him accredited to the team as official psychologist.

I found his ideas very interesting. He told us about the skills of visualization and everything fell into place. I had been developing ideas like that myself, naturally, over the years. It would have been useful if someone had told me seven or eight years before, at the start of my career. During the intervening period I had been teaching myself, without really realizing it. It takes a considerable period of time to develop natural sporting mental skills.

Either together or separately, we'd sit down and talk through each race and how we saw it developing; we'd then lie down, and Simon would tell us to think about our breathing and relax everything from the toes right up to the head. He would go through each part of the body in turn and get you to relax them. The legs would become leaden. The whole body would feel very heavy. Mike Spracklen would join in the sessions as well, but he'd just fall asleep. In a sense, I suppose we were in a semi-trance-like state. It was that borderline between being awake and asleep.

You think you know what's going on around you, but your body is so heavy you think, 'I'm not sure whether I believe in this, but I'm just going to lie here a bit longer because I'm quite comfortable.' You remain in control of what's going on, and mentally remain very much alert. 'If I wanted to, I could get up and walk out,' you reassure yourself. 'But I'm quite content.'

When we were totally relaxed, Simon would talk to us about what to expect and what we wanted out of the race. It became ingrained deeply into the mind. It was close to being under hypnosis, although we're not talking Paul McKenna here. It wasn't someone saying, 'You're going out to race 2000 metres, it's not going to hurt you at all, and you'll have loads of energy.' Nothing like that at all. I don't know if I believe in hypnosis – and I've never actually been put in a complete trance – so I'm not sure how it would compare.

This was purely designed to get you completely relaxed, but in a state where you were still totally aware of what was going on. That was the difference. As I understand it, under full hypnosis you have no recall of what has happened to you.

What Simon said to us was nothing different from what we'd been through as a group before. There was nothing clever or mystical about his words. It concerned the concentration within the warm-up, certain points within the race that he'd pick on, the mental awareness when sitting on the start, after 15 strokes, the stride and the rhythm that you're going to get into. Practical things, tactics. But we were doing this in a totally relaxed state, with everything else blacked out.

I can't say whether it helped or it didn't, except that after one session we went out and set an unofficial world record in the coxless pairs. Andy said later that there had only been one time when he had been forced to row to his absolute limit just to keep up with me. It was on that occasion.

In some ways, it's an obvious asset to any sportsman. Athletes train their body to incredible levels. Everything is put into the physical training. Yet very little is done mentally. Most of the time, the limiting factor is the mind, not the body. Sports psychology is still in its infancy in some respects. Now and then, it gets a big boost of publicity. In an Olympic final, there's very little difference between the athletes in percentage terms. What is the factor that makes someone better than their nearest rival? Most of the time, it's their mental state.

I talk about visualization when I give motivational talks now; of being aware of time and making time. As a society, we have less, although in theory we're supposed to have more time on our hands for leisure. But my experience is that we tend to be rushing around from one thing to another. Very rarely do we have time to sit down and think. That's a very important part of whatever you're trying to do. Even top businessman should occasionally lock the door of their office, and think problems through. It's exactly the same with sportsmen, and that's what we do with what I call visualization. Put yourself in the situation of foreseeing problems before they arrive, to try to cure them in advance.

Visualization can put people off because it's modern jargon. Perhaps it could be better described as day-dreaming. As children, if you do that at school, it's classed as a bad habit. But sports psychologists now will say that in fact it's a good thing. That it's positive, though it's a question of maintaining a balance.

Since those Games, I have always maintained that I don't need a psychologist or hypnotherapist. That's not to denigrate those professional men and women. I just felt my own psychology was adequate.

What I did during the four years up to Sydney, for instance, was to constantly visualize what was going to happen at those Games. A day did not pass when I didn't think about what was going to happen on that momentous date, the day of the coxless fours final, Saturday 23 September. I call it the 'what if' situation.

Rowers take part so little in major international events – far less than top footballers, for example – that we don't really get that much experience, although I've got more than most. Because of that, you have to continually picture yourself in situations, and work out how you're going to respond to them. That's really important, if you're favourites to win, as we were. What you don't want is surprises. That could mean catastrophe from a favourite's point of view.

So you have to say to yourself: 'What if somebody leads off the start? What are you going to do about it?' or 'What happens if you get a really good start and something happens in the middle period? How are you going to respond to that?' Certainly for me, questions like that are vital to consider constantly, because it's my job to do the calls and direct the tactics of the race.

Yes, we'd have set tactics going out, but if somebody produces something unexpected, we'd have to respond to that. You'd either have to say 'they've gone off too hard' or 'we've gone off too hard'. You put yourself into thousands and thousands of different situations and plan how you, and the crew as a whole, are going to react to that. When it comes to that final race, whatever happens you've been through that scenario before, albeit in your head. I don't like surprises of any kind, and certainly not in an Olympic final.

In the four years up to the Olympics, when I was driving, or maybe pushing the trolley around the supermarket, I'd be thinking, 'I wonder how the Australians are preparing? How are they looking to try and beat us? And what about the New Zealanders? They weren't thinking, "Oh, if we could come second that would be fantastic," were they? They were dreaming about winning the gold medal. They were trying to come up with a plan to beat us. I wondered what that plan was. How were we going to counter that?' All these thoughts were going on all the time, so when it actually came to the race, whatever was thrown at us, we could respond to it.

It's not negative thinking. It's very positive. It's very professional. Preparing for different situations. The perfect row is to go off into the lead at the start, keep moving away from your opposition with every stroke, and win by a long way. There's no doubt in your mind for any period of the race. That's a nice situation to be in. The reality is that it doesn't work like that.

The worst situation is for you to go into the race with all your plans, then for somebody to do something unexpected, and for you to take no notice of it. You may decide not do anything about it; but you have to be aware of it. It's crossing the line first that's the important thing. That would get you in the history books as a winner at the 2000 Olympics. It doesn't matter how much you win by – or lose by.

I used to train with the Evans brothers, Mike and Mark, who were in the Canadian eight and went to Oxford. That eight won in Los Angeles in 1984 by just blasting out of the start and establishing a reasonably big lead. Everybody rowed back at them and closed them down really fast.

As they crossed the line, they must have been a metre or two in front, but just past the line they were in third position. People said afterwards: 'You were really lucky to hang on to that. Two strokes after the line you were only third.' They just turned round and said, 'It doesn't matter; it's who crosses the line at 2000 metres that counts. It's a 2000-metre race, not a 2002-metre race.'

Similarly, Jonny and Greg Searle were fourth with 500 metres gone, third at 1000 metres, still third with 500 metres to go, and only led with 10 metres to go against the Abbagnales at Barcelona in 1992. But they walked away as Olympic champions.

In more recent years the British team had a psychologist named Brian Miller, who was very good, although he didn't really work with us. He had a saying that Matthew and I used a lot: 'If not now, when? If not you, who?' I tend to agree with that.

People would say to me, 'Do you think you can win the Olympics again?' The facts were that the Sydney Games would go ahead in September. There would be a coxless fours final on the 23rd, and somebody would win that. Why shouldn't it be me? If I don't do it now, when am I going to do it? If it's not going to be me, who am I going to let beat me?

It's a positive line of thought. To get that far, you must have a belief that you are capable of winning. If you can't do it on the day, when are you going to do it? It was no good saying, 'Well, I'm not that bothered if I get beaten. There's always another time.'

For me, there wasn't another time anyway. Not at 38. For the others there's not going to be too many more occasions when they'll get the opportunity. It's got to be right now. This was the day we had to do it, one way or another.

People used to say to Brian, 'You don't seem to do any work with Steve and Matt. Why's that?' He would just shrug and say, 'What they do is pretty good. They're successful. There's very little I can do to help them. The day that they come and ask me for help, it will be too late. The moment will have passed.'

The 1987 World Championships, when Andy and I had won the gold and silver, had instilled a lot of confidence in our bid to win two events in Seoul. It would mean we'd have six races at the Olympics in six days of racing. We would really have to be switched on, because all our opposition would be having only three races. It was all about conserving energy in the early part of the week. Semi-finals day would be the really tough one because we'd have two races on the same day.

We won our coxless pairs heat, and that put us straight through into the semi-finals. The next day in the coxed pairs we had a much tougher draw, with the Abbagnales and the Romanians, who were said to be a reasonable pair, amongst the opposition.

The first three would qualify for the semi-finals. In theory, we could do that without too much trouble, but if we finished first or third we worked out that we would meet the Abbagnales again in the semi-finals. We wanted to avoid that. There was also a concern that we'd meet the East Germans, who also worried us, in the same semi-final. Our coach, Mike Spracklen, had worked out that if the Abbagnales won and we finished second, we'd go into the easier semi-final. So, we set out deliberately to finish second, which is not that simple.

The Abbagnales did what they normally do and blasted off into the lead, with us slightly behind them, but Romania were pushing quite hard as well because they also wanted to avoid third place. Pat Sweeney had the unenviable task of attempting to judge it just right so that we finished second. It was all thoroughly confusing.

I thought the Abbagnales were further ahead than they were. Pat told us to 'easy' it before the line, and, in doing so, we nearly got beaten by Romania. I hadn't realized that if we hadn't 'eased' it, we'd have probably have rowed through and won. In the end, it was a blanket finish, with the Abbagnales just getting home first.

Still, we had the semi-final draw that we wanted. So far, so good. We had the following day free. But we then faced two semi-finals on the same day. In theory, that shouldn't have troubled us unduly, except for the timing of the races. The coxless pairs was the second to last event in the morning, and the coxed pairs the first race in the afternoon. It didn't give us much time to recover.

It got worse. There were very strong cross-winds in the morning, and the start of racing was postponed. In the World Championships the year before the conditions had also been very rough, there had been a lot of turmoil and complaints from competitors, and the officials were determined not to have further controversy. They would not race until the wind had dropped to acceptable levels. However, they delayed racing in the morning only.

When our race went out to warm up, there was eventually a collision between two of the boats, America and Austria. Some on-the-spot repairs were done, but the result was that our race was last off in the morning. The afternoon programme remained the same. This was not what we had expected at all, and all our plans were going awry.

It came down to just over an hour between the start of the coxless pairs semi-finals and the start of the coxed pairs semi-finals. We requested that the coxed pair race should be delayed. The FISA officials said they had no problem with that, but it was up to all the other countries we were racing against to agree. Nobody had any objections, with the exception of the Soviet Union and Czechoslovakia, who both realized that if we were exhausted they'd have more chance of progressing to the final.

The race timing remained unchanged, which was frustrating, although we had the satisfaction of seeing Czechoslovakia eliminated. We won our coxless pairs semi-final comfortably from Belgium, climbed out of the boat and walked around for 10 minutes to keep the blood flowing, and to ensure that our leg muscles did not stiffen up. Meanwhile, our coxed pair boat had been put on the water for us by Mike and Pat, and soon we were back in action.

At least, we didn't have to do a full warm-up! I remember that semi-final being quite severe on the legs. It was a reasonably tough race. But, with three going through to the final, we achieved that relatively comfortably by finishing second to Bulgaria.

The journalists weren't allowed to come down to the boating area and after our coxless pairs semi-final win we did not go up to the press tent, because we just wanted to recover. However, we'd arranged to see a few of the media who came down to the gate next to the boating area. I knew Neil Allen of the London *Evening Standard* reasonably well because he was married to Helen Bristow, who used to be the physiotherapist on the rowing team. He said to me: 'Your legs must be really tired now.' 'Yes,' I retorted, 'but they're still stronger than yours.' He said: 'Fair point.'

At an international regatta, you would normally do a heat and a semi-final on the same day, but you've hours between one and the other. Also, if you had a real chance of winning the event, it's unlikely that you'd be absolutely flat out in the heat. You'd also be racing oarsmen who would be in exactly the same position as you.

But here on the Han River Basin, we were taking on fresh athletes in the coxed pairs. It was hard, but I wouldn't describe it as punishing. We had to keep reminding ourselves that it was only the fourth race of six. You didn't go out to try to win the semi-final just for the sake of it. You had to keep your powder dry. We had no doubts at that stage; Andy and I were still convinced we could win both.

Penny Chuter had once more given our plans her blessing, although she stressed that our priority was gold in the first final, the coxless pairs. Nobody could really object to what Andy and I were attempting. In the World Championship the year before, Great Britain had ranked third of all the rowing teams because of two people – Andy and me. So we had a considerable amount of power over the situation.

The final of the coxless pairs was effectively a match between us and Romania. We knew beforehand that we were going to win. Otherwise, why try two events? If we had harboured any doubts, we wouldn't have contemplated the task. However, you still have to go out there and do the job.

The conundrum was: how could we win this without putting everything we possibly could into it? The plan was a very fast start, as always. One of the assets I've brought to most of the crews I've been in has been my explosive start, the ability to get the boat off the line and moving fast pretty quickly. Rowing is different from other sports, like cycling or running, where normally it's a disadvantage to be out in front and have people sitting on your shoulder. In rowing, it's an advantage to be out in front because you can see what your opponents are doing. You can relax more than when you're behind.

In that case, we got off to a very quick start. We were very comfortable and settled into a nice rhythm. We normally rated about 35 strokes a minute and here we were at 37, but it felt a smooth, easy pace. The Romanians came back at us in the middle thousand, but, although they edged back, they never got closer than half a length. Never once in the race did I think: 'Shit, we're going to struggle here.' I just felt in total control the whole time. That rarely happens to me. There are periods in most races when you think, 'God, I'm knackered.' Never for one second did I have any doubts. I felt totally confident, even though we were quite close together by the finish.

It was the best race that Andy and I ever rowed together. Very professional, very controlled; all the elements that you'd like to have in the perfect race were there. In my career, I've enjoyed four or five really top-class performances and that was the first. The next would be the three in Barcelona in four years' time.

That's why we felt confident for the following day. Everything had just fallen into place. Obviously, to win a gold you've got to put something in. But this had been easy, or relatively so, in Olympic terms.

When the union flag was raised, an incredible feeling of satisfaction and pride flooded through me. It was better, in truth, than when I received my first Olympic gold at Los Angeles. The Eastern bloc boycott in 1984 meant that medal was definitely tainted because the top rowing nation wasn't there, nor several other strong ones. Los Angeles had been more about relief that we had justified what had been expected of us.

Four years before, everything had happened so quickly that I didn't feel that I enjoyed the moment as much as I should have done. In Seoul I did, because it was the last race of the day. It was something to savour, and we made the most of it. That proved to be one of the causes of our downfall the following day.

Quite simply, I enjoyed the crowd's reaction too much. We'd have been better off if we had just taken our medals and disappeared, to prepare mentally for the coxed pair. But no, we went through all the social niceties that go with winning a gold medal, talking at length to family and friends and dealing with press and media requests. The race took some energy out of us, and the excitement of all the celebrations drained us even more. We didn't realize it at the time, of course. That's where we should have been more sensible.

How different it had been the year before in Copenhagen when we had struggled to win the coxless pairs. We disappeared immediately afterwards and rested. We also thought to ourselves: 'God, this is going to be really tough tomorrow.' We were in that frame of mind. Yet, when it actually came to the race it was not as bad as we feared. That tends to pick you up and keeps you going.

We enjoyed all the excitement and emotions of victory, but to excess. When your medal presentation is the last of the day, you can take your time. There's nobody to usher you away; you can savour the moment. Andy went off and found a union flag and wrapped it around his shoulders, there were interviews with both BBC and ITV and then Ann came down and joined us. It was a real party atmosphere – but not quite what you want to be doing the day before an Olympic final. Yes, we'd just won one. But we had to prepare for another.

Looking back, it reminds me of Seb Coe and Steve Ovett in 1980. Steve had won the 800 metres, thinking 'the 1500 is my event', but with an Olympic medal already round his neck. Seb, who was best at 800 metres, may have been disappointed but that also gave him extra determination to do something in his 'weaker' event. Seb walked away with a gold and a silver, and Steve with a gold and a bronze. I'm convinced that it was just because of their respective attitudes to each race. It's one of the learning curves you have to go through. Unfortunately, learning curves in Olympics don't come around often enough to put them right. If we'd done those two events again, with the benefit of hindsight, we'd probably have won them both.

In the coxed pairs final, we again lined up against those formidable brothers from Naples, the Abbagnales. There were also the East Germans to consider. You expected them to be very consistent. They had been at every World Championships I'd been to, though more recently they'd slipped away a little.

Of the Western crews, very few were consistent except the Abbagnales. They kept themselves to themselves, but possessed an aura of arrogance. That didn't come so much from themselves, but their coach. He was very critical of their performances.

In Seoul, before that coxed pairs, I probably had a similar feeling to Steve Ovett before the 1500 metres. I was thinking to myself: 'I feel really good. I feel really strong' because of winning the afternoon before. But probably it would have been better if I feared it was going to be really hard. Maybe I'd have had more fight in me.

Once the race began, after a false start, I had an ominous feeling in my stomach as it became a real struggle right from the first few metres. I found it exhausting. We were left by the Abbagnales, and were last after 500 metres. Although we reduced the Italians' lead to a length by the finish, the East Germans had also passed us and we had to accept third. The disappointment was acute. We knew we had the horse-power to beat the Italians over any one-off event when reasonably fresh, but not after six races. The first race had taken the edge off us more than we had anticipated.

Some people at the Games thought we were insane attempting to do two events. Oarsmen have done that at World Championships. In Copenhagen, there had been an East German who lifted a gold and a silver. He won a gold in the coxed four, and then went into the stroke seat of the eight who had no chance of winning anything at that stage, and hauled them up to winning a silver. However, most people knew how dominant we were in the coxless pairs, and it did not entirely surprise them that we were trying to do something outstanding.

It was a great day for the Abbagnale family, by trade a family of gladioli growers. Another brother, Agostino, had already collected a gold in the quadruple sculls. They would also collect £15,000 apiece from their Olympic association. We received a thousand handshakes but nothing more.

Not winning gold in that race didn't make me a failure. The disappointment of it wasn't as great as people might imagine it to be. You feel satisfied because you've won a gold; that was what it was all about. I've been to World Championships and not won a medal. That hurts more than going to an Olympic Games and winning a gold and a bronze. Steve Ovett wouldn't have been disappointed that he lost the race he should have won in 1980, because he already had that gold medal in his pocket. The Olympic Games is about being a champion for another four years. That's what I had become.

People tend to forget about the bronze, anyway. They don't say: 'Oh, Steve Redgrave has won five golds and a bronze.' They say, 'He's won five consecutive gold medals.' That's what it means to the world, and to myself. More than anything, I just felt really upset for Pat Sweeney. He'd put in a lot of effort into both boats and helped on the coaching side, working with Mike. All Pat had to console himself with was that he was a bronze medallist. Mike had walked away as a coach to an Olympic gold medallist crew.

Pat deserved far more as part of the unit than an Olympic bronze following a gold medal at the 1986 World Championships and a silver medal the next year. But then again, you had to place it in perspective; three years before when he received that phone call from Penny Chuter he was sitting there eating burgers, drinking beer and not even dreaming that he'd go to an Olympic Games again and have a chance of winning a medal of any colour.

Seoul had been full of fine memories. Also some strange ones, none more so the previous day when our coxless pairs race had been delayed. Belgium, in the lane next to us, had found that their stretcher bar was cracked. Everyone else was told that the race would be postponed, and that they'd put the singles final, which was to have been the last, on before us.

Everybody else started paddling back down to the finish. But Andy and I thought that was a waste of time, because as soon as we got there it would be time to come back. We decided to stay close to the start. We spotted an official car on the bank, with its doors open, and because there was a little pontoon nearby decided to get out and sit in that vehicle. We just wanted to get out of the sun and relax for a few minutes.

Andy was sitting in the front and I was sprawled out across the back seat when there was a knock on the driving side window. It was a fellow named Tommy Keller, who was then President of FISA. 'Sorry boys, this is Princess Anne's car,' he told us. 'She wants to watch the start of the single sculls race which is just going off.' So we both got kicked out, politely, and rather sheepishly removed ourselves. Princess Anne then appeared, and said to us: 'I thought it was only horse races that had delays like this.'

After our race, she wasn't officially supposed to present the medals, but did so anyway because we were the winners, which I thought was a nice touch.

I'm not a strident royalist, but I am a traditionalist and overall I think the royal family do an excellent job. A lot of people are very cynical about our heritage, but the royal family do have the opportunity to do good, not just for this country but world-wide. I believe that they should remain largely as they are, and not respond too far to suggestions that they should be 'modernized'.

Having been in close company of some members of the royal family, especially the Princess Royal, I can appreciate the workload they have is quite incredible. Much of it is self-generated, just because of personal interests they have.

The Princess Royal has many sporting links. I spent two and a half days with her on a tour in America in 1994 – fund-raising for the BOA appeal amongst Britons out in the USA – and I was absolutely shattered at the end of it. I needed a rest. She flew back to England and just carried on the same kind of schedule of making two or three appearances a day.

I first got involved in that appeal by making an appearance when the BOA held a conference at Wembley. From that, I became their principal fund-raising celebrity in Atlanta.

I did a tour which started with a dinner in Atlanta, followed by a lunch in Philadelphia, a dinner in Boston, a lunch in Washington, then back to Atlanta. I was training out there at the time. The idea was to get the British to empty their pockets for the BOA.

The Princess Royal's a very down-to-earth person and that's why I like her. I've been to several functions with her. The thing she dislikes most is the formal line-ups at functions to be presented. She prefers just a group of people and to have an informal chat. She's then more relaxed and everyone else feels more at ease. We've spoken quite a bit, about my health problems and rowing generally.

In the States, we had one of Coca-Cola's private jets loaned to us. She was with a bodyguard and personal aide. You are given a list of dos and don'ts, and one is that while you're travelling, you don't make conversation with royalty. You have to wait until they talk to you. It's understandable. It's their rest time between engagements.

The funniest occasion was at Atlanta. I had Natalie with me at the time. Natalie was then about five, and I said, 'Do you want to meet the Princess?' She said excitedly, 'Oh, yes.' It was all very embarrassing because Natalie just kept making pig noises as the Princess Royal and I attempted to have a conversation. I was trying desperately to keep a straight face.

Strangely enough, that bronze medal I won at Seoul was the one I had stolen a few years later. I was at an Olympic fund-raising lunch in Atlanta and my medals had been passed round for everyone to take a look.

At the end of the lunch, the three golds I then had all returned, but not the bronze. I was on the top table, and one of the officials next to me got up to the microphone and said, 'Could we have all the medals back, please.' Still no sign of the bronze. The staff went through all the bins. It was Christmas and they thought it might have gone out with the hats and crackers. The organizers were extremely embarrassed and upset. Ann was also very annoyed. I wouldn't have liked to lose it, although I have always believed that winning gold is important for the memories you have, not for the medal itself. I just thought, 'Why walk away with the bronze?' I assumed it was a mistake.

When we left the next day, it still hadn't been found. Then somebody contacted the British Olympic representatives in Atlanta, saying the medal must have been slipped into their pocket and they would like to return it. It eventually arrived in a plain brown envelope, with no name or address of the sender. It remains a mystery.

Andy flew straight back from Seoul, while I attended the closing ceremony. Ann and I also went to watch some of the other sports. I knew the British sports minister at those Games quite well. Colin Moynihan had coxed the Olympic eight in Moscow in 1980 and also in Los Angeles 1984, when we were on the same team. I happened to meet him at a function in the second week, and, following that, Ann and I were chauffeured round with him. We joined the hockey team's celebrations after they won their gold medal and watched Neil Adams in action at the judo.

Only three Britons had won Olympic golds at successive Games, and the last two were water-polo players at the Antwerp Olympics in 1920. But when I eventually returned to Britain I wasn't expecting much of a home-coming. In that, I wasn't disappointed. Marlow held a reception, but very much smaller than four years before. There was almost a blasé feeling about it. When an area produces an Olympic gold medallist there's great excitement, but if that person keeps on winning people start to take their success for granted.

I was left with very much an empty, deflated feeling when it was all over, a reaction, I suppose, to all the effort that had been put in, the excitement of winning something and achieving what I set out to do, even though I had not fulfilled that completely at Seoul.

Also, from a 16-year-old, my aim had always been to step up on to that podium and have a gold medal ribbon encircle my neck at the 1988 Games. The bonus was that I had got one in 1984, too. It was very much in my mind to stop. I certainly wasn't clear in my own mind whether I did want to carry on. I told the journalists out there that, as I was now married, it was about time I started a career. Eventually, in a sense, I did, but it was just a continuation of the one I'd already started: British elite oarsman.

It was all or nothing for me, but Andy had other plans. He had already made it clear that he did not propose to carry on for another Olympiad, but would continue rowing for another year to try to get some financial benefit out of it. Soon we were to go our separate ways.

CHAPTER 13

LOSING MY PARTNER –
AND MY FOCUS

Andy and I rowed for only one year in the coxed four and for a total of three years as a pair. But because of what we achieved, the public perception was that we were together for an eternity. By the end of 1988 we had won two Olympic golds apiece, and two World Championships, and, in Britain, that takes you into the realms of legendary status, alongside such people as Seb Coe and Daley Thompson.

Of course, what happened out in Seoul didn't quite tally with the suggestions by some people that we weren't in harmony, and that we had a vehement dislike for each other. A pair like that could not possibly complement each other, could they? They'd be spending too much time having rows.

Those who said, and wrote, that just didn't understand us. I rated Andy very highly. I saw him as the best we had at that time, apart from myself. But it was his attitude and determination, his sheer guts, that had impressed me. When he wanted to achieve something, Andy gave it everything. When it's pretty tough going, you need somebody who will grab the race by the scruff of the neck and say 'let's go'. He was that type of character.

At that time, as I have stressed, I was very much guided by Mike Spracklen. His forte was seeing something in rowers and believing they could make the grade. That's what he achieved with Andy, who had arrived in the four with a reputation as something of a professional loser. Indeed, I welcomed that objective view from someone like Mike. I knew that I was far better than Andy and all the others in the British team. But it is very difficult to make judgements when you're head and shoulders above those around you.

If you're involved in a team sport, it doesn't matter how good the best person is. As I constantly advise young rowers, what matters is how good the weakest person is. You could have the four best oarsmen in the world. That doesn't guarantee it being the fastest crew in the world. It's how they work together, and blend together, and get the best out of each other. And, in putting together a winning boat, first in the fours and then in the pairs, Mike had no peers in this country.

What is important about a successful boat is that all its crew must feel they are contributing something. That they're not second best at everything. I was way ahead of everyone at that time on tests and assessments, a bit like Matthew Pinsent is now. It must have been quite difficult for Andy to sit in the boat and say: 'Well, I'm second to this guy on everything.' Andy was aware that, technically and in terms of strength and ability, he was not of the same standard as me. The qualities that Andy possessed were consistency and guts.

As far as my own future was concerned, I had said to myself in 1978, when a 16-year-old schoolboy, that I'd win an Olympic gold in the single scull. That had not worked out; yet, here I was with two Olympic gold medals and a bronze, two World Championship golds, and three Commonwealth Games golds. My achievement in Seoul had been the target that I had trained all my sights on for the past 10 years. I had walked away with a gold in the coxless pairs and a bronze in the coxed pairs. I was thoroughly satisfied with what I'd achieved.

But where did I go from there? Sir Edmund Hillary could have said the same after conquering Everest in 1953. Instead he sought a new challenge: the South Pole.

In my own way, I had arrived at the summit. All I could do now was search for another to ascend. I thought, 'Do I actually want to carry on, or not?' If I did, it would be for one reason only: to try to win in four years' time in Barcelona. I could have walked away to a more settled existence. But what would I do? I could have tried another walk of life. But there probably wouldn't have been the excitement there that I got from rowing.

At this point, there would be those who would have analyzed it as an addiction. That's a bit of an exaggeration. I have said that I could give it up, at any time I choose to do so. But isn't that what the drug addict claims?

Maybe, if I'd boasted degrees and qualifications, I'd have thought far more seriously about the alternatives. But, educationally, I didn't have anything behind me. I would have been a retired Olympian with a CSE in woodwork, and nothing more. Glory, like a gold mine, becomes exhausted at some time. All that's left is an empty shaft in your life. People would have wanted to congratulate me, but would not have been queuing up to employ me. Even if I could find the work I wanted, I just couldn't see myself settling down as someone else's employee after a decade of being part-time self-employed and unemployed.

As an elite rower, you're very much your own boss. You commit yourself to an Olympics and then go off and train for four years and race at those Games. You're very much in charge of your own destiny.

I have to concede that, financially, it was proving difficult. I had earned some money from TV and personal appearances as a spin-off of my success. There was also our sponsorship. Leyland DAF wanted to stay with us. But, in truth, I wasn't making any money from the sport. I was just about surviving. I was always in the red, but I had a standard of living with which I was happy. The rewards were just about sufficient to justify me carrying on.

Nevertheless, for the next six weeks until I met up with Andy again, the thought was constantly going through my mind, 'What do I really want to do?' I decided that I did want to carry on, but this time I would not attempt to resurrect my original desire to go single sculling. Events in 1986 had taught me that. I should continue in a pair. But with whom?

I knew Andy wanted to continue for another year after 1988 to capitalize on the Olympics. In other words, to milk the gold medal for what it was worth before calling it a day. That was anathema to me. Of course, I desired the financial rewards, but I thought in terms of four-year cycles. Andy even went so far as to obtain the services of an agent, Athole Still, the former international swimmer, opera singer, broadcaster and journalist, to advise us both, even though we had already talked about going in different directions. As it turned out, Andy did eventually retire and Athole stayed with me, and he and his daughter Roxane remain my business advisers to this day.

Staying in a pair with Andy simply wasn't an option because he wasn't going to be rowing in four years' time. Yes, we could have rowed with each other for one more year; we could have attracted quite a good sponsorship deal because we had crossed that threshold between sporting excellence and sporting celebrity. It was abundantly clear that if I did carry on, I would have to find someone as good as Andy, if not better. That would not be easy, because at the time there didn't appear to be anyone around with his quality.

Our relationship finally came to an end for good at, of all places, the Motor Show at the NEC in Birmingham. Andy and I were there as guests of our sponsors, Leyland DAF, at the end of 1988. When Andy asked me about my plans, I told him: 'I'm not prepared to row for one year. I'm aiming for '92 and I'm going to try and find someone to row with for then.'

Pat Sweeney was astounded. 'You're mad,' he told me. 'You should continue rowing with Andy.' Presumably, he thought that if we stayed together, Andy would be persuaded to carry on for longer. 'I'm sorry, Pat,' I replied. 'But I don't think I can.'

I was so determined that I shouldn't do anything for mere short-term gain. I knew that I had to make definite plans now if I was going to savour victory again in four years' time. Never in my career have I said to myself: 'I'll give it a go for one or two years and see how I feel.' It's always been all or nothing.

When our decision was revealed to the world, it was not without some acrimony on Andy's part. 'Steve believes in devoting himself to rowing, to the exclusion of everything else, but that is not my approach,' he was quoted as saying. 'I think he resented my other interests. I just did not understand his motivation.' I accepted the first part, but the remainder of it was simply untrue.

A *Daily Mail* cartoon summed up the public and media perception of our relationship and parting. It featured a rowing boat wrenched apart by two oarsmen rowing in different directions, and the caption 'Holmes and Redgrave, I presume'.

Probably the best judge was Mike Spracklen, whom I was delighted to discover had been awarded an OBE in the New Year's Honours list of 1988. If anyone deserved one, he did. Mike simply reflected of me and Andy: 'They did not fight or argue like other rowing crews. There was no hate, but also no love; just a highly successful unit.'

It was my old mentor, Mike, whom I turned to, inevitably, to consult about possible replacements. He came up with two names: John Garrett and Simon Berrisford.

John had rowed in the British eight, but more recently had been in the coxed four and was in the crew that finished fourth in Seoul in a boat stroked by Martin Cross. Mike evidently saw some potential. But John was a civil servant, who felt that his career was more important than rowing, so he was never really an option.

Simon was in the coxless four that had finished fourth at Seoul. He was bitterly disappointed that his crew hadn't won a medal. Obviously they were all upset in their own way. But, out of the four people in the boat, he was the only one who seemed to want to do something about it. He had determination and his attitude was:

'I can do better than this. I can achieve something.' I felt that there was the opportunity with him to create a potentially good boat.

The only possible obstacle was that we both rowed on stroke side and one of us would have to swap over. I didn't regard that as a problem; in fact the idea of changing sides actually appealed to me. I wanted to be the first person to win an Olympic gold on both sides of a boat. To my knowledge, no one had ever done that at Olympic or World Championship level.

It was quite a motivational challenge for me. And it compensated, in part, for not having rowed in the single scull at an Olympics, which would have been the ultimate experience. It added some excitement to the whole project.

In truth, it was easier for me to change than most other people. Because I'd done so much sculling it made it easier to adapt. Even during that period, up to 1988, I'd continued doing a fair amount of single sculling. It was certainly never a big issue for me to change to bowside, although it caused some astonishment within the rowing fraternity. In fact, for reasons which I will explain later, bowside was to become my established position.

Simon and I got together in November, and we started training at the Leander Club, where he was a member and had been since leaving Shiplake School, a few miles further up the Thames. He lived in Henley. I subsequently joined Leander myself and it was at that stage that we began use it as a base for all our formal training. There used to be just two of us out on the water. Now the river downstream towards Hambleden Mill has quite a lot of rowing traffic on a weekday.

The Leander is ideally located, just downstream of the 18th-century Henley Bridge, and is a temple of rowing tradition. It has been described as the Lord's of rowing. It is one of the most famous rowing clubs in the world. The club was born in 1818, when some 'gentlemen' set out on the Tideway in a new six-oar cutter from Westminster Bridge. The boat was called the *Leander* and subsequently a London club was formed under that name.

When the people of Henley decided to stage their own regatta in 1839, the club was asked to provide an umpire. The following year, it won the Grand Challenge Cup, the first of many successes. Finally, in 1897, Leander moved to a permanent home in Henley, where it has remained. Today, it combines a fashionable clubhouse for its members and a centre of rowing excellence.

The club's official colours are cerise, but Leander members are recognized the world over in rowing circles by the pink socks they wear, and the hippo emblem on the club tie. I used to wear the pink Leander socks. But I had the mickey taken out of me so much when wearing them, together with a pink bow-tie, when I went to a boxing dinner and had to climb into the ring to make a presentation, that they're now left in my sock drawer.

Leander is synonymous with Henley Royal Regatta. As a member of the former and a steward of the latter, as well as being on its management committee since 1998, I am a great supporter of both. Knowing my original rowing background, that frequently surprises people. Not a year goes past when I'm not asked questions like, 'What do you think of all these people getting dressed up?' and, 'Surely, they're only here for the social side of the regatta?' In the media, it's still represented as all the toffs getting into their finery and going to the Regatta. It's an easy target. But that is only because they don't understand what either institution represents.

I'm a great supporter of keeping our traditions alive, events like Henley, which are part of our heritage. Henley is something that oarsmen and their families and friends attend because of the tradition, not because they associate it with being upper class. The reality is that, yes, the event does attract quite a lot of crews from Oxford and Cambridge and other red-brick universities, but there are also boats from what might be described as 'working-class' clubs, like the Poplar, Blackwall and District Rowing Club, down on the Isle of Dogs. Their supporters love to get dressed up and come along to Henley and be part of the whole atmosphere.

There are those who believe that no one watches the rowing, that it's all about socializing, networking and guzzling Pimm's. That's certainly not been the case since I've been competing there. It's the nearest thing to rowing in a stadium and, having won 19 trophies over the years there, I can testify to the fact that each one has been the equivalent of lifting the FA Cup. I love it. It's great to be involved in as an elite sportsman, but it also welcomes the grass roots of our sport. That's what makes it such a special event and why oarsmen enjoy rowing there. Ann and I are also patrons of Henley Women's Regatta, which takes place two weeks before the main event.

Henley is very strict on tradition, and its insistence on certain standards, like the length of women's skirts being not above the knee, is often ridiculed. But a dress code is part of its identity. I think those traditions should stay. People used to get dressed up for the regatta when it first began 160 years ago. I believe we should retain that element, but make sure that we run it as a modern event, and very professionally. If I were chairman of Henley Royal

Regatta, I wouldn't make any changes to the image. If you start to tamper with that, it could affect its survival.

I've never come across any snobbery personally at either Leander or the Royal Regatta, but maybe because I've forced myself to the forefront of the sport I'm treated differently. Leander is a high-performance club and to gain membership there you have to have done something within the sport, to have rowed or helped someone achieve a certain level at any sport.

Undoubtedly, there has been snobbery at Leander, and it comes across slightly at Henley Regatta, because of the era the people concerned have come from. Ten years ago, those who were sitting on committees making decisions on who should become members all went to public school. Leander was set up as a club for those who had rowed at Oxford and Cambridge because their standard was so much better than anyone else's in the country. But that has all changed. Elite rowers come from all backgrounds now.

People who are running the sport are my generation and beyond. It's when my generation and below come to take over that the snobbery that still exists today will be completely eradicated.

Returning to my new partner Simon, he had been on the team for two or three years and was basically quite shy, but if you had met him then, you wouldn't have thought so. That sounds strange, but his shyness manifested itself in him being quite loud and outrageous. He had plenty to say for himself, but not all of it constructive – certainly not from a rowing point of view.

He used to like shouting abuse at people on the bank and generally making a spectacle of himself. In particular, he was excellent at making squealing pig noises. On the whole, I found him quite amusing. I can't say his behaviour irritated me too much.

I thought he had a lot of potential, and so did he. In the boats that Simon had rowed in previously, he always felt that he was the star turn and far better than the people with whom he rowed. I got the impression that sometimes they didn't get the best out of him because of that. With me, he was, if anything, the opposite. He lacked confidence and took quite a long time to find his feet. But then it was always going to be a daunting situation for him, forming a pair with me, considering what I'd achieved with Andy. He was almost literally stepping straight into Andy's shoes.

I had brought the Leyland DAF sponsorship to the table, so there was money for him as well. In addition, there were grants from the Sports Aid Foundation. Basically he was, like me, a rowing buff, with no distractions like employment to concern him.

Simon and I jumped into the deep end. We planned to carry on with the two events and initially we proceeded to win everything we competed in except the coxed pair at Lucerne regatta.

That was a classic race, the closest finish I've ever been in. We were quite a long way adrift, and in the last 500 metres we really picked up the pace and came steaming back on everybody else. There were four boats all in a line, which is rare in rowing. Indeed, we were probably all closer at the finish there than we would have been on the start. There was less than a tenth of a second between all four boats, which is pretty damn close. Simon and I came fourth.

We didn't contest the coxless pairs because it was on the same day, but the British duo that did, John Garrett and Salih Hassan, finished second to the East Germans. We knew we could defeat John and Salih quite comfortably, so that put us in confident mood for completing a double at the World Championships in Bled, Yugoslavia. After all, we'd raced at every other regatta and won.

That year the East German coxless pair was Thomas Jung and Uwe Kellner, a couple of young guys. But at those World Championships they just stormed home from us and we had to console ourselves with silver medals. In the coxed pair we could only manage fifth, so overall Simon and I were very disappointed.

Well, maybe not Simon. I think he was secretly quite pleased, having been to two World Championships and an Olympic Games and finished seventh, fourth and fourth respectively. To actually receive a medal of any colour was a significant step forward for him. It also turned out that Jung and Kellner were an outstanding pair. The following year, they beat Matthew Pinsent and me in the World Championships very convincingly. They dominated the event in the same way that I had dominated it with Andy and then with Simon up until those World Championships. They were a class act.

We had trained very intensively, but we didn't get the results in Yugoslavia that we might have got because, as I was to realize later, I had taken a back seat mentally.

For 10 years I had eaten, slept and lived rowing – apart from those excursions into bobsleighing and the trip to Australia after Belinda and I broke up. I felt that was the way to do it; there was no alternative to complete dedication, to the exclusion of everything else.

Maybe it was inevitable that at some stage I would feel the need to switch off. I simply felt at that time that I couldn't maintain that intensity of devotion to the sport for another four years. In training,

I continued to do everything expected of me; yet, my mind was not completely attuned to it. I wasn't 100 per cent committed and, to be frank, I thought I'd cruise for a couple of years. I still had every intention of competing at the Barcelona Olympics, but didn't really want to do four years' hard graft to get there.

Not that I let everything go. The fact was that Simon and I would have been world champions if it hadn't been for that East German pair who were brilliant for two years.

The problem remained, however: how were we going to come back from that defeat? I went away on my last ever bobsleighing trip, in the winter of '89, determined to close the gap in the following season. I was confident that we could do that.

Fate again took a hand. Just as I left, Simon was out training at Henley when he was hit by a sculling boat. The rigger hit him in the middle of his back and he was in a lot of pain for a long time. All the time I was away Simon was having treatment on the injury. He eventually returned to the water, but it had a devastating effect on the performances of our pair. Some days, his back would be fine and there would be no problem at all. Other times, he would be in serious difficulties and struggle to walk out to the boat, let alone row it effectively.

The damage was quite severe. The vertebrae have little nodules on them, with tendons attached, and some had broken. Simon didn't have surgery, but had a couple of epidurals – a spinal anaesthetic, normally used on women during childbirth – and ongoing rehabilitation treatment. It was very much hit and miss in training. We got a lot of work done, but you could never be sure that he would be fit.

At that time, it didn't really occur to me that it could be a permanent problem. I just accepted that it would take a long time for him to recover fully. We raced in the early international regattas and performed reasonably, but it was at Henley Royal Regatta that things came to a head.

We completed our first race on the Thursday and he was obviously in a lot of pain. At that particular time, he had to hobble to the boat. Rowing on the injury was certainly doing him no good at all. Clearly it was getting worse, and as the season wears on the training gets more intensive rather than the low-endurance work that we start off with. It was taking its toll.

It was actually my wife Ann who decided that enough was enough. She wasn't the team doctor at that time, but musculoskeletal medicine was her field of expertise. She advised him to have time

out and receive treatment on a proper training rehabilitation programme to ensure that he wasn't doing himself any long-term injury.

It goes without saying that the back is crucial to rowing. It's the
centre of a complicated leverage system that creates boat-speed.
The power comes from the legs, which are connected to the boat
through the shoes on the stretcher, then is transferred to the blades
through a leverage mechanism which involves the hands, the
shoulders and the back. The latter is the key element.

The back has got to be able to hold the power of the legs and
be the connecting linch-pin. It's a sport that's going to expose you
if there's anything suspect about the back. Most of the injuries
within the sport are back-related.

After that first race, Simon was pulled out and it was clear that it
would be some time before he returned. In any other year, it would
have been too late for me to form another boat for the World Championships. Usually, once Henley was over, it was followed by
Lucerne the next week, then there were only four or five weeks
before the World Championships. However, because that year the
Championships were in Tasmania the date was much later. They
were to take place at the end of September – their spring, approaching summer – to make sure the weather was suitable. It gave me
plenty of time to find a replacement for Simon.

For the moment, I had to suffer the annoyance of sitting and
watching Henley Royal Regatta, where I had regularly competed
and which I so much enjoyed. It was particularly difficult not to be
taking part that year, because we wanted to take on the two pairs
who had been put together to row the coxless four at that time:
Tim Foster, a 20-year-old student and world junior champion; my
old Los Angeles crew-mate and sometime adversary, Martin Cross;
Pete Mulkerrins, who had developed a habit of finishing fourth in
every boat he raced in at World Championships and Olympics; and
a towering 19-year-old Oxford University student named Matthew
Pinsent, who had already caught my eye with his rowing prowess.

CHAPTER 14

TORMENT IN TASMANIA

I had first become aware of Matthew Pinsent in 1988 when Andy Holmes and I were training for the Seoul Olympics. We had been asked if the junior pair could come and train with us for one session at Molesey. We agreed, and it turned out that they were Tim Foster and Matthew. They joined in with us, and I was rather disappointed to find that we were considerably quicker than them. 'Well, if this is the best boat the juniors have got, God help them,' I thought. 'They're not going to do very well.'

How wrong you can be.

When I had been a junior you had to be close to senior standard to have a chance of winning a medal. What has happened, since my early days, is that juniors' training is limited by their schooling, while seniors have gone through a transition from being very amateur to very professional. From doing just one or two sessions a day, before or after work, they have become full-time athletes. Simultaneously the difference between juniors and seniors has become more marked. The other fact was, of course, that Tim and Matthew were up against Olympic champions.

Nevertheless, I was really surprised when I heard that they'd gone on to take the gold in the World Junior Rowing Championships. That was a second for Tim, who had won one in the coxless four the previous year, too.

The next occasion when our paths crossed was in a BBC 'Children In Need' item the following year, when six oarsmen had to race for a minute on rowing machines. Matthew was included because of his involvement with the Oxford Boat Race crew. We were all in a line, but the ergos were set up on the shiny floor of a gym, and if you don't get your timing right and you're really putting everything into it, you start sliding across the floor. That's what Matthew did, much to my amusement. He nearly ended up on the adjacent judo mat where some other activity was going on.

Even then, as an 18-year-old, he stood out as incredibly big and powerful. At that time, in 1989, he was being coached by Mike Spracklen, who was trying to put an eight together, although for some reason that didn't work.

He ended up in a coxed four. They went to the 1989 World Championships and came third, which was a really good result for him, only a year out of juniors.

The following winter, Matthew rowed with Pete Mulkerrins in a pair which came second to Simon and me at the national trials and pushed us quite hard. We crossed the line almost simultaneously. Admittedly, this was during a period when Simon's back problems made it an unreliable guide.

Pete was a decent oarsman, but something of a Jonah. He was always known as the guy that finished fourth, which he did with crews at no fewer than four World Championships and one Olympics. Matthew, an Old Etonian, was a geography student at St Catherine's College, Oxford, at that time. He always looked an outstanding athlete and I was pretty impressed. I thought to myself, 'If I ever get an opportunity, because of Simon's injury, I wouldn't mind doing a pair with him.' It was a partnership that had medal potential written all over it.

At that 1990 Henley Regatta, when Simon was forced to pull out of our pair, Matthew was doing a coxless four with Tim, Pete and Martin Cross. That quartet did the pair and four at Henley, and I'm certain Pete and Matthew fancied their chances of beating Simon and me in the Silver Goblets, of which we were holders. There was always a friendly rivalry between that four and Simon and me. There was definitely a bit of feeling between Pete and Simon because they'd rowed together in the four, and several other times – including that fourth in the 1988 Olympics – after which Simon had started rowing with me, the best oarsman in the British team. Anyway, we could never respond to that challenge because Simon was injured.

I was forced to sit, frustrated, on the bank during the regatta as Matthew and Pete were beaten in the semi-finals by the Austrian pair, Karl Sinzinger and Hermann Bauer, World Championship bronze medallists behind Simon and me the previous year. The British pair were leading up until the final stages, but were forced to stop to avoid Pete's oar striking one of the wooden booms, which mark out the course, after being warned – erroneously, according to most observers – to change course by the umpire. It left their rivals to come through and win. To add to my chagrin, Martin and Tim were also defeated by that same crew in the final – a pair I was never beaten by when partnered by either Simon or Matthew.

We went to race at Lucerne the following week, in an eight. With Simon still out, I was substitute in a boat which consisted of a combination of the coxed four and the coxless four. One of the guys in the coxed four had a back injury and I replaced him on the 'wrong' side to what I had recently been accustomed. I had rowed strokeside with Andy; bowside with Simon; and here I was back on strokeside. Rowing on the same side in that victorious eight was Matthew.

He always seemed to have the vital components to make it to the top. I never doubted that he had the ability to do so. He was a strapping 6ft 6in and 15 stone – similar to my own physique, although I am slightly smaller – and was technically well endowed, which is always potentially a good combination.

The next venue for those two fours was the Goodwill Games – rather like a mini-Olympics – in Seattle the following weekend. Matthew did the coxless fours, while I rowed in the coxed four, and then both boats came together to race in the eight. There was a fair amount of spare time and Matthew and I spent quite a lot of it together.

In terms of personality, we clicked virtually immediately. There was a rapport between us which exists to this day. As someone once said, 'Matthew and Steve are as natural a partnership as Marks and Spencer.' There was an amusement arcade with a football game and we were always taking each other on. We were very competitive with each other. I liked that. It was something that did not exist between Andy and myself.

Later in the year, while we were out in Canada, I introduced Matthew to golf on the pitch-and-putt course at Victoria Island. Since then, we've become regular opponents on the fairways, and again there's fierce rivalry. The competition between us off the water used to be quite unhealthy on occasions, even when just playing cards. On training camps and at regattas, four of us would sit down to play a few hands and there'd be real needle. If I wasn't going to win, I'd do anything to ensure that Matthew didn't either. He'd do the same back to me.

By that stage it was quite evident that Simon was not going to be fit for the World Championships. Because they were in September, it gave me more time to organize a boat for myself, although, by that stage, I was definitely very keen to get a pair together with Matthew. There is an etiquette about these things, however. I didn't come out and ask him outright, because he was rowing with

Pete Mulkerrins in a pair, and I didn't want to muscle my way in uninvited. It would have been a bit like asking out someone else's wife.

Mike Spracklen had been my friend and rowing guru for 10 years up until that time, but he was now off to Canada to coach. Although I was then being coached by Pat Sweeney who had coxed Andy and me at Seoul, I turned to Mike, whose views I obviously respected, for his advice. He had also coached Matthew to a bronze medal in the coxed four in 1989. 'He's a top guy,' Mike said unhesitatingly. 'I can see that being a good unit.' That backed up my intuition that it was something worth doing.

On my return from the Goodwill Games, I spoke to David Tanner, who was now in charge of the British team. David decided that the way ahead was to experiment by trying out both Matthew and Pete Mulkerrins with me in a pair. They would just go out for a paddle with me and see how it felt. Of course, I'd have to swap over, depending whom I was partnering. Although I'd won Olympic medals on strokeside, I had the flexibility of being able row on both sides.

On that morning in early August, David arrived to say that Pete had changed his mind. He was no longer interested in doing the trial. Matthew then arrived very late. But once we got in a boat together, we had a reasonable session. We came off the water and both agreed that, yes, we'd like to take the partnership further. There were trials a week later at Nottingham, which gave us a week to prepare to take on Tim Foster, who had been Matthew's partner as a junior, and Martin Cross in a pair, then row in a four with them in a time trial. Whichever combination looked to have the best potential was the one that would go forward for the World Championships.

As it turned out, we beat Martin and Tim reasonably comfortably. David Tanner was already talking enthusiastically of a 'dynamic partnership'. The four also performed well. It looked like both boats could win a medal. The best pair around at that time were Jung and Kellner of East Germany, that outstanding combination which had beaten Simon and me the year before. East Germany paraded probably the top crew in the four as well. But the possibility of winning a silver in either boat looked possible.

I thought the world of Mike and having Pat coaching us was like settling for second best, even though he was our choice. At least Pat was a realist. He was quite aware that you have a cox in a coxed pair not because you need them to steer, but because there is a category for it. Pat's humility contrasted greatly with the demeanour of Adrian Ellison, who steered the coxed four at Los Angeles.

Pat and I got on really well, but the problem was that, as the senior figure, I could dominate what we were doing more than with Mike, and certainly with Jurgen Grobler, who, it would be confirmed at those 1990 World Championships, would be joining us from East Germany. That made it difficult for all three of us. However, it helped that we went out to Canada and had three weeks' training with Mike Spracklen before coming back and then going out to Australia.

Before departing, we studied the depth of competition we would probably face, and our likely rivals in the fours looked far more daunting. We might not even get amongst the medals in that discipline, while there appeared to be definite gold medal possibilities in the pairs. Only having had a couple of months to prepare we weren't going to be in the best possible shape, but we felt that if we got it right we could win the coxless pairs and if we got it wrong we'd come second. That's always a bad attitude with which to approach an event. As it turned out, we did get it wrong – and came third!

Before going out to Canada, I was really very ill. It came on overnight and I suffered from vomiting, diarrhoea and acute stomach pains. Ann took me into hospital, where they put me on a drip for two days and I recovered. However, it was obviously very worrying at the time. I lost a lot of weight, about 10kg (22lb), and there was no real explanation. We all assumed it was food poisoning of some sort.

It took me quite a long time to recover my strength fully and to put that weight back on. I was used to having the occasional minor medical problem. Now and again, you'll miss a couple of days' training. This was a more serious incident than I'd been used to, but I was back on the water within four days so I didn't miss much training, which thus far had seemed to be going reasonably well.

It was as we prepared to return home that we made the decision to train through the night back in England.

We would only be back in England a week before the circus moved on to Australia and the preparations for the World Championships. So, we decided that, instead of reverting to English time and then moving our body-clocks forward to Australian time, we'd go directly from Canadian to Australian time. We would train at the times that we would do in Australia, but back at home. The idea sounds crazy, but it worked.

It meant that we stayed at Leander and got up at midnight, had breakfast, went out for our first row, a warm-up, then the second work session would be just as dawn arrived, about 6 a.m. By the time we got back, it would be daylight and the rest of the world would be on its way to offices and factories. We'd go off home for a few hours, and then come back at lunchtime ready to go bed again during the afternoon.

The flight to Australia for a week's training camp prior to the World Championships was quite interesting. It departed late in the evening, at about 10.30, so the other passengers had mostly been to work and everyone fell asleep quite quickly. We had to get up a bit earlier than usual. But for us it was the equivalent of early morning and we got on the flight wide awake.

When we landed first thing in the morning, Australia-time, we were fit and ready for the day, while everyone else wanted to sleep. We slotted into the day-night Australian time very easily indeed. We were ready to train and our body-clocks were well prepared.

Unfortunately, that was where our problems began. Our training camp was at Geelong, just outside Melbourne, and because it was their spring, there was a lot of floodwater. We couldn't find a lake, so we had to train on the river, which had burst its banks. It was 50 metres from the boathouse to the river, and water had risen up to just short of the boathouse entrance. Henley can be tricky at times when the water is fast and high, but this was far worse to prepare on, especially with a small boat like the pair. The camp did not go well. The conditions affected us more than they should have done. It was one of the reasons why we didn't perform very well when we flew up to Lake Barrington in Tasmania for the championships at the end of October.

In our heat, Matthew and I had the misfortune of being drawn against the reigning world champions Jung and Kellner. At the 1250-metre stage we were leading them, having seen off the Austrians. But the East Germans slowly came back at us and pulled clear. That was the only time in my career – apart from that incident at Henley Regatta when I was beaten by Eltang – when a boat I've been rowing in actually stopped and we just paddled home. We simply accepted defeat. I just didn't have the fight in me to repel them. I rationalized it by saying to myself, 'Let's save our energy and keep our powder dry for the final.'

It was an ominous portent for the final, but first we had to qualify from our semi-final. We achieved that without any frights, leading all the way to defeat the Soviet brothers Nicolai and Yuri

Pimenov again. They actually finished third behind the Yugoslavs, but still qualified.

In the final, the conditions were really rough. The boats that performed well were the ones that had been together for a long period of time. The effect of choppy water is exaggerated more in the smaller boats and it can take a long time of rowing together to get used to that kind of hazard. Jung and Kellner, who had been together for a number of years, revelled in the conditions and won convincingly.

That is not to seek excuses. It was a poor performance by us and we lost the race between the 500- and 1000-metre marks. We were even deprived of second place. To illustrate the paucity of our display, it was the only time that the Pimenov brothers had beaten me in all the times I raced them. Matthew and I were devastated by what had happened. We thought the worst possible scenario would be that we would come second. As we crossed the line, we turned to one another and said, 'We're never going to get beaten again.'

One of the East German coaches at those Tasmania championships was of the opinion that 'Redgrave looked lazy.' There may have been more than a hint of truth in that. I had gone though a period, particularly with Simon and even when Matthew first came on the scene, when some of my drive and purpose had deserted me. During that time, I probably only applied myself three-quarters of the time to rowing. But to be a top athlete, you've got to be committed 100 per cent. It was not until the end of 1990 that I really threw myself into rowing body and soul once more and I thought to myself, 'If I want to win in Barcelona, I've got to pull my finger out now.' That was a turning point because I knew that I really had to get my priorities right and improve my attitude if I was to be an Olympic champion again in 18 months' time. I'd had my cruising period, and it was time to buckle down to some serious work and get focused once more.

It was also a significant moment when our new coach Jurgen Grobler arrived at the beginning of 1991. Here, I thought, was someone with new ideas of how to guide us to the Olympic Games the following year. Mentally, by then, I was in the right frame of mind. If he had come the year before, I don't think we would have hit it off at all. I simply wouldn't have been prepared to do what he demanded.

To be quite honest, if Jurgen had said to Simon and me in 1989, 'Right, we're changing the training methods and you've got to do this, this and this,' I'd have turned round and said, 'Get stuffed,' or words to that effect. 'There's no way I'm going to do that. I'm going to continue doing it my way.' That was the kind of mood I was in.

Simon, incidentally, recovered fully and raced at the Barcelona Olympics with Pete Mulkerrins again, back in a coxless four. They put in some really good results through the 1991 season and I was convinced they'd win a medal at the World Championships, but they didn't produce much in the final and finished fourth. They failed to improve on that in Barcelona.

I could only sympathize with Simon. Matthew and I had got only the bronze in that first World Championships and Simon would, understandably, have said to himself, 'Well, I got a silver with Steve the year before.' But there was just something about the pair once Matthew and I got together. We both knew that it was something special.

That first winter, Matthew was preparing for the Boat Race with Oxford, so I was training at Henley on my own. Traditionally, we train in singles through the first part of the season. Simon was also back there by then and, quite often, he'd say, 'Why don't we get back in a pair, and do this or that event?' That was quite a difficult time for both of us.

It was never a huge issue, but I knew that, ideally, Simon would have liked to carry on rowing with me. Frankly, although he had apparently got over his injury, I still harboured doubts over whether his back could take it once we got into the racing season again.

But regardless of that, to me, and to most observers, the pair with Matthew and myself just looked better and stronger, and that seemed the way forward. Jurgen had just arrived, too, and he was keen to carry on coaching Matthew and myself as a pair.

It would have been fascinating to see what would have happened if Simon hadn't got that injury. I certainly don't think of myself as acting selfishly and with only my own interests at heart.

I believe that, essentially, I'm a very loyal person. If Simon hadn't got injured, and we were performing very well, we'd have carried on as a pair right the way through. I'm sure of it. But because there was a break, and I started rowing with someone else, and we rowed to the World Championships, that chapter had closed and the next one had started. It's rather like your girlfriend travelling abroad and falling head over heels in love with someone else. When she returns, there's no point in trying to continue the relationship, just for the sake of it, when it's clearly over.

When Matthew came into the pair, he did feel a little bit daunted about rowing with me and what I'd achieved up until that time. But he told me later that he just put it out of his mind. 'I can't think about filling Andy's shoes,' he said. Again, providence took a hand. All the timing was right. After that initial period of rowing with Matthew, everything seemed to be right; whereas Simon had to take Andy's place directly and row with someone who had swapped from strokeside to bowside, which is not an easy thing to do immediately.

I should explain the problem, because the assumption might be made, 'Well, you've rowed on one side of the boat. Why can't you row on the other?' But it took a long time to get the confidence. On flat water there's no problem at all; but go out on rough water and you get quite tense. It's the inside hand that turns the blade and it rotates in the outside hand. When water gets rough, the natural instinct is to revert to how you had rowed previously.

Then you start turning the blade with both hands, get yourself in a tangle and hit the water. There was also the fact, as I have already mentioned, that I had this slightly laid-back attitude when I was doing a pair with Simon, who, himself, lacked some confidence. There was a combination of factors that made the whole situation very difficult.

I have always treated any newcomer to a boat I have been in, whether a pair or a four, as a rowing partner, an equal. There are no egos involved. My attitude is straightforward: 'We've got a job to do. Let's get on with it.' I hope that I have never given the impression of lording it over anybody. I have always tried to avoid intimidating people or giving the impression of: 'I'm a double Olympic champion and you've got to do what I do and what I say.'

I'm sure that in some quarters there's an assumption that 'rowing with that Redgrave must be difficult because he's so high and mighty'. Certainly on the journalistic side. That was particularly the case when I got together with Matthew. Media commentators were convinced that I was going to be the dominant partner. After all, I was a double Olympic champion rowing with a teenager, as Matthew was then.

It was immediately perceived as 'my' boat. But it wasn't like that at all. I've always looked on it as an equal partnership, although I'd obviously use my experiences from other combinations.

CHAPTER 15

FRUSTRATION AS JURGEN
PULLS A STROKE

Our new coach, Jurgen Grobler arrived in January 1991, two months after the historic fall of the Berlin Wall. He was the first rowing coach to leave East Germany. It must have been a traumatic moment for him coming to a country of which he knew little, and a vocabulary of only a few words of English.

I knew very little about him and hadn't really given much thought to coaches in East Germany, or their systems. As a junior, though, I had my suspicions, along with many of my British team-mates, about how the East Germans had achieved their remarkable results in rowing.

When I won my junior silver medal with Adam Clift in the double sculls back in 1980 my immediate thoughts had been: 'We'd have won that if the East Germans hadn't been cheating.' Not that I could be certain, of course; it was just the generally accepted view at the time that the Eastern bloc countries as a whole were using artificial stimulants to enhance their performances.

When I began to be successful, I changed my mind. Quite simply, I had no reason to be suspicious. It is a subject I will return to later, but my belief is that if they were cheating, it obviously wasn't doing them any good because the crews I was involved in were beating them regardless.

It was while I was at the indoor rowing championships in Boston, USA that Jurgen's name was suggested to me by a fellow named Ian Wilson, a lightweight world championship gold medallist in the four in 1979, who trained up at Nottingham. Ian was coming to the end of his career when I started. He said to me: 'I hear rumours that you're looking for a coach at Leander?' I confirmed that we were because Mike was about to depart. He added: 'There's a guy who'd be brilliant.'

I passed on Jurgen's details to the powers-that-be at the club and he came over for an interview in June, 1990 which happened to be

Henley Regatta time. For a rowing coach from the Eastern bloc, to witness the Regatta, with all the social side in full flow for the first time, must have been a surreal experience after the austere locations of his homeland.

He was put up at a huge mansion, and couldn't believe that only one person lived there. In a house like that you'd have three or four families in Magdeburg, where he came from. The Leander people had picked him and his wife Angela up in a Jaguar, which also must have impressed.

I sat in on part of the interview. He told us about what would happen when the Berlin Wall came down, and how his country would cease to exist. Jurgen didn't want to go to West Germany, and although he'd had offers to go to several different countries, he was keen to come to England.

Jurgen added that he wanted to be involved with me and help me win my third Olympic gold medal. I had to keep reminding him, 'It's not just my third, Jurgen. There's my fourth as well.'

By the time he started, in January 1991, Matthew was preparing for that year's Boat Race with Oxford. Jurgen was initially just employed to coach at Leander – it was not until after Barcelona that he became chief coach to the British men's team – so we had a virtual one-to-one relationship.

I knew how many gold medal-winning crews he'd been involved with in his career in East Germany which spanned 19 years. In nine years, between 1981 and 1990, his East German women's squad had accrued 21 world titles and five Olympic golds.

Impressive credentials indeed; but it didn't cut that much ice with me then. In my opinion, at that stage, although the coaches had their place, the most important people were the athletes.

Initially, I was not totally convinced by what he had to offer. To my mind, he had to prove himself. I vowed to myself that I'd give Jurgen a year and do exactly what he said. I'd follow his ways to the letter. If it worked, fair enough. If not, then I'd have to reconsider whether I wanted to continue with him.

Yes, he'd come from the top rowing nation over the last decade, but you knew all about their screening policies, of getting the right sized athlete, of training them full-time. It was a completely different set-up from what we were used to in this country. How was this East German going to fit into the Western world and the way that we coached our athletes?

He came with a glowing reputation, and we knew how successful he'd been in coaching the women crews in East Germany, but I was certainly a sceptic. To my mind, we just didn't know what we were getting. His presence could revolutionize British rowing and help me to more success; but, equally, it could be a disaster. However, I felt that, as one of the people instrumental in getting him over in the first place, I had to be seen to support the appointment.

My views have altered since Jurgen has been involved. Indeed, I have come to the conclusion that coaches have just about equal influence on results as athletes. When they present the gold medals at championships I believe that the coaches should be there on the podium as well, receiving their recognition. It's really no different from football and rugby, where the coach has a much higher-profile role and far greater status.

Jurgen had left a country where the state controlled virtually every part of people's life, including sport. One of the first things he said to me was: 'I need to have a meeting with the sports minister.' I asked him why. He replied: 'We need to organize things better than it is now.' I asked him why that should involve the sports minister. 'Surely that's the person who runs sport?' he said. I had news for him. 'Sorry, Jurgen. Not in this country, it's not.'

In East Germany sport was ranked very highly, and the minister in charge did have real power, which involved regular meetings with their head of state. If you were head coach of a particular sport you could go right to the top to make sure that your needs were met, whereas in this country 'sports minister' is little more than a title, with no teeth as such.

Possibly the sports minister here has rather more influence under Labour. When the Conservatives were in power, it was the job nobody really wanted. That was particularly the case in the eighties, principally because, if there were any major problems, like football hooliganism, it was your responsibility and it did little for your political image.

That wasn't the only misapprehension on Jurgen's part about England. When he heard that I had an MBE, he thought that it was the equivalent of a knighthood. A German magazine writer came over and interviewed Jurgen and me and, when the article was published it referred to me as 'Sir Steven Redgrave'. I assumed it was a light-hearted reference. Unfortunately, it was taken seriously in some quarters and when I turned up to obtain my accreditation for the 1991 World Championships, I was welcomed as Sir Steven and given a special VIP pass.

That story did the rounds for several years, and one time at Mannheim in 1996, members of the American women's eight came up to me and said: 'Are you really knighted?' Before I could answer, Matthew butted in and said, 'Oh, yes. Of course he is.' They were fascinated. We then started spinning a yarn about what the benefits are of being a knight. We told them how you are given many acres of land containing a few villages, and some peasants, and how I would ride around on a fine stallion.

They swallowed the lot. It was a couple of regattas later that they discovered the truth. At Lucerne that year we took our boat out on to the water, and when we tried to put our feet into the shoes of our boat we each found that one was blocked. A toy horse had been stuffed into each of them.

Matthew returned from the Tasmania World Championships to begin his second year at Oxford and prepare for that year's Boat Race, although we did some training together as winter approached. Jurgen had sent a programme over for everyone to follow. I just sculled during that period and, when he arrived, fitted in with what he asked me to do.

The way I was brought up with Mike, to win a gold medal you had to be very single-minded and do things a certain way. What I've learnt since then is that there are alternative ways to get to the top. I didn't find it easy, initially, committing myself to Jurgen's methods.

The main difference was that Jurgen introduced weight-training, which I hadn't done for a number of years. There was also less water-work than I had done under Mike, with whom I used to do a lot of mileage but nothing else.

It was when I was training for the Eights' Head of the River of 1991, one of the principal early season events, that I gained my first real insight into Jurgen's expertise. In previous years, we used to practise at normal race-pace for most of the time. Suddenly, on the Tideway, he had us doing this long-distance, slow, plodding training. I was saying politely but forcibly, 'Come on, Jurgen. It's the last week before the Head. We've got to go on and practise race-pace.'

He'd respond with, 'No, no. This is what goes.' He didn't seem to realize that though it was a long race – at four and a quarter miles, the same as the Boat Race – crews would strike at the same kind of rate that is achieved at World Championships. If you're just plodding round doing steady work, there's just no way that you'll be prepared to do this. But I thought to myself, 'OK. He's convinced this is right; this is what we'll do.' We went out and won quite comfortably. He had immediately instilled confidence in me that what he was making us do seemed to work.

Two weeks later, I did the Scullers' Head over the same distance, an event with which I never seemed to hit it off. Traditionally, I'd always performed badly. I wasn't convinced I'd do any better that year. I'd done all this low-rate striking, working on power and length of stroke, all through the winter with Jurgen. A lot of the scullers who had come up to Henley to join with the work we were doing would beat me. Jurgen was unperturbed. Just before the race, he said to me: 'Right, for the first 2000 metres don't overdo it. Just go a comfortable pace. Then after that, that's when you really start racing.' That's what I did, and I won that as well.

Once the Boat Race was over – Oxford having won in one of the fastest times ever – Matthew and I only had 10 days before the national trials at Nottingham. We jumped straight back into the pair to prepare for them. I was at stroke, as normal. We won the trials reasonably comfortably, and it was when we returned to Henley that Jurgen sprung a novel suggestion on me one day. 'Matthew's been doing Blue Boat training and now he's got to increase his fitness,' he told me. 'I think for three weeks we'll put him in the stroke seat. That will put him under pressure and get his fitness levels much higher, much quicker.'

My reply was: 'I've got no problem with that.' Three weeks came and went, and Jurgen decided to keep him there for the first international regatta in Cologne. There didn't seem to be too much quality in opposition, but it turned out to be reasonable. We won very convincingly. Matthew stayed in the stroke seat from that period on.

I have to confess that Jurgen's decision had frustrated me. Earlier in this book, I have stressed the importance of the stroke, and the fact that he is traditionally the guiding force in a boat. I had always relished that role with Andy and, before that, in the coxed four. Subconsciously, at least, I felt that this decision was a blow to my esteem.

It also had an effect on the boat in some of the training we did in that first year simply because I was then so much stronger than Matthew. Being in the bow seat you've got so much more leverage because you're closer to the end of the boat. That meant I could pull him round the river. In my frustration of thinking I should be in the stroke seat because the boat would go faster if I was there, I was in danger of pulling the boat apart.

It's been said that I was very opposed to Matthew stroking the boat and it's true that I honestly believe that in that first year we would have been a faster crew with me stroking it. I was fitter and stronger. My strength was always speed from the start. Whichever crew I was in, we'd get the boat speed up and running very quickly. We would have got clear earlier within races. Comfortable as we were in them, we could have dominated even more. Matthew was very good at one pace, but we'd never storm away from anybody into a big lead. However, we were stronger in the middle with him in the stroke seat than with myself.

During that first season with Matthew at stroke, I gradually accepted that my role had changed. There were two reasons. Firstly, the way I looked at it was that Jurgen had come over to this country and had taken over a pair that was the best in the country, and had been put together by somebody else. I felt that he needed to do something to make the pair his entity. He had to identify it as his boat and not mine. He'd swapped us about just for the sake of it, but because it had gone so well he'd felt no reason to swap it back. Secondly, my own role had changed. I'd always been the driving influence in all the boats I'd been in. Now, it had to be a partnership and that change was all part of that.

In truth, over the months, I came to realize that it made the boat much stronger. It gave Matthew much more confidence to sit in the stroke seat, though I used to give out the commands either way. In fact, it's easier reading a race from the bow seat than the stroke seat. You can see more of what's going on and it's much easier to talk to the oarsman who's in front of you rather than turning over your shoulder and shouting out commands. In a race, it has the added benefit of you being able to issue commands quite quietly. The opposition doesn't really know what you're doing.

When it came to racing, I would immediately slot into a role of supporting Matthew to get the best out of the boat, and that used to work really well. My forcing the pace in training helped him because he had to develop quicker. By the end of the first year we were compatible in that format and I was convinced that I was better in the bows position. It made it a much more complete unit than it would have done if it had been the other way round.

Now and again, Jurgen would swap us about. Notably, in 1996, at a pre-Atlanta training camp in Seville, he said: 'Oh, this is quite good. We might leave this for a few weeks.' A few weeks came and went, and I was still at stroke. Then we went to Banyoles for another camp, had a meeting out there, and both of us said, 'No, we're happier with it the other way round.' We felt more confident about how we'd developed it over the previous five years.

Once that season came and went, I felt happy and was totally confident about our future. We won all the races we entered very comfortably, including at Lucerne. We were winning by times like 10 seconds. Yet, when we travelled out to the World Championships in Vienna, I felt very nervous. Having Matthew, who was eight years younger than me, I felt quite burdened. I felt I had to be seen to be over-relaxed and not under pressure to give Matthew confidence. In fact I was far from it.

Jurgen used to come up to me when I was on my own and say, 'You've got to support Matthew; give him the confidence,' things like that. That made me worry even more about him.

Despite those reservations, our heat went well and we qualified for the semi-finals very comfortably, won that easily, maybe too easily, and moved into the final. Jurgen sent us on a walk as a warm-up to one of the sessions. We were talking about by what margin we would win. We were so supremely confident at that time that we felt we could win our World Championship event by several seconds, which was ridiculous.

During the final, there was a slight following breeze, which makes the conditions really quick but not enough to make the water rough. Just enough to help you along. That always makes boats finish much closer together at the end. Yugoslavia forged into quite a lead; we weren't dominating as normal. We were a couple of lengths down. At one stage the Pimenovs, who had got silver the previous year, and ourselves were fighting for fourth and fifth place, with 500 metres to go. I was thinking: 'What's happening here? We shouldn't be here. We should be up there at the front.'

Through that whole race, we were pushing hard and having to dig well into our reserves. Either other crews had paced it wrong, and were going to suffer at some stage, or there was something wrong with us. We weren't performing at our normal standards. As it turned out, we started picking off boats and coming back. We won by about half a length from Yugoslavia, a decent margin considering our early position, in the end.

As we crossed the line, Matthew thrust his hands in the air in celebration. That was perfectly understandable because it was his first World Championship victory. Without appearing blasé, to me it was just another World Championship. My third. I felt it was only half the job done. Barcelona was the following year and that was the real test of our merit. Then I happened to glance up at the scoreboard. We had broken the world record.

Jurgen's methods included predicting times, which you had to be capable of achieving in perfect conditions. All our training was based on the clock, and you worked to a percentage of that target in your endurance work. You didn't always try to get the top speed on a day-to-day basis, but tried to work towards percentages.

His predicted time for the coxless pairs in Barcelona was 6 minutes 22 seconds. If that was correct, and you clocked it, that should mean, by Jurgen's estimation, that you should be capable of winning the gold at the Olympics. Our time was 6 minutes 21 seconds. My delight at breaking the world record was immediately diminished by one thought. 'Oh, shit,' I said to Matthew, 'Jurgen's going to make our target time even quicker now.' In fact, he didn't. Jurgen felt that it was the right time to win the Olympics, and so it proved the following year.

After our usual three-week break – the only real holiday we got – we were back training at Leander. It felt good. It was the Olympic season again, if not quite in Olympic year. One of our first trials, in December, was at Henley. We beat the next boat by 10 seconds over a 3-km time trial. With winter not even yet fully upon us, Matthew and I were extremely satisfied with how things were going. We were head and shoulders better than anybody else in the team and, seemingly, with normal progress nothing could deny us an Olympic gold. Could it?

CHAPTER 16

THE PAIN AND THE GLORY

By the winter of 1991, and with the Barcelona Olympics less than a year away, Matthew and I had established ourselves as a formidable duo. We were winning all our trials. But, as it does for the man who has come to believe that he can't lose at the casino, life has a habit of dealing you a bad hand at such moments.

It began when we travelled out to a three-week training-camp in South Africa early in the New Year. It was a historic trip because we were the first team to go to the republic after apartheid had ended. Overall, it was a productive camp, except that I picked up a stomach bug and had diarrhoea the whole time I was there. It was not, shall we say, uncontrollable, but my system was certainly not right. I found the whole camp quite hard to cope with because of the debilitating effects of dehydration, caused by the diarrhoea.

At the end of the camp, Matthew and I competed in a pairs race just outside Johannesburg, winning very easily, and then we joined in an eight and that was successful, too, although it was a very tough race. When I returned, I was still having stomach problems. It was now February, and I had it checked out by my own GP. After analysis of a stool sample, it transpired that I had picked up salmonella poisoning of some sort while out in South Africa.

I took medication for that and the symptoms cleared up for a few weeks. But they returned and, simultaneously, my performances started to tail off quite quickly. On the rowing machine, even when doing a fairly steady session, I'd really be struggling to hold split times that I would easily achieve normally.

On the river, I felt that I could do the work and there wasn't the same problem. Out on the water, you go at the pace at which you feel comfortable, whereas on the ergo there's a digital read-out telling you precisely how hard you're pulling, and that puts extra demands on you.

You know what you normally pull, and I was struggling to do that. Mentally, that was very tough to deal with at the time. I was also struggling with the diarrhoea symptoms. Anybody who has suffered from that after a heavy night will testify to how unpleasant it is for the next 24 hours. In that period I'd be going to the toilet five, six times a day.

I'd arrive at Leander in the morning and go to the toilet before a warm-up run, which usually lasts only about five or six minutes along the river bank. By the time I'd returned, I'd have go to the toilet again before we went out on to the water. That's how my life was. I was also becoming increasingly fatigued. When I came back from training in the afternoons, I'd just lie on the settee and fall asleep for the rest of the day. However, I was not suffering any weight loss, which reassured me slightly.

I was not used to this kind of problem. Other than that occasion in 1990 when I had to go to hospital with similar symptoms, and the odd bruise and broken limb when I was a child, I had always been generally healthy. I knew that I was not quite right, but not to the extent that I was soon to discover.

Although my health was affecting our performances and the boat was not working brilliantly, Matthew and I went to the national trials at Nottingham. The standard of the other crews was such that we felt we'd win regardless. There was no point in pulling out because of sickness. However, Matthew and I were beaten by Greg and Jonny Searle in the pairs trials. They were two relatively inexperienced but very talented rowers, coached by Steve Gunn. He had been one of their teachers at Hampton School.

Considering what the brothers produced later that year at Barcelona, it was not altogether surprising, particularly in view of my condition. However, apart from the obvious disappointment, we also had to accept the possibility that the selectors could decide that Greg and Jonny would be the pair at Barcelona and we'd have to find something else to do. That is how the system worked in Jurgen's former home country. Fortunately, in Britain it doesn't quite work out that way. We don't have the talent to rely on first past the post. Selection is based on a number of assessments as well as the trials.

The selectors, in their wisdom, decided that both boats should go on to the international circuit and row in regattas against each other. Normally, everything about my training and racing is controlled, but this was a rare occasion when I knew it would be down to pure blood and guts if we were going to prevail against two very able athletes.

Before the first regatta, in Cologne, Matthew and I vowed that we just had to make it work and buckled down to training, and gave it everything in the build-up. Ultimately, it was just determination and digging really deep that got us through. It was decided that Greg and Jonny should race in the coxless pairs on the first day and the coxed pair on the second. We did the coxless pairs both days.

We both made the coxless pairs final, as expected. We were ready for a real showdown with them. Unfortunately, Greg and Jonny were left at the start. They protested that they weren't ready and had put their hand up to signal that. Whatever the explanation, they didn't race. We had won both days in the coxless pair. The Searles had done quite well in the coxed pair, but nothing had been proved between the rival crews.

It was decided that we would race again two weeks later at Essen, where the competition was expected to be much stronger. We finished third on the first day, while Jonny and Greg did not make the final. Also, the pair that put the Searles out were beaten by us in the final. By that calculation, our performance was better than theirs.

However, we came off the water after the worst performance that Matthew and I had ever rowed. We had been beaten by the young Slovenian pair Iztok Cop and Denis Zvegelj (who had rowed as the Yugoslav pair that won the silver medal at the previous year's World Championships).

While our poor display had obviously been the result of my illness, we were none too optimistic about our future plans when we were approached by the chairman of selectors, Mark Lees, and the team manager, who was then Brian Armstrong. But their first words were: 'Right, we're selecting you for the Olympic Games.' We could hardly believe it after an exhibition like that. Obviously, they were aware of my condition and Brian's advice was, 'Right, you've got two and a half months. Go away and do what you have to do, get yourself sorted out for the Olympic Games, but there's no selection problem. You don't have to race if you don't want to.'

That was comforting to know, and good management on their part. But the illness persisted and the symptoms became worse. Now, it was not just diarrhoea. I was also suffering from terrible stomach cramps.

One minute I would be fine, and then suddenly I would feel such excruciating pain in my stomach that'd I'd have to crouch down until it abated. Sometimes I was doubled up on the floor. It was now May and I went to see a specialist.

We talked through what had happened and the consultant produced a whole list of possible explanations. He said, 'Let's work our way down until we can find it.' At the bottom was a condition called ulcerative colitis, but he said, 'There's no way it could be that.'

I underwent all sorts of tests, which included an intestine biopsy. That is not a pleasant experience. On that occasion, the doctors took four samples of my intestine. Not to put too fine a point on it, to achieve that they insert a tube up your backside. There's no anaesthetic, because they need you to move the body around. I drove straight back to Leander after it was done, and it felt as though I'd been kicked several times in the stomach. A few years later, I went through that indignity again and had 12 samples taken. Thankfully, that time I was put under anaesthetic.

It revealed what the specialist had least expected, that I *did* have ulcerative colitis. While I was relieved that a cause had at last been established for my sickness, I was also acutely aware that it was, by now, only 10 weeks before the Barcelona Olympic Games.

Jurgen and Matthew were obviously as concerned as I was and had already discussed possible options. At the same moment that I had discovered the extent of my illness, Jurgen had told Matthew: 'Right, we're going to give Steve two more weeks. If it doesn't improve we're going to have to do something else.' Suddenly, all my plans had been thrown into disarray. It wasn't a question of whether I would be competing for a medal; it was whether I'd go to Barcelona at all.

Throughout all this uncertain period, however, I was still out there on the river on a daily basis and doing all the training expected of me. That was the key element to how I got through it and came back to standard quite quickly. I'd hardly missed a training session through the whole of that time, even when I was very sick. The performances may not have been 100 per cent, but as Jurgen said, 'Your body's still got to do it, and you're getting some effect from it.'

To compensate for the energy I obviously lacked, I was putting in even more work than normal. That was actually to benefit me later. I was going through ridiculously hard training just to maintain my body at its normal levels. It wasn't a case of me sitting around and saying, 'Well, when I get better, I'll get back into training,' and then fight my way back to fitness. The fitness had to be there. If I'd even started to miss sessions and rest, as you might normally with a serious illness, as this was, I'd have gone. I'd have lost the battle. It was, I suppose, a question of mind over matter, of refusing to allow the condition to defeat me.

Once the cause was known, the consultant was utterly amazed by how inflamed the intestines were and the fact that I was actually completing the workload that I forced on myself. He found it impossible to comprehend that I could put myself through the rigours I did. It is normally such a debilitating disease that the last thing you'd want to do is physical exertion. That's why he had ruled colitis out initially.

Looking back, the odd times that I'd missed training throughout the years tended to be stomach-related. It all fell into place. There had always been an underlying problem. When I had gone into hospital two years earlier, it had been the first indication of colitis, without me or the medical people realizing it. That time, it had settled down without treatment. Now, there was no alternative to medication.

Once I was put on the right treatment, I began to improve immediately. Fortunately, I never had to have surgery, which some sufferers of colitis have to undergo, but the medication still continues once a day, and will until I die.

Although the Olympics were approaching far more quickly than I would ideally have liked, there wasn't any time when I didn't think I'd make it. I repeatedly told myself: 'I'm going to be there,' even though I knew that some other members of the British team and officials were thinking, 'There's no way he's going to recover from that.'

My performance levels started to return quite quickly. We didn't race at the last international regatta at Lucerne or at Henley because the Games would have been too soon afterwards and instead we went away to training camps. It meant that Matthew and I did not race again until the Olympics themselves. At the time Henley was taking place we were away at altitude camp in the Austrian Alps, which went well, before moving on to Varese, in Italy, for warm-weather training.

I experienced a great sense of relief as everything appeared to return to normal and our training times compared well with those of the other British boats. And yet, something was niggling away at me. In the back of my mind was that nagging doubt about what had happened before. I couldn't help recalling that incident in 1990 when I'd had to go into hospital with the intestinal problem and been put on a drip for three days. Then, I had felt fine when I left hospital, but when it had actually come to the racing, I felt wiped out. At the Olympics you've got to be at your absolute best. A voice in my head kept saying to me: 'Are you going to break down?'

Mentally, it was far from ideal preparation. But then something happened which not only filled me with pride but psychologically helped sustain me through that difficult time. At the first team managers' meeting at the Olympics, every sport can put forward one person from their team to carry the British flag at the opening ceremony. Then the team managers all vote for their preference from that list.

Our then team manager, Brian Armstrong, had a quiet word about a month before to ask me if I was willing to accept the honour, if asked. 'Yes,' I replied without hesitation. 'I'd be very keen to do that.' However, when it got closer, and he checked again just before the managers' meeting, I had to say 'No'. We were situated out in Banyoles, which was 75 miles and well over an hour's drive from the main Olympic stadium. Our races were all in the morning, so we were getting up early again, as we had at Los Angeles, and getting into a similar routine. The opening ceremony was on the Friday night, which meant that I wouldn't be leaving that until about 11.30 at night because it's one big party, and we started racing on the Sunday.

It would be like going out to a night-club just before you took the most important examination of your life. You just wouldn't do it. However, Jurgen and Matthew both insisted that I should say 'Yes' and if I got the vote, I should do it. There was no question about it. They said it would be a great honour for me and the sport.

As it turned out, I won the vote. The most pleasing aspect of it was that, once I was told that I had been given the honour, it was announced to the whole team. Not many people were aware that I had even been put forward. There was a standing ovation from the other rowers. That really shocked me, and brought home to me more what an honour it was and how the other people in the team regarded me as a representative of our sport. There were several rowers from other countries who also carried flags.

We got over the logistical problems quite simply. In the event, I got picked up by a car, organized by the BOA, which drove me down to Barcelona, I stayed in the main Olympic village overnight and was brought back by car the following morning. We only had one session on the Saturday, which was in the afternoon. I was also brought into the Olympic stadium area relatively late, so I avoided all the standing around which occurs as a result of the parade of teams being the last element of the opening show.

We were all grouped together in the gymnastic hall adjacent to the Olympic stadium, and then brought out and queued up ready for our grand entrance. After I had been told I would be Britain's flag-bearer my mind went back to the Moscow Olympics.

Probably nobody else even noticed, but I had always been fascinated by the Soviet weight-lifter who carried his nation's flag in one hand outstretched. I discussed it with Matthew, and he said: 'I bet you couldn't do that.' That familiar desire to achieve a new challenge had returned. When I mentioned it to some of the other rowers, they insisted: 'You're crazy. You'll damage your arm. You shouldn't do it.'

I accepted the pouch they had given me but, on the spur of the moment, I walked out there in the Olympic stadium and held the flag in front of me with my left hand. The pole is an alloy tube, which is relatively light, but the breeze in the flag makes it heavy. I didn't find it too difficult until I got to the back of the track, and then you walk across the turf into the allotted position for your country. That was when the wind was at its strongest. It picked up the flag, which was pretty large, and only then did my arm start shaking.

The strange thing was that I had never been in a stadium before as a competitor. To walk out before an 85,000 crowd was very special. The best way I can describe it is to say that you feel you're leading the entire nation. It was something that will remain with me. I soaked it all up, and took in everything that was going on around me. It was the first opening ceremony I'd ever been to, not having attended Los Angeles or Seoul.

If there was a minor disappointment it was that I was expecting more noise, but then you don't expect Great Britain to get a massive ovation when you're in Spain and possibly people are starting to get bored by that stage. It was a fantastic moment as I prepared myself to equal Jack Beresford's record of three Olympic gold medals, set in the single sculls in 1924, the coxless fours in 1932, and the double sculls in 1936. He actually went to five Olympics and won two silvers as well. When he won his last gold, he also carried the flag. My thoughts were, 'Well, if he could do it and win three golds, why can't I?'

Having had no racing build-up to the Games, we wanted to draw one of the major contenders for a medal in the heat to test ourselves. We were granted that wish in the form of Slovenia, whom we regarded as the next best pair. Normally, we would not have been happy with such a draw at that early stage, but on Lake Banyoles it suited us perfectly. It would also give us the chance to demonstrate to those crews who had arrived at Barcelona, hovering like vultures, that despite my illness we were nobody's easy pickings. We went out there and dominated the Slovenians from start to finish. The crew that had defeated us at Essen, when I had been suffering badly with colitis, just weren't in the race at all.

People always used to ask Matthew and me which were our best races. Our answer has always been the same. The three we contested in Barcelona – the heat, semi-final and final – would rank right at the top. We were, in all modesty, pretty impressive. Those performances were as close to perfect as you ever get.

In that heat, we cruised to the line, and although Slovenia closed us down slightly towards the finish that was only because we let them. We were totally in control. After we crossed the line Matthew and I just paddled quietly out of the way. Slovenia crossed the line and collapsed. Their heads went down and they just drifted for a while.

That heat was a crucial part of my rehabilitation. As we paddled back past the grandstand to the landing stage, I had goose pimples and the hair stood up on the back of my neck. I knew at that moment, after all the problems we'd had, all the discomfort I'd endured in the six months leading up to Barcelona, that we were going to win the gold medal.

We could tell that Slovenia were absolutely devastated. Having beaten us at the second international regatta, they were convinced for two or three months coming into the Games, that they were going to claim an Olympic gold. Suddenly, six days before the final, they had experienced a stab of apprehension as they came face to face with the realization that somebody was about to snatch it away from under their noses.

Of course, they still had six days to do something about it, but mentally they had lost it completely. In fact, they ended up getting the bronze, and not even the silver. I'm sure it was because of the manner in which we had annihilated them. One of them just sat there with his head in his hands afterwards. He did not move for three-quarters of an hour, so badly had he been affected. Then they had to go out and do it all again in the repechage, and they won through to semi-finals, where they met us again.

As well as Ann and Natalie – she was by now one year old – my parents and sisters had all came out to Barcelona and had rented a farmhouse outside the city. Matthew's parents were staying with them. It's important to be able to get away from the pressure of the Olympic regatta, if at all possible, and after that first race we both cycled up there one day to see them.

Apart from the Slovenians, the Germans were our principal competition in the semi-finals. But once again, we overwhelmed our rivals and were able to cruise home as the others behind us fought for a place in the final.

Although we had been rowing superbly, and well within our capabilities, we were aware that we might not have things our own way in the final. We were thinking, 'There's five other boats and one of them is going to come out and give it a go. Maybe it'll be Slovenia. They'll get their act together and really come out firing. Or maybe France. Germany too.' We had to be alert to that. There's always somebody who, instead of pacing it as they should do to try and get their best result, will say, 'Sod this, we've got nothing to lose. We'll give it our best crack. We'll just go blast off and see how long we can hang on for.' Very rarely does it work. They normally blow up and do not win anything.

On the morning of our final on 1 August, however, it was soon evident that the German thinking had been: 'We're not going to win this. We'll race for second place. Our race is against Slovenia.' That made the task even easier for us.

The Germans surged into an immediate lead, but by the time Matthew and I crossed the 250-metre mark we had taken over and continued to extend our advantage. It was obvious that no one was racing us. They were merely competing for minor medals. It was a joyful moment as we crossed the line. Matthew thrust his right arm into the air, one finger erect. I confined myself to patting him on the shoulder. It is usually my way. A journalist asked me later why I had been so restrained. I told him: 'I'm not an outwardly emotional person. I see no need to inflict how I feel on others.'

That makes me sound almost like an automaton, which is actually far from the truth. I know people look at me and think I'm very calm and in control and not very emotional, but underneath I am quite sensitive. To be more accurate, I'd say the Redgraves are quite an emotional family, but very British with it. So it never shows. I wouldn't say it manifests itself as being cold, but sometimes it makes us appear quite hard. Many times, I've been accused by Ann of not being very emotional, of not reacting to a situation, and I'm sure it's an infuriating trait, but we Redgraves tend to keep our feelings to ourselves. We bottle it all up. We epitomize the stiff British upper lip. That's how my father was brought up – with the belief that overt displays of your feelings are perceived to be a weakness.

The receipt of my third Olympic gold and Matthew's first probably changed our rowing relationship from that moment. Subconsciously, on both our parts we hadn't been equals. Now there was no disputing that we were. Matthew was to reflect later in an interview: 'Until Barcelona, Steve had to be seen to be the boss. It took me a long time to realize he needed as much from me as I needed from him.'

I read later that Andy Holmes was staying only two miles from the regatta course at Banyoles during the Olympics. I never saw him, and in articles he denied he would watch our races, even on TV. But he made one interesting observation about me: 'If he gets over this gut trouble something spectacular could happen, because he's rowing with this young kid Pinsent who, if he wants it enough, has it in him to be one of the stars of all time. He is the most extraordinary prospect.' In that, Andy wasn't far wrong. Matthew had lifted his first gold and, at 21, he had barely started his career.

Neither had the Searle brothers, who, following our success, proceeded to overcome the mighty Abbagnales, with whom Andy and I had enjoyed some spirited duels over the years. The Italian brothers were also bidding for a third Olympic gold themselves, when they were beaten by Jonny and Greg – not forgetting the tearful coxswain Garry Herbert – in the coxed pairs. Our race had been all about dominance and control, but you couldn't beat the Searles' brilliantly judged surge for the line to claim the prize for sheer excitement.

Once you've completed your event, you're urged to move away and let other athletes enjoy the Olympic experience. Ann and I departed and drove back through France, having a holiday on the way. But once we arrived home, she bought me a ticket for the closing ceremony and I returned just for that night.

Away from the rowing lake, Linford Christie had successfully staked his claim to be the world's fastest man, by powering to victory in the 100 metres. Together with our gold medal triumphs, it lifted the cloud that had appeared over British sport, when three athletes had been expelled for drug abuse.

Afterwards, my thoughts returned inevitably to my illness. During that prelude to Barcelona, I'd tended to put the causes and future implications to the back of my mind as far as possible. I'd only really been concerned when I didn't know what was wrong with me. I'm no different from anybody else in that. It's better to know what you've got so you can get on and deal with it. I'd had 17 weeks of those symptoms, which is a hell of a long time.

What the specialist had told me is that the intestine gets red raw and hasn't got the capacity to hold anything. What I hadn't realized is that the intestine absorbs a lot of goodness and produces a lot of energy; it's not all confined to the stomach.

It was also emphasized to me that colitis is a very serious condition. Some people have one bout of it, and it never returns. In other patients, it recurs often. You hear stories of people who have had to have most of their intestine removed, people who have to use a colostomy bag. Worse, you hear about people getting colon cancer and dying from it. Colitis can be a precursor to that.

Back in the summer of 1992, I didn't think too much about the prognosis, but I must admit that the older I get, the more concerned I become. The experts say that it is not known for certain what causes colitis. Some suggest that it is stress-related; others that it is connected to diet. I can't believe the latter because, as an athlete, I've always eaten pretty good-quality food.

As far as the former is concerned, my immediate thought was: 'I don't lead a particularly stressful life. I do what I want to do.' But when I began to ponder that at greater length, I came to the conclusion that being in a must-win situation nearly every time you go out and race must be stressful. And it was made worse by the fact that during most of my rowing career I'd had financial problems. I've been constantly in the red, and not having enough money to train and prepare as I would have liked was another source of worry.

It was for that reason that, after Barcelona, I decided that if I was able to secure a good sponsorship deal, I'd carry on. That was definitely my intention.

However, if that contract was not forthcoming, I accepted reluctantly that I'd have to retire and find a 'proper' job. As the father of a young daughter, I had the responsibility of supporting that child. Rowing for me had gone way beyond just being a pastime at which I excelled. It was a career, and when you have a career, it's assumed that you'll at least survive on the proceeds, if not actually prosper from it. Frankly, I wasn't doing that.

When Ann married me, she knew what she was letting herself in for; she had been a rower herself, and she understood intimately the life-style I was leading. She also appreciated what I was aiming to do. But it's different when you bring a child into the world. They've got no choice about the way they're brought up. You feel very responsible for the child in that situation. Fortunately, sponsorship was to materialize, but not before I had seriously considered laying down my oars for good.

The strangest thing was that when I got back from Barcelona the colitis returned. What was remarkable – and again providence was surely taking a hand – was that there was a two-month 'window', if you like, when I was healthy. The Olympics were in the middle of that. Either side of that period, I was an extremely sick person. But was it fate? Or was it mental strength that pulled me through?

CHAPTER 17

MATTHEW: LAID-BACK TO A FAULT

O n or off the water, I am, by nature, a competitor. That factor has undoubtedly contributed to making me what I am today. I'd be competitive if I was with friends on a boating lake, the kind where they shout: 'Come in number eight. Your time is up.'

That is where Matthew and I differ. Apart from in the throes of combat in major competitions, he's exceptionally laid-back. Nothing really seems to worry him. He's Mister Cool. Sometimes I got frustrated with that when we were out training. If another boat went past us, I thought we should have been trying to match their speed. The urge was within me to take them on. Matthew could switch off and just let it go. For instance, when we were out at a regatta at Lucerne one year a Dutch lightweight sculler passed us as we were paddling around the lake. Matthew hardly took any notice. If I had been on my own, I wouldn't have let him do that. I said to Matthew: 'How can you let a lightweight sculler overtake you?' He just shrugged and replied wryly, 'Well, he is world champion.' Of course, it didn't really matter. Not in the grand design of things; not even in the world of rowing was it of any consequence. Yet, it irritated me. It was the principle behind it. If that sculler had been out there paddling against me, he wouldn't just have let me pull away from him. We're athletes. We're competitive whatever situation you put us in. Aren't we? But in the decade I've known him, and shared a boat with him, Matthew simply has never been like that. He can switch off within his own sport, one at which he is outstanding, to let crews that are supposed to be slower than his go more quickly. The truth is that he is very lazy. Matthew is capable of doing much more than he does on a day-to-day basis and that used to rile me at times. But you can't really fault the guy, because when he's got to produce something on the big occasion he never fails to do so.

I know that Matthew's attitude used to frustrate James Cracknell, another member of the Sydney coxless four, as well. James was one of those characters who'd give it his all at every training session. He'd watch Matthew on the ergo to establish how he was doing and quite often he'd beat him. Since the four was formed in 1996 Matthew was consistently the best on the rowing machines. But being beaten never worried him, or didn't seem to do so. Yet, when it came to a serious test, Matthew would beat James every time. I've never been quite certain if that's a fault or a virtue. I think it just illustrates that he's got great confidence in what he does and how he does it. Maybe if you're not quite so confident, you feel that you have to prove it all the time. Maybe that's how I was, and how James was in the build-up to the Olympics. Every training session he had to prove something. One of the most frustrating things was when we were out on the Thames at Henley, doing our training sessions. You could guarantee that on different occasions in the year a crew from another club would come along and try to take us on. They'd be pulling harder and rating higher and 'beating' us. It would infuriate me, because I knew we could have defeated them comfortably if we wanted to. I'd have loved to just put them in their place.

But you had to look at the overall picture and get on with your own work. It didn't worry Matthew at all, or didn't seem to. Only occasionally would it annoy him, but he'd still just get on with what he was doing. Inevitably, after such incidents you'd then hear all the stories circulating about 'how such and such a crew is faster than Steve Redgrave's' and 'we're quicker than the British four'.

Matthew is the son of a retired clergyman from Dorset, Ewen, and his wife Jean. I would imagine that, by nature, he is quite shy and retiring, but the environment he has been brought up in and particularly the education he has gone through have brought him out of himself to a nice level, where he is confident in whatever he does. I'd describe him as quite a balanced person.

Some people who go through that type of education – Eton and Oxford – can be unbearably pompous and arrogant; perhaps they need that to be the leaders of industry, business and politics that many of them become. A public school education gears you up for success in life much better than a comprehensive. If you are a confident, intelligent person then you are quite likely to be pretty unbearable when you come out the other side of one of those institutions.

It never worried me that Matthew would be like that. I'd seen enough of him to build a picture, and I knew that he wasn't a loud person, not someone who would be trying to be constantly the centre of attention. Simon Berrisford was the complete opposite.

He was quite insecure and tried to be the showman. I was quite aware of that before we got together.

I believe you are significantly conditioned by your environment. When I was young, because my sisters were quite a bit older than me, I spent quite a lot of time with my parents and their friends. I found myself growing up faster than others of my age, because I was around adults. I was a child, but I was having more adult conversations, rather than indulging in a lot of schoolboy giggling.

I have made rowing my career, at least in part, because I was not qualified to do anything else. Some people are surprised that Matthew has carried on even to this stage. He celebrated his 30th birthday just after the Sydney Olympics, yet with his qualifications and background it might be supposed that he would have become embroiled in the world of business or commerce well before now.

It doesn't surprise me in the least that Matthew has continued as an oarsmen. If he had been in my circumstances when I was starting out, though, I don't think he would have made rowing his career. I did so because I had no qualifications or desire to do anything else. Back in the late seventies, when I began, those with academic gifts went to university, they studied, they rowed for a number of years, and won or lost. They'd then settle down and move on to their career. That's what Matthew would have done.

But sport, even some of the traditionally amateur ones like rowing, has, in the last 10 years, become a career. With sponsorship, the money you can earn can provide you with a comfortable living. After a long struggle, I now have a home in Marlow Bottom of which I'm extremely proud. Matthew has bought himself quite a large house in Henley.

Matthew's girlfriend and many people he knows from his university days have gone into quite high-powered jobs with blue-chip companies and they get paid very well. But they have to work very hard, and long hours. The attitude has to be: while you're good at a sport, and surviving quite comfortably, why not continue?

Matthew has had a few girlfriends since I've known him, but his relationship with Dee, as we know her, is very serious. She's Canadian, from Toronto, although her parents are Greek, and she works for a firm of consultant trouble-shooters. They met when she was a mature student at Oxford.

In fact, their relationship appeared so serious that when we received a very formal invitation to go to Matthew's cousin's home for Sunday lunch in April 2000, Ann and I thought there might just be an engagement announcement in the air. In fact, it turned out to be a birthday lunch to celebrate Matthew's 30th and his father's 70th birthdays, giving them a combined age of 100. They hadn't put a reason on the invitation because they didn't want everybody bringing presents.

Matthew is eight years younger than me and there's no reason why he couldn't equal my tally of Olympic golds. Who knows? He could actually surpass me. Matthew jokes about that now and again. But realistically, I couldn't see him rowing when he's 42, any more than I will be. That would require so much commitment.

There's only been one British rower who's won a gold medal at 42. Guy Nickalls had actually retired, but was asked to come back and row in the gold-medallist eight in the 1908 Olympics. He was a Leander man, like myself, and I believe his concession to renewed fitness was giving up port and investing in a heavier overcoat for his training walks down to Temple Island!

I think Matthew will continue rowing up to the next Olympics and then stop. But it wouldn't totally surprise me if he carries on until he's 38. However, it's getting tougher all the time. We're doing much more training than we were four years ago, and then we were doing considerably more than four years before that.

That's what I don't like about the sport at our level. The amount of time we have to put into it. It requires far more training than most so-called 'professional' sports, and then there's the require-ments of your sponsors to consider. Also, it's inevitable that, as a successful sportsman, you should be asked to support numerous charities and appeals. I'm happy to do that, wherever possible, but it all restricts your time. It never used to worry me at all as a young man, but if I were starting off today I think I'd find it extremely daunting.

In many ways, it's a peculiar job, this one of mine. To spend a fair percentage of your time within inches of the back of your crew-mate's head, ploughing up and down the same stretch of the Thames – often in winter with the wind and spray penetrating even the layers of protective clothing we wear – and occasionally issu-ing commands, as I did with Matthew in the pair. It can be seen that however different you are as characters, you must comple-ment each other. In that, Matthew and I were always near-perfect partners.

There's a saying in rowing that 'a happy crew is a slow crew'. I've never believed that. It may have been the case in more amateur days when the fellowship of people rowing was more important than their aims. Now the pursuit of an Olympic gold medal attracts such huge media interest and is potentially so lucrative that it's no longer a pastime, but a deadly serious business. If you want to be successful, it doesn't matter whom you row with as long as they're the best. Andy Holmes proved that. I knew Matthew was the right man to partner me from the start. We also happen to be good friends.

In the good old days of two training sessions a day, we used to finish at lunch-time at the latest. We'd go and play golf or go, with another guy called Mark Hall, who trained with us and was trying to get into the team, back to his house and play on his computer. It was not until Ann and I started having children that I took a step backwards and started to question my priorities.

I thought so much of Matthew that I asked him to be godfather to Natalie, our first child, who was born in 1991. You don't do that if you feel the other person is just passing through your life. I felt that whatever happened to our futures in rowing, we'd still be friends after we retired. I'm still sure that will be the case.

There was tension at times between us, of course. It's difficult to avoid that when there are two of you in close proximity. When you are sitting in the bow seat, traditionally you're the person who gives the commands in day-to-day training as James did with the Sydney four. It's a responsibility that somebody has to take, but it does mean that you are effectively telling other people how to do their job. Sometimes with James I used to think, 'Oh, God. Here we go again. Same old thing' – which is not actually very fair.

All that an oarsman is trying to do is get the best out of the boat. Sometimes the things you are saying are for your own benefit, not just for the crew's. But it has the effect of a foreman sitting next to three other workers on the production line, constantly barking at them.

You can imagine what it's like when there's a two-man boat, with somebody saying: 'Right we're going to do such and such now' or 'We've got to think about this.' Sometimes that would get a little bit too much. You intend it to refer to both of you, but it can sound like it's one instructing the other.

I would have hated somebody doing that to me all the time. Fortunately, Matthew was so laid-back that he accepted it and just got on with it. Even then, there were times when you realized it was a bit too much, and you just shut up.

Your low points were as hard to accept as for any other sportsman. You might not have rowed badly that often, but you were looking to try to row perfectly. You were constantly saying, 'I want more speed out of this boat.' When that wasn't happening, which was most of the time, it got frustrating. You were clearly not trying hard enough.

The truth is, of course, that you can't be the world's best, most technically perfect oarsman every day you go out on the water. But you want to be. I could never have changed and been like Matthew, because I got my success from the way I am. I would get frustrated because I always demanded so much from myself and those around me while Matthew could plod along, if necessary.

Yet, we weren't a pair who argued. On the occasions when we hadn't been happy with the way the boat had been moving, there was just a mutual silence. However, invariably, by the time we'd put the boat away, got changed, and were having our lunch up in the crew room the tensions had disappeared. We worked well together, partly because once we got out of the boat we switched off and into a more light-hearted mode.

If I *did* get wound up, it could be for a long period of time. It would build and build until I thought to myself, 'This is stupid. I don't really know what I got upset about in the first place.' Matthew never seemed to be fazed by it all. Only very occasionally would that happen.

People find it surprising that we never fell out, like any other two other people at work. But most people don't choose their work colleague. With Matthew I did. If I had felt he wasn't right, he wouldn't have joined me in the boat.

One of our problems was complacency. When you win so many races it is difficult to retain the drive to go out and do it again. Apart from beating rivals by ever-increasing margins, where do you go from there? It's like winning the first international regatta of the season; yes, I wanted to do it, but as a race it didn't mean anything.

That wasn't the motivation for getting out of bed in the mornings to do the training. To other people, it meant something, possibly their selection for the Olympics. If they didn't perform well enough they wouldn't be going. But for us it was different. When you're number one in the world, your place is secure, barring injury or massive loss of form. Domestic trials were even less of a motivation.

When I started, every race had to be won. In the four years up to Sydney, there was only one race of true significance and that took place on 23 September 2000. As Matthew used to say, when we enjoyed a long unbeaten run, we'd have traded in all those medals and races we'd ever won to make sure we won that one in September. There was only one race that mattered. After Atlanta, the motivation was not about lifting big weights, producing good ergo scores, winning domestic trials, gaining successes at Henley, being victorious in World Championships. It was about winning the Olympic Games at Sydney Regatta Park.

To build yourself up to being at fever-pitch at exactly the right moment is really a difficult thing to do. But we were favourites, and most of the time favourites do win. I didn't expect to need passion to win on that day. That wasn't a factor. Many sportsmen talk about passion or spirit within them, or within their teams. And that may well be the case. But to us, passion was just the final gear into which we rarely have to move.

The fierce intensity with which we trained took the passion out of what we did. It's just competitive conditioning. We became like robots. Hopefully, until we came to that final race, we wouldn't need it. If you start needing passion to win anything, there's more than a hint of desperation; that your natural ability is not sufficient. And that's not a situation I ever wanted to be in.

After Barcelona, we were naturally satisfied with what we'd done and, initially, Matthew and I found it quite difficult to keep the motivation going. The closer to the Olympics, the easier work became, and vice versa. Normally, we were just programmed to do the training. But that year after the Olympics we weren't so committed as we should have been. Matthew and I would row down and hide behind Temple Island, and just hang on to a tree. We'd check on our watches to make sure we were back at Leander, and in Jurgen's vision at the correct time.

As a rule, though, Matthew and I had the utmost respect for Jurgen. He brought consistency to our pair with the knowledge that had accrued from being a top international coach. It was in the small details. There was a lot more planning and structure behind everything.

I found it bizarre when he came along and marked out the whole river in 500-metre stretches, and recorded everything. But there was always a purpose to everything. He brought in training to percentages. Now we were not looking to go as fast as we possibly could all the time. We might be working at 75 per cent of our maximum speed. After all, Linford Christie didn't go out every day and try to run 100 metres as fast as possible.

With Mike Spracklen, I achieved some outstanding performances, and took the sport in this country to new heights. But it was rather hit and miss, and now that is not the case. With Jurgen, I've always been able to perform at the right level, at the right time. That was not the case beforehand.

He was crucial to my development and success during the nineties. It was good having somebody with more knowledge than myself, although I like to think he has learnt from me, as well.

Just occasionally, he would make it clear that he thought I was doing too much on the promotional and after-dinner front. 'I think you're doing a bit too much, Steve,' he'd say. 'Be careful. You're not as young as you used to be. I want to try and make you a winner as much as you want it yourself.'

He had a very dry sense of humour. He had his little jokes, like telling Matthew that he'd changed the training programme, and that we were doing something totally ridiculous. He thought that was hilarious.

I'm sure Jurgen found it difficult initially to assimilate himself into an alien culture, but as he used to say, he couldn't be homesick, because he didn't have a home. His country had ceased to exist. Angela, his wife, could speak reasonable English and she has been a great support to him. They have a son, Bjorn, who is now at Oxford University.

Leander initially provided Jurgen with a house, but then he bought his own. Any time he got any money, he'd cycle straight across the bridge into town to the building society and pay a cheque in or give them cash to pay his mortgage off. He has found it difficult to relate to that concept. He was horrified by having a huge debt.

In 1993, we did all the training that we were asked to do. But that's it. Nothing more. Sometimes we were reluctant to do that. But if we could do that, without killing ourselves physically or mentally, and still get the results we wanted, it left us with higher gears into which we could move in Olympic year. Where Matthew and I were concerned, we were just biding our time between one Olympics and the next. The fact that we didn't lose any races in between, or very few, was amazing, considering the attitude that we had.

The World Championships in 1993 were held at Roundice, near Prague. We made it through to the final, and had one of the toughest races of our careers, beating Germany, Slovenia and Belgium, but only narrowly. It wasn't helped by the fact that we were given an unfavourable outside lane in a strong cross-wind. We emerged from the pack in the last 500 metres, which was unusual for us, rather than asserting ourselves early on. When we crossed the line, there wasn't the elation that we'd just won the World Championships. Matthew turned around to me, and said: 'We're never going to hide behind that island again.'

The last 10 strokes were really quite painful. Slovenia put everything into it to try to expose us, so much so that one of their crew, which actually finished third behind the Germans, collapsed with exhaustion after the medal ceremony. It was one of the few occasions when we've done the rowing equivalent of staggering across the line.

By the following two years' World Championships, at Indianapolis and Tampere in Finland, normal Redgrave–Pinsent service had been resumed. Indeed, in 1994 at Indianapolis, we actually set a time of 6 minutes 18.34 seconds, which was a new world record. We beat a very tough German pair, who had rowed for Cambridge in the Boat Race. Although we always knew we were going to win, we only edged in front in the last 100 metres.

Departing from Barcelona, Matthew and I had confidently predicted to family and friends that 'in four years' time we'll be at Atlanta and we're going to win gold medals'. That hadn't been the wisest move we'd ever made. Such statements have a habit of being flung back at you. We were relieved that, half-way to Atlanta, we remained on course to fulfil that bold pronouncement.

CHAPTER 18

BREAKING POINT
AT ATLANTA

M y decision to aim for a fourth Olympic gold at Atlanta was not one I took lightly. In fact, after Barcelona, I was within weeks of giving it all up and thinking seriously about an alternative career. The overriding factor which persuaded me to carry on was the sponsorship. With Natalie by then aged one, I had to feel financially secure to be able to commit myself to continuing the pair with Matthew in the next Olympics. The motivation was there, but for a worrying period not the money.

I didn't want to be in a situation I'd known for so many years when I didn't know where the next cheque was coming from, and whether I could pay my mortgage off that month. It's not an environment you want to live in when you've got children. There were rumours that the British Olympic Association was going to make some financial support available, presumably on the basis that it would have been a national disgrace if a three-times British Olympic champion was forced to retire because of lack of funds. I've heard since that they would have done it, too, but, understandably, it's a precedent that they didn't really want to set.

Fortunately, a new sponsor miraculously appeared. It was ManuLife, which became Canada Life. Our deal with the company started in 1993 and was worth £25,000 a year to both Matthew and me through to Atlanta. It allowed us to survive, nothing more. It was not until 1996 that I was able to bring a smile to my bank manager's face – by not being in debt.

These days we have the National Lottery money on board, which is excellent, up to a point. But four athletes out of the team didn't get any funding from it: Matthew, myself and Greg and Jonny Searle. The reason is that we were receiving our own sponsorship money. Fine, it might be assumed. But I believe I was being hard done by. Would footballer David Beckham, for example, forego his salary because he receives x-million pounds for a boot deal? Of course not.

For our sponsorship, we had to go out and work for that money. We'd also reached the pinnacle of our sport to make ourselves marketable. Those getting Lottery money don't have to do anything for it. The best-funded person from the Lottery fund was Peter Haining, who has, admittedly, been world lightweight champion three times, but at two Olympic Games he'd never made the top 10. Yet, Peter has been funded better than anybody else. If you related that to football or other professional sports, it would be considered obscene.

However, that situation appears to be regarded as acceptable for an 'amateur' sport. We were told that is all because of the 'level playing field' approach that's taken in sports such as ours. It's just accepted that there isn't an elite and everyone is the same when palpably that's not the case.

It is not just the method by which rowers today are funded that irritates me – it is the attitude of some of them to it. When I started to receive sponsorship income from DAF Trucks and then Canada Life, my priority was how it was going to prepare me best for the next Olympic Games, with all the cost of training camps and attending regattas. Rowers these days have no such problems. It has all changed dramatically since the advent of National Lottery grants, which have made rowing the biggest funded of all sports. You do sometimes wonder, though, if it is really appreciated by its beneficiaries. Or does it all come too easy?

In 1999, at our altitude camp, there were so many athletes with mobile phones and Walkmans, it might have been an upmarket holiday resort. I know they're both common now and not a luxury, and I'm not suggesting that you require austerity to be a 'real' sportsman, but I did reflect on what I'd been through in the past and think to myself, 'Are these funds being spent in the right way?'

Of course, you need leisure items, especially when you're in some isolated mountain base, and there's nothing else much going on, but there was one athlete who didn't eat properly, and was always moaning about not having enough money to pay his rent. Yet, he was able to buy himself a CD Walkman. I had to say to myself: 'Is he focused in the right direction?' Or maybe it's just me, looking from a different perspective. If I was given a considerable grant now, I'd immediately start evaluating how it could benefit me for the following year. But there again, I suppose if somebody had given that kind of money to me at 18, I might have thought, 'What can I go and spend it on?' Perhaps it's just down to my age and experience.

I've never had any money from the Lottery, at least not directly, because of my Lombard sponsorship. To qualify for Lottery money you have to respond to a list of questions, such as: Do you work? How much do you earn? Do you receive sponsorship? Appearance money? What are your travel/training/coaching/equipment costs? Are you married? How many children? and so on. Then it was all worked out, and the end result was that I received nothing.

Under our system, once you earn between £20,000 and £30,000 that reduces your Lottery funding. Anything over that, and your Lottery money is stopped. There are, however, two pots: one for direct grants to individuals and one for financing travel to regattas and training camps, from which we all benefit.

My situation has always been complicated by the fact that Ann is part of the British team. As doctor, which was a voluntary post until 1996 when it became part-funded by the Lottery money, she is away on a lot of trips. When that happened, we had to pay for the children to come with us, or find somebody to look after them.

For the Atlanta Olympics, we were away for a total of 11 weeks from the start of the first training camp. My parents travelled out to look after Natalie and Sophie but we paid to fly them there and provided a house for them. The children travelled out with us, and I reimbursed the ARA for their tickets, so we could all travel on the same plane. Yet, for Atlanta, we were receiving just a few hundred pounds a child, although the family had two people on the team. There were other costs involved with taking the children.

Since then, nothing has changed and the way the money is distributed is very amateurish. I understand that it's a very difficult job. But the view seems to be, because it's public money, it's got to be seen to be fair. It's got to be even-handed for everybody.

But I would suggest that if you go and ask members of the public who buy their Lottery tickets: 'Of the percentage that goes to sport, where would you want your money to go? To somebody who may just get selected and go to the Olympics? Or to somebody who is a potential medal-winner?' I'd say a high percentage would prefer to see their money go to the better-prepared athlete than somebody who is just going there to achieve the highest level of which they're capable. I'm not denigrating such athletes; however, I do feel that when there is only a certain amount of funding, it has to be prioritized.

It would probably astound the public to learn that, before the advent of Lottery grants, competitors actually had to pay to be a member of the British team. The exception is the Olympics – the

BOA covers the cost of that – but we had to pay for the overheads of attending World Championships, international regattas and training camps. Olympic athletes paid less, while coaches and back-up staff didn't pay at all, and their costs were spread around.

Yet the reality was that at the Indianapolis World Championships, two years before Atlanta, non-Olympic rowers had to contribute near enough £2000. That was for just one event. As an Olympic athlete, it cost me less. But even so, I was spending thousands of pounds a year. That's when my overdraft built up. The costs for me in Atlanta year were quite incredible.

As a man who began with aspirations to be a champion single sculler, I always used to say that if that discipline was better financed and was supported by a better coaching set-up, we could turn out some world-class performers. The truth is that there's been a hell of a lot of money put into sculling, and a lot of time and effort, without it yielding real results. Just throwing money at part of the sport doesn't work. I'd like to see a slightly different structure where an oarsman or oarswoman achieves a bonus for attaining good results at major competitions.

Sponsorship and endorsements are of such importance today that, for a sporting 'celebrity', hiring the right agent is as important as having the right coach. Athole Still, my representative, handled the ManuLife deal, as he does all my business affairs. His organization suits me because it's a family business and he's well respected in his field. I'm looked after on a day-to-day basis by his daughter Roxane, and Athole's wife Isobel is also involved on the accounts side. It's been an excellent relationship. Athole and I also go to watch Chelsea together. I have been a fan since the late 1960s.

Initially, Athole found it difficult to arrange commercial deals with sponsors and find endorsement opportunities because of the upper-class image of the sport. To an extent, some companies still regard rowing as being all about public schoolboy/university types, and accessible only to a privileged few.

But things have changed. Everyone appreciates by now that my background is far from privileged, but it's the elitist image of rowing overall – evoked by Henley Royal Regatta and the Boat Race, in particular – that remains an obstacle to be overcome. I hope that, in some way, I've been able to destroy that prejudice.

My only involvement with the Boat Race has been helping out with Oxford at one stage. I have certainly never had anything against the event. Yet, somehow I managed to become involved in a pre-race controversy in the week I was asked to present the trophy to the winners in 1997.

The Boat Race started in 1829, and continues to attract a huge TV audience – an estimated 400 million viewers world-wide. I watched it before I even got involved with rowing. Sometimes the standard is very poor. Pretty near damn rubbish, I'd say. Sometimes it's very high, and the highs are very high indeed, because there are often several internationals involved.

I gave my opinions in an interview I did before the race and the article made it appear that I was opposed to the event. If that was the case, I wouldn't have gone near it. Anyway, the piece particularly offended Dan Topolski, the two-times Oxford Blue and Oxford coach, and son of the world-famous artist, Felix. I've been very good friends with Dan for a long time.

What happened was that I was asked the question, 'What does the Boat Race do for international rowing?' I tried to answer honestly, as I always do, and said, 'Absolutely nothing.' It's quite true. The annual four-and-a-half-mile event on the Thames Tideway gives rowing a profile, but it's a different sport, in some respects. The same as Head of River races are different from international regattas. Henley is different again. They are many different sports, all under the same title.

I said that the last time that Oxford or Cambridge actually produced anyone who had progressed to race in the British team was Gavin Stewart, who in 1987 was going to be in the 'second' Oxford boat and, when the Americans dropped out, ended up stroking the first boat and they won – the subject of Dan's book and feature film *True Blue*. Gavin subsequently got into the international team. But that was rare.

I went further and said that what the Boat Race does for international rowing is what go-karting does for Formula One. I made it worse by saying that, in fact, that was not true, because go-karting was a good basis for getting into motor-racing and progressing to F1. In the context of what we were talking about, that is exactly correct.

I also appeared on Alan Green's Radio 5-Live show the night before and called the Boat Race a Mickey Mouse event, which Dan also didn't appreciate. That was probably a little bit too strong. It annoyed a few other people, like Duncan Clegg, the Boat Race organizer, but did not appear to bother the rowers who were just really pleased that I was giving the medals out. Matthew, who's rowed in the Boat Race, agreed with my views exactly.

Dan never said anything to me, but it was made known to me through Matthew that he wasn't very happy. I would have preferred it if he had called me himself and had it out. Maybe I should have rung him to explain and put it in context. He didn't talk to me for a long time, although we now seem to be back on good terms. It probably didn't help that the Boat Race's Beefeater sponsorship was coming to an end and they were trying to find new backers and didn't want any bad press. Though I stand by what I said, that was never my intention.

Just occasionally, though, in my career, I have uttered something I wish had remained unsaid. That bullish prediction by Matthew and me, coming out of Barcelona, that we were going to win golds at Atlanta was one such example. Of course, we were confident about victory, even that far ahead, and knew what we were capable of achieving, and it's great motivation four, three, two years away from the next Games.

But once it gets into Olympic year, and you've told thousands of people what you're going to do on a certain day and at a certain time, as it gets nearer and nearer, that puts a lot of pressure on you. The media and the public, not just in Britain but world-wide, want you to succeed, want you to win four golds which no other rower has ever done. I found that very difficult to deal with.

As we got closer to that date with destiny, the expectation we had heaped on ourselves had begun to take its toll. By the time we had reached our final month's preparation the pressure had built up so much that I was terrified of letting my country, and all those supporters, down. In some ways, looking back, it was very arrogant. Also, it was giving the opposition an incentive to knock us down, to put us in our place.

That's the reason why, since Atlanta, I just maintained that we were going to give it 'our best shot' in Sydney and generally played it all down. It's not what the journalists and headline writers want to hear, but it had to be done. I still felt the same inside, that I was supremely confident, but I just didn't articulate it. Never, during those four years did I pronounce: 'On 23 September 2000 we are going to win a gold medal.'

Atlanta 1996, the so-called Billion Dollar Games, was an organizational shambles right from the start of what turned out to be the longest opening ceremony of all time. Baron Pierre de Coubertin, whose aim in the late 19th century was 'to bring the young people of the world together every four years to celebrate sport in its purest form', would have been horrified.

Those Games had little in common with ancient Greek traditions. The most moving moment was the opening of the Olympics by Muhammad Ali, who was presented with a special medal 36 years after he'd thrown the one he won in 1960 into a Kentucky river as a protest against racism.

Just about everything that could go wrong did. The transport system was chaotic, and I spent too much of my time complaining about that before Matthew and I eventually moved out of the village. The opening ceremony, at which again I was asked to be flag-bearer, was not only far too long but also badly planned. Then there was the bomb outrage, in which one person was killed and hundreds injured, in Centennial Park.

Not the organizers' fault of course, but it cast such a shadow over the remainder of the event that I was in two minds whether to continue.

To go back to the beginning of that period, I discovered that I had been chosen to carry the flag just as I was complaining bitterly about the transport problems we had been encountering in trying to get from the village to Lake Lanier. Brian Armstrong, as team manager, had originally asked me if I would perform the task. I thought that if a rower was to be selected it was Matthew who should get the honour. However, because rowing had been chosen four years previously, I was convinced that it wouldn't come back to our sport again. They'd give it to track or field.

For that reason, I said 'Yes'. I was sure I wouldn't get it, but that it would give Matthew far more chance of getting the honour in four years' time at Sydney. He would be the prime candidate then if we carried on our success and I felt that I was giving him a 'banker'.

I never considered for a moment that I'd actually get it again. When I was told, about three days before the Games started, I had just been on a coach that got lost on the way to the rowing lake, about 40 miles north-east of the city itself. Once we reached the lake, I went up to Brian and had a real blast at him about the transport. I was half-way through remonstrating with him, when he interrupted me and declared: 'They've asked you to carry the flag again.' I was so furious that I didn't take it in. It went completely over the top of my head. I was still raging on: 'Something's got to be done about this transport...'

Brian interrupted me and said patiently: 'Didn't you hear me?' I said: 'What?' He repeated it: 'The BOA have asked you to carry the flag again.' I was totally dumbstruck. I hadn't even been thinking about it, because nobody gets to carry the flag twice. It's just not etiquette.

I told Matthew and Jurgen, who were delighted for me. Matthew hadn't come to the Barcelona opening ceremony, but he said this time: 'If you're doing that, I'm definitely coming down.' In fact, all the rowers attended.

The whole thing was appallingly stage-managed. In my view, that bad organization was probably responsible for the death of the Polish team manager, who died of a heart attack. It really surprised us that there was so little media interest in that incident.

We were all asked to gather in the adjacent baseball stadium, where instead of the normal military precision at these events it was absolute chaos. The British traditionally try to organize themselves so that the flag-bearer is followed into the parade by the team officials, then the women, smallest throughout to tallest, and the same with the men.

It's normally all quite regimented and ordered, but here the organizers, whether overwhelmed by the scale of the event or the number of athletes involved, failed to line everyone up correctly in order. Suddenly, someone started shouting, 'Go, go!'

We all ended up charging out of that stadium into the Olympic stadium, which was a fair distance. In the ensuing mayhem, the Polish team manager collapsed and died. We didn't find out until the following day, but we were stunned.

When we arrived in the stadium, the athletes, being fitter, were in front of the officials. I was somewhere in the middle of the group. I had the union flag shoved at me by someone, and as we entered the Olympic stadium we were just a disorganized rabble.

There just wasn't the sense of decorum or formality that I'd experienced at Barcelona. It seemed to affect the athletes. I remember Greg Searle and others started chanting 'Stevo, Stevo,' which was quite amusing, but just would never have happened four years earlier. They also all gathered around me, like bees round a honeypot, because they knew that the flag-bearer is always picked up on TV and they wanted their friends to see them back home. Despite all the mayhem, I couldn't resist my usual challenge to myself. This time, I decided to carry the flag out in front with my right hand, just to prove a point that it could be done with both arms.

After we won our heat, the media attention directed at Matthew and me was quite incredible; nothing like I'd ever experienced before. I realized for the first time how much interest had been generated in us. Four years previously at Barcelona, after our victory in the final, there had been no more than 30 people at the press conference, mostly British journalists, many of them former rowers, some of them internationals who'd been quite successful, but all old faces that we knew.

Here, after our heat at Atlanta, we were mobbed. I was shocked at how many people were there. There must have been a couple of hundred journalists. There was a press centre in an air-conditioned marquee away from the water-front. But David Tanner, who was responsible for the media, decided he did not want to move the journalists away from the lake-side because they would miss other races with British interest, so we were taken into the press tent overlooking the course.

It was the first time I'd seen the children for a week, although Ann had been with them daily because my parents had brought them along. I had Natalie and Sophie, one in each arm, and I could feel myself being pressed further and further back into a corner of this tent and felt really claustrophobic. I thought to myself, 'I can't handle this at the moment. I just don't want this.' I answered two or three questions and the girls started to play up, so I forced my way out and left Matthew there on his own.

I had never experienced that amount of pressure before. This little sport suddenly meant so much to other people. That's when it dawned on me how what I was trying to do as an individual, and Matthew and I as a pair, had captured the imagination of the media. Each day, it got worse. Two or three days before the final I could see myself blowing it by the sheer pressure I had been putting myself under by that ill-thought-out prediction after Barcelona.

The interest in us had gone from one extreme to another – from indifference to overkill.

I try to maintain a good relationship with the media. It's important for the sport, and the exposure I have had over the years has helped me. There have been one or two that have suggested that I'm a 'miserable bastard' or something similar. People close to me would probably say that's true! After Atlanta, there was one particular article in the *Guardian* by a woman writer which posed the question: why were Matthew and I so miserable? It accused us of being sullen and generally rude. I still don't really understand why. I tried to be as pleasant to her as I am to everyone else; it's the way I've been brought up.

That article didn't upset me; I just found it quite amusing. What did she expect us to be like? Cracking jokes like Frank Carson, relating anecdotes like Peter Ustinov? Most sportsmen and sportswomen tend to be more introverted than extrovert, with some obvious exceptions, of course.

Once we'd qualified for the semi-finals we had to wait while everyone else went out and did the repechage. We had to sit around watching everybody else strive for qualification, even though we knew that the crews in the repechage were not going to be our main rivals. Then we had to kill more time to when it really counted – the final. The waiting was the worst part. I used to hate it.

You've got so much time at the Olympics for waiting and thinking about what might happen. You'd get these thoughts as you walked around beforehand, such as, 'Physically, I just can't get in this boat and row,' but then I'd visualize myself doing it, as I've described earlier. It looked like Australia was going to be our main opposition, and I'd think, 'Right, if I'm out on the water, rowing along side by side, there's just no way they could beat us, there's no way I'm going to let them.' By doing that, I was safe, locked into my own environment, concentrating on the thing I knew best.

When the bomb exploded, it was on the eve of our final. We were nowhere near where it happened. Matthew and I were staying at a hotel at that stage, having departed the Olympic village because we were concerned that we might contract a viral infection, to which James Cracknell, another rower in our apartment, had already succumbed. As a consequence of this infection he was unable to race. Speculation that we left the village to avoid the transport problems was merely a smokescreen to prevent panic spreading through the entire British team. We arose at 5.30a.m. that particular day and turned on the television to find pictures of carnage and presenters telling us that 'a bomb has gone off at the Olympics'.

We had no idea of the scale of the blast, and in those circumstances you automatically assume the worst. Many thoughts go through your head. Some people assume that athletes are oblivious to the real world, and pretend that such political and global issues do not exist; that we are, essentially, only interested in our sport, and nothing else.

Not for a moment would I consider myself 'holier than thou' in that respect, but I do believe in surveying life from a wide perspective. I found that I started asking myself, 'Why are you are doing this when there are people losing their lives?'

Suddenly your sporting endeavours appeared so irrelevant and trivial in such a context. My immediate thought was that I must accept my share of responsibility for the bombing; that an event, of which we were admittedly only a small part, had given someone the opportunity to make a 'political' statement.

My assumption was that the whole thing would be cancelled, but an Olympic spokesman, interviewed on the news, soon reassured everyone that the Games would continue. For a moment, I considered whether I should carry on as though the deaths – of which there could have been tens, hundreds – had been a minor irritation. I just sat there, with the TV images in the background, thinking: 'Do you really want to go on? What is the whole point of actually racing and being part of all this?'

Then your rational side takes over, and you say to yourself: 'Well, if we don't go out and race, somebody else will. Somebody else will be Olympic champions in the coxless pairs that Matthew and I would feel we should have won. Somebody else is going to steal our glory.' If we didn't go ahead and row on a point of principle, what would that achieve?

It was not easy to switch back to the job in hand. All I could do was to psych myself up and just try to get on with what I do best. We went down to the course for our pre-race paddle, returned and were lying back in the rest tent. That was when my mind began playing its tricks again. I started thinking: 'What the hell are you doing this for anyway? This is absolutely crazy.' On top of my normal fears about the race, I still had no idea how many people had died, just that it had been a very crowded area. You imagined it was going to be hundreds killed, which thankfully wasn't the case. It wasn't easy to put all that out of my mind and focus. But I managed it.

Our final was first thing in the morning. On the way to the start, I heard Natalie shouting, 'Come on, dad.' That sent pins and needles up and down my spine. Hairs stood up on the back of my neck. Within the race, we didn't have any problems. I felt in control the whole time, although we did change race tactics because we got such a good start.

Originally, Matthew and I thought the third 500 metres was where we'd have to really push on to make sure we won the gold, but we didn't have to do that. What happened was that, at the start, our boat just shot away from everyone else. We had certainly been 'up for it', probably because of all the hype and the pressure. That just translated itself into sheer boat speed.

We were a length and a half up inside the first 45 seconds to a minute. The question in my mind was, 'What's going to go wrong?'

There was a possibility that we'd gone off too hard. We'd put too much energy in. We were not going to last the distance. I had to take that into account with all my commands. Anyway, we settled down into our race pace, and we were holding everybody. Nobody was coming back at us. We felt pretty comfortable and relaxed. But the energy can go without any warning. You never really know at what stage you will lose it.

When we passed 1000 metres, the point we'd trained for and discussed how we were going to push on, I said to Matthew, 'We're just going to maintain this speed.' It felt good and we had struck a smooth rhythm; there was no reason to try to extend the lead we already had, put more effort in, and die in the last 500 metres with everyone storming past us. So we rowed through the third 500 metres, came out of that still controlled, and I said, 'We're going to maintain this again.'

From 750 metres out, maybe 500 metres, but certainly before 250 metres, crews will always start picking it up, put everything into it; they'll go and go, right until the line. What happened here was that we came through with 500 metres remaining, and we were still in charge. I thought, 'No, this is good. We're going to stay at this speed.' I just said, 'We'll stay like this until 250.'

Now, 250 metres is 30–35 strokes from winning an Olympic gold; it's your final spurt. And we were still at our cruising speed. What happened was that the principal danger, the Australians, were increasing their rate and coming back at us. Only at that moment did we actually pick it up again, because they were coming back so quickly at us from about 350 metres. But never, at any stage, did I think, 'I'm knackered here. I'm never going to be able to keep this up.' It was totally controlled. It was covering tactics. The energy we had put in to get that lead at the start had to be paid back at some point. If we'd carried on our pre-race tactics, we could have died.

In fact, I don't think we would have done. I think we would have won by more. But we couldn't take that chance. People say, 'those Australians were close to you, and coming back.' I just reply, 'They weren't as close as they were at the start.' That's what's it's all about.

As we approached the finish at Lake Lanier, there was a tremendous roar from the 20,000 crowd, which included a lot of Britons. When we crossed the line in front, there was a real feeling of sheer relief that we'd achieved what we'd set out to do and that we hadn't let those people down. The further you get in your career, the worse

Toasting an honour. A proud occasion as my family celebrates the news that I have been awarded an MBE for services to rowing in the 1987 New Year's Honours List. Behind me are (from left) my wife Ann, my sister Christine, my father Geoff, my younger sister Jane, and my mother Sheila.

LEFT A profitable partnership. Andy Holmes and me in the coxless pairs at the 1986 Commonwealth Games.

RIGHT Family backing. My mother Sheila and my elder daughter Natalie, leading the cheering during the coxless pairs final at Atlanta, when I won my fourth gold. I doubt whether I would have achieved all that I did without my mother's support.

LEFT Victory salute at Seoul 1988. A gold for Andy Holmes and me in the coxless pairs.

ABOVE Medallion men. Andy and I show off our gold medals.

LEFT Hats off to Great Britain. A fantastic feeling as I carry the flag and lead the British team into the opening ceremony of the Barcelona Olympics in 1992.

RIGHT The golden boys. Matthew Pinsent and me with our medals after winning the coxless pairs at the Barcelona Olympics in 1992. It was my third, and Matthew's first, Olympic gold.

BELOW A deadly duo. Matthew Pinsent and me during the coxless pairs at the Barcelona Olympics in 1992. It was one of our finest performances together as we took gold.

ABOVE A picture for the world's media. Matthew Pinsent and I display
our golds after the coxless pairs final at Atlanta in 1996.
BELOW A great reception from our British supporters after we take gold
at Sydney in 2000.

ABOVE Made it! We cross the line in our final at Sydney's Penrith Lakes, beating the Italians by just .38 of a second. The Australians were third and the Slovenians fourth.

LEFT A study in concentration and determination as we repel the challenge of the Italians.

LEFT A wonderful feeling as we celebrate receiving our golds, which were presented by Princess Anne.

ABOVE An ecstatic moment. I come to terms with our achievement as
Matthew clambers up the boat to share his delight at winning gold.

the pressure becomes, especially when you've had a highly successful one like mine. Not only had we been favourites, but I was also
thinking: 'If I am going to walk away from it now, I don't want it
to be with a bad result.'

People say I looked absolutely shattered during and after the
race, but physically I felt really strong. It was, admittedly, a
different finish from Barcelona, where we had wanted to win by as
much as we possibly could, and did so by five seconds, and everyone said 'what a performance'. But two years afterwards, nobody
remembers how far you won by. As far as they were concerned, it
was a fourth Olympic gold for me, and a second for Matthew.

I was mentally exhausted more than anything. Because I'd convinced myself six or seven weeks beforehand that it was going to
be my last race, that's why I came out with that much-repeated
statement to Dan Topolski.

After Dan's brief interview, we paddled quietly back in front of
the grandstand to the medal rostrum. In the time between crossing
the line and the 10, 15 minutes it takes to get to the rostrum I saw
and heard Natalie and Sophie. Ann and I had promised to take
them to Disney World in Orlando. 'When are we going to see Mickey
Mouse?' Natalie was saying. 'When are we going?'

Ours were the first gold medals presented since the bomb had
gone off. I felt that the national anthem was being played for me
alone. It was a highly emotional moment.

After numerous TV, radio and press interviews, we were
whisked away to the BBC studios in Atlanta, to be interviewed by
Des Lynam. Then, finally, we were able to go out for a meal with
our families.

That was quite bizarre in itself. We went to a country club outside the city, recommended by the people with whom Matthew's
and my parents were staying. It was quite a staid jacket-and-tie
place. Because we had been conveyed in a mini-bus from one interview to the next we were still in shorts and tee-shirts. We walked
into this dining area and it all went deathly quiet. We were seriously under-dressed and we had obviously committed a major *faux
pas*. But then it was announced that we had won Olympic gold
medals, and the whole attitude changed. Everybody wanted to talk
to us, and the staff couldn't do enough for us. If there's one thing
the Americans like it's a winner.

Ann was still on duty as team doctor for another day, and the
children and I went to watch some of the races and had photographs taken of us and the family at the rowing venue. I had seen

little of the girls in the preceding 11 weeks, when I had been away at training camps in France and Canada, before heading for Atlanta. My parents had looked after them during the Games.

I valued greatly my family being with me at all my Olympics: Ann, the children, my parents and sometimes my sisters. They go through all the emotions that I do, and in a strange kind of way that is a comfort rather than a concern. We've always been a very close family, but when you're a close family living just down the road from each other, you don't see each other that often. We're not on top of each other. Jane, my younger sister, will perhaps pick me up from the airport sometimes, or look after our Old English sheepdog, Thea, while I'm away. That kind of thing. If we lived far apart, we'd probably all keep in contact more.

The biggest surprise for my sisters and me was when our parents moved to Spain in 1989 after my father retired. The timing was strange. It was just after Jane had her twins and mum had always wanted grandchildren. I couldn't believe that they would leave then. But my father, who had continued to do the odd piece of building work, buy an old house and do it up, or buy a plot of land and build a house, said he wanted to go somewhere warm. He liked the climate in Spain and was fed up with it here. Like his brother Bill, he'd always had itchy feet and wanted to travel.

They went out there to look at a plot of land between Alicante and Valencia. Oddly enough, my father came back a bit indecisive while mum was very keen. The upshot was that they had a house built out there. My mother actually got quite homesick, and I think it helped that they were able to follow me around Europe, wherever possible, in a small camper. Now they've bought a bigger one. They'd spend the winter in Spain, return here for Henley, then go to Lucerne, before travelling round the continent, often taking their grandchildren, and visiting World Championships and regattas. It meant they were away from Spain for the really hot part of the year, but enjoyed the benefit of a warm winter.

They sold that house in 1999, and bought one in England, but are renting it out. They still enjoy living out of their camper van. Even in retirement, my father has never lost his inclination for anything practical. He helped out with the construction of our current home and also with improvements to Ann's practice in Bourne End, about four miles from Marlow. He insisted on staying there overnight during the work, even though the roof was off. It was autumn time, but he'd sleep on a camp bed with just a few sheets over him looking at the stars through the roof. He wouldn't come and stay with us. He's very much a loner in some respects; a very quiet sort of man, who doesn't like to impose himself. But I've got tremendous respect for him.

When I used to work for him at about the time I started rowing seriously, he used to call me 'the foreman'. It was because I always had my hands in my pockets and never did any work. When he decided it was about time that I got my hands dirty, I'd say: 'I've got to go off rowing now, Dad,' and disappear. He's still very fit and will quite happily carry RSJs about and do all the work himself. He refuses to get somebody else in to do it unless absolutely necessary. I think in many ways I take after my father, although I'm a bit more outgoing, but that's because of my situation. I've had to be. I'm definitely more like him than like my mother.

Ten years ago, I would have said that my father wasn't emotional at all, but now I know that's not true. I wasn't there, but there was an incident at a reception given for us by the family who were looking after our children before semi-finals day at Atlanta.

Somebody mentioned me to my father, just something simple like 'How do you think he's going to do?' and he had to walk away because he was overcome with emotion. I've never seen my father in tears, or break down in any way. It made me realize that my parents are both struggling with the pressures of what I'm doing.

At the time, I was finding it hard to deal with the pressure I was under in Atlanta, and when I heard that I must admit I cried as well. I felt very emotional about the whole situation and what was expected of Matthew and me. It's very easy to look back now and think 'how stupid to let an event like the Olympic Games screw you up so much that you become emotional about it', but that's what it's all about. You feel so isolated, so helpless with all that expectation. Everything is on your shoulders and nobody else's. But that incident showed me that I was not the only person who was worried about the race. That thought helped me through it.

I know the pressures that Ann has to go through being team doctor, looking after the rest of the team as well as having me on the team and trying to be a wife to me. It's extremely difficult for her. It showed itself at the World Championships in 1998. Ann was being interviewed in the grandstand on the final day and she started crying; Natalie, who was then seven and getting to the age of understanding, was getting really upset and she was in tears, and I had to walk away. Yet, in a way, I was glad that I was not the only one getting in a state. And, for all that people believe that

I'm the epitome of composure and coolness before a race, in fact at an Olympics I'm the opposite.

After the Atlanta finals, my parents departed quite quickly. As we had the children back with us, it was not really practical for us to be involved in the second week of the Games. Two days after our event, I travelled down to Orlando with Ann and the children. We tried to follow what was happening in the Olympics on American TV which was virtually impossible. As far as the Americans were concerned, the rest of the world might as well not have been competing. I was interested in the men's tennis final, but had to ring the BOA in the Olympic village to find out that Tim Henman and Neil Broad had won one of eight silver medals and seven bronzes, which was the total of Britain's haul, other than our gold.

America's media coverage of sport makes an interesting comparison with ours. In Britain, if you do badly you get a real slating because there's nothing else for the media to talk about. If an American performs poorly, they're simply ignored because there's somebody else who's done well anyway. In a sense, as an athlete, I think I'd prefer receiving no publicity to a kick in the teeth.

I've always been fortunate in that I haven't often been ignored, and very rarely received a journalistic kicking. Few top British sportsmen can say that. It was probably because I was successful. I was cynical enough to realize that Matthew and me losing was always a bigger story than us winning, even though I found the concept obscene. Unfortunately, it's how we treat top sportsmen in this country.

It happened to me during 2000 in the build-up to Sydney. After our coxless four's first pre-Olympic event of the season, the first World Cup at Munich, there was one newspaper suggestion that I'd become the 'weak link' of the crew. That was far from the truth, but it did cross my mind that, for once, criticism was going to be levelled at me. Perhaps the media were bored with this notion of an invincible, awe-inspiring oarsman, and preferred instead to witness his downfall? I've always said that wouldn't bother me, anyway. I just hoped that continued to be the case as Sydney approached.

Frankly, I don't hark back to past glories much, nor do I dwell on disappointments, although it's all there in mental storage somewhere. It's the way I lead my life. Everything is about here and now. What's happening in the next 24 hours is what's important to me; not yesterday, not next week. Of course, I have revelled in the glow of satisfaction from winning each of those five gold medals, but only at the time; once it's over, that's it. The feeling died and all I had in mind was my next challenge. The only time that I really get nostalgic is every four years when I attend dinners, and fund-raising activities for the British Olympic Fund, and I meet other athletes there, both from the past and those from my own era.

Post-Atlanta, after returning to England from Orlando, I thought I'd made a terrible mistake in what I'd said to Dan Topolski. I knew for certain that I didn't really want to retire. I just wanted a long break. In fact, it was to be my longest period off the water in 21 years. When I did climb into a boat again on 1 December 1996, it gave me a comfortable feeling, like a baby that's been returned to its mother. This was a familiar environment and I felt pleased to be back. Ann was not so sure.

CHAPTER 19

HELL TO LIVE WITH

Few women would have supported me in my rowing career as Ann has, and I have always appreciated that. I'd go as far as to say that if I hadn't been with somebody who was a source of such encouragement and who was also a top-level sportswoman herself, I wouldn't have been able to achieve what I have done.

To look at it from the another viewpoint, if I'd been married to a woman not involved with sport at all, would I still have been allowed to do what I did for the 12 years leading up to Sydney? Would it have been acceptable to that woman? Or would our relationship have broken up because of the long periods of being apart, and the single-mindedness required to train seven days a week for 49 weeks a year, year in year out? Those are questions I have often thought about, but which are impossible to answer. Certainly, I don't know if I could have been such a bedrock to Ann if it had been the other way round. I like to think so, but you don't know.

Inevitably, we've had our difficulties over 12 years of marriage because of the pressures we are both under from time to time. There are inevitably going to be rough periods. It's reassuring to have Ann as the team doctor because I get to see her more often than I would normally. But when we're away on training camps and international events, I have to accept that she's not there for my benefit. She's working for the team. Sometimes, that can cause friction.

Some people say that when you get married you try to find a good mother figure. Although I never set out deliberately to find a person who fitted that description, Ann's certainly that. She's an excellent mother to our children.

The way we lead our lives has made our own relationship quite difficult at times, with me doing the amount of training that I had to do, and Ann also having her own business as well as being involved in the British rowing team. There were also the three children to consider, Sophie having arrived in February 1994, and Zak being born in February 1998. As if Ann and I didn't have a hectic enough lifestyle anyway, we seem to spend most of our spare time conveying the children round to different activities. It's what you have children for, and I wouldn't have it any other way, but at times it makes our own relationship very difficult. From my own point of view, I have had to juggle a family life and rowing, as well as public speaking and other engagements since I became successful. It seemed to take up all my time.

The worst thing is finding time to be together. When we had problems with our relationship, which we have in the past, we always used to agree that we'd do something together at least once a week. It would be just our time. Unfortunately, that's not realistic. So instead you'd say, 'OK, well, every two weeks, but it's got to happen.' You do that for a couple of weeks and that's it. You're back to where you were. If you're not careful, you begin to take each other for granted a lot of the time because of that lifestyle. That's obviously not good for a relationship.

I'm probably not the easiest person to get on with for the people who matter to me. Part of the reason is complacency. Being naturally quite lazy, I did my training, then went home, where I was quite happy to flop down in front of the TV. If you've been out to two or three business or charity dinners a week, you don't really want to go out and socialize again with your wife. However, Ann's stuck at home with the children a lot of the time and feels claustrophobic in that situation.

She suffers a lot from my lifestyle, and so do our friends. We don't get to see them as often as we'd like to. My close friends understand the situation really well. That's why they are my close friends. We can go a for long time without seeing them, but when we do it's like we've never been apart. It's never 'Hello, stranger, where have you been?' I get a lot of comfort from that. There's a sense of continuity, despite everything I've done.

I know that I can be quite irritating at times. In particular, Ann doesn't like being left in the dark about things. When I was training, I'd sometimes play golf afterwards and normally get back at, say, 3.30. Most of the time she would be reasonably happy with that. She might have had a moan and said, 'You're never around. You never look after the kids and I want to do some training. I'd like to go running' – that sort of thing. But basically she accepted it. It was when I didn't turn up as expected that Ann got annoyed.

When I first started the pairs with Matthew, when I was married but before we had kids, I used to go off and play golf quite regularly. Matthew and I spent time with each other a lot more than we do now. In recent years, if we did fit in golf, we usually had only a couple of hours, which wasn't really enough. We tried to sneak out as much as we could, even if it was for only a few holes. There was one occasion when we were scheduled to have three training sessions, but it was cut down to two. I didn't tell Ann that, and went to play golf during the afternoon. That evening, she asked me matter of factly, 'So how was golf?' I thought, 'How did she know?' There was no point denying it, so I said, rather tamely, 'Really good, actually,' and left it like that. But she wasn't very happy.

I wouldn't say that I was chauvinistic, more that I don't go out of my way to do the things that I know should be done. You wouldn't often find me going to the shops, for instance. Maybe if that's being chauvinistic, then I am. I see myself as being lazy, but if there were things that were absolutely imperative, I would do them.

In the evenings, Ann had to deal with a lot of the paperwork involved in her practice. She also had to return the many phone calls a week that she received from different rowers and other athletes who wanted to discuss problems they had. While she was doing all that, I watched the sport on TV. At 10 o'clock, I'd say: 'Right, I'm off to bed.' Meanwhile, she had to get all the uniforms out for the children, clean their shoes and do the ironing. If the children got up in the night, they didn't wake me, they woke her. At home, I generally had a very cushy life, while Ann had all the graft.

The other problem was that, because of my dyslexia, I found it quite difficult to write letters. That creates problems when you're self-employed and VAT registered. Ann had to do all her paperwork and quite a lot of mine as well. Now and again, I'd complain and say, 'Why hasn't this or that been done?' which also caused discord.

At end of the month, completing VAT returns is always a very stressful time. We'd have rows about getting it all completed. The demands that I was putting on Ann made it all quite difficult. Now Melanie, Adam Clift's wife and my personal assistant, deals with the accounts.

I know that my single-mindedness has, at times, put strains on the relationship and I'm not always the most communicative of husbands. Very occasionally, it has got that bit too much for Ann and she once chastised me with the words: 'Get out and do some work. You haven't done any for 20 years!' but I think it was said in irritation, rather than with real feeling.

According to Ann, in an interview she once did, it's 'too often been a "him and us" situation. He switches off and becomes very selfish. The first few weeks after an event are not very pleasant. He just wants to escape and do his own thing.'

Certainly, we have gone through some turbulent periods. But that's probably true of most relationships today because of all the pressures. In modern marriages, 12 years is quite a long time. From the outside people think, 'What a perfect relationship they have,' but the reality is not always what it appears. As people say, you have to work at a marriage. It doesn't just happen.

People might assume that we had most of our problems earlier in my career, when we had less money. But that was never a factor. In fact, things were very much easier then in a way. Money can cause problems because of all the side issues that go with it. It's one problem going without because you do not have enough money in your pocket; it's quite another having to give the VAT man a size-able amount of money that you've already spent!

Most relationships have problems when children come along. When you live with somebody, you are initially devoted to each other. Then, when you bring children into the equation, there are third, fourth and fifth parties involved, all competing with you for the mother's emotions. Inevitably, the mother is more intimately involved with the children in the early stages, certainly when they're very young and dependent on the mother. All our three were breast-fed.

As the male, you sometimes feel left out and, however hard you try to rationalize it, that causes friction within the relationship. For the man that's the hardest part about having children. It had all appeared so perfect; you have found the person that you want to spend the rest of your life with, you've had children that you both always wanted as well. Yet the ground rules have suddenly changed. You are no longer the priority in your partner's life. It's understandable, but I found it hard to come to terms with that fact.

It was not such a problem with our first child. We carried on our lives very much as normal when Natalie came along. It was when our second child was born that the problems started. By that time, Natalie was getting to an age of being quite active, and looking after her and a new baby, Sophie, took up Ann's time even more. Then a third child, Zak, made it even more difficult. As I write, our children's ages range from 10 to three. The demands are very different. It takes a long time to realize that.

A relationship subtly changes as the children are born. You find yourself in conflict with your emotions. Their birth gives you great joy and each one was a thrill. Yet you're saying to yourself: 'I don't want our lives to change. I want everything to stay as it was.' As their grandparents say, 'It's nice to have grandchildren because it means that you can give them back when you want to.' As parents, you've got them all the time. I would imagine that a lot of relationships struggle through that period of starting families.

Things did look quite bleak for a while, and we've gone through some seriously tough times, although never bad enough for us to contemplate splitting up. Ann and I were both quite determined to get through it, which I think we've done.

When we first discovered that Ann was pregnant with Natalie in late 1990, it was a thrilling moment, but also a considerable shock. It wasn't planned at all, other than the fact that we knew we both wanted children at some time. We both assumed that it would happen when my rowing career was over. Mind you, at that stage, I had no idea that I would still be rowing 10 years later...

We thought it would be difficult to carry on as we had. That proved to be true. But in my case, Jurgen was extremely flexible. It was only between Barcelona and Atlanta that it started to become an issue as far as training went. Ann's busy morning was Thursday, and I would take Natalie to a gym class once she reached the age of two. We wanted Natalie to do that, in fact all three children have. That meant rearranging our training schedules, which was not entirely popular. I just had to tell Jurgen that it was a fact of life, those were the things that had to be done, and everything had to be adapted around it.

Once we'd had Natalie, I thought, 'I'm happy with one, that'll do.' Then another one came along. Then another. Ann's always made it clear that she wanted more than one or two. Only recently, she's been saying, 'Shall we have any more kids?' And I reply, 'In some ways it'd be nice, and in other ways, no.' We're not getting any younger.

Now Zak has started to sleep through the night, it's made a tremendous difference to Ann's life and our relationship. Having had years of my sleep broken up by babies, do we want to go through that traumatic period again? It wouldn't be until they go to university, or leave home, that you can start having a normal life together again.

That could be 19, 20 years away. I'll be very surprised if we have any more. For the first time, Ann's given me the inkling that she's not quite so sure.

Ann doesn't really like the limelight. She'll be around at rowing championships, but does not want to be in photographs, and avoids them if she can. I can understand that, although my first thought after a major win is of Ann and the children. I want to share my triumphs with them, and of course the occasional defeats. They're always there. As far as I'm concerned, it's us as a family achieving something. It's a whole family effort, although the kids are a bit young to realize it at the moment.

Natalie and Sophie missed three weeks of school to be at Sydney. Natalie was not entirely certain about that. She's a bright girl who enjoys school. Initially she wasn't sure if she wanted to come to the Olympics. But it was important to me that she was there, together with the rest of the family.

The children were with us in Australia up until we moved into the Olympic Village two weeks before the Olympic final. In the build-up to a major event, I valued that because it brought an air of normality to my preparations and was what I was used to. If you've got to go and change nappies or try to stop your children pestering other members of the team, it helps you keep your feet on the ground. Also, perhaps it means that you have less time to think about what lies ahead.

In the months before the Olympics, I hardly stopped thinking about our coxless four final; not a day passed without me contemplating how it was going to turn out, who our rivals might be, what their tactics would be. Those thoughts just kept multiplying the closer we got to it.

In the immediate build-up to a championship, it's sometimes not been easy for the children. They found it difficult that one day everyone appeared so nice and relaxed and wanted to play and another day, when things had not gone so well rowing-wise, they didn't want to know.

But generally, most people, including the team manager, David Tanner, have said they liked having the children around because it made for a more pleasant atmosphere. It ensured that the athletes were not quite so intense.

In training camps, there was plenty of space, so the children were not too much of a distraction for the other rowers. You weren't on top of each other. There has always been a policy with training camps, certainly since I've been involved, that nobody goes with their other half. Even when I went away, I shared a room with Matthew and spent most of my time with him. I wasn't with Ann, although I could go and see her when I wanted to.

Everybody accepted that I was on the team and everybody wanted Ann to be the team doctor. If that was the case, then everybody had to accept that my family had to come along. Because we were away for such a long period of time, that was the accepted norm. To my knowledge nobody ever said, 'This isn't right.'

Once inside the Olympic Village, however, I had to put the children to the back of my mind until it was all over. That may sound rather uncaring, but that's the way it had to be during that time. My thought processes had to be entirely focused on rowing.

Returning to the end of 1999, as the calendar turned to the new millennium, the year of Sydney, I thought ahead to the Games and didn't feel any great emotion at all. But I knew that once I arrived there and the expectations of millions of people were accompanying us, expecting us to win, the pressure would have built to fever pitch.

We would be favourites in probably 95 per cent of people's minds, even if we had not been going that well and had lost all the regattas in the meantime. When you're under such intense stress, your true emotions will emerge, even if normally you are very British and reserved.

The stress of what I went through was even harder for the family. Every day, I went out there and was in control of my destiny. They felt the tension, but were not in control of it. It's a bit like the driver of a bobsleigh and his team. I decided what to do and when. The family were like the brakemen. If I were to crash, they would suffer just as much as me.

CHAPTER 20

A NEW CREW,
A FRESH CHALLENGE

While Britain's Olympic team had little to boast about at Atlanta, Ireland certainly did. Michelle Smith, now de Bruin, had won three golds in the swimming pool and, despite being the subject of much innuendo about her miraculous improvement in form, she was greeted as a national heroine back in Dublin. There was an estimated crowd of 50,000 including the Irish Prime Minister.

Ann and I were met at Gatwick by my mother, my sisters, my brother-in-law and my niece and nephew. Yet, in a way, it was the people of Marlow who meant most to me. A procession was organized in my honour, starting at the Barn Club in Marlow Bottom, passing through the High Street in Marlow, and ending on a boat on the Thames. I was more confident about making a speech than I had been back in 1984. I said that I was born and bred in Marlow and very proud of that. 'And I'm going to stay here.' Later, I attended a reception in London, where I met the 1932 coxless four gold medallist Roland George, then 91. He had won his gold in Los Angeles after he and his crew had taken 10 days to get there, five of which were spent crossing the desert in fierce temperatures.

Despite my low-key arrival, though, I soon found that I had been elevated to a sporting celebrity. Not one mobbed and besieged by fans outside my house, but the favourite, according to the bookmakers, to lift the BBC's 'Sports Personality of the Year' trophy for 1996, presented in December. It actually became quite an issue. In November, *Rowing Magazine*, edited by the *Guardian*'s rowing correspondent Christopher Dodd, devoted its front cover to the programme with a plea to its readers to 'Vote! Vote! Vote Redgrave X'. The BBC got sniffy and its then sports publicity officer, Jenny Hickman, now Jenny Searle (wife of Greg), said in the *Daily Mail*, 'Campaigning distorts voting. We just want it to be fun.' Chris responded, 'It's is my duty to encourage everyone to acknowledge his feat.' Then the *Sporting Life* pitched in, suggesting that 'Steve is not a life-and-soul-of-the-party character', unlike racing's beloved Frankie Dettori. Neither of us won. The winner was Damon Hill. I came second.

I have found the winners of the award a bit perverse at times. We're a nation that seems rather embarrassed by our successes and we give awards because somebody has had the bad luck of a tyre blowing up in Adelaide, and not completing. We prefer heroic failures. We also go for those who get a lot of air-time on TV.

From now on, we'll probably get more footballers winning now that votes are also allowed by e-mail and telephone. In the old days, voters had to write out and send coupons from the *Radio Times*. I think that will have the effect of pushing out the minority sports. I hope I'm not being churlish to suggest that, until Sydney, I've always done better in the sports writers' awards because they know more about the overall picture of sport than simply what people are shown on TV.

In fact I get very frustrated with the BBC's 'Sports Personality of the Year' because I think it should be a 'Sports Achievement of the Year' award, like the one they have in Australia. They don't care if you've won an Olympics, a World Championship, or even a domestic title. If you have performed to an outstanding level, you'll be recognized for that. And it doesn't matter which sport you're involved in.

What happens in Britain is that a two-hour programme is dominated by the domestic seasons of football, rugby, cricket, and our international failures, and then they say, 'By the way, we've got 54 world champions this year', and they're all crammed into a two-minute slot. Despite finally winning in 2000, after 16 years of turning up, as I joked to the audience, I still feel that I should not have been honoured in that way. The BBC's annual award should be for achievement and in 2000 that shouldn't have been awarded to me. I was just one of four oarsmen in our crew, one of whom, James Cracknell, actually won more than me last year, and there were other British gold medallists. If there was an award for outstanding lifetime achievement, that's fine. That said, I regard it as a great honour, particularly coming from a sport which is not a major media attraction.

One of my favourite moments, however, was when, at the 1999 Sports Review of the Year, Muhammad Ali was named 'Sports Personality of the Century'. Though I have reservations about boxing as a sport, I have great respect for him. I was brought up in that era when he was in action and used to see many of his fights. It was the charisma of the guy. He always seemed to be such big news. It was his cockiness the public loved. People get annoyed with the way Prince Hamed regards himself, and it was the same with Chris Eubank, too, but Ali always got away with it because he had style.

It was very special at the end of 1999 being in a room with mainly sports people and experiencing the aura Ali created around him when he entered it. It was the same sort of atmosphere he brought to the Atlanta opening ceremony. You felt his presence. It was even more intimate at that BBC review. I enjoyed it greatly.

There were so many people who just wanted to meet him and shake his hand. I've always respected him, but I didn't expect others to see him in the same light. It's not just because of what he's achieved in boxing, but in all sorts of different ways. Like refusing to fight in Vietnam and being shunned by his boxing association and by some of his countrymen; though it turned out that he was supported by public opinion on the question of the war.

Ilie Nastase came up afterwards because they were apparently quite good friends at one time. They were sitting very near me. Ilie said, 'Do you remember me?' He was getting a bit concerned that he was not getting the message through. Ali's face is so blank these days because of his Parkinson's disease. You don't know whether he's taking it in. Ali's wife said, 'Yes, he remembers you and he wants you to kiss him on the cheek.' His mind is still very sharp. You can understand the frustration he must have with his own body; possessing the intelligence, but not being able to communicate it.

The morning after that I was presented with the Sports Writers' Association award of 'Sportsman of the Year'. That was one of many accolades. I was nominated for the 'UNICEF Sportsman of the Century' award in the water sports category, and received one of the 'People of the Year' awards at the Hilton Hotel. I was also named with Richard Branson, Maurice Saatchi and Tessa Sanderson as a possible 'Motivator of the Year' by one magazine. I was even in *She* magazine, listed among 'Sporty Sexy' men, which is not to brag but to illustrate how I had finally made that breakthrough in terms of public perception. Suddenly, I was overwhelmed with requests to appear on all kinds of television programmes. I was a mystery guest on the BBC's *They Think It's All Over*, and on *Noel's House Party*. I was also asked to support numerous charities, including a SportsAid Ball, Comic Relief, Henley Alternative

Regatta – dragon boat racing – for a cancer charity, and one particularly dear to my heart, the National Association for Colitis and Crohn's Disease.

I was also asked to play in a number of golf tournaments, which pleased me greatly. In Atlanta year, I took part in a Pro-Am contest with Sam Torrance before the British Masters at Collingtree Park, Northampton.

I was asked to appear on the National Lottery show. There I got a major surprise. Or should have done. It all began when Ann and the children and I went down to Orlando after the Olympics. Athole Still's daughter Roxane had called the apartment we were at and spoken to Ann, who has a habit of doodling when she's on the phone. Without realizing it, she had written 'This Is Your Life' on the pad. When I saw it, I didn't have to be a nuclear physicist to work out that I was due to become a recipient of Michael Aspel's big red book.

That night in bed, I said casually, 'Oh, when are they going to record the programme?' She said, 'What programme?' I said, 'This Is Your Life.'

'What are you talking about?'

I said, 'You wrote it on the pad.' Ann couldn't believe it. She thought she'd be in big trouble, because the subject isn't supposed to know in advance. I said that I wouldn't let on that I knew as long as she kept me informed about what was going on, because I hate surprises.

It was never mentioned again until several weeks later when a trailer for the programme appeared on TV. I asked if there had been any developments. Ann said 'No,' and stupidly I believed her! That was on the Wednesday. On the Saturday, Matthew and I went down to Southampton for an event staged by Canada Life, our Olympic sponsors, and then appeared at the Boat Show for our boat manufacturers, Aylings. Finally, we were driven to the *Lottery Live* programme, on which we had been asked to appear. I thought it was a National Lottery car driving us around. But it wasn't, it was from *This Is Your Life*.

Bob Monkhouse was compering the *Lottery Live* programme. He was dropping hints all over the place, and I just did not pick up anything at all. He kept telling the audience that at three minutes past eight 'there's going to be a really big surprise, but I can't tell you much at the moment'. It really didn't click ... until Michael Aspel walked in the door with his red book. Then I knew it was for me. If I hadn't been forewarned, I would have assumed it was for someone else.

I was taken to Teddington, where the programme was recorded. I hadn't seen Ann all day. One of the first people they bring out is your wife. I went up to her, gave her a kiss and a hug, and whispered 'You bastard' in her ear. You could just about hear it, too.

I wouldn't have liked it if it had been a complete surprise and I have to say I did enjoy it. Fortunately, I recognized all the voices! The last guest they brought on was Pertti Karppinen, which was a nice touch. The story was told of how I met him for the first time in the drugs testing room in 1984 after our Olympic triumphs.

It was on *This Is Your Life* that Ann confessed that she hoped I wouldn't carry on rowing and would lead a normal life – whatever that is – but by that time I had already made my mind up to aim for Sydney. I'm sure she was aware deep down that I would continue. What she missed most was our spending weekends with the children. Very occasionally we did get a Sunday off, but that was rare. When I *was* at home on a Sunday, it was very noticeable how much she appreciated the family atmosphere. However, the reality was that even if I had been home every Sunday, I'd have done a bit more with the family, but not much. I'd have ended up cutting the grass or tidying the garage. I wouldn't necessarily have been kicking a ball with the children.

I've never felt guilty about the kind of father I am. Why should I? I saw and still see the children a lot more than most fathers. I am around the home more than the fathers who commute to London from our area. My children were up before I left in the morning, and I was there when they got back from school. The only difference was that I might go away for a three-week period, or 10 days, or long weekends. But that didn't happen often. They know who their father is; other dads commute to and from London while their kids are in bed, so they don't see them half as much of their families as I do.

The other advantage of my occupation – with my Lombard sponsorship and other spin-offs of the Olympic campaign – has been that I've been able to bring financial stability to the family. That hasn't always been the case by any means, and certainly wasn't when we first got married.

I have the BBC sports presenter Steve Rider to thank the original contact with Lombard. We had been talking about sponsorship during a game of golf, and as Steve had been involved with Lombard when they backed the RAC Rally, he suggested they sponsor Matthew and me. Practically within a week they had agreed terms and, after Athole had completed the negotiations, a deal was signed worth one million pounds, including bonuses, over four years.

Brand exposure was one of the main reasons Lombard entered into the sponsorship, but the company couldn't believe the amount of coverage it received in prime media. Over the four years Lombard estimates that the company received an eight-fold return on its million-pound investment. Lombard also saw the sponsorship as a way of motivating the company's employees; judging by the enthusiastic reception we got at staff events, it worked.

When I first decided to continue to Sydney, I hadn't thought about what kind of boat it'd be in. I still thought that there was a bit more to come from Matthew and me in the coxless pair. However, Matthew was quite emphatic when told my decision by Jurgen, 'I don't want to carry on in a pair. I want to do something different.' He was right. We discussed it on the way to a function and we were both keen to do a four. I had been doing the coxless pair for the last 10 years, and we'd been competing in it for six years with each other. I still felt that we could go faster and achieve more, but it was the right time to try a new challenge. As I told journalists at the press conference to reveal the new crew, 'A four can give us more variety, enthusiasm and drive.'

Of the oarsmen from the Atlanta Olympic team, the principal candidates to make up the four, apart from Matthew and me, were James Cracknell, Tim Foster and Greg Searle. James, who had been on the senior team for five years, after winning a gold in the coxless fours at the 1990 World Junior Championships, had gone down with tonsillitis on the day of the opening ceremony at Atlanta and was unable to take part in the double sculls. Tim and Greg had been in the coxless four crew that won bronze at Atlanta, together with Greg's brother Jonny, and Rupert Obholzer. Greg had ruled himself out because he had decided to concentrate on single sculling. That left four contenders, including Matthew and me. However, it was not a foregone conclusion. We all still had to go through a winter of training and assessment, and undergo trials at Nottingham's Holme Pierrepont course before the four was officially named.

As a group we went to Hazewinkel, Belgium, for the final selection, and Jurgen swapped people around to determine what combinations worked. Unfortunately, I came down with appendicitis and was in hospital during that period. In my absence, it was decided that the four would be me, Matthew, Tim and James.

When we returned there was more mixing and matching. First Matthew was in the stroke seat and I was at three, but that didn't work well. Then we tried James at stroke. It wasn't bad but didn't really gel. Finally we came up with the combination that went to Sydney: Matthew at stroke, Tim at three, me at two and James at bow. Traditionally, in a four, the oarsmen are positioned alternately on either side: bow and number three on bowside and number two and stroke on strokeside. However, our new combination meant that we had the two bowside oars rowing next to each other in the middle of the boat. The theory is that it's more efficient from a racing point of view. The forces are more likely to make the boat move in a straight line.

Our first race as a four in 1997 was at Munich. It was the first round of the inaugural World Cup, an event which had replaced the old international regattas. There was a very strong head-wind, and it was quite rough, particularly off the start. We had Poland in our heat, an inconsistent crew, but they had been world silver medallists, so it was a fair test. We just moved straight into the lead, right from the start, and dominated the race. We competed in the final the following day, beating Germany by a comfortable length and a half. It was the perfect start.

Three weeks later, we moved on to Paris. The French, who had been silver medallists at the Olympics, had been absent at the first World Cup. Obviously, they would compete in their home event. We expected them to be reasonable. Conditions were the complete opposite of those in Munich and there was a strong tail wind. In the final, we established a slight lead, the French came back at us, but we stayed a few feet in front of them. In the second half of the race, it was very rough, but we concentrated on maintaining a clean technique. We felt quite comfortable, although it was actually quite close by the end. It made us firm favourites for the third, and final, World Cup event at Lucerne, which we duly won.

In the meantime we rowed at Henley and were successful there, too. The first season had gone just about perfectly, with only the World Championships remaining. Matthew and I had taken the view at the start that, if the four didn't work out, we had the option of moving back into a pair for the Sydney Olympics. However, we had quickly discovered that the four had the potential to win the World Championships and Olympics.

The 1997 World Championships were held at Lac d'Aiguebelette in France. On the day that we arrived and started racing we learned of the death of Diana, Princess of Wales, in a car crash in Paris. It was an extraordinary period. We knew what was happening because of the news programmes we were receiving. But because we were also isolated from all the reaction to it, it was a very surreal experience.

It evoked similar thoughts to when I heard about the bomb in Atlanta. It makes you realize that what you do is actually a very insignificant act on the world stage. What you are doing doesn't really affect that many people's lives. In comparison, Diana had touched many people in her too-short life. Not many people in the world wouldn't have heard of her. A small percentage of the world know what we do.

You have to respect everything she did. I never met her personally, but she was around the same age as me, so to me it was a tragically short life. She was such a public figure worldwide. Everyone knew what pressure she was under with the break-up of her marriage, and media-wise she had been such a significant personality, right from word of her engagement. Overall, I believe she handled herself very well in a very difficult situation, considering her personal problems. She still put a lot of energy into her various charities and appeals.

All sport in Britain was cancelled on the Saturday, the day of her funeral, which also coincided with our World Championship final. There were suggestions in some quarters that we shouldn't take part, as a mark of respect, or that the competition should be delayed. However, the event continued as normal.

When the FA cancelled all the football games on the Saturday, that was perfectly understandable. But we were abroad, in a World Championship. Just because something traumatic happens in your own country you can't expect the rest of the world to stop whatever it's doing.

For us, that day was so important. Our sponsorship, our rankings in the world, all revolved around that one moment in the year. The sports fixtures back home were merely rescheduled. That was impossible for us. I think we handled the situation well. The funeral was going on at the time we were warming up for the final, and we had our own one-minute silence. We sat motionless on the water. We were very distant from what was going on back home; yet, for us, it was very emotional.

The race itself went very well. Having cruised through the heats and semi-final, we dominated all the boats in the final. The French were runners-up, and the Italians third. Messages were emanating from Australia, home of the self-styled 'Oarsome Foursome' – who had 'retired' after winning their second Olympic gold at Atlanta – about how impressed they were that we could go out really hard, take a lead, but not suffer from the speed we'd put into it, and take control. Then we could move on again within the middle of the race.

That was the best we'd raced since we'd been together. But it had to be put into perspective. It was only a year on from the Olympics, a point when the standard is traditionally at its lowest. Crews always get more focused as the Olympics approach.

By the end of the 1997 season, the Australian four were saying that they were going to return and race in another Olympics. That didn't entirely surprise me. As it transpired, they were beaten at their trials and decided to do a coxed four at the next World Championships, and then split up into a coxless and coxed pair.

After those 1997 World Championships, we had our usual three-week break before starting back in winter's training again ready for our second season. I spent a week at home. Then Ann and I went to the Bahamas for a fortnight, leaving the children with my parents. The weekend I came back from that holiday, we arrived on the Saturday morning and I spoke at a Thames Tradesmen's Rowing Club supper that evening. On the Sunday lunchtime we went to a 60th birthday party for my former coach, Mike Spracklen, just outside Wallingford.

In the evening, we were supposed to go down to a wedding reception in London. But we were both so exhausted we decided not to go, particularly as training started again on the Monday. On that first day back I came down to Leander, did two quite light sessions, and then went home. I had a terrible thirst and just started drinking pint after pint of blackcurrant juice. It was clear that something was not right. Your immediate assumption is that it's a combination of the first day of training, a change of situation. In fact, that had nothing to do with it.

It was the beginning of a period that was to test the patience and resolve of all of our crew, and our coach.

CHAPTER 21

DEPTHS OF DESPAIR

I was desperately worried that October day in 1997 when I drove to High Wycombe to see a specialist named Ian Gallen. There are always urine-testing strips around the house – we use them at training camps to test for dehydration – and I knew enough about the possibilities to check myself for sugar in the urine. I had tested positive and that almost certainly meant one thing: diabetes. I also understood enough about the condition to fear that it would be the end of my career because my lifestyle would have to change so radically.

I was aware that some sportsmen, such as footballer Gary Mabbutt and cricketer Wasim Akram, suffered from the condition, but with due respect to them, their sports didn't require anything like the energy levels that mine did. And energy was going to be the crucial factor if I was to continue.

Three per cent of the UK population have been diagnosed with diabetes, about 1.4 million, and there are probably the same number again who are unaware they have it. Everybody knows of somebody who suffers from the condition. Diabetes mellitus, Latin for sugar and syphon, is a deficiency in insulin, the hormone secreted by the pancreas. Without insulin, the cells of the body, particularly muscle and fat cells, are unable to take up sugar from the blood. The blood sugar concentration becomes abnormally high and sugar is excreted in the urine. It can lead to minor symptoms such as excessive thirst and dehydration, passing abnormal quantities of urine and weight loss, or to more traumatic effects.

In fact diabetes is the single biggest cause of blindness among adults of working age; it also increases the chance of heart disease, can cause kidney damage and can affect the circulation in the feet so severely that amputations might eventually be required.

There are two types of diabetes. Type 1 is usually associated with the young, and those suffering from it are insulin-dependent for the rest of their lives. Type 2 is called late-onset diabetes; it can often be hereditary, and occurs when the supply of insulin is deficient. Both are incurable, but they are treatable. There is a history of diabetes in my family: my grandfather developed type 2 in old age. When I first had medication for colitis in 1992, I had been warned that I might become diabetic in later life. I always assumed that if I ever suffered from the condition it would be in my seventies or eighties, like my grandfather. Not at my age then, 35. Initially, it was thought that I had type 1, until it was found that I was still producing some of my own insulin. So it is now thought that I have type 2.

Type 2 diabetes is normally treated by a strict diet, a campaign of weight loss and decreasing the intake of sweet foods, or possibly by slow-release medication. The diet means restricting yourself to the suggested maximum of 2000 calories a day by reducing saturated fats and severely reducing your intake of sugar while increasing the amount of carbohydrates, like pasta, potatoes and bread, you consume. If I had been someone in a normal sedentary occupation, that would have been no problem. But such a regime immediately created difficulties for me. My energy levels dropped drastically, and I began to feel quite ill and sorry for myself.

At the end of November, we were scheduled to go out to a training camp near Cape Town. Before leaving, I went for an early season medical screening at the British Olympic Medical Centre at Northwick Park Hospital in north-west London. That is something we do regularly, anyway, but on this occasion it was for my own peace of mind. I wanted to know how my body was coping with the diabetes physiologically. It was the worst test I had ever done by a long way, but I was expecting that.

One of my immediate problems was that there was no real medical expertise on diabetes and rowing, presumably because, if you're suffering from the one condition, you normally don't carry on with the other. That made it very difficult to start with. Initially, I just ran out of energy and was not performing well.

However, I remained optimistic because I was told that, although, physiologically, there were no records of anyone having continued to perform at the top level, there was no reason why I shouldn't. It would not be easy, though.

The problem was trying to get enough energy inside me to feed the demands that I have without it dangerously affecting my sugar levels. Somebody training two, three or even four times a day in a sport like rowing needs enormous funds of energy. I was told that

I required a 6000-calorie diet, and that's a huge amount of food. You've got to have quite a lot of sweet foods and for a diabetic that's pretty difficult. This is an idea of the typical daily diet that was necessary to maintain the energy levels I required for training and racing. I started with a large bowl of cereal at breakfast, perhaps four Weetabix; between our first two sessions I had a bowl of porridge with a lot of brown sugar, or scrambled eggs on toast and a large jug of juice; then between the next two sessions, I had soup followed by a large pasta dish and a pudding with another jug of juice; back home I may have had toast or malted loaf and then for my main meal, the biggest of the day, I'd have, say, spaghetti bolognese followed by rice pudding or apple pie and ice-cream; I'd have more cereal before going to bed. When I was out driving and stopped for petrol, I'd invariably pick up some chocolate or doughnuts as well. Alcohol was generally ruled out, although if I was at a dinner, I might have a glass of champagne or wine.

My problem was being able to get enough insulin into my system to counter the effects of what I ate. With the help of Ian Gallen, I worked out a system of controlling my blood sugar levels, without the need to change my diet drastically. It involved injecting myself subcutaneously, normally in the abdomen, with insulin six times a day. I did the injections so discreetly that people rarely knew that I was doing it, even at a dinner.

However, it is more complicated than that, for a simple reason. Intensive exercise, like the training I did, brings blood sugar levels down considerably, anyway. Therefore it was a constant juggling act with my metabolism. If there was too much insulin in my body when I was training hard, my blood sugar levels could decrease so low that I began to feel vague.

If your blood sugar levels drop too low, without taking any preventative action – usually eating chocolate or having a sweet drink – you suffer from hypoglaecemia, or a 'hypo' as it is usually known. Without treatment that can eventually lead to a coma, and even death. I have had those symptoms only twice, and fortunately never on the water.

From that initial diagnosis, I have had to carry with me, at all times, a blood glucose monitor, a device for pricking my finger, a syringe and a supply of insulin. It was a question of balance, of understanding diabetes and getting things right. It has been a complicated business, and certainly no easy matter.

That training camp near Cape Town was a real struggle. It was land-based, which meant that it consisted predominantly of working with weights, on rowing machines, and cycling. Despite feeling very low, I took great pride in the fact that I did every session in Jurgen's programme, even the cycling. I have never been a great cyclist. It is not my forte, especially uphill. If I can hang on to the group, then I've normally got a good finish. At previous camps, I would stay with the others, albeit at the back, but here I struggled to stay with them at all and did most of the sessions on my own, which makes it even more difficult. If you're with a group, even at the rear, you have the advantage of 'slipstreaming', but here I was exposed. There was no respite.

At somewhere like Tallahassee, in Florida, which is virtually flat, there is not so much of a problem, but here it was all steep hills and I felt very ill. It was out at that camp that I descended into such despair that I had a long telephone conversation with Ann, who brought some light to my dark mood.

One day was particularly bad. It was a long-distance session which started with an uphill climb, and, within five minutes of starting, I got a puncture. I repaired it, but by then I was well behind. I eventually caught the others because they had stopped for a break. Jurgen accompanied us with a van containing liquid and food. But I decided that I wouldn't have a break myself, but just grabbed a banana and carried on so that I could continue with the group. At least I had the relief of a long downhill stretch.

At the bottom of the hill, I got another puncture. The rest disappeared into the distance once more. Again, I repaired it. Then Jurgen appeared. He was quite well aware of how hard I had been struggling, of course. He told me to put the bicycle in the van, and call it a day. But I refused. I insisted that I would complete the session. I just had to do it. I knew there was no quality about the session I was doing, but I refused to yield and take the easy way out. In fact, there were only two of us who completed every cycling session, Matthew, the best in the group, and myself.

That whole period, from then until early in the New Year, was a complete nightmare for me. There was an obvious connection between the two illnesses. Colitis is stress-related. When I was diagnosed with diabetes, it was a pretty stressful situation. Undoubtedly, it had caused a flare-up of the colitis. I continued to complete all the training that I was supposed to do, but I knew that I could not carry on like this.

When I returned from South Africa I went for another series of tests at the British Olympic Medical Centre. I was at my lowest ebb, physically and mentally. I thought that the results would be awful, even worse than the start of the season. In fact, although they weren't brilliant, they weren't as bad as they might have been. However, that didn't alter the fact that I just didn't have the energy I required.

Jurgen told me that I didn't have to do the sculling trials that we normally do before the turn of the year, but to continue on my own training regime, and try to sort out my problems.

I had been advised to have more tests done on the colitis. The last biopsies of the large intestine had involved four samples, but this time they took 12. The specialist was concerned that some spots he had found on my intestines might indicate that I had Crohn's disease, which is related to colitis, but even more chronic. They gave me an anaesthetic but it was still a thoroughly unpleasant experience. Driving back from London, I had to stop on the M4 to throw up, and Ann took over the driving. I was very low. I was so dejected that it was the only time in my rowing career that I went AWOL. Ann and I had actually planned a holiday some time before, and we just went off without telling Jurgen and the rest of the boys.

I didn't tell Jurgen where I was going or when I'd be back. I just disappeared. In fact, I went away for two weeks on a skiing holiday with the family. One of Ann's sisters and my old friend Eric Sims came along as well. It was on that holiday that I took a long hard look at the future. That first week away, I felt awful. It was as if everything was conspiring against me and I knew that I was not producing the level of performances that were adequate. One illness I could deal with. But two was proving too great an obstacle. It was the lowest point of my career, other than 1985, when I'd had that back problem.

I can't say that I actually considered giving up the sport to which I had dedicated my life. It was more a case of it quitting me. It was not me saying to myself, 'OK, I've given it a good go, I think I'll stop.' It was simply that I was not performing at levels that justified me being a top athlete. My performances in training were not just below par – we all go through that from time to time – but were really poor. This is no disrespect to them, but at the time I would have struggled to win a place in the women's team. In fact, I was barely up to ordinary club standard.

But I was lifted somewhat by the news from my specialist when I phoned him from the resort. The tests had shown that symptoms I had been experiencing, which were slightly different from the original ones, *were* colitis, and the spots had proved negative. I felt reassured by that, and immediately began taking a new course of tablets which I had been prescribed, and only a week later I was feeling better within myself.

When I returned, Jurgen made no comment about me disappearing. I think he was waiting to see how I performed in some pairs trials. In fact, although I was bottom of the four of us, we were all well clear of everybody else in the British squad. I was pleasantly surprised with that, and so was he.

Altitude training doesn't help with control of the condition, as I was to find in February 1998 when we had a camp at the Drakensberg Mountains, near Johannesburg. There, we raced in the Riviera Vaal Regatta in the pair and in the coxless four. But I returned early, because Ann was just about to give birth to our son, Zak. As I did so, Jürgen was about to become embroiled in controversy.

The rowing community had been shaken by another kind of problem completely. It was as I returned from that training camp that we all became aware that the *Mail On Sunday* had published some serious allegations against Jurgen. The paper reported that files kept by East Germany's reviled Stasi Security Police had revealed the extent of the Communist regime's use of illegal drugs in sport. Jurgen was accused of a central role in the drug programme.

According to the newspaper, Jurgen was a graduate of Leipzig's College for Physical Culture, the nerve centre of East German sport since the fifties and an institution that had earned itself a reputation as a leader in hormone-doping research. Two performance-enhancing drugs had been produced for use in rowing, Clomiphen and Oral-Turinabol. They were used to boost growth hormones, mainly in women, but also in men, and were developed during the build-up to the 1980 Olympics in which East Germany won 11 of 14 golds. The drugs were issued to athletes as young as 10, and they produced side-effects such as steroid acne, which left its victims scarred for life.

Jurgen's response to the newspaper was: 'I spent time trying to find new ways to develop performance. I understand training and its effect on the body. Of course, you saw things and asked questions. But I am convinced that, in rowing, doping was never the number one priority in the GDR.

'Some of the things may have gone on at that time which might not have been correct. But I can look everybody in the eye. I am not a doping coach. I am not a chemist. I had to live with a system I knew was wrong.' The ARA backed him, and its president,

Martin Brandon-Bravo, said that he was certain that rowing in Britain was a clean sport. He had full confidence in him.

Of course, we had asked questions about the drug situation as soon as Jurgen arrived in England. Jurgen told us they had done some experimenting in the sixties and early seventies and found that drugs in rowing were of no benefit. You could relate to that.

The fact was that East Germany was better than everybody else in many rowing disciplines because they got the right athletes into the sport and trained them extremely well. They didn't need drugs.

I never really sat down and talked to him about it. Frankly, I didn't confront him. I just knew how he had trained us. Even if Jurgen had been involved, it didn't worry or shock me. I was only interested in the person that I knew. And I knew that he has a strong moral sense of what is right and wrong.

Yes, there was evidence that there was drug-taking in a lot of their sports, and apparently amongst their juniors, according to a TV programme I saw at that time featuring young East German rowers saying they been told to take tablets. But if they were, they didn't work. East Germany's juniors were good, but if you trained hard, as I did, you were on par with them, if not better.

I'd known Jurgen for eight years at that time. There'd never been any suggestion that, when performances had not been going as well for us as they might have, he would introduce drugs that could improve matters.

That's all I could go by. Being with somebody in such a close environment, closer than most other sports, because of unity within the crew, there may have been certain times when you would have thought, 'Hey, that's a bit odd.' But there was nothing at any stage that would make you think that Jurgen would be involved with anything of that nature.

In our sport, there are very open drug tests. FISA can come along at any stage and do mandatory tests. Never once were East German rowers ever caught drug-taking. Potentially, every time you raced, you could be drug-tested. When did they take these drugs?

If it was going on in East Germany and he was involved, and that's a big 'if', that was the country and environment that he was involved in. It was difficult to say morally whether that was right or wrong. A country lays down its own laws and you follow them.

If the powers-that-be instructed our athletes to take drugs and you didn't think it was a problem, then that's the policy you would follow. That, or get out. If by following that line you got a better house in a nicer environment, a better job and a car, and the whole practice was acceptable in your country, 99.9 per cent of people would go along with it, wouldn't they? It's black and white.

Admittedly, Jonny and Greg Searle were very sceptical of Jurgen's past when he first came over. At one international regatta, Jurgen produced a gold sachet containing a substance which was some kind of energy-restoring health drink. He'd been give it by one of his former colleagues in East Germany. Jurgen said to us all, 'This is an isotonic drink. Make sure you keep up your fluid intake, and drink some of this.' We didn't think anything of it, other than to drink it.

Jonny was aghast. He said, 'You took that without even knowing what was in it. You're absolutely crazy.'

But having known Jurgen for a couple of years then, there was no way there was going to be anything in that. Jurgen knew as well as we did the chances of being drug-tested. If there was something in it and we were caught, we'd say, 'Well, we've been given this stuff by our coach.' His career could be over.

I was very surprised by Jonny's attitude. He kept saying, 'Didn't you ask him any questions about what was in it? It looks very dodgy to me.' Yet if Jonny had been given something by Steve Gunn, who coached him at the time, he'd have taken it with no questions asked.

In 24 years of rowing, I've witnessed the odd case of a positive drugs test in the sport and a lot of innuendo and rumour. In the early eighties, a Romanian was tested positive. He was banned for life and so was the team doctor. In July 2000, three scullers, a Cuban man and two Belarus women suffered the same fate after testing positive for anabolic steroids. There was also one particular country which was very open about using 'medical' help but frankly they were poor rowers, so if they were using drugs it wasn't doing them any good.

In British rowing, there's been only one incident and that's just hearsay. One of the junior athletes is supposed to have consulted his GP at that time and said, 'I'm going to go on steroids. I want you to advise me.' The doctor simply told him to get his life in gear and get himself sorted out. It was something that he shouldn't be doing. I don't know whether the junior concerned actually did anything, but he never made the senior team anyway.

I'm pleased to be involved in a sport that doesn't have that problem. As a sport, we're adamant that, if you're caught, it's a life ban, no second chances, no excuses. Most of the drugs that will ban you from the sport shouldn't be anywhere near your system. It's crazy when people in some sports are banned and then come back, like Ben Johnson. He was banned, had it lifted, then was caught again. It's completely crazy. It's sending out all the wrong messages.

If they want to do blood tests instead of urine tests as a form of doping control because abuse is easier to identify by this method, I'm all for that. There are sports that are very anti-blood testing because it's more difficult to disguise some of the substances you may be taking. There's the old civil liberties argument. But it's all nonsense. If you haven't got anything to hide, you should be willing to do any test that is required.

I am totally opposed to any performance-enhancing drugs in sport, even the so-called 'harmless' ones, for which the IOC president Juan Antonio Samaranch called for restrictions to be eased in 1998. Morally, I feel that it is totally wrong.

As I've stressed before, an athlete with excess muscles is not going to succeed at rowing any more than he or she will in marathons. That's not the case in other sports. Mark Tout, the bobsleigh driver with whom I was involved in the mid-eighties, actually tested positive for anabolic steroids in 1996. Bobsleighing is a very explosive sport. You require sheer power to get the sled up and running, but no stamina.

I feel that rowing has been able to remain clean worldwide because of one simple reason. Yes, you have to be powerfully built, but it is also endurance-based. You have to be more of an all-rounder. To my knowledge, among sport drugs there's nothing that enhances both areas or improves one without harming the other. Fortunately, for everyone concerned, the initial furore over Jurgen quickly died down.

Returning to my own medical problems, by March 1999 I was still not happy with what I was achieving. My training was what I'd call 'bitty'. As that 1998–99 season had progressed, my performance levels were still up and down. If I was, say, doing a test on the ergo, my performance would be good, and then I'd suddenly stop, as though my energy sources had run out. I had lost a stone of my muscle bulk over that winter. My strength was ebbing away, slowly but significantly. I was 30 seconds off my usual pace in gym tests. I used to be able to bench-press 120 kg (265 lb), but now all I could manage was 105 kg (230 lb).

One day a group of us got together at my home to discuss the whole issue of my diabetes. They were Jurgen, Craig Sharpe, professor of exercise physiology, and a real expert in this particular field, my wife Ann as team doctor, and Ian Gallen, my diabetologist.

There were various suggestions, including having muscle biopsies, to establish whether I was getting enough energy through to them. But we decided against that and instead took the radical decision to greatly increase the amount of insulin I was injecting into myself in an attempt to increase my energy levels. Previously, I had tried to keep it to a minimum, but diabetes is actually easier to control and more flexible the more insulin you take.

The problem was that, initially, I had been saying to myself: 'I don't want to be a diabetic, and I want to avoid taking insulin.' That's a natural reaction. Now, I had to be realistic and say, 'I am a diabetic, and will be for the rest of my life.' I must control the situation, not let it control me. I would have to change, to get as much insulin in my body as possible. However, that would also mean that I would have to alter my work programme. I wanted to maximize my energy levels, but had to be careful that my blood sugar didn't plummet to a level where I might suffer from a 'hypo'.

What had been discovered was that the medication I had been taking for my colitis was making my diabetes worse. I couldn't keep my blood sugar levels under control. Then, I was running on glycogen which was taken from my muscles. I was fine up to a certain level, but when I needed to dip into reserves of my energy there was nothing there. Fortunately, during that time, Jurgen and the others alternately pushed me and made allowances for me, depending on what they thought I needed at any particular time. Once I changed my medication, my overall condition improved.

It required a great deal of balancing, and, slowly, I was able to return to consistent output. Although my advancing years and the effects of diabetes meant that I would never produce the levels of performance that I had in my prime, as I prepared for the World Championships at St Catharine's, Ontario, in the summer of 1999, I felt that at last I had the problem relatively under control.

Meanwhile, the four had continued its build-up towards those 1999 World Championships. In April, Tim and James had won the pairs trials at Nottingham. Matthew and I didn't take part because he had a rib injury. We then had four or five weeks to the first World Cup race in Munich. Three weeks to the day before that race, Tim had a party at his home and put his hand through a window.

The first I knew about it was coming down to training on the Sunday morning. I was told he'd had an accident but nobody knew how bad it was; just that he'd cut his hand and had stitches.

He was in hospital all night and the first impression was that he'd got drunk and was involved in a fight, but I couldn't see that. Tim, who was then studying for an MSc in sports science at Brunel University and in his spare time played lead guitar in a group, was not a violent type. He just wasn't that kind of character.

However, James was really very annoyed about it all, probably assuming at the time that Tim had been totally irresponsible. Jurgen was also extremely irritated, more because he hadn't been contacted and had to establish what had gone on from other sources.

What we eventually pieced together was that the incident had happened during a get-together after that year's Boat Race in the old Oxford University boathouse where Tim lives with his girlfriend, Beth. There had not been a fight. In typically garrulous mood, Tim had just tried to emphasize a point to Luka Grubor, one of the oarsmen at Leander, and had flung his hand back and put it through the window.

He had severed tendons in his little finger, cut deep into his ring finger and sliced his thumb down to the bone. The glass also lacerated an artery. He lost about 1 litre (2 pints) of blood and he arrived at hospital looking like a victim from a Michael Winner film. The doctors had even more of a shock when he arrived because he'd recently had his hair dyed red. They couldn't believe he was a professional sportsman. They thought he was a punk rocker.

I suppose my thoughts were, so close to the first World Cup race, that if the first report of severed tendons was correct, it was unlikely that he'd be able to race. He'd had surgery to repair them. Yet, we had no idea how long it would take him to recover, if he did at all.

It may sound callous, but I was probably the least agitated about it, because physically Tim had the least strength of all the oarsmen in the four. I thought that if we had to find a substitute for anybody, Tim would be the one who was most easily replaced. It didn't concern me that much. I thought, 'We'll just get somebody else and carry on.'

Tim suggested afterwards that Matthew and I were somewhat cold towards him, and gave him the silent treatment, as though we were really annoyed. But that wasn't actually true. I think it was just his own guilt, that he had let the rest of us down, manifesting itself in his mind. It was an irritating situation because it interrupted our progress. But I wasn't really upset with Tim personally. I'm fairly philosophical and I just thought that it was one of those things.

What can you do? Do you stop going to parties, do you stop dancing? How far do you wrap yourself in cotton wool during a four-year campaign of trying to win the Olympics? You could get ridiculous. Not crossing roads, not driving. What happens if you get an illness? You have to lead as near normal a life as you possibly can. I've been skiing during winters, and doing that makes you extremely accident-prone. It was an accident. What can you do about it?

There was plenty of time before the World Championships to find a temporary replacement, and we knew we had a good enough crew to support that person. But we all wanted to get back on the river as soon as possible. The decision was made that either Luka, ironically enough the guy talking to Tim when he damaged his hand, or Simon Dennis would row in the four with us. Both were in the eights group.

We went to Docklands to do some timed pieces with both, and raced against some other fours who were going to make up the eight. There was little to choose between them. The decision was made that it would be Luka because he was living in Henley. Simon was in London. It was decided really just on convenience.

James was very pleased because he and Luka, the Zagreb-born son of a Croatian export company representative, were good friends and shared a house.

The steady-state training, which is what we do most of, actually went better with Luka than it had done with Tim. We were actually going faster in our endurance work. That felt good. But when we did timed pieces it was very hit and miss. Sometimes it would go well, and sometimes not. But we still felt that we were good enough to go to Munich and win.

That first World Cup race about two weeks after the new four got together was at the end of May. We won our heat and the Romanians won theirs. We felt that we weren't moving together, so we swapped the boat around. For the final on Sunday, I rowed behind Matthew at three, and Luka rowed behind me at two. It was Jurgen's decision. He hoped it would kick-start us and we'd go forward from there.

But it didn't work at all. We came fourth, behind the Romanians and two German crews, one of whom we'd beaten the day before. The winners defeated us by nearly seven seconds. For Matthew and me, it was a devastating reverse. It was our first defeat in a championship race since 1995.

'It's a feeling I'm not used to, and one I hope I'm not going to get used to,' was my terse comment at the time to the media.

We returned home extremely dispirited, but were lifted by the news that Tim had been making great progress with his hand. The rehabilitation process had been going well. He should be back in the boat within the next training week.

At Lilleshall, where he had gone for rehabilitation, Tim had met some professional footballers. They'd asked what we were like. He described Matthew as being like Alan Shearer, very reliable and leading the line; behind him, himself, the creative midfielder, like David Beckham, skilful but occasionally having moments of career-threatening stupidity. I was like Tony Adams, apparently, leading from the back, the motivator who got stuck in, and at bow James was the David Seaman, the last line of defence. He also described how we complemented each other, saying: 'If there were four Steves in the boat it would tear itself apart. If there were four like me [Tim], we'd probably not get up in the morning.'

The decision was made that we would carry on training as a three, and Luka would return to the eights group. We would wait for Tim. It was at that stage that it became apparent to me what Tim added to the boat, despite his lack of power, and how important he was.

Over the last couple of years, Matthew had become physically the strongest on all the tests that we do to monitor our progress. He was a long way ahead of the rest of us. But then different people bring different elements to a crew. That's something I've learnt over the years.

I felt at the beginning that the weakest link was always going to be Tim because his ergo scores were not very good, and his weights likewise. To be frank, the physical side was not his forte. But the one thing that Tim has is that when he gets in a boat he moves it very well. He gets the best out of himself. When Tim damaged his hand I thought, 'Well, it's a shame, but I'm sure we can find someone to replace him who would take his place without too much being lost.'

The fact of it was that when we put Luka in the four, although in fairness we only had three weeks before we started racing, the boat was never the same. When Tim came back in after six or seven weeks out it was immediately a different crew. He put a spark back into it. Even the crew members who are weaker on paper are still important.

CHAPTER 22

TESTING TIME FOR TIM

That failure at Munich gave us all a good jab in the ribs. The attitude was, 'Right, we've got to do something about this.' We decided not to do the second World Cup race, but instead went up to the north-east for the 164th Durham Regatta, on the River Wear. It is the second biggest event in the domestic rowing calendar, after Henley. That year, it attracted no fewer than 580 crews.

There was a charity dinner and they auctioned seats in two eights, in which two of our four, James and myself, would row in one and the other two, Tim and Matthew, in the other. They bid £300–£400 a seat.

Over the 750-metre course, our four also took on the Durham eight in a challenge match, watched by 3000 along the banks. Durham University are not a top crew, but good enough standard, who've won medals at Henley. A four should have the acceleration over the first two or three strokes, but from there on, against an eight, you're really struggling. We got a slight lead, rated very high, and were neck and neck. As we crossed the line, we did a mock celebration although we knew that we'd lost. It was that kind of occasion. It was a nice relaxed weekend away before Henley Royal Regatta and we also did a bit of training up there. The most important part of the trip was having Tim back in the boat. Immediately, it seemed to have more life and rhythm about it.

Tim emphasized once again how you don't have to be the strongest rower to contribute to the success of a boat. As I have said previously, rowing is a power and endurance sport. Although the key element you need to make a boat go fast is power, it's also a very technical sport; what I call an alien sport. When I say that, I mean that you will never do anything like rowing until you get in a boat. From birth, you learn to stand up, you learn to walk, you learn to run; all a natural progression. If you become an athlete it's just extending what you can already do to a higher level. Every child can run. But nobody knows how to row or understands the correct movements until they get in a rowing boat.

You have to learn quite subtle movements on a platform that is really very unstable. Without the oars to stabilize it, the boat would turn over. You are trying to row on the recovery (when the blades are returning for the next stroke), without blades on the water, to make the shell move very quickly. The fact of having to balance it as well complicates it further.

It's very difficult to teach someone about the body movements, to hold on to the blade correctly, and get the blade into the water at the right time and with the right angle (where it doesn't dredge the bottom or skid across the top), all on an unstable platform.

I had to learn everything out on the water because, in my early days, there were no rowing machines of any quality. I started off in a tub pair, which is a big wide boat that's very stable. Rowing clubs don't have that kind of boat any more, and I think it's a pity, because they are excellent for giving you early practical experience of a boat's stability on water.

These days, all the initial work is done on ergos. The advantage of rowing machines is that they're a very stable environment. You can teach people the body movements to give them confidence, so that it becomes more of a natural technique without having to worry about the stability of a boat on water.

Once you've mastered the technique, you must still have the power. But the skill factor is very important. If you want to be the best oarsman in the world, you're ideally tall and strong because rowing is a sport of leverage, but also very technical as well, in terms of using the blades in the water to optimum effect. The perfect rower is as strong as an ox, as fit as a cheetah, and technically superb. He doesn't exist, but that's the ideal. Because nobody possesses all those qualities you have to compromise.

To take myself, I've always been a very strong athlete. Not the strongest, but at the top end. I was quite technical, but not the best technician. Physiologically, I wasn't the best, either, but still right at the top. In fact, I wasn't at the top in any of the demands of my sport, but my strength lay in being close to the top in all its basic requirements, with my particular assets being power and mental toughness.

Tim's great asset is his technique, but physically he's a bit lower, and power-wise a bit lower still. However, the important thing is that if you put Tim in a boat with some really strong guys, it's a good balance of resources.

Of the remainder of the Sydney coxless four, Matthew's qualities were all about power and endurance. James was a good all-
rounder. It was the combination that was important.

If there's one athlete I believe has approached the optimum in
all aspects of rowing it is the Finn Pertti Karppinen. I really looked
up to him as an international. He was a huge athlete. To win three
Olympic golds you've got to have something pretty special about
you. He was technically quite good, power-wise excellent; he's one
of the prime specimens ever in our sport.

Greg Searle, who won Olympic gold in 1992 with his brother
Jonny in the coxed pairs, is still one of the best athletes that we
have. But he has suffered by being successful in a rowing boat, then
moving into sculling.

The advantage I had is that I was single sculling before having
any success. That built me into a stronger person. You would have
said five or six years ago that Greg was going to be the best oarsman coming through from the juniors, better even than Matthew.
His potential was outstanding. If you look at ergo scores, Greg
held the British record until 1999, although now he's been beaten.
He's lost something since he's been sculling, whereas I gained a lot
of physical and mental strength from it. Greg was a successful
rower before and has has taken a step back since sculling. He may
yet be outstanding. He's got time.

Returning to our coxless four, Tim was back in full fitness again
in time for Henley Royal Regatta. In the Stewards Cup, we were
due to meet the Australian crew, the so-called 'Oarsome Foursome'
who had taken the gold at Atlanta. It was quite nerve-wracking
because they were reigning Olympic champions and we would be
trying to wrest their title away from them. They were an outstanding crew, no doubt about that. We had to be at our best. We'd
done the fun thing up at Durham but that didn't tell us whether we
were back to our top international form.

There were only two entries apart from us, the Australians
and the Danish lightweight four. We were drawn against the
Australians in the semi-final. We started well, got a length to three-
quarter length lead, and although they rowed really well in the
middle part of the race, they never came back at us. In the closing
stages we moved away from them again. However, we knew we
had been in a race with them; they'd raised their game to take us
on. It had confirmed that we were back on target.

So exhilarated was Matthew that he twice punched the air, once
before the line and once after. He was later accused in the media

by Henley chairman Mike Sweeney, umpiring from the race launch, of a breach of etiquette. Matthew said it was just an instinctive reaction to the tension of the race.

The race times of the Danish lightweight fours have always been similar to ours at international regattas. We knew it was going to be in a rigorous test against them, perhaps tougher than against the Australians. But our speed off the start gave us the lead and we stayed about a length or so in front for the rest of the course. That was very satisfying.

The following weekend we headed for Lucerne, where we re-opposed the Romanians, winners of the first World Cup race, and the Australians, who had won the second World Cup race which we missed. The Romanians had been runners-up in that second race and led us on points. We knew we did not have a chance of winning the World Cup but needed to win at Lucerne to demonstrate our form.

Yet again, we dominated right from the start and secured the victory, with the Australians second, and the Romanians third. Tim raised his repaired right arm in a symbolic acknowledgement that he had recovered after four weeks out. They were notable scalps and it put us in excellent heart for the World Championships in Cologne.

Perhaps at this point I should explain how our four prepared for an international event, and what happens during one. In general, we got together for a serious crew meeting the night before a race. We went into detail about how the race could go, depending on what we knew of our opposition. Also, what we wanted to get out of it. We'd meet again an hour before our race, to go through a warm-up and then review what we were expecting. Jurgen started it off, and then there was an opportunity for anyone to come up with new ideas. At the end, I went through the strategy, talking about the calls and how we would all respond to those. The idea was to make sure we were all focused as one. From that point on, we were not just four individuals.

In the race itself, the ideal performance was to equal-split, in terms of speed, the first and second halves of the race. Normally, the first 500 metres is the fastest, the second 500 metres the second slowest, the third 500 is the slowest, and the last 500 is the second quickest. The first and second 500 are when you're at your cruising pace, the hardest pace you can possibly move at without going over the top. If you've got any energy left, you push it up at the end to try to go that little bit quicker. Most crews will follow that, but sometimes they'll change tactics to suit. The Italian brothers, the Abbagnales, used to go as fast as they could in the first 1000, establish as significant a lead as they possibly could, and then just try to hang on. Most of the time it worked, sometimes it didn't.

Competitors of boats I've raced used to look at us and, most of the time, thought, 'Well, overall, they're better than us. They've got more speed than us, and their cruising speed is better than ours, and they've got a faster finishing speed. How can we counter that?' The only tactics were to try to catch us unawares. What used to happen to Matthew and me in the pairs was that people tried to surprise us by getting away quicker and hoping that we didn't respond. Unfortunately for them, invariably we did.

It might be assumed that a lot of tactical calls and sheer demands for more effort are made in a race. In fact, that's not the case, principally because you always discuss race tactics before you go out and everyone knows what is expected of them at any time. The inboard computer tells you how many strokes per minute you are doing. Off the start, we knew that we would be in the high 40s. After around 15, 20 strokes we'd be in our stride and I'd say, 'Stride, now.' And I'd give the rate, say, '47'. Between the 15th stroke and the minute, which was my next call, we knew we had to come down steadily to 38, 39, maybe 40. Then I'd say, 'One minute, now,' and I'd give another rate. Then after another minute we'd be at our race pace, which would be 36 unless there was a really strong head-wind.

It's that straightforward. Just key words. 'Now' at every 500. The third 500 was always an area that we tried to move on because that was the slowest part of the race. Because it's a very physical sport, you neither have the time or energy for inspirational speeches.

A lot of the preparation for an event is done informally. At regattas and training camps, I nearly always roomed with Matthew, both when we did the pair and, later, when we were in the four. We spent quite a lot of time in our room and it's inevitable that we talked about our performances. 'What do you think such and such will do?' We always assumed there was going to be a surprise from somebody. 'Who will it be this year?' All the time, it was on your mind. When it came to formal meetings, a lot of talk had happened beforehand.

At our altitude camp in 1999, we did have our own rooms. I quite liked that. You can do what you want when you want to do it. If you're not sleeping very well, you can read. When you're in a stressful situation, little things like that can bug you.

At training camps and regattas I didn't used to like sleeping during the day. I would want to stay awake in the afternoons. If I rested during the day, I wouldn't sleep very well at night, which would really annoy me. Matthew, however, is one of those people who sleeps anywhere, anytime. At altitude, for example, we would train twice in the morning, have lunch, then there'd be a few hours to kill before the next training session. Everybody would have a rest, except me. I'd just go and watch TV, or something.

The problem was that at night I'd go to bed about 10.30, but if Matthew was not in the crew room watching a film, he'd go to bed and read a book. That would keep me awake. Then just as I was still attempting to get some much-needed sleep, he'd close his book, turn the light off and be straight off, with me mentally cursing him.

Also, when I'm very tired, I tend to snore. Matthew's favourite trick, which was taught him by another rower that he used to share a room with, is, if someone snores, to clap his hands very loudly. Just once. The noise would wake me up, but I had no idea what the source was. But it was enough to get me to turn over. Eventually, because he'd done it so many times, I caught on.

He was only disturbing my sleep because he'd been napping in the afternoon and was in a light sleep himself. Yet, I didn't disturb him in the afternoons. It sounds quite trivial, but when you're isolated up a mountain for three weeks, living almost like monks, and there's nothing to do other than train and eat and sleep, little things like that start to get on your nerves. It wasn't a big issue, though. Most of the time, it was comforting to have someone to talk to, or, say, watch the golf with, if there was any on TV.

Sharing rooms was necessary to keep costs down, rowing being an 'amateur' sport. All through my career, I was used to cheap travel, on the cheapest route, everything economy class, and accommodation to match. People could never believe that, as representatives of our country, we didn't go business class, or, if we did, very rarely.

Similarly, on training camps, we were only offered water with meals. In many ways, it was quite primitive. You'd have got better looked after in prison. Why not have other drinks? Coffee or tea? It would be the social thing to do, and should be part of the meal. In recent times, we advanced tremendously and we could have food and drink any time we wanted. When we went on altitude training, Jurgen introduced tea and cakes at 4 p.m. before going off and doing our third session of the day. A very English idea, that!

However, we always had to bear in mind the costs of major international events, like World Championships. At St Catharine's, in Canada, location of the last World Championships before Sydney, there were 67 rowers, plus back-up staff. These days, apart from a doctor, we have physiotherapists and even a masseur. It's nearly 100 people in total, and that's huge when compared to a professional football team, considering what financial backing they would have.

What irked me most, though, as I have already alluded to, is that everything had to be seen to be absolutely fair. There is more of a communist society within our sport than communist societies used to have within their sports. There's a constant feeling that you can't have this or that because nobody else has it.

Yet, our team benefited financially from the Lottery because of the results we'd got. If you studied the results at the Olympic Games and those competitions that affected the amount of money, it's Matthew and myself who were the primary Lottery-earners. You used to think, 'Well, we've put our fair share into the team budget. Shouldn't there be a reward, even if that reward may be benefiting us on a performance level as well?'

To return to that World Championship final at Cologne, our team discussion inevitably involved the conditions. The event was staged very late in the season, the weather had turned, and it was quite windy, creating unpleasant water. In particular, there was an extremely strong tail wind. We thought the water would be very choppy in the last 500 metres, so our tactics were to really go out and get a big lead in the first half, so that we could relax if the water was bad in the final stages. That's what we did, although we struggled in the final stages as we paid for earlier efforts.

We found it difficult to shake off the Italians and French, the Olympic silver medallists, although neither had produced anything all season. But with Matthew lifting the rate to 45, we eventually won by a third of length from the latter, only a fifth of a second outside the world record. With the Italians third it meant the medallists were the same as in the previous year's World Championships. The first four crews home all beat 5 minutes 50 seconds, but you never win by much in a tailwind.

It was, as I was to tell the media, as I held Zak, Sophie and Natalie, who were holding union flags, an 'off day'. Yet, my slight disappointment could not detract from the fact that it was my eighth World Championship gold. I had become the first rower in the history of the sport to do so.

Back home, we attended the opening of the impressive River and Rowing Museum at Henley. I met the artist Justin Mortimer, who had painted an oil of me for the museum. I was in good company. He had previously been commissioned to paint the Queen's portrait.

There was a high flood stream that day, and we were out in the morning training. The wash was even stronger than usual because there were around 17 police and Thames Conservancy launches out, ready to accompany the Queen's launch from where she'd arrived by helicopter. Not for the first time in my career, the crew of a boat I was in was warned about going out on a strong flood tide. The danger is getting too close to Hambleden Weir which is about two miles downstream from Leander.

It is a dangerous sport, and we could turn round Temple Island, which is much nearer. But when you're doing a 20-km (12-mile) session, completing that five times is a bit of a pain. The lock-keeper at Hambleden used to get really very uptight. If we turned too close, he came rushing out, shaking his fist. But we feel that we spend most of our time on the river and know it better than most people who assess what is safe. If you're training for the Olympics or a World Championships and have spent the last 20-odd years living most days of your life on the river, then you should know what you're doing.

As the water undulates through Buckinghamshire and Berkshire, the Thames looks so serene and unthreatening. I enjoy the quietness of the river. In fact, I used to like rowing at night, from when I was a schoolboy right through to the early eighties, and occasionally with Matthew when we trained for the Eights Head of the River on the Tideway. The tranquillity at night helps produce a closer harmony between crew and boat.

However, although I have a great fondness for the river, it must be respected. I was reminded of that one February morning in the eighties, when I was training for the Eights Head at Molesey, coached by Mike Spracklen. We took on so much water because the river was so rough that we had to abandon the boat. The water was freezing and we got a good soaking, but fortunately we were close enough to the bank to struggle out. We were in no real danger, but two incidents in 2000 illustrate how treacherous the Thames can be: firstly when a young man died after jumping off Henley Bridge for a bet; then, a Durham University women's eight was dragged towards the weir at Hambleden and, although they tried to turn, the boat was snapped in half. They escaped unscathed, but it could have been pretty unpleasant.

We began the penultimate season, 1998–99, before the Sydney Olympics in buoyant mood. With Tim back on board, we all felt that everything was definitely back on track. After a week's training here we travelled out to Orlando, where the BOA has a training base.

We took road bikes and did a lot of gym and ergo work. It was there that Tim suffered a serious back problem. It turned out to be a torn disc in his lower back. It was a recurrence of trouble he had in the early nineties. After travelling, we had completed a really hard hour session on the rowing machines and Tim really struggled with it. However, he managed to do all the training.

When we returned, there were a couple of weeks before the Fours Head of the River Race in mid-November, and it was decided that he would get some treatment on his back and we would row with a replacement.

As the end of the year approached, so did decision time for Tim. He had either the option of retiring, or continuing with injections and physiotherapy or surgery on his bulging disc. He opted for surgery on 18 December at Harpenden Hospital. It must have been a distressing time for him. After his operation, he had to lie flat on his back for a month, and could not move outside home for two months. It was not until 18 March that he actually returned to the water.

Meanwhile, it was not all serious work on the water. In February, Matthew was part of a 10-man team that broke the record for rowing 100 km (60 miles) at the River and Rowing Museum, and in doing so raised £6000 for Comic Relief. They completed it as a relay, and their time of 4 hours 42 minutes was nearly 18 minutes better than the previous best, set by Nottingham University. I couldn't take part because of 'flu.

We went to Seville for the spring regatta, and it was there that Ed Coode came and rowed in a four with us in place of Tim. Ed was, like Matthew, an Old Etonian, and the son of a solicitor from Cornwall. He had also rowed for Oxford in 1998. Ed proved himself a more than capable substitute.

It just all clicked. It seemed to be an excellent combination. Some of the long endurance training sessions were some of the best we've ever done within a fours group. It was so relaxed, so flowing. But what about the real thing, the 2000-metre races? We knew what had happened with Luka the year before.

Tim was starting to get back into a boat as we approached the time of the first World Cup race at Hazewinkel, but it was decided that he would not train with us, but would return gradually, going out in the single and doing a bit of light ergo work.

When it came to the race itself, Jurgen decided that Ed would be in the four for that World Cup race and that Tim would go in the single. I thought this was absolutely bizarre. I thought to myself: if he was going to race in the single, he had got to be in reasonable shape and his back strong enough. If that was the case, surely he should be back in the four?

We secured a comfortable victory from Poland, our first competitive 2000-metre race since the last World Championships in Cologne, eight and a half months previously. Tim did reasonably in the single sculls, though he did not make the final. He described the change of disciplines as being like a flat jockey going national hunt racing, or a 400 metres hurdles runner switching to hurdles.

Jurgen approached Matthew and myself at the airport afterwards and said: 'I've decided to keep Ed in the four for the next World Cup race and still work on Tim's fitness and make sure he's fine'. I can't say I agreed with his decision. But somebody had to make one, and I was just glad it wasn't me.

It would then be assessed after the following World Cup race in Vienna in three weeks' time. However, during that period, Tim was pulled into the eight for that event at the New Danube Lake. Again, it was very odd. If he was capable of rowing, and good enough to row in the eight, why wasn't he good enough to row with us?

Anyway, we won, the eight came second, and my thoughts were, 'What's going to happen now?' It was only 10 days before Henley, which finished less than a week before Lucerne. This was a difficult time to change. I felt that Tim would be back in the boat after Lucerne, and Ed would go back into the eight.

Again, at the airport after the regatta, Jurgen reiterated that Ed would stay with us. Ed didn't actually know until Matthew read it out from a newspaper that he was in a four for Henley and Lucerne. Tim would remain in the eight.

There was no consultation with us. It was very much Jurgen's decree of what was going to happen. I would have thought we would have been asked for our views. Certainly, if I'd been in charge, I'd have brought Tim back in as soon as he was fit. I really couldn't understand it.

As an athlete, Tim was, at that stage, slightly better than Ed. You only had to look at his previous record – bronze at the Olympics and silver at the World Championships. To my mind, we *were* the four. Not that Ed was the outsider coming in, because it was never like that.

When Matthew and I were in the pair, we never had to make the same kind of decision, anyway, but it was very much a close-knit relationship between the three of us. All the training sessions and planning were a three-man effort. I felt that once the four was created, generally, there wasn't the same harmony between athletes and coach.

In his defence, Jurgen always made it very clear that Tim was not out of the four, but was still very much involved. He was still going through rehabilitation, even though he was racing internationals in the eight. I'm not sure what kind of rehab it was which allowed him to exert himself fully in World Cup races!

When Jurgen did eventually ask us three what we thought, we said that if Tim was fit and his back was showing no reactions, he was the one who should be in the crew. Having said that, we could not fault Ed, because ever since he'd been with us, we'd won in good style. That included the final World Cup event at Lucerne, when we defeated the Norwegian crew who actually broke the world record in the heats, admittedly in very fast conditions.

We had an excellent build-up to the 1999 World Championships at St Catharine's, near Niagara Falls. The training went superbly and we stepped up a gear during our races, especially our final which was probably the best World Championship row I've ever had. It was a first World Championship gold for Ed, and a ninth world title for me. And we had plenty in reserve.

It was the last major championships before the Sydney Olympics, albeit over a year away, and it was important that we put a marker down for the opposition; that we set a standard to give them something to think about. Then, inevitably, you start thinking, 'Should we still be thinking in terms of Tim coming back into it?' However, we couldn't fail to notice that the eight had done really well to secure a silver, and Tim had played a big part in raising their level.

It was an intriguing dilemma. Was Jurgen going to put the four best people in the four – or was he going to stick with a unit that looked like it could win the Olympics, and an eight that Tim could strengthen to win another medal at Sydney? During our last camp out in Australia in September 1999 Jurgen told me that 'The four best people will be in the four. There will be no compromising.' He was adamant that his priority was that we should win the gold. If we did that and the other crews came last in everything else, to him that was far preferable than coming second in two events.

I could understand Tim's frustration with the situation, which was highlighted in the BBC's *Gold Fever*, the video diaries recording our preparations for Sydney.

Maybe he felt he was banging his head against a brick wall. However, the way I would have looked at it was the eight was a stepping stone to getting me back into the four. There was not a stage where Jurgen ever said to him: 'there's no way you're going to go back into the four.' Sensibly, that's the way that Tim approached it. The door was never closed on him returning.

When we travelled out to that camp, it was September 1999, a year away from the serious business at Sydney. The England rugby players had their own test that month, the Rugby World Cup, and just before I departed, their coach Clive Woodward asked me to go along to Twickenham and give a talk to his players nine days before the competition began. I have always been a great rugby fan, although the highest level I attained was turning out for Maidenhead fifths.

It was basically a question-and-answer session, in which they talked to me about how I motivated myself. I spoke a little about visualization, and by all accounts it went down very well. Unfortunately, I missed attending the matches live because of being away, but watched as much as possible on TV out in Australia.

We had travelled out there to the City of the Gold Coast, with whom the BOA had a contract for provision of exclusive facilities, including the Hinze Dam, where only the British team trained.

When you actually make the transformation into the calendar year of the Olympics, it is an exhilarating moment. The Games have taken a big step nearer. But I was impatient. I just wished it was sooner. When you start thinking that, it's always a good sign.

For Ann and me, New Year's Eve was quite a fun occasion. We had been among those invited to the special celebrations at the millennium dome. Personally, I wouldn't have been particularly keen to attend, bearing in mind all the problems with transport. But Natalie demanded to go as soon as we received the invitation, and we didn't want to let her down. We also had a holiday away skiing, knowing that there would be no more chance for relaxation until after Sydney.

I could turn my mind off our preparations for the Olympics. That was the theory. It didn't happen, of course; my thoughts constantly turned to how I might be feeling in a year's time. I also felt that it could be a period of uncertainty for some of those involved. It that, I was proved correct.

CHAPTER 23

'SORRY, BUT I'VE GOT TO BE SELFISH'

A year away from the big event, it was comforting to know that we were well ahead of our rivals. However, we could not be complacent. We knew full well that a lot of people make massive progress as the Olympics approach. At the start of the year, I looked back at our progress. When we had set up the new crew, we had no real idea how we would perform. We went to the first international regatta thinking, 'We haven't got a clue of where we're going to finish this. We could win it, we could be in the top few, we could be anywhere.' We just didn't know.

However, we won it, so you start thinking, 'Well, we could go the whole season without being beaten.' Then we won the 1997 World Championships. But after that, you go through a difficult period, where you are aware that you have to do two more World Championships before the Olympics. Just repeating what you have already achieved can be hard.

It was even more difficult for Matthew and me in the pair when we won the 1991 World Championships, followed by the Olympics the next year. Then, we said we were going to do the same thing for another four years. We didn't even have the excitement of doing something new, like the four, and of not knowing what was in store for us. The most difficult part of it is to keep the intensity up, and keep your performance up, so that nobody feels they can successfully intrude on your success.

The media tend to pick up on unbeaten runs, and it's targets like that which helped keep us motivated. I had to keep saying to myself, 'I've got to do the training now to do well in the trials in a month's time' or whenever they were, even though they didn't excite me very much. I used that to get the best out of myself.

From a personal point of view, the year leading up to Sydney was one of the most challenging of my career, not merely in physical terms, but mentally, too. I was not performing to my expectations, despite my colitis and diabetes then being under control.

I had also to come to terms with the fact that gradually, over the years, Matthew had taken over as the prime mover of the boat. It was the master yielding to his one-time apprentice. I felt vulnerable. It was inevitable that it should happen at some time. Nobody has a divine right to defy the years, and in March I turned 38, an advanced age for any athlete, but particularly one involved in a power and endurance sport. However, it was not easy to come to terms with.

Through the mid-1980s and 1990s I had reigned supreme in British rowing, both in championships and assessments. Now it was Matthew who was turning on the power at will, not me. In my younger years, it never used to worry me that one day I'd have to do an ergo test. I'd just go down to Leander and do it. I knew that I was better than everybody else in the country. Even if I did badly my score would still be better than anybody else's.

During the last four years when my health hasn't been good and the years have began to take their toll, I have not been quite as consistent as I'd like to have been. I couldn't expect to be in perfect condition and do personal bests every time I did a session on the rowing machine.

Jurgen told me between Barcelona and Atlanta that he always knew that, at some stage, Matthew would be better than me. I accepted it but the realization came in the last two years, certainly in the last 18 months up to Sydney, when Matthew stepped up quite a few gears. His best ergo score until the winter before the Olympics was exactly the same as mine. Potentially, I believe he was capable of performing better a long time ago, perhaps back to before Atlanta. But only in those 18 months did he actually put in some outstanding performances, above what I'd done. For example, on the bench press, which is not rowing-related but is a good guide, Matthew was lifting more weight than I'd ever done. The best I ever lifted was 127.5 kg (281 lb), in Australia. In 1999, at altitude, Matthew lifted 130 kg (287 lb). Now he can lift 135 kg (297 lb). That's some progression.

I remember when we first trained at Leander together I'd be training on 20 kg (44 lb) heavier weights than him. He just couldn't do it. Jurgen used to joke, tongue in cheek, that he had women in his East German squad who could lift more than Matthew. Now he's Mr Atlas.

In the Olympics build-up I believed I was as strong as I'd ever been. I couldn't bench-press very well at one time because of an arm injury. (It sounds ridiculous, I know, but I fell off a giant medicine ball and fractured a bone in my arm. It means I still can't straighten it properly.) There were only two people in the whole British team who were better than me on the bench-pull, which is more rowing related than the bench-press. One of those is Matthew.

To do an ergo test, I had to gear myself up mentally and physically to that particular day, whereas 10 years previously I'd just turn up and put in a good performance. Now I had to focus and prepare for it carefully, to ensure my blood sugar levels were right.

What I did know is that if we had to do an ergo test and it was the most important one of the season, I'd be second or third best in the country, after Matthew and Greg Searle. I couldn't touch Matthew. Greg was British record-holder until Matthew beat him in the winter of 1999.

I had to be realistic about myself. Look at any sport and who stays at the top for more than 10 years? I had 16 years performing in a crew at the top level. I used to be the driving force and outstanding athlete within those boats; now I was just a member of that crew, rowing with somebody else who was the outstanding athlete.

At times, over the last year or two, I would sit down and say to myself, 'Do I really want this? To be second-best?' But, to look at it from a different perspective, people would often say to me, 'What's the ideal make-up of a boat?' And the logical answer, as I've stressed before, is that you want to be the weakest in it. You want to be rowing with people who are better than you are.

I'd been gradually approaching that situation and if I had not retired would have continued to do so. I had accepted that in the last year of my career, I was no longer the top performer within that boat. Yet, not to be the best man in a crew for one or two years when you'd been rowing for 24 years was not exactly a bad record.

When I was younger I was very much like Matthew is now, although I was always far more consumed by the sport. Rowing was my whole world. That was partly because I was attempting to win gold in a sport in which we, as a country, hadn't been successful for a long time. In terms of training, I had to do things differently from how they had been done in Britain traditionally, to break the mould. I was guided by Mike Spracklen, who was also very focused and single-minded. His view was that, to be a champion, you had to concentrate your whole being on that goal. Methods changed when Jurgen appeared. Although we had more training sessions, there was less intensity about them.

That doesn't mean that they weren't, at times, gruelling. To give some idea, this is the kind of schedule that Jurgen planned for us. Firstly, let's get rid of one misconception: the commonly held belief that rowers are up at 5 a.m. every morning, which is far from the truth. We actually had 'hands on boat' at 8 a.m. Tim was dead against going any earlier. His philosophy was that 'we're supposed to be professional sportsmen. We train all day. Why do we have to get up really early to go out training?' In fact, we only tended to train early to avoid the other river traffic, particularly from Easter onwards.

Normally, the first session was on the water. We'd be on the river at 8.20, and be finished by 9.45. After a short break, the second session started at 11 a.m., either back out on the water or doing weights, or on the ergo. Then four to five times a week, after lunch, we'd do a third session, starting at 3 p.m.

In all, spread over seven days, there were 18 sessions a week, mostly between one hour and two, 90 per cent on water, and all endurance-based, normally over 16 km (10 miles). Gym work would include circuit training – body curls, sit-ups, lateral pulls, leg extensions and weights – all without a break. We'd have a day off every month. We trained 49 weeks a year.

Training was never really enjoyable. It had to be done. Indeed, perhaps there was an element of masochism about it. That it was no good unless it hurt. On the water, freezing fog was the worst. Early in the year, right up to April, there was often a wind against the flood stream, which created waves like something you'd normally find off the coast. But what kept us going was the thought that somewhere another crew might be training that bit harder than us.

We had begun 2000 with the crew of the coxless four still unconfirmed by Jurgen. By early in the New Year, the general consensus was that Greg Searle would be the basis of the coxless pair, together with Ed, while Matthew, James, Tim and myself, would be the four. There was supposed to be a final decision at the end of February, before we went to a training camp near Seville, but it appeared that there was not much between Tim and Ed.

Eleven months of rowing in a four could become monotonous, which is why we also train in singles and pairs, and occasionally eights. It is to relieve the boredom, as much as anything else. Last year, for example, the first trials of the season were the singles, in December. So we tended to work in singles up to that point. Then we concentrated on pairs until mid-February, after which we moved into the fours before going away on that camp to Seville.

There we had a mixture of rowing in the eight, the four and the pairs. That was followed by the Eights Head of the River, two or three weeks before the final trials at Nottingham in April. For that, we were back in pairs again. Immediately they finished, we moved into the four, although now and again we still went out in pairs. In fact, Jurgen didn't announce the final four until after the trials.

Out in Seville, we did a series of trials, called 'seat races', in which Matthew and I stayed in one boat, but were joined alternately by two from the four others in our group – Tim and James and Greg and Ed – and did four races over 1500 metres with different combinations. The idea is that you take all the times each person has achieved in every combination, and the one who scores the lowest is the 'best'. It is an adoption of a system used at junior level in Britain, and not one that I like. In fact, I think it's a farce. Jurgen had never heard of the system when he came over from East Germany. It would only have some merit if the conditions were similar on every occasion, and in our case if Matthew and I rowed to exactly the same standard each time, but, of course, that's impossible.

It emerged that James was better than Greg, and Tim did slightly better than Ed. But, as James pointed out, when the line-up was Matthew, himself, Ed and myself, it would be the first time we had used that combination since the World Championship finals. That made it unfair to Ed because most of training had been with Tim in the boat. What all this confirmed was that Tim appeared to have got a grip on the seat. But having said that, we had one outing in the second week in Seville with Ed, and it was probably the best session we'd had. I honestly didn't know which was the best four, and thankfully it was not my decision.

Obviously, you don't want to give too much away to our opposition until you start the international season, but while we were out in Seville, we took part in a race against a crew of Danish lightweights. In theory, we were putting ourselves at a disadvantage because we had not done much as a four up until that time.

If we went out and raced badly, word would spread and, no doubt, delight our potential Olympic opponents. We raced 1000 metres on the first day, with Tim, and beat the Danes quite comfortably. Jurgen wanted to swap us around and bring in Ed for the second day when we were due to race the same opponents again. We told Jurgen we weren't prepared to do that because it would be sending out the wrong message to other countries if we lost. James was particularly vociferous that we should stay the same.

We argued that it was no slight on Ed, but that we had to be aware of the psychological effect of a defeat. As a unit, we did not want to be seen as weak. Eventually, Jurgen agreed. I think that is one of the qualities that make him a good coach. He said what he was thinking, but allowed us to give our views. He was always open to persuasion.

The uncertainty about the final four, and the fact that the Olympics was increasingly dominating our every waking thought and often our sleeping ones, too, inevitably created tension. There was one occasion, only a week before we were due to go away to Seville, when it all got to me and I did get annoyed with Jurgen.

During one training session at Henley, Jurgen decided to put out two fours, one in which he kept Tim, myself and James together and, for reasons best known to himself, replaced Matthew with first Greg Searle and then Steve Williams, who had been in the coxless pairs for the last two years.

Jurgen's intention, by bringing other oarsmen in, was clearly to bring them up to a better standard. James and Tim did not appear to mind. In fact, James said it made him realize the difference between a good and an ordinary crew and claimed it gave him confidence. There was so much difference between Steve Williams and Matthew being in the crew.

But Matthew and I were definitely unhappy. Matthew complained because he was the one moved out into the other four, who were all good athletes but not used to rowing with each other. I was frustrated because we had got our four set up really well, and we all felt comfortable. It was a good platform to work on.

What Jurgen had done was to upset the whole basis of our preparations by putting somebody new in the stroke seat whom everybody had to follow. Tim, myself and James were sitting behind that person. It would have been easier for Steve to come into James's seat and James to take over the stroke seat, because the three of us were used to rowing a certain way and style. It was confusing, and, to my mind, a retrograde step. Just about the only positive effect it did have was to confirm that our original four was the right combination.

Athough I could understand Jurgen's thinking, I made my irritation clear. 'I'm happy to do an outing,' I told him. 'But outside our normal schedule. This is an Olympic year. We're not here to teach people how to row. Yes, you're chief coach, and the aim is to get people to achieve the best they can, but in my book there's only one thing I'm interested in this year. That means I need to be selfish about everything I do.'

CHAPTER 24

TASTING BLOOD,
TASTING DEFEAT

How much does it hurt? That's the question that must pass through many people's mind as they watch the end of any boat race. The features contorted into gargoyles of agony, with some of the participants barely able to lift themselves back into their seats after they have collapsed over the line.

Like all endurance sports, whether marathon running, cycling or rowing, it's inevitable that you will suffer at some stage as the lungs desperately seek oxygen to fuel the muscles, but the strange thing is that the bigger the event, the less likely you are to feel the pain. In the build-up, you can't help thinking, 'Oh, bloody hell. I've got to go out and row. This is going to be really painful. This is going to really hurt.' Yet, I've found over the years that when you go into an event with that mental attitude, it actually turns out to be a lot less painful than you expect it to be. It does hurt, of course, but maybe mentally you switch off from it. You get used to it.

You're so finely tuned for the last race, the final of an Olympics, that, if you're getting problems of the limbs screaming, then you're not in the physical shape to win anyway. It's all about pacing, about getting the best out of yourself, to go as fast as possible between A and B. If you start feeling your chest tighten and your legs are working harder than they should be, you're not going to last the distance.

There is one certain truth about rowing. When you win, it's not as painful as when you lose. In Atlanta, for example, physically I felt fine, although I admit that on TV I looked absolutely drained. It might have been thought, 'How could he row another stroke?' In reality, the expression was one of relief, that I'd been released from the mental pressures, not the physical demands of the race itself.

It's what you've trained to do. You've been through the process so many times in the build-up towards the event. It's easier within a race than it is when you're preparing for it. When you're training and doing race-pace pieces it seems to be so much more painful. All you're thinking about is trying to row well and trying to clock a fast time, competing against other boats which are not actually alongside you.

There are races, particularly early-season, when you're side by side and you've got to push harder than you want to push. That's when it's not very nice. But I've done that so many times that I'm almost immune to it. Maybe you will go to the first World Cup race, and after crossing the line, you'll taste blood from your lungs, because, however hard you've trained, you can't reproduce the effects of a race. You're using parts of the lungs that you don't normally need.

You get that a small amount within the earlier races, but you're fine-tuning your body so that when it comes to your last race, your legs are not hurting, at least not so much. The whole body runs on automatic as you settle into the pace required to get the best out of yourself and your crew for that middle part of the race.

I like to race next to another boat rather than against the clock. Maybe it's because I'm lazy. I just do what I have to do to beat that crew, and no more, whereas in a time-trial you have to row as fast as you possibly can against the clock. Racing side by side, once you've taken the initiative you can relax and take control. Conversely, if you're down, the effort required in closing that gap can be excruciatingly painful. That's how it felt in our pairs trials final in April 2000, with the Olympics just five months away.

We had reached that point with the formation of the four still not formally clarified, although we all knew in reality that Jurgen's decision was a foregone conclusion. Until that time we had been training in pairs, but once these national trials were over, we would move into a four in readiness for the first World Cup races. It had been evident since the turn of the year that the four would be Matthew, myself, James and Tim.

On the face of it, the only possible doubt involved Tim and Ed. Tim, it will be recalled, had been training with us until December 1998, then went off for his operation and it was hoped he would be back. When it became obvious that he would not be for perhaps three months, Ed was brought in. It was always said by Jurgen that Tim had not lost his place. Ed was just being brought in as cover.

As it happened, Ed took part in the 1999 World Championships and we had a fantastic row. Tim also performed very well in the eight, but it was very difficult to say: 'Well, thanks Ed, you've been a great sub, but you're out of it again now and Tim's back in.'

That's why it was dragged out as long as it was – to be fair to Ed. But a decision had to be made, with the first international regatta, the first World Cup at Munich, looming in June.

In theory, the crew would consist of those who had performed best over the winter in the various assessments, a 2000-metre ergo test, and a British 'regatta' of coxless pairs at Nottingham, in conjunction with the continual monitoring of performances in training by Jurgen. After the seat-racing in Seville, we all knew what the score was. Matthew and I had been in every combination of the four, and Tim and James had come out best of the others.

During the national trials at Nottingham, 22 oarsmen would be competing for 14 Olympic places – the eight, coxless four and coxless pair. Although I felt that most of the seats had already been decided in Jurgen's mind, it was considered a last-chance saloon for eight rowers.

Assuming that I didn't continue after Sydney, this would be the last time that Matthew and I would row together seriously in a pair, and it was a strange feeling as we prepared for it. Before then, I would also do my last ergo test. For that I was thankful.

It took place on my birthday, 23 March. They were never my favourite days, and as this would almost certainly be my last-ever ergo test, I'd built it up in my mind. With the problems I'd had I could never predict when I would be at my best and when not.

Ed went before me and wasn't going well, so he stopped. He knew that he'd have to do it again. When I got on the machine, I felt quite good. I thought, 'Yes, I can do quite a good test here...'

I knew that if I stopped I wouldn't want to do it again. I finished the distance, although going very slowly by the end of it, and on the video clip that was shown on television it appears as though I blacked out and collapsed. It was true that I was physically and mentally exhausted, but I knew what was going on around me. It just takes a little while to recover. The oxygen demands that you put on your body are so great that your body automatically closes down areas that are not being used to try and fuel other areas that demand it. I felt pretty similar to that, as I will relate later, when we crossed the line in our final in Sydney.

When you're fully fit, you always get close to that state. James always collapses and falls all over the place after an ergo test. He's done what he's supposed to be doing but you know he's not quite all there, but I think that's more the mental than the physical effect of the exertion. I came last in the group and I had the option of doing the test again, as Ed did, but decided against it. I remained confident that I was still as good as anybody once I got out on the water.

As Matthew and I prepared for the pairs in the two and a half weeks before the Nottingham trials, there was never a stage when Matthew and I felt that it was going well and we were in command of what we were doing. I don't know why that should have been. It was certainly not complacency.

Matthew and I were well aware that Tim and James, in particular, were determined to beat us. They rarely got that opportunity, so you couldn't blame them, and, anyway, James was always slightly nervous, if unnecessarily so, about his seat because of the threat from Greg Searle. 'The satisfaction gained from beating the best pair in history,' James had said in a *Daily Telegraph* article he wrote, 'will be immeasurable.' We knew we were in for a tough period.

James likes to tell the story of how the first time I met him, he was trialling for the coxless pairs in the Junior World Championships. I was coaching the group. James forgot to do up the gate that keeps the oar in place and after a couple of strokes he fell in. Not the most auspicious of starts.

You can't fail to notice James amongst most rowers. He wears an ear-ring, has a penchant for dying his hair and has a tattoo on his left ankle. He also possesses an almost obsessive desire to win. While there was a tendency for some of us to be occasionally lax in training, James, a former junior world gold medallist, wouldn't allow that.

He was so ferociously hungry for an Olympic gold that he was constantly seeking perfection, even in training. He was forever haranguing Matthew and me. It did provoke disagreements. We'd all go out for a certain session, and Matthew and I would want to do the work in a certain way, leaving something in hand, while James would want to approach it like a bull in a china shop. It didn't matter how well we'd done, it wasn't good enough for James. He was not used to success and that made him so intense that it boiled over at times.

However, James responded to the challenges he was set really well during the winter of 1999–2000. Even when we had those seat races in Seville, when Matthew and I were ever-constant in the four, it boosted James' confidence that he came out slightly better than Greg Searle.

There was a period later in the year when James and his Danish girlfriend, Emily, the daughter of an Olympic gold medallist in the coxless fours, split up. They were sharing their house with Luka Grubor and, by all accounts, it was slightly reminiscent of TV's *Men Behaving Badly*. Emily, who was a student in Reading, moved out and went to live closer to her college for a while. James was pretty shocked about the whole thing and it hit him rather hard. His initial thoughts were that his relationship was more important than anything else he was doing. He lost all his motivation to train. He did the work, but his heart wasn't in it: that was obvious for a while. We did discuss it as a group, but we played it down. I didn't think it would jeopardize everything. It just took James a while to get his head round it. He wears his heart on his sleeve and is up and down about a lot of different things. Anyway, before the Olympics he and Emily got back together and she travelled over to Sydney.

Returning to those Nottingham trials, Matthew and I knew what we would be up against when we completed a timed piece of work over 2000 metres at Leander, 10 days before. We finished over 10 seconds behind Tim and James. The following day, we came down for training and I went to go straight in the boat, but Matthew insisted we went for a jog first, which we don't enjoy. As we did so, Matthew looked at me intently and said: 'We're going to win this trial.' I replied, 'OK, then. But how are we going to do it?'

Matthew's answer was, 'Right, we're 10 seconds behind. We've got 10 days. We've got to look to improve by a second a day'. It was a lot to ask for, but that gave us the motivation, having been thumped, to do something about it.

In fact, so concerned was I about my performance at that moment that I went to see Jurgen to discuss the situation. The fact that Matthew and I weren't working very well in the pair was, frankly, to a great extent my responsibility. It's like tennis, in which, even between matches, players talk about losing their timing of shots. The same kind of thing had happened to us. It was probably because we were trying too hard, knowing that, compared to others, we'd missed quite a lot of work in the pairs. Out in Seville, for instance, Matthew and I were always in the four, whereas the others were in the pair or the four. Certainly, they were in pairs a lot more than we were.

Then, after Seville, we had two weeks to the Eights Head, which again is very different from fours rowing and pairs. Looking back, we'd probably been out of the pair for too long and were technically not rowing that discipline enough to get the best out of it. I found it very frustrating. Flat out for short bursts we were still the best in the country; but at cruising speed we were putting more energy in than we were getting out. It was certainly not for any lack of trying. In fact, we were trying to use pure power to compensate, and were pulling the boat apart rather than in the same direction. When we got back into the four it all clicked again.

I'd experienced the phenomenon before, and eventually you correct it. But I have to confess that I even went so far as to suggest to Jurgen that Matthew would go better with Ed at the trials. I knew I was taking a major risk with my whole future by being so candid. If I stepped out of that door, albeit temporarily, would I have it slammed back in my face? Even as I said it, my thoughts were, 'How am I going to get back in? Have I put myself on a slippery slope from which I won't recover?'

I was in a difficult situation because I felt confident that when we got into September I would be in the right physical and mental shape to do what had to be done to win. I always felt really confident of that, even through all the low points. But I had to do what was right for the boat as a four, not as one individual.

You have a loyalty not just to yourself, but to the crew. Yes, I was trying to win an Olympic gold medal, but I knew that I couldn't live with myself if, by trying to achieve that, I destroyed everyone else's dreams. I have always believed in loyalty to your crew-mates. If I felt that I was going to stop the crew achieving what it could, it would be very hard, but there was no question about it. I'd have to step down, hard though such a decision would be to make.

However, when I told Jurgen how I felt, he was almost angry in his response. 'No, that's rubbish,' he said. 'Why do you put yourself under this sort of pressure? Why are you putting yourself down? There's no reason for it. There's no problem with you. This four needs you. In my eyes there's no question that you should be in the boat, and there's no question in the minds of other people in the boat that you should be in the crew.'

I have much for which to thank Jurgen. People may ask how much difference a coach actually makes in the success of a crew. Personally, I don't think I'd have done it without him over those last four years. Much depends on the belief of the coach being right. It was his faith that saw me through. People don't realize the intensity and direction that coaches put into the unit and athletes. Other coaches wouldn't have put up with the inconsistency in my performances over the last three years caused by the diabetes. They'd have got cold feet and thrown me overboard. Most coaches would have been scared that things were not going to sort themselves out, and would have gone with a different combination.

If Jurgen had accepted my suggestion and put Ed with Matthew, I'd have been thoroughly dejected at realizing that I wasn't going to achieve what I'd set out to do. That pairing might have worked, and I'd never have got back into the four. What would have been my reaction? It's difficult to say. It would have been tempting just to chuck it all in. But I would probably have rationalized it and reminded myself that although I was not performing consistently at that moment, I was still better than most other people in the team – and it was a very strong team. So would I have rowed in the pair with Greg? I had never rowed with him, but it might have gone well. Or would I have joined the eight? Both were always medal prospects. Neither would have been quite what I was aiming for. But six months away from the Games, having put in three and a half years of training, you don't just throw all that preparation away.

During my low points, there have always been things that have given me that little shaft of light to lead to my objective. That was the case here. As we got closer to the trials, Matthew and I picked up a reasonable amount of speed – not enough, but it was coming back. I still felt that Matthew and I were the fastest pair.

The trials at Nottingham's Holme Pierrepont course are run like a mini-regatta, with heats and a final. It was an extremely fraught week for everyone. Even Jurgen got upset when I appeared on BBC Breakfast TV on the morning of the trials final. The television crew caught me just as I was leaving for the water sports centre. I said, 'Everybody is fighting for their Olympic place. This is the last opportunity that people have got to show that they're good enough for a place in the boat.' The reporter responded: 'You can't be worried about your selection?' and I said, 'Everybody is in the trials and has to produce a performance of some sort.' To be honest I was just trying to put myself under pressure because I wanted to perform well. If I convinced myself that my seat was on the line, it could help persuade me to pull my finger out.

That had been my attitude right up until those trials. Though it was really two people – Tim and Ed – fighting for one seat on bowside, I emphasized in various team meetings that there were actually three of us fighting for two seats. I didn't want to fall into the trap of complacency and think, 'Well, I'm in regardless' and cruise it and suddenly think, 'Oh shit' because they're battling against each other to get in, and I find myself not at the level I'm supposed to be.

Yet, in reality, I knew that, out of the three pairs, Matthew and I were the only ones who knew, 100 per cent, that we would be going, regardless of our results at Nottingham. Even if we got beaten by the other pairs in the group, as indeed we did, it would have made Jurgen's decision a bit harder. But he'd made his mind up before then.

When the item was broadcast the implication was that I was fighting for my Olympic seat. Everybody picked up on it, and Jurgen got quite irritated because that's not the way he does things. Under his system, if you've done a good performance at the World Championships and there's no suggestion that you're not performing at a good enough level, your Olympic seat is secure. His mentality is, 'If you've done nothing wrong and performed OK, why should you lose your seat?' The obvious answer to that is, of course, 'If there's somebody better, then that person should be in.'

I don't really agree with his strategy. If I were in charge, I'd make it more open and competitive. It might create tension, but that exists anyway. The problem is that his oarsmen don't always understand the way that Jurgen works and haven't got the confidence in him that they should have. As head coach, he is interested, ultimately, in the long term, in what happens at the Olympics. Not at the trials or the first international regatta. He keeps his job if the boats perform well at the Olympics, not how they do early-season. In team meetings, he tends to tell everyone 'no problem' and encourages them to worry about what they're doing and not everybody else, but it's very hard for people to accept that at times.

That Nottingham final was so much harder than any other pairs race I've ever done. What Tim and James did to Matthew and me is what we had become used to doing to the rest of the world. They rowed away quite early and took a reasonable lead, which they maintained comfortably. Not only did they beat us, but Ed and Greg did, too, albeit narrowly. We felt we were never in the race.

It was one of those rare occasions when Matthew and I were completely dominated by another boat. It made you realize how all those victims of ours had felt, the crews that knew they didn't have a chance, like those at Atlanta and Barcelona. Yet they'd kept coming back for more and racing us again; in some cases, time after time. I would never have been able to cope with constant defeats. I was annoyed with myself after this one setback. This was not what Matthew and I were used to at all. It was all blood and guts on our part. We were putting in far more effort than we normally would have done if we had been on top of our game, but still to no avail.

In the last 10 or 15 years I became so familiar with victory that if ever I'd been regularly beaten I'm not sure whether I could have accepted it, and I might have had to give up. As a pair, Matthew and I had to win. There was no question about it. End of story. Everybody else says that, of course, but what they mean is that a medal of any colour would have been good enough, or maybe just getting into a final – that would have been an achievement for them. Not for us.

James said after we'd raced that, although on paper it was obvious they were in better form than us, they never felt that they were definitely going to win. That was because they knew what Matthew and I had done in the past. If we'd won, it wouldn't have surprised him. It would certainly have surprised me!

In that race, we made the best of a bad two and a half weeks. If we had got beaten by other pairs outside our group as well that would have been really disconcerting. But as James and Tim say, the motivation of beating Matthew and me was so much greater for other people than the race itself was for us. They raised their game, just like football teams do against Manchester United. We were always on show and there to be shot at.

The only satisfaction we got out of that final was that we were improving all the time. That's how we approached it mentally. We were still behind, but we felt that we were closing the gap. Jurgen said afterwards, 'Another week and you would have won.' It was frustrating. Certainly, if we'd both raced as pairs at Sydney, I feel Matthew and I would have won.

I never spoke to Matthew about my suggestion that he should partner Ed instead of me, and neither did Jurgen. On reflection, it wasn't just me that caused the trials not to go as well as they should have done. It was a combination of both of us. It came up at one of our meetings after the trials, and Matthew said there had never been any doubt that we'd row in the pair together.

While the result had no effect on Jurgen's decision, everyone was more on edge because the trial was open to the media. In all the trials I'd done before, the media had never been invited. Times were just kept between the crews and coach. In a similar trial in 1992, Matthew and I had been beaten by Greg and Jonny Searle, which was an even worse experience than Sydney. We thought, initially, that we wouldn't be going to Barcelona in the coxless pairs. But nobody knew about that, apart from a few rumours that got round. However, that was different from the times appearing in the newspapers, as ours had in 2000. Jurgen was adamantly against it. When he first came over to England, he insisted that timed pieces and trials were to be kept private.

Before the Barcelona Olympics, we did a timed piece in Varese, having missed two regattas before the Games, because of my colitis. We'd lost our last race in May. People were very interested to know whether we were back on form, or not. The times were actually pretty quick and everybody knew about them afterwards, because they were leaked by the British coaches, maybe on purpose.

In hindsight, I don't think publicizing those Nottingham trials results did any harm. I don't think it will have pleased our opponents that Tim and James, who were due to make up the four with us, were obviously so good. It was clearly not just a case of Matthew and me taking them along for the ride. There might have been a few crews around the world who thought, 'Oh, Redgrave and Pinsent aren't as good as they used to be,' but I was convinced that once we got to Munich for the first World Cup race of the season we'd show them. There was no doubt in my mind.

It was also an important boost for James and Tim. Although they don't get as much coverage as me, media-wise, it did enhance their reputation. Yet, James remained frustrated, despite what they had achieved. He felt that, if you read the reports, he wasn't even in that boat with Tim. The accent was very much on Tim, because of all he'd been through, and how he'd fought his way back.

As far as James was concerned, it was all about 'Foster's done this and Foster's done that.' He added, sarcastically: 'Bloody hell, wasn't I in that boat? Apparently Tim did it all on his own.' He said it without malice, but nevertheless there was that little bit of feeling behind the scenes. Somebody had to point out to him that it was exactly what Matthew had felt like in the last 10 years of rowing with me. Not just at national trials but at Olympic Games.

The newspapers had been labouring the point about Tim's back, but he hadn't had a problem with that for nine months. He'd trained every day on his own, or with the eight squad. We knew he hadn't got a problem and how well he was performing. But it was only seized upon by the media because he'd actually demonstrated his well-being in a race. It was understandable, but nevertheless very difficult for all the athletes.

The press announcement of who was in the four was made officially on Friday morning, 14 April, at Leander. It still had to be formally confirmed to us, too. Jurgen called us all together, including Ed, at 7.30 that morning and told us what was happening. He said that Matthew had performed outstandingly during the winter and had demonstrated that he'd moved on in all aspects. James had also made a big improvement. Jurgen said that I had done enough to keep my position and that he had no doubts about me at all, and finally told us that it was, as we'd always known, between Tim and Ed. He said, 'Tim's in, but Ed shouldn't think of himself as a loser.' Ed would go for the pair with Greg, with whom he been rowing almost constantly since February.

Jurgen asked if anyone wanted to say anything. Matthew said it was obvious to all of us that Tim was back to where he was before, and above Ed. I said nothing. Ed then said that it had been totally fair. 'I'm not surprised at the decision,' he said. 'Now I can concentrate on the pair and get going as well as possible. But if anyone's got a problem on bowside, I'm ready and available.' Ed was very philosophical about it all, at least on the surface. He told one reporter, tongue-in-cheek, 'I enjoyed the four, I've done a lot in the four and achieved a lot, but eventually you outgrow that and you've got to move on. It's that time for me.' That made me laugh. I thought it was a nice touch.

In truth, I felt for him. It had never happened to me – not being selected for a crew – at least, not since those Abingdon boys spurned the chance of rowing with me back in 1978, and I had known nothing about that until later. In the whole of my career, I've never known that situation. Perhaps it's as well. I don't know how I would have responded. Being the best for so long has sustained me, even in low moments, and in recent years there have been many of those. Fortunately, there have also been the glorious ones.

When the four was announced to the media, Jurgen made a speech about the selection, in which he emphasized that it had not been a 'a gift shop for Steve'. He was anxious to dispel any suggestion that it was 'my' boat and that I had got my place automatically. While I had certainly done enough over the year, Jurgen would have been pragmatic enough to drop me if I really hadn't been up to standard. Jurgen is employed to coach boats to win medals, not be the choreographer of romantic fairytales that end in nightmares.

We knew that the first international regatta in Munich would be quite tough because we hadn't had that much time together in the four. Other countries would be more focused for that first race. That's how it turned out. Although we always felt in control of events, France chased us hard to the line and we won by a quarter of a second. Three weeks later in the next World Cup regatta at Vienna, we took on tougher opposition, including New Zealand, Italy and Australia, but still came out on top, winning from New Zealand by just under two seconds. When we defeated the Australians at Henley Royal Regatta, everything appeared to be going smoothly.

By that stage, after two of the three events, we had already won the World Cup. Nobody could beat us. The final regatta was at Lucerne. I had the feeling that we could give that one a miss, even though it is regarded as the top international regatta. But then you think: 'Well, we're going to win anyway, even if we're not completely right.'

Jurgen had given us the week off after Lucerne, but it did seem to me that in the build-up to Henley, and afterwards, we were doing more work than we would normally do. The attitude seemed to be, 'Right, boys, you're having that week off, but we're getting the work done now.' In hindsight, we certainly did too much training in that period before Lucerne. It took the edge off us.

The semi-final gave ample warning. We rowed well enough in the first 1500 metres and appeared to be in charge, but then we failed to respond effectively when New Zealand challenged us. As we tried to take the rate up, our rowing became disjointed. New Zealand beat us by a tenth of a second – the first time our coxless four line-up had been beaten since its formation. Matthew swore a little bit. I just said, 'Let's keep our focus. It's tomorrow that's the important thing.' That evening, we discussed what we were going to do in the final, where our opponents would include Italy, Australia and New Zealand. We agreed we'd have to be more committed and rely on our power more. We still felt that we could win it.

Yet, the race started for us in the way that we'd finished the semi-final. In simple terms, there wasn't enough oomph about it. There wasn't anything to give. We were tired, just as we'd been at the end of the semi-final. When the time came to step it up, we just didn't have the speed or know-how to do it. That was a real shock to the system. The race became a slog and we knew we weren't in it. When that's the case, it's difficult to summon the fight. Italy and New Zealand were ahead of us, but we were still level with the Australians with 750 metres to go. I remember calling, 'Let's use the Australians' – in other words, let's use them as a target to get back into the race. We couldn't even do that. In fact, the Aussies nearly caught New Zealand on the line for second place behind the victors, Italy.

We finished fourth, over six seconds behind the winners. There were no cross words. In fact, very little was said. Normally, when we finished a race, we turned round very quickly and got on with the wind-down, or paddled towards the medal podium. On that occasion, we just drifted for a while.

Initially, we weren't sure if we should go to the medal raft, as we'd finished only fourth. But as we'd already won the World Cup, we discovered that we should go and receive that, together with our medals. James didn't want to go at all. I was a bit annoyed with him because he was so down and negative. He didn't want to shake the hands of the people he'd just rowed against. He felt himself better than them. But if it had been the other way round and he'd been standing in the middle of the medal rostrum, he'd have expected everybody to congratulate him. Inside you may be feeling dreadful and would rather just hide away, but you've got to be as good a loser as a winner.

We'd lost. There was nothing we could do about it. It didn't matter how much you sulked, or hid away, that was fact and you had to deal with it. I said to him, 'Look, I know how you're feeling. Don't show them how much it's hurting you.' He shrugged his shoulders and didn't take too much notice, to be honest. That was his way of dealing with it. He just finds his emotions difficult to control. James's mood was improved, however, when he later went and rowed in the eight, replacing the injured Louis Attrill in their final, which they won.

We went round and received our World Cup. It was not a pleasant experience. I remember saying, 'We none of us want to be here, but we've got to use this to make sure that we're not in this situation in ten weeks' time.' Maybe I'm too good at putting on a face. Even after that defeat, we went to see the press. They said, 'It's really good that you come, win, lose or draw…you're always here.' I think that's important. You take the accolades when you win, so you've got to be sporting when you lose.

Ever since that first World Cup race, which we'd won, there had been a few questions posed about my condition in the media. Now they increased. 'Is Steve Redgrave over the hill?' Christopher Dodd asked in the *Guardian*, although, admittedly, he answered it by saying I was still good for gold. Hugh Matheson in the *Independent* suggested, 'for the first time Redgrave looked his 38 years and that, perhaps, he'd rather be somewhere else'.

Sadly, it's a typical trait of British journalism. As soon as things don't go the way they hope, the coverage becomes negative and personal. I find that very sad. You would think that a past international like Hugh would remember situations he's been in. Knowing me as he did, I'd hoped for more sensible comments than that.

However, those kinds of observation never spurred me on or held me back. It wasn't a one-person calamity. I was just glad it happened then and not the next time. To be honest, others were more concerned about the reaction than me. Jurgen wasn't happy. He said, 'It's terrible, after what you've done for British sport and British rowing, how they're having a go at you.' But I just replied, 'Look, Jurgen, if we win, I'll get most of the attention, and if we lose, it'll be my fault.'

Defeat. That was a concept I had tried to block out of my mind until then. I didn't even want to think about what would happen if we lost. Of course, as we looked ahead to Sydney, it did cross my mind. Questions like that have to be answered. The only way you can answer them is out on the water. There is a fear of losing, but you have to use that to motivate you. I don't believe any top athlete, in the build-up to a big race, doesn't think about what happens if it all goes wrong.

That failure at Lucerne wasn't as catastrophic as it may have appeared. I can't say that it wasn't a major problem, because it was. But I believed that it would spur us on. It had also taken quite a bit of pressure off us. When you win every race, people expect you to carry on doing that. They get blasé about winning. That defeat had proved to other people, as well as to ourselves, that it wasn't a matter of just turning up at the Olympics to collect our gold medals. Of course, there was a downside, too. Other crews were now saying, 'Well, they are beatable.' Instead of thinking, 'We could win, but only if Britain get it wrong,' they could now cling to the belief, 'We can actually win this in our own right.' What we had to do now in the heat and semi-final at Sydney was to row in a way that told them 'You're *not* going to win'. I still believed that once we got there, if any of the other boats were asked who they had to beat to win, they'd still say us.

There was no attribution of blame, although Jurgen tried to accept it. He said he'd over-trained us and felt that, in hindsight, we shouldn't have raced. We wouldn't accept that. We didn't get to talk about it until after our week off, but when we did, we all took a percentage of the blame. Even if we had over-trained, we should have put up a reasonable show, but we were just not in the race. Strangely enough, I had felt quite strong at Lucerne throughout the whole of the race. I told Matthew that later. He said, 'I felt absolutely f****** knackered.' There've been other races where I hadn't been up to the level that I'd like to have been, but we'd still won. That shows you it's about four, not one individual.

Inevitably, that reverse cast doubts in our minds. All you think is, 'Why have we been as good as we are, and suddenly we're nowhere? Perhaps our time has been and gone.' Yet, it never really affected our confidence. We still felt that, man for man, we were better than anybody we were due to meet at Sydney. There was no need to go back to the drawing-board and start again from scratch. All five of us discussed it, and all five of us took the blame.

When we returned to Britain, it was a bit like having a death in the family. Nobody quite knew what to say to us or how to approach the matter, even Ann's mother, who had been looking after the children. It was the same with other children's mothers when I picked ours up from school. Everybody wanted to skirt around the issue. Nobody was quite sure what to say, so they didn't say anything. The defeat affected other people more than me.

In fact, it definitely helped us. We trained much better and were much more focused. But then it probably helped the winners, Italy, as well. It gave them confidence that they had a chance, and I put it no stronger than that, that they could repeat the feat in Sydney. By this stage, there were four crews that I thought could win gold – the top four at Lucerne – and eight crews that I thought could medal. Although the Italians would obviously be a threat, they had blown it in the 1996 Olympics after two World Championship victories leading up to Atlanta. They had virtually the same crew that time as this. Would they do the same again? I thought New Zealand, who had been consistent without actually winning anything, could be a greater danger. They had been second at the two World Cup races. I couldn't really see Australia winning it.

Just over a week later, we attended a major event at the River and Rowing Museum, when the British rowing team, all kitted out in our Marks and Spencer (BOA sponsors) suits, were introduced to the national media. Someone asked whether I was in as good condition as I had been before previous Olympics. 'I don't think I'm as good as I have been,' I replied, then after a pause, added, 'I'm better.'

I really believed that was true. Admittedly, elements such as ergo scores were not as good as they had been, but my basic power was about the same. Significantly, however, I was mentally stronger because of what I'd been through. I had to be better than four years previously, otherwise I'd be in trouble.

Obviously, there were times when I felt that I wasn't quite the same athlete that I would have been if I hadn't had my illnesses. That needs saying. The challenges over the last six to eight years had been more about getting over health problems than trying to establish personal bests. Up until that time, it had always been, 'Can I do better ergo scores? Can I improve my performances on the water?' There were no barriers to continual improvement. It's the situation that Matthew's in now. It's just a question of how hard he wants to push himself, how far he wants to go.

For me, over the three years leading up to Sydney, it wasn't a question of how hard I wanted to push myself. I had to drive myself pretty hard just to keep a reasonable level that normally I would have achieved quite easily. That was very frustrating and hard to cope with. As we made our final preparations before leaving Britain, whether it would be all worthwhile, only the next month would tell.

CHAPTER 25

THE COUNTDOWN
BEGINS

As we flew out of Heathrow at the end of August, *en route* for Australia, I had just one date in my mind, Saturday 23 September. I couldn't think about what might happen afterwards. Beyond were just the mists of time, in which I would discover Life After Rowing. Even basic logistical plans, such as where my parents would be on the day following our final, and when we'd pick up the children from them...that was all for 24 September. Certainly, there was no thought of what it might be like coming home to British soil. It was a matter of keeping the focus on what I was doing.

Before Sydney, we prepared at the BOA training camp on the Gold Coast. I shared a room, as usual, with Matthew. Neither of us was as anxious as we had been four years previously and we enjoyed these Olympics far more than Atlanta. At the camp, it was good to mix with other athletes at mealtimes, particularly with the swimmers, who were getting up for training at the same time as us.

We all got into a routine of waking at 4.30 a.m. That caused some dissent, principally because Tim wasn't happy about it. I should stress that we got up at that time not because of masochism, but because once we moved to the Olympic Village we would start training at 5.15 a.m. I said, 'Well, we know we're going to have to get up early once we get to Sydney, so why don't we start getting used to that routine?' It wasn't vitally important, but I felt it could add a little to our performance.

The reason for the early start was that each day of the rowing competition began at 8.30 a.m., and you had to be off the water half an hour before racing started. The course opened at 6.30, and you could not go out on the water until then. So there was only a limited time for working on the water before racing.

As I've emphasized, Tim is always remarkably laid-back, except on the subject of his sleep schedule. He has always preferred to keep Count Dracula's hours. He was quite happy to stay up late and watch TV, then moan about how early he had to get up. Tim insisted that his body is geared to that, and that's his natural way of doing things. I don't agree. I think you attune your body to what you want it to do. If you're working night-shifts, then you sleep through the day. When we arrived on the Gold Coast, we were all getting up naturally early anyway because of the effect of jetlag on our body clocks.

However, Tim argued: 'Oh, no. I'm not having that problem. I'm quite happy to sleep in until 10 o'clock.' His argument was, 'We've got all day to train. Why don't we do that? Why get up at the crack of dawn?' They were pretty pointless discussions. We all knew what had to be done. Suffice to say, we got up early.

During our stay at the Gold Coast, Matthew and I played golf against the British javelin throwers Steve Backley and Mick Hill, which was great fun. They're both good golfers. Mick plays off five and Steve off seven, while Matthew and I are both 162-handicappers. We were one up after nine holes, and at one time three up. Steve and Mick won, but did not take the lead until the 18th, so we thought we'd done pretty well.

We spent two and a half weeks at the training camp before moving to the Olympic Village. We'd done most of our endurance preparation by then, including the work at our altitude camp at Silvretta, in Switzerland, where we'd spent a fortnight before travelling out to Australia. Now it was down to set pieces. It was more intensive, but there were fewer training sessions. For two or three days we continued to do three sessions a day. Then we reduced it to two sessions. By the end of that period, we were down to a warm-up and just one work session.

Off the water, there was a sense of anticipation, but I felt calm and confident, so much so that it began to concern me that I wasn't getting nervous enough. It wasn't until just before the heat that I started to feel the first real twinges. By the final, real nerves had set in. But that was fine. You need that. The timing was just about right.

By all accounts, Ann and David Tanner were slightly perturbed that I was too relaxed. This was not the Redgrave they had known in Olympics past. But I didn't want to be in the state of mind I had been in four years previously. I didn't want to go through that kind of hell again.

We arrived at the Olympic Village on the Tuesday, four days before our event was due to start. The following day, we attended a reception in Sydney, where it was announced that Matthew would be carrying the Great Britain flag at the opening ceremony. In fact, Matthew had said to me at Henley, just before we left, 'Do you have any thoughts about carrying the flag?' I replied, 'No, and I'm not expecting that at all, but if it was offered to me, yes, I would take it.' I asked him if he would like the honour. When Matthew replied that he would, I asked him if he wanted me to speak to David Tanner about it. Matthew retorted, 'No, I'll do it.'

I couldn't have been more pleased that Matthew got the opportunity to carry the flag. It gives you an incomparable buzz and, privately, I'd hoped it would happen to him. Jack Beresford had enjoyed that honour when he won his third Olympic gold medal, as I had at Barcelona when I won my third. It was, therefore, very apt that Matthew should be doing it as he prepared for what he hoped would be his third Olympic gold. I know the rest of the British Olympic team also thought it was the right decision, although I believe that the boxer Audley Harrison was a little bit upset that he wasn't asked.

Matthew did the job far better than I did it. That might sound bizarre. How many ways, you may ask, are there of holding a flag? The difference was that I'm far more conservative with my emotions than he is and, although it was a great honour to carry the flag, I kept the pleasure I was feeling within myself. For me, it was more a personal thing. Matthew spread his around. At Atlanta they were chanting 'Stevo', which brought a smile to my face, but otherwise I didn't betray that much emotion.

It's not a matter of just walking into the stadium. It's the whole occasion. Matthew was utterly overjoyed and he managed to convey that feeling so that it spread through the whole team. When he was given the Union flag as we were walking towards the stadium, he walked back through the whole British team, draping it over everybody's head, then back again to the front. I thought that was a nice touch. The feeling on his face, the sheer joy that he was clearly deriving from the experience, was contagious.

James wasn't going to go to the opening ceremony at first, Tim was in two minds, and I wasn't sure, but when Matthew was asked to carry the flag, we all wanted to be there for that. We wanted to share in his moment. It goes on for some time and we would be racing in two days' time, so it could be a tiring distraction. But we weren't unduly worried. Yes, we wanted to win that heat on the Sunday morning and reassert ourselves, but the bottom line was that to qualify directly for the semi-finals all we had to do was finish in the first three.

One thing that surprised me about our four was how much respect we were shown not only by the other athletes from Great Britain, but also other countries. Competitors are not supposed to take cameras into the opening ceremony, but of course people do, and everybody wanted a picture of us together. It was a nice feeling.

There were a few strange comments made to me before the rowing got under way, which summed up the attitude towards what I was attempting. An Australian fellow turned up at the training base on the Gold Coast and told me, 'I want the Aussies to win, but I want you to win. I'll be happy if you win and these three [Matthew, Tim and James] lose.' I thought that was quite bizarre.

Later, at the course, a New Zealander came up and said, 'I'd really like you to win, but I have a problem. You're racing my son.' Again, I found that really odd. I couldn't imagine my parents going up to another rower and saying, 'Good luck. We hope you do well, but we only want Steve to win.'

I spent quite a lot of time with Ann at the opening ceremony. Even for me, attending my fifth Games, it was still an uplifting experience. You have to be there, to taste the atmosphere of the Olympics to appreciate what it's all about.

In the village, we were aware of the other British competitors, but we had to concentrate on our own business. Everyone had a job to do. There would be plenty of time to socialize after our events had finished. I was glad that our event was over after the first week. It must be hell for marathon runners: they have to wait right until the end.

Several of the athletes came up and said how they thought the BBC's *Gold Fever* series, our Olympic video diaries recorded over the previous four years, had made great viewing. One was swimmer Karen Pickering, whom I knew quite well, having been on the Great Britain team together a number of times. She thought the programmes were excellent, not just from our point of view, but for sport generally. They gave an insight into what all athletes go through. Even close friends don't realize how much time, effort and commitment goes into being an Olympic athlete, and 94 per cent of competitors come back as losers.

We also got on well with the British trampolinists, who were training next to where we were doing weights. Their coach invited my daughters, Natalie and Sophie, to try trampolining, and the girls soon befriended the competitors.

As far as our base was concerned, there was a school of thought that we should be staying near the Penrith Lakes course. There were some spare beds in houses nearby, which would have allowed us to stay in bed an hour longer. But I felt we should be up and awake anyway. The only downside of our arrangements was that we had a 45-minute bus ride. It's still dark at that time, and the tendency is to drift off to sleep again.

Matthew is the type who can sleep any time, anywhere, and he and James invariably used to nod off. I didn't feel we should be doing that. We should have been awake. However, there was one morning when we all fell asleep, even Tim. That morning, the outing didn't go well and we weren't very happy with it. As it transpired, when we came off the water, Matthew reported that he had a back problem, so that most probably accounted for our poor session.

That was something of a concern to us, coming as it did between the heat and the semi-final, but I always felt extremely confident that the injury would settle down. Matthew had suffered from odd back injuries before. Fortunately, we got through the semi-final fine, and it didn't become an issue. That was our only worry in those days before the final.

During the build-up to the Games, drug-taking by athletes was once again in the forefront of public debate. In rowing, there were many people tested, before and during competition, from Lucerne right the way through to the Games. All countries were targeted. For the first time during a major championship, an oarsman – a Latvian sculler – tested positive for drugs. He finished tenth, before being disqualified, which led me to the conclusion that if the people they catch are performing so poorly, it's not a very good advert for the advantages of drug-taking.

There were four bodies doing testing: our Sports Council, the Australian equivalent, the IOC and FISA. That's how it should be. It's very difficult for anyone to slip through the net. I was required to do a random test at Lucerne, and another at the Gold Coast. James was also tested at Lucerne and had an EPO (blood test) when he arrived in Sydney. Matthew was tested at the Gold Coast and twice during the Games. But you know beforehand that if you are medallists, one of the crew will be tested.

As we awaited the draw for our heat, we discovered that we had been seeded fourth. It's normally calculated on the last result, which is an absolutely crazy system. How could we be seeded fourth when, in four years of rowing, we'd lost two events and three races? Everyone else we'd raced had lost more races in one regatta than we've lost in four years. Still, we had to ignore that indignity. What was more important was that our opponents included a serious contender in that first race and it emerged that we would face one of the top boats, Australia, in our heat. In that regard, it was a good draw because it would give us the chance to prove to ourselves and everyone else that Lucerne was just an aberration and that we were back on form.

On the Sunday, the morning of our heat, I could hardly believe the number of spectators. There had been 22,000 in Atlanta, but most of them were located in a massive 18,000 grandstand. Here, they were spread round a bit more, but it must have been pretty close to the capacity of 24,000. In fact, I had warned the guys before the heats, 'Be prepared for the noise. There's a big gathering at 750 metres to go.' Having raced at Henley when there's a lot of cheering, we were all used to it, but I was still surprised at how many people were there so early in the competition.

We were in heat one, together with Australia, Slovenia, Romania and Yugoslavia, and it went even better than we could have hoped for. We dominated the race, right from the word go, defeating the Australians comfortably. We won by 3.45 seconds, in a time of 6 minutes 1.58 seconds, and progressed through to Thursday's semifinal as the fastest qualifiers from the three heats. Significantly, our time was much better than Italy's in their heat. They recorded 6 minutes 4.59 seconds.

It was a good test, though, because Australia had been second to us at the World Championships the previous year. They were a very professional crew and would keep going whatever...unlike some, who would accept defeat readily. Also, a lot of boats believed that we weren't as dominant in the last 500 metres as they used to think we were because of what had happened at Lucerne. The Aussies were clearly thinking, 'Perhaps we *can* catch them' and kept going.

There was no chance that we would settle for second or third in the heats. Victory would mean that we would be allocated one of the best lanes in the semi-final, those in the centre of the course. That was important because of the unpredictability of the wind. Unlike track events, heats and semi-finals tend to be rowed true. Winners of a discipline will normally win every stage, right the way through. Often, like us, they will be leading at 500 metres and never relinquish that advantage. Similarly, 50 per cent of winners of the previous year's World Championships will go on to win the Olympics. It's quite a predictable sport, and that's why our Lucerne defeat was a major shock to a lot of people.

I would have liked us to race the Italians in the semi-finals four days later. As the winners at Lucerne, it would have been a great psychological bonus if we could have beaten them, too. But that didn't work out, and our main opponents turned out to be France and the USA. Slovenia and Romania comprised the remainder of the competition. The crews I believed were the principal threats to our gold medal ambitions – Australia, New Zealand, Italy and Norway – were all drawn in the other semi-final, which promised to be a real dog-fight, with three to qualify.

Slovenia were fast away in our semi-final, but we soon took control. Without unduly exerting ourselves, we qualified for the final, defeating runners-up Slovenia by half a length. It was a surprisingly good performance by the Slovenians, who showed that it was no fluke in the final. The USA took the final place by finishing third. It meant that France, whom we thought had been performing well, and whom I expected to be seriously in the medal hunt, were eliminated. But in fact they were very disappointing.

Australia beat Italy by the narrowest of margins in the second semi-final, and although both crews recorded times marginally better than ours, they had done so in a race when both had been flat out. We knew, however, that our boat could go a lot faster if it had to, and that we hadn't put everything into it. The way the heat and semi-final had unfolded for us boded extremely well for the final. It was ideal preparation. From that stage, there was little doubt in my mind that we were going to win. The bookmakers, I'm told, made us 3-1 on to win gold, which made us very hot favourites. To my mind, that was pretty fair odds. Yet there was never any complacency, even after the semi-final.

The day before the final, we met at 5 p.m., went out in front of the accommodation block and did a bit of gentle stretching. Then it was up to Jurgen's room to discuss the race. We all chatted through what we felt, and focused on every aspect of the race so that we were absolutely clear what we were doing. There were no changes to strategy. All the races leading up to the final were part of a learning curve towards that race. We had total belief in what we were doing. We all had quite a lot to say. Jurgen and I talked most. My contribution was mostly motivational. I reminded everyone of all the hard work we'd done and how we mustn't squander it now.

Tim reminded us of the last time he was at an Olympics in the coxless four and how they had won their semi-final, but in the final they got to a certain part of the race and everyone moved on and they got left behind. He didn't want to be in that situation again, not that they had been anywhere as consistent as we had. That four would have lost more races in one regatta than we had in four years. James didn't have much to say, but that's not unusual. You could see him getting nervous in crew meetings, but in a productive sense. Overall, I thought it was a good sign.

By that stage, we had assured ourselves that our defeat in Lucerne had probably been the result of over-training. It was almost certainly a one-off, but we had to avoid complacency. It was a matter of getting the balance right. You have to recognize the enormity of what you're trying to achieve, but neither get carried away and build it up nor play it down too much. Our attitude had changed slightly. What it came down to was that we felt we had to row our best to guarantee a win, whereas in the past, if we performed well, we'd win. I felt that was quite a good way of focusing our minds.

We also talked tactics – what I expected to be calling, although you never know quite what words you'll use. There was some discussion about the opposition, but not much. We always felt that what we did was important, not what all the opposition did. If we rowed the way we could row, we'd row our best. And we had to row our best to win. If we didn't, we had Lucerne to remind us of what could go wrong.

Somewhere, at their own pre-race meetings, the Australians and Italians would be focusing on each other, not on us. I really believed that they were not plotting to beat us, but the other finalists. Their philosophy would have been making sure that they came second, in the knowledge that 'If the British row like they did at Lucerne, we can win it.'

I told the meeting I expected the Italians to do something a little different from what they had done before. Although they'd been very close to Australia, when they'd raced side by side, they'd come off worst both times. Everyone had his own say. To some extent, it's to cope with your own nerves. A way of biding your time. It's the waiting that's the worst part of it. The dividing line between a good row and bad row can be very little, and the more relaxed you are, the better you perform.

It's not a reflective time. It's one when you have to start concentrating, although it's important not to get too wound up about it, otherwise you won't perform at the right level. We had to keep reminding ourselves that it was just another race, because the danger is that the enormity of the situation can take the edge off you.

That's why occasionally you get surprise winners, because nobody expects anything from them and they just get a thrill out of the whole experience. They'll perform better than the crews who are supposed to do well.

It was only Tim's second Olympics and James's first, but I had no worries whatsoever about their ability to rise to the occasion. They were both experienced enough to know what was expected of them. I was certain they would do everything at the right time and not do anything crazy. James was the youngest at 28, but to put his age and experience in perspective, if he'd been in the eight he would have been the oldest. He'd won three World Championships. It's not quite the same as winning an Olympic gold, but the next best thing.

You can't carry people. It's important that everyone in a boat can take responsibility for themselves and not need to be mollycoddled. You have to be confident in them. From my earliest years on the water, I learnt that you have to look after yourself, make sure what you do is right for yourself, and do what makes the boat go best. You have to rely on everyone else doing the same. If that is the case and everyone is correctly prepared, physically and mentally, there won't be a problem. For that boat to go its best, you all need each other. If you're worried or concerned in the slightest about anyone you're rowing with, that can detract from what you're striving to achieve. Back in 1991, at those first World Championships with Matthew, I had felt under pressure. I was the experienced one, having won two Olympic golds. This guy had been a junior champion and been third at a World Championships, but I still felt that I was carrying the pressure for both of us then, yet I had to be seen to be really relaxed. It was crazy.

Back to Sydney 2000. As our meeting broke up and we went to our rooms, I was supremely confident that we were all ready, mentally and physically, for the following day. We had the race in our hands. Only the four of us could throw it away.

CHAPTER 26

DATE WITH DESTINY

The morning of the final I woke from a good sleep just before half past four. I lay there for a while, waiting for the alarm to go off, just turning over the race ahead in my mind. As usual, Matthew and I were not at our most talkative at that time as we walked to the dining hall together. Although I wasn't that hungry, I knew I had to eat something to maintain my blood sugar at the correct level once we got out on the water.

Ann drove us all down to the course in a mini-bus. Dawn was breaking as we went through our warm-up routine. We completed our stretching exercises, then did our warm-up on the water. As we paddled down the course, I talked through the race again, repeating what I was going to call and what we were looking for in each individual area, making sure we were absolutely focused.

I was surprised by the number of spectators who were arriving at that time, when it was still getting light. Those early birds included a large numbers of Britons, who cheered us loudly. Despite our concentration, I could hear people yelling, 'C'mon Steve, C'mon Matt.' Everybody's name was called out. And, of course, 'C'mon Great Britain.' The whole area was festooned with Union flags.

It was a wonderful feeling and those supporters created a great atmosphere, but we didn't acknowledge them. We wanted to try and stay relaxed, not get caught up by the fever of anticipation. I had to keep the crew calm throughout that period. We did a series of warm-up bursts and, even then, they were a little bit livelier than normal because of our nerves. You don't want to get carried away with the excitement of it all two or three hours before you actually go out to race. It can take the edge off you.

An hour before the race, we went for our warm-up jog along the ridge at the top of the course. It was very brief, but coincided with the time of the coxless pairs event, in which Greg Searle and Ed

Coode were competing. In their heat, Greg and Ed had won with a fast time in the coxless pairs. I thought, 'Hmm, that's good for them, but that's also a good sign for us, and the eight, the whole team.' They went on to the semi-final, so the British camp had been very hopeful of a medal.

We were about 750 metres from the finish and had a good view of the closing stages. By then, it was obviously going to be the French who would win. They'd taken the race by the scruff of the neck and were looking quite impressive. Matthew and I had raced them at two Olympics, when they'd come sixth and third, so we knew them very well. Greg and Ed were still second at that stage, having been in the lead earlier on, and our main concern was whether they'd still get a medal. Towards the line, Matthew was still shouting them on, saying, 'They're going to get the bronze.' I had my doubts. 'They're going to be fourth,' I said. Sadly, I was right. Greg and Ed were pipped for third place.

I was really pleased for the French, who must have found it frustrating that all the times we'd raced them they'd never had a look in. In fact, they had thought about giving up after Atlanta, but because the World Championships were in France in 1997, they had stayed together. They also knew by then that they wouldn't be racing Matthew and me. They won those Championships, retired, and then thought, 'No, let's go for the Olympics.'

For Britain, the result of the coxless pairs was hugely disappointing, and not just for Greg and Ed. The better the pair did, the better it would make us feel. If they went well, we knew we were going to go better. At the time, though, we couldn't afford to feel any pity for them. We were only 40 minutes away from our own race. That was the only matter on my mind.

We returned to the boat for a brief chat, just going over details. Again, I went over what I'd call during the race. Then we just strolled about for five or six minutes until 'hands on boat' time, which is 35 minutes before the race. Jurgen approached me, as he often had at that point before races. He would just ask me quietly to go and speak to James, or Matthew, or whoever, and reassure them. At the previous year's World Championships, it had been Ed Coode, the least experienced.

On this occasion, Jurgen said, 'Just have a word with James.' In truth, I was anxious to keep my own focus and thoughts, but I walked up to him. As I have already said, I was aware that James had been a little uptight for some time before the final. At crew meetings, you could see him getting nervous and twitchy. He had his back to me, so I just patted him on the shoulder and said, 'It's all right, James. We're going to win this. No problem.' He turned round, and you could see that he was very emotional. Although he had his sunglasses on, his eyes were filling up and he was pretty close to crying. I thought to myself, 'This is the last thing I need at the moment.' To be honest, I was feeling like that as well.

We walked off in opposite directions before meeting up again at the boat. I knew it was important that I controlled myself and didn't get carried away by the enormity of the moment. That is not to say that you try to suppress your feelings. But it is important that you use them to your advantage.

We paddled to the start. As we went through our immediate pre-race ritual, I happened to notice that the Australian boat was called 'Peter Anthony'. It was named after an outstanding Aussie lightweight who had actually won the open double sculls at Barcelona. Normally, I was never too aware of the boats around me. I didn't go out of my way to look at the opposition. If all went to plan, it should be out of our rivals' hands anyway.

As usual, I had warmed up in a cotton t-shirt for comfort, so just before the start, I stripped it off and pulled up my all-in-one suit, cleaned my sunglasses and checked my stroke-coach (the inboard computer, which gives the rate of stroking). I didn't set it at zero yet, though, because once the roll-call of crews started, I knew Tim would slide forward and set the thing off. So I had to wait until he had done that before re-setting it. Then I took a last mouthful of water from a bottle.

Tim turned round and wished me and Matthew luck, while James patted me on the back. We never went in for ostentatious gestures of encouragement before a race. I said, 'Let's make sure that we're keeping it long,' and made a few final points about staying relaxed and in control of what we were doing.

Before the start of the rowing regatta, all the crews were concerned about the weather, and rightly so, because it could turn at any time. We were very fortunate. We had nothing like the poor conditions the canoeists had to contend with. By the time the canoe finals were held on the same course on the last day of the Olympics, it was really rough and would have been unrowable. Knowing that the regatta had to finish at a certain time, what would the organizers have done? Cancel it, with no Olympic medals presented? Or awarded medals on the basis of time trials? It doesn't bear thinking about.

In fact, conditions were excellent. The water was fairly calm and, as we had paddled down, a very light wind was blowing straight across from the direction of lane one. Just before the start, it changed to a very slight head-wind, which I was sure wouldn't suit our rivals. I couldn't have felt more pleased. Our warm-up bursts had gone well. Everything felt good. I thought, 'We're going to win this. We're going to win this by quite a long way.'

In fact, the wind was changing all the time, almost between one minute and the next. I knew that if it turned into a slight tail wind, it would favour lane six; if it stayed as a slight head-wind, it would favour lane one. We were in lane three. My only concern was that if it turned into more of a cross-head wind, the Americans in lane one would have a huge advantage. But I couldn't really see them doing anything, anyway. If it came down to a tail wind, then New Zealand, Australia and Italy would have a slight advantage. However, there would never be that much difference from one lane to the next, and Italy were adjacent to us. As there was hardly any wind, it was not a big issue.

With two minutes to go, the clogs that held the bows of the boats in position rose out of the water. These devices are used nowadays in championship events and, as well as keeping the boats straight, which is particularly important in a cross-wind, they also avoid false starts. As we were sitting there, I looked round instinctively to reassure myself that we were straight and thought, 'This is a bit unreal, really, but I'm not quite ready for this now.' It was almost as though I had enjoyed it so much, I didn't want to disturb the moment.

I've never had that feeling before. It was nothing like Los Angeles, where I went through a controlled panic, when I was asking myself whether I could actually become Olympic champion. Nor like Atlanta, where I had felt a lot of pressure on me, mostly self-inflicted. Here I felt very laid-back about it all. I had made a very conscious effort to achieve that when we arrived at the Gold Coast, because I had got too involved emotionally in the whole situation four years ago. I had thought to myself, 'This is going to be the last time. This is one I've always looked forward to, ever since they were awarded the Games. Let's enjoy it.'

Anyway, I forced myself to return to reality and told myself, 'Ready or not, the race is going to start. You'd better get on with it.' And with that, the starter began going through the roll-call. I slid forward and got into my start position, re-setting the stroke-coach as I did.

The starter called the names of all the finalists, from the USA in lane one, and the light turned to green. This was it. We made an excellent start, and after eight strikes we had already forged into a lead. Once we began moving out, my thoughts were, 'This is comfortable. I'm rowing hard, but well within myself and in control of what's going on.' My first call was 'Stride' at the 15th stroke. Then I gave the rate, '44'. The rate came down slightly because I was not looking to overpower it. We continued for a minute. Then I said, 'One minute, now.' Another rate. Then we settled into our race pace. We'd go through 500 metres at that rate. All I'd say was, 'Keep it solid,' 'Keep it long,' or 'Quick catches.'

Relatively quickly, we established a lead of half or three-quarters of a length and the thought again went through my mind, 'We're going to win this by quite a long way. We're going to keep moving away. This is what it's meant to feel like.' We were .88 seconds ahead of second-placed Australia after the first 500 metres, but then, for some reason, we failed to increase our advantage. I was reassured by the knowledge that as we were working quite hard, obviously everybody else had to be doing so, too, just to stay with us. If someone was within range, scrapping with us, I'd always feel that they were putting more effort in than we were and they would suffer for it eventually. The Italians had the fastest second 500, but they were coming back at Australia. We were quickest in the third 500, traditionally our strongest stage, but it was Slovenia who did the fastest last 500. I never noticed them at all in the race, although they actually finished only two seconds behind us. Other boats were having good spells, but they weren't really making an impact on us. Nobody could make a sustained challenge.

In the second 500 metres, there was the least amount of calling from me. We were aware of everything going on around us and we'd respond to anything if we had to. We had talked about that stage being the key to it. We felt that the Italians would try to make their move then and do what they had at Lucerne, even though they knew that if we were back on form, that would only get them level with us and not a length in front, as it had back in July.

In the event, I was reasonably pleased with the second 500 metres, even though we didn't continue to move away from everybody else, which would have been ideal. The Italians had closed us down slightly and after 1000 metres our lead had been reduced to .46 seconds.

The third 500 metres is where we always attempted to assert ourselves emphatically. We treated it by splitting that distance into two 250s, with the second of them, at 750 to go, the start of the build home. At that moment, I said, 'Gold medal catches,' which seemed to have a good response. In the training and build-up, that expression referred to getting a quicker entry of the oar into the water, what we needed to win us a gold medal. It told the crew just be that little bit sharper, without losing our power and rhythm.

At 500 metres to go, we were .99 seconds ahead of the Italians, and as we entered the last quarter of the race, I called for us to step it up again. As I did so, the thought went through my mind, 'This is tough and I'm working hard, but we're doing all right, and as long as we don't make any big mistakes, it's our race.' It might be suggested that any assumption that the race was in the bag could be fatal thinking because, relatively speaking, other crews were still close enough to inflict damage. More than two decades of experience told me that they wouldn't. There was no stage when I thought that anyone was going to row through us. All you're thinking about is how far there is to go. A study of the split times later showed that it didn't go precisely to plan. The Italians went slightly quicker and inched back at us in that last 500 metres, while the Australians also put in a faster time, but they weren't really troubling us. We were actually the fourth fastest boat in the last 500 metres overall. But there were different times when we would have been moving quicker than anybody else. There was no panic, no negative feelings at all. Everything was in control. The feeling was, 'The race is won; all we've got to do is to complete the distance.'

It may sound strange, but sometimes you know you're going to win the race, yet you've still got to win it. That can sometimes be tougher than being side by side, battling stroke for stroke, and your mind is completely on the threat from the opposition.

So, to the final 250 metres. As we had paddled down the course in the morning, we had gone through the calls as if it was a perfect situation. In the last 250 metres we planned to 'lift it' at several stages. Every time something was called we moved really well again. I'd say, 'First lift – go. Second lift – go. Up again – go. Last time – go.' We'd just keep raising it as much as it needed, but I actually cut out some of the lifts that we could have put in if we had to. There was more in our reserves, if needed. In fact, it wasn't necessary.

In that last 500 metres, I knew we were going to win, but the Italians were making it pretty hard for us. They weren't handing it to us on a plate. But it was just a matter of keeping the length, not panicking, sticking to our lifting routine and not doing anything silly.

In that last 250 metres, we stepped it up every 10 strokes. That's three lifts, because there are roughly 30 strokes to go. I remember calling for one just before the last 250, and we increased the rate by two pips. That's earlier than normal, but I felt we needed to do something earlier than later. That gave it the necessary impetus. After the next 10, I missed out. However, it would have been there if we'd wanted it. By that stage, the colour of the lane-marker buoys had turned to mauve. What a welcome sight that was. With 100 metres remaining, they changed to red. You're still talking of six, seven strokes to the finish, but by then we knew we were there.

I don't know quite how I did it, but I can remember looking under my armpit for the finish line, which is a line of bubbles across the water and quite distinctive even from some distance. You can see it from 50 metres away. That's three or four strokes before you cross the line. There was no doubt then that we'd done it. That's why suddenly, the boats behind closed us down quite quickly. We eased off because there was no way we were going to lose it, even though our winning time of 5 minutes 56.24 was only .38 seconds faster than the Italians. It wasn't the runners-up going faster, it was us going slower. The one thing I didn't have to say at the end was 'Wind down'. Everybody took that one for granted. We hadn't rowed at our best, but it had been enough. We had won!

As we crossed the line, the pain that had accumulated with the amount of effort that had gone in suddenly hit me. Throughout the race, the lactic acid has been building up; your legs are hurting, but mentally you are so focused on what's going on around you, and, in my case, concentrating on giving commands, being aware of what the crew should be doing and what everybody else was doing, you don't really notice it. Or, at least, not until you cross the line and stop. Then it's like a seizure. Everything suddenly gets thrown back at you. You have to deal with it then.

All I remember thinking is, 'God, this is hurting at the moment.' It was probably more excruciating than anything I had experienced before. I knew it would pass, but I suffered for a few minutes. Atlanta was more about mental tiredness. This was mental and physical torment. People talk about the *Gold Fever* series and how I fell off the rowing machine after that 2k test and how much it appeared to hurt. This was similarly painful, but instead of falling off an ergo and thinking, 'Shit, that's the last ever ergo I'm ever going to do and I've got a crap score. That's really disappointing,' I was thinking, 'This is going to hurt for maybe five, 10, maybe 15 minutes, but I'm going to be five-times Olympic champion for the rest of my life. I can put up with this bit of pain for a short period of time.'

I just wish I had been a little bit more with it and could have enjoyed those first moments of triumph more. All I can recall in the seconds immediately after the finish was giving a half-hearted wave of acknowledgement for their efforts to the Australians and the Italians. The next thing I knew, Matthew was standing up, moving along the boat and trying to clamber over Tim to get to me. My only thought was, 'What the bloody hell is he doing?' I didn't know if he was coming towards me or to James. Matthew can't really remember why he did it. I was so out of it that I didn't feel I wanted to talk. In fact, I couldn't talk. I was still desperately trying to catch my breath; my legs and chest were screaming.

Frankly, I couldn't understand how Matthew could raise a smile, let alone raise his body into an upright position. You can see on the video, as we crossed the line, the exhaustion on the features of Tim, James and myself, but Matthew had his arms raised! We said to him later, 'What the f*** have you been doing? No wonder we're tired. We've been pulling you along!'

As he clambered over Tim, it was not the most elegant bit of manoeuvring I've ever seen. Tim said later that it wasn't his most treasured Olympic moment either. As he put it, 'It's not quite how I want to remember the Olympic Games, having a sweaty crotch over the top of my head!'

Eventually, Matthew got to me and bent down to hug me. Quite how he made it, I don't know. The rigger was actually level with the water, so the boat was at quite an angle. Tim was desperately leaning the other way, trying to keep it balanced. Meanwhile, I'd got this blubbery whale on top of me and my only thought was, 'Oh, shit, we're going to go in.' As Matthew gently fell backwards overboard, my biggest fear was that he would take me with him. That may sound amusing, but the truth was that if I had gone over the side, I'd have been seriously struggling. I'd have had no strength whatsoever, let alone the mental reflexes, to make it back up. Even Matthew said that he could remember falling over the side and going down, and having to remind himself, 'I've got to kick my legs out, or I'm going to drown.' It was only a split second's thought process, but it seemed to take ages to take effect.

Meanwhile, all I could do was reassure myself that I was going to be OK – eventually. I just needed time to recover, because I felt pretty damn rough. Even when we paddled across to where a lot of British supporters were situated on the opposite side to the grandstand, I could hardly row. I was just going through the motions. But then the roar from the crowd and all the excitement really got the adrenaline pumping; the blood began flowing and I started to feel a little more human. Suddenly, I felt fine again, but it had taken that reaction from our supporters to bring me back to life.

Emotionally, I felt pretty choked up. If we had gone straight to the medal ceremony, I think I might have shed a few tears, but because of the time lapse we released quite a lot of emotion over on that side of the water. I have to admit that a few tears flowed, but just from joy. By the time it came to the presentation we were composed.

It was my job to be aware of the post-race and medal routine. Immediately after the race, you were supposed to turn and go straight towards the TV cameras, do your interviews and when the previous medal ceremony has finished in front of you, move on to the pontoon to receive yours. However, I had said to Matthew beforehand that I wasn't happy about going straight back to be interviewed (assuming we had won, of course). He had agreed. There were a hell of a lot of Brits out there to support us, most of whom had paid an awful lot of money, and I believed our first duty was to them. In my view, the Olympics are not just about athletes and their performances. What makes the Olympics is the expectations of people back at home and the crowds that are out there encouraging you. If one of those elements is missing, it wouldn't be the same event. You've got to give your time to everyone. The medal ceremony for the men's double sculls was going on, so we went across to the opposite bank and took the applause and returned the appreciation of those who had supported us, not just from our own country, but from many countries.

When we returned eventually, we found the BBC's Steve Rider desperate to get hold of us to do an interview. But to me, the most important thing about sport is your rivals. Normally, you stay out on your boats, then come into the medal rostrum and congratulate or commiserate with the other crews before the presentation ceremony. That, for me, is correct. It's a poignant moment. You don't go off and do TV interviews until later. Doing it this way round was quite wrong. It was giving in to the world's media before the sporting moment was over. It was how the Olympic hierarchy wanted it to happen, but that annoyed me.

Once we got on to the holding pontoon, the first thing I wanted to do was go up to the Italians and the bronze medallists, Australia, and congratulate them on their performances, for making the race as special, and as hard, as it was. One of the Aussies told me, 'You're a real hero within the sport,' while the Italians said it was their best row ever. That's what you want to hear. The Italian stroke man told me that the result was really good for the sport, even though they were gutted. He conceded, 'It's our best row we could have hoped for.' If they had to be beaten by anyone, they were pleased it was by our crew. That was quite an honour.

I have to say that there was one man in our boat who wouldn't have done that if we'd lost. But that's just James's make-up, and it's the one thing about him that disappoints me. As I reflected after Lucerne, if you're not good enough on that day, you've got to be man enough to stand up there and say 'Well done' to those who have beaten you. It doesn't matter what the reason was for the defeat.

Although most other people in world wanted us to win, five other boats in that race were hoping it wouldn't be the case on that particular day. The Italians were clearly overjoyed at getting silver. The Australians experienced mixed emotions. They had also hoped for silver, but knew the Italians would be tough because they had beaten them at Lucerne. However, the Australians had defeated them in the Olympic semi-final and also the year before, when silver medallists at the World Championships. Despite some disappointment, they had bronze medals and would soon be standing on the Olympic rostrum.

Eventually, once I'd completed the formalities, I spoke to Steve Rider. It meant the BBC had to wait, and I don't suppose they were terribly happy, but it wasn't done for effect. It was simply that I thought it was the correct way to behave.

Steve's first question was, 'Do you get that sense of history?' 'No,' I replied. 'Every day's history, isn't it? It's just another day that's passed.' I was not trying to be smart or glib. It was just not a question that I really wanted to answer. All the interviews beforehand had demanded, 'Can you be the best Olympic rower that's ever been?' I accept that the question had captured people's imagination over the last four years, and particularly the last few months. But you still had to be aware that what we had just achieved was about a team, not an individual.

I would have been betraying the others if I had immediately gushed on about my own feelings. It seemed to have been forgotten that our team included a man – Matthew – who had just won his third Olympic gold medal. That was a fantastic achievement, as it had been for me at Barcelona. Only three or four people have achieved that in British Olympic history, but there was hardly any recognition of that in Matthew's case because of the spotlight on me. Afterwards, I felt not so much triumphant, but satisfied with the job I'd done *with three other guys*. I have said it before, but it's worth repeating. I had not gone for a fifth gold medal; I had gone for the one I hadn't got, the one at Sydney.

I don't consciously hold myself back. That's just me. I've never been an exhibitionist. I'm never going to react like the American sprinters, pointing at the camera and having to tell the world that I'm the best. You have established that by crossing the line first. If people can't see that, or you have to go and tell them, perhaps your actions on the track weren't as good as they could have been?

People ask me which Olympics has been the best experience. Each is special in its own way. To try and pick out one Games is like saying which is your favourite child. They're all favourites in different ways. Sydney was special because of the problems we had to overcome – my diabetes, Tim's hand and back. We had just crossed the line as a unit, having spent four years together. I found it disrespectful to the others that all the attention centred on me winning five consecutive golds. That made it harder for me to enjoy the moment because I really felt for the other people in the crew. Maybe I shouldn't have, but it's a fact. I remember James speaking at the annual Leander dinner in 1999. He said, 'I want to try and get Steve to win five Olympic gold medals, I want Matthew to win his third, but, most importantly, I want to get my first.'

Finally, we stood on the pontoon, waiting to receive our medals from IOC member, Princess Anne. We normally receive them in the order that we are positioned in the boat. James, as bow-man, should get his first, but the Princess said to him, while gesturing at me, 'I hope you don't mind if I go to *this* man first.' She told me, with a smile, 'This is the second time I've given you an Olympic gold medal. I don't think I'll be doing it for a third.' I wasn't quite sure what she meant. Since it was two Olympics since she gave me that last, did she mean that she wouldn't be around in 12 years' time to give me another, or that she didn't think I would be around?

Then came an unexpected honour, when the President of the IOC, Juan Antonio Samaranch, emerged to present me with a pin, which is a mark of his personal respect for a person. Most, if not all IOC members, have the pin, and it's also given by him to a few performers who have achieved special feats. He's never a man of many words, but he told me mine was an outstanding achievement. I was totally stunned.

Afterwards, it was inevitably hectic. Speaking to the media, meeting up with my wife Ann and our children, my parents and my sisters, who had all been besieged by the press seeking their comments, I couldn't get away and back to the village until about 9.30. I was absolutely shattered by then. The other three had gone their separate ways, Matthew off with girlfriend, Dee. Ann was working the next day and needed an early night.

It's difficult to know what to do next after winning an Olympic medal. People think you should be dancing in the streets and getting drunk on champagne, but it's not like that. It was not until after the closing ceremony, the morning that we came home, that I lay on the bed and thought, 'That's it. Yes, I've done it!' But that feeling lasted for only half an hour or so. It will probably be something I'll appreciate more in years to come.

I remember after our final at Barcelona, Matthew went off to lunch with his parents, while I went back to the village and watched a bit of TV. Then I thought, 'What do I do now?' So I went to do my washing at the launderette. When Matthew returned, I was out, so he went to do his washing, too. It's crazy. You've won an Olympic gold medal two or three hours before. Now you're sitting in a launderette watching your clothes spin round.

This time, I went down to the coaches' floor, on which Ann was staying, and watched some of the Olympic coverage on TV. I saw Steve Backley throw, but I was so tired I couldn't even wait to see the last round. I saw him later in the week, and said, 'Sorry, but I couldn't stay up for your last round.' He said, rather ruefully, 'I felt the same.'

During the racing, my parents looked after the children at a house they had rented up in the Blue Mountains. My sisters and their families also stayed there. Mum and Dad left on the Tuesday after our final, while Ann and I and the children moved into an apartment at Darling Harbour.

We bought tickets for the last day of the gymnastics, and for the tennis finals of the men's singles and the women's doubles. It was nice to see the children, particularly Natalie, get pleasure out of that. She's reasonable at tennis herself and really enjoyed the women's doubles final because the Williams sisters were playing.

I have looked at a complete re-run of our final only once since that day, but been asked about it countless times. Strangely enough, watching it again didn't excite me – perhaps because I'm still living the real thing. I've heard the last bit of Alan Green's Radio 5-Live commentary, with Richard Phelps shouting in the background, and that makes me smile. But at the moment it doesn't stir me, although I know that many listeners found it very emotional.

On reflection, I'd say, yes, the race was tough, but every question that was asked of us we answered. Having said that, when I studied the video, Tim looked absolutely exhausted. He was really struggling in the last few strokes. But by then the race was over and, anyway, there's struggling, knowing that you're going to win and struggling, knowing that you're going to lose. They are very different.

In our own minds, there was absolutely no way that we were going to lose that race, even in the last 500 metres when the other boats were coming back at us. We were surprised when we saw the video clips immediately we got off the water. Our reaction was, 'Shit, that's quite close.' People still say to me, 'Oh, the Italians were really coming back at you.' Well, the Italians certainly did appear to be coming up to us pretty fast as the camera angle changed to that final shot. But we never got that impression on the water. We knew that we'd won that race with four or five strokes to go, and instinctively took our feet off the gas so the field closed up pretty quickly. It's all about judgement, and we got it right. It didn't matter as long as we didn't catch a crab or do something really stupid. It's like a middle-distance runner knowing that the race is in the bag, cruising to the line and stopping almost immediately afterwards.

I said soon after the race that, with 250 metres gone, I knew we would win. I still maintain that belief. People have misread the race. It was always my impression in the race, and it is supported by the video evidence, that the Italians, who were second most of the time, didn't really have us in their sights. They were far more concerned about what was going on behind them. Towards the finish, one of the guys looked round once to see where we were, or possibly just to see where the finish was. In their hearts, though, they were fighting for silver. It was only as close as it was because of a very fast finish by the Slovenians, who were the fly in the ointment. They were among my outsiders for a medal, yet they were only two seconds behind us and came fourth.

We all thought we could beat them without a problem, but once they started pushing hard, the fear within the Italians and Australians was that they'd be rowed down and finish without a

medal. If a crew starts pushing you hard, you become more concerned about not getting anything than where you finish. It means
there's a mini-battle going on behind you. The simple fact is that if
we raced any of those boats individually on that particular day,
we'd have won by a long way. There'd have been clear water. The
others in our crew all agree with that. Talking to the Australians
and Italians afterwards, they know it as well. The winning margin
may have been only .38 seconds, but in 10 years' time, nobody's
going to say, 'Well, they only just won.' What people will say until
the day we die is, 'They were Olympic champions.'

The clearest memories I have of an actual race at an Olympics
is 1984. The recollections that will live with me this time are not
of the race, but of the reaction to it; the genuine good feeling from
the other athletes from other countries, some of whom I'd never
seen before and would never see again, coming up and saying,
'That was brilliant!' There were British athletes – major names like
Seb Coe, who was working for Australia's Channel 7 – coming up
and saying, 'You're a legend.'

Seb had been at his height when I was just coming on to the
international scene. 'Awesome,' he told me, 'absolutely awesome.'
That was remarkable, at least in my eyes, coming from someone of
such stature. Apparently, when we crossed the line, Seb and the
Australian presenters were all hugging each other and shouting at
the TV. I found that very difficult to come to terms with. But it felt
good that something I did purely for the enjoyment of it had given
so much pleasure to other people.

CHAPTER 27

GLORIOUS RETURN

This time, the crowds were there to greet us on our home-coming when we arrived back at Heathrow at 7 a.m. on the Tuesday after the closing ceremony.

If we thought the response to our victory was remarkable in Sydney, nothing could have prepared us for the reception we received back in Britain. I was astonished by the emotion of it all – how much it meant to others. There were people who had spent the whole night at the airport, ready to welcome us, and members of the Great Britain team. Some were family and friends and people from Leander, but others were complete strangers. For me, that was really bizarre. There was a great commotion as we were inundated with requests for TV, radio and newspaper interviews. Police had to quell irate press photographers at Heathrow as they literally fought to take my picture with my new Jaguar XJR.

I never had an inkling that it would be there for me. When I walked out of Terminal 4, I saw the car standing there in all its gleaming glory and thought it had been laid on by Athole Still or Lombard, just to get us home, and I'd have to give it virtually straight back. But then Ann turned to me, handed me the keys and said, 'This is a present from me to you.'

It had always been a dream of mine to own one. She'd known that since the occasion, some years earlier, when I was watching Jeremy Clarkson driving one on *Top Gear*. Ann said nonchalantly, 'Is that the kind of car that you'd want?' I nodded, and that was it.

In the early seventies, I got a big glass bottle in which I started collecting pennies and two pence pieces to save up to buy one. It was so long ago there are probably half-pence as well. The XJR cost about £10,000 when I started. I've still got the bottle, and it's only half full...

There had been a few whispered conversations between Ann and Roxane Still at the airport – Roxane and her father had organized the car – so I had a feeling that something was going on. I thought it might be another appearance on *This Is Your Life* or something like that. Then it crossed my mind that maybe *Changing Rooms* had done an extension on the house while we were away, or Alan Titchmarsh had been along with his *Ground Force* team, and I'd come back to a beautiful garden.

Anyway, after we eventually escaped the commotion at the airport, Ann and I drove back to the house. My parents arrived with the children, and Matthew came along for a while. There were many things I wanted to say to him but it was difficult with other people around. The only chance I got was when, eventually, he went to leave and got in his car. I just went up to him and said, 'The last 10 years were fun.' He boomed, 'You're not going to go all weepy on me, are you?' He drove away, and although we have continued to see a lot of each other since, and will continue to do so, from a rowing point of view, that was a symbolic parting of the ways. Unlike Atlanta, this time it was for good.

Words were superfluous anyway. He knows how I feel about him. That I think he's a pretty incredible guy, with the patience of a saint to put up with me for over 10 years. That's been the case especially in recent years, when he's been the top dog performance-wise, but come off second-best publicity-wise, and taken it totally in his stride. I've got an enormous amount of respect for his rowing ability and just as much respect for the way he conducts himself. I hope he carries on and is as successful as he has been with me, if not more so. I also hope he gets as much pleasure out of the sport as I've had out of it. It will give me real delight to see that happen.

Although I didn't announce it until later, there was never any chance that I would continue on the water. I always remembered what Andy Holmes said about me after Matthew and I had won at Barcelona: 'Life should be more about gold medals, shouldn't it? He'll go on rowing until he drops. He'll carry on rowing even when he starts to lose regularly.'

He was wrong, at least on the second count. On the first, he missed the point. Of course, life is not only about gold medals. But who, blessed with the talent to win one and simultaneously earn a comfortable living, would reject that opportunity? No one, I hazard a guess.

He was incorrect in his assertion that I was so obsessed with the sport that I would continue regardless. There comes a time when your body tells you 'no more', at least at the highest level. And I would only contemplate continuing if I could do so for another four-year cycle. Rowing in internationals at the age of 42? I don't think so.

During the last season, it did cross my mind that I would go for another World Championship in an attempt to bring my victories up to 10. There would have been a nice symmetry to it. I did contemplate the idea of forming another pair with Ben Hunt-Davis, who rowed in the successful eight, and with whom I've rowed in a pair a couple of times, when we went quite well together. He was getting married, going on honeymoon and not returning to the water until early in 2001. I did think it would be a possibility, if we both kept ourselves fit, to try to do a coxed pair at the World Championships.

But then I thought seriously about it and realized that I didn't want to be back, ploughing up and down the river, going through all the physical demands of building up for those championships. I just didn't see any point in that at all. People have asked if my decision would have been different if I didn't have the diabetes and colitis to consider. The answer is an emphatic 'No'. You can continue serious rowing into your thirties, but not into your forties. Sport is a young person's thing. That doesn't mean you can't continue when you're older, but it's different when you're talking about top-line competition.

In fact, it was on the second day of the Olympics that I said to Matthew, 'I'm definitely going to retire. There's no question about it. There's no way I can do this again. I want you to know that.' I never really said that to him four years previously, at least not so forcefully.

For that reason, I was determined not to make the same kind of statement that I had made before. I had regretted that, having my words constantly thrown back at me. I had every intention of announcing my retirement in my own time.

Quite simply, I wanted to announce it under the banner of Lombard, the people who had supported us so well on the way to our Olympic golds. If I had done it during the Olympics or just afterwards, it would have been the IOC or BOA sponsors in the backdrop behind me.

So I ended my career formally with an early morning press conference on 31 October at Coutts Bank on The Strand in London. I had deliberately picked that day. Jurgen had reminded me when we both appeared on *This Is Your Life* for Matthew that training started again on 1 November. 'That's when I'm expecting to start preparing a team for the next Olympics,' he said, although he was well aware that I wouldn't be there. It had also been four years ago to the day that I told Jurgen that I had wanted to carry on to Sydney. I thought it would be a suitably poignant date to announce my retirement.

I have no intention of going out in a boat again. I will continue to train as part of a general winding-down programme, but I've got no yearning to do that in a rowing boat, and certainly not on an ergo. I think I've done my fair share of rowing. I'm sure Ann and the children would agree. In fact, when I told Zak, jokingly, that I was carrying on he said, 'No, no, you've got to stop. I'm locking the door.'

In Atlanta I made that immediate post-final statement, declaring my retirement, which was how I felt at that precise moment. But literally hours after it, I started to reconsider. I knew that I wanted to be part of it for another Olympiad. After success and some time to ponder, you think: 'Yes, that wasn't so bad. I'd love to continue.' But this time, no. There has been no inclination at all. There wasn't a fibre in my body that made me feel: 'Yes, let's go and do it all again.' That chapter in my life had now come to a close with no sadness, no regrets. I did race once more in the Supersprint Rowing Grand Prix at Dorney Lake, where I was involved in the organization, but, frankly, I didn't really want to do that.

The Supersprints attracted at least 10,000 spectators, some say close to 15,000, so many, in fact, that the queues stopped the traffic on the M4 motorway. The reception we had on our open-topped bus parade through Marlow was just as incredible. These are just two examples of the impact that I – though I'd prefer to say we – had made. I just couldn't comprehend it at all. I hadn't done anything different from what I'd been doing for the past 16 years at Olympic level, and 25 years in my career.

I was nominated for World Sportsman of the Year in the water sports category. My rivals were four swimmers, including Ian Thorpe, who had just won three Olympic gold medals. An Aussie journalist said to me that it was only fair that Ian Thorpe won that. I said, 'Ian who?' That was sacrilege to an Australian. He looked startled, but then realized I was only joking. In the list of nominations, there were achievements by each name, three or four lines of success in the past year. They were all multi-medallists. Next to mine it read, 'Five gold medals over five Olympics'. Just one line. It's the impact of that fifth gold that had made me a contender.

But should it? In a sense, it was the same with the BBC's Sports Personality of the Year award, which I won at the end of the year. What I achieved in 2000 was nothing more than the other oarsmen in the coxless four. So, really, if I won anything it should have been a lifetime achievement award.

Of course, I had to accept that our victory, and my part in it, had captured the imagination. There had been a lot of interest because of the Olympic video diaries. There were undoubtedly viewers who had probably never watched rowing before and we had tapped into a new source. People were fascinated by whether we could overcome what had happened at Lucerne and the problems we had over the last four years. Obviously, those racing against us wanted to win, but I think people within rowing generally feel that my winning five gold medals has done a lot for the sport. It has put it on a different pedestal. And if that's the case, I'm delighted.

I was regarded as such a certainty to win the BBC's prestigious award that the bookmakers stopped offering odds on me well before the event. Yet, as I was driven down to the London Arena, for the first of three appearances on the BBC Sports Review of the Year, I was still not totally convinced that I would win the trophy. I did, however, think to myself, 'I'd better prepare what I'm going to say.' But then I thought, 'this is crazy, if I start planning my speech I'll get jumbled up and it'll be terrible.' In the end, when it was announced that the viewers had voted for me, my response was completely off the cuff. People told me later that I spoke so well it must have come off an autocue, but it didn't. I can honestly say it was straight from the heart.

There was one particular person that I didn't mention in my acceptance speech and should have, and that was Ann. But, nobody's perfect, especially me. If she had been annoyed she'd have let me know, which she didn't, so I think I got away with that one. I would have liked to have mentioned my parents, the rest of my family and my doctors and consultants too.

Earlier that day, I had gone to the London Arena to receive the *Smash Hits* award for Hero of the Year. That was an incredible experience, with thousands of young people screaming their heads off. I was also voted runner-up, behind David Beckham, in the magazine's Sports Person of the Year category. That kind of event made me aware what a great impact our feat had had. People from all walks of life want to tell you about the feelings they experienced on 'that' night when we won our final. It's really humbling, but also very satisfying when you get standing ovations and when you get people referring to you as the 'best Olympian ever' and 'everyone's hero'. I still have to remind myself that it's me they're talking about. I don't think I'll ever take it in fully. It's not what I did all the training for over all those years, but it's a wonderful feeling all the same.

From there I went straight on to the Football Association's headquarters in Soho Square where Matthew and I did the draw for the third round of the FA Cup, before finally going on to the Sports Review of the Year.

That was just before Christmas, and by then I was already aware that I had been made a knight in the forthcoming New Year's Honours list. There had been so much speculation that it wasn't a shock when the letter arrived. In fact, as far as my family and friends were concerned, it would have been more of a surprise if it hadn't happened. But, it was still a great honour, particularly as I am still relatively young. This government has been very good at recognizing the achievements of sports people, especially Olympic sportsmen and women, but the fact is that knighthoods tend to be awarded to older people. It's unusual for someone my age to be honoured with one.

It brought great joy to my parents. Their pride is greater than anybody's. They couldn't have imagined that the baby they produced would become an Olympic gold medallist, let alone a multiple one – and achieve all the recognition and profile that I've got now. Coming from the family background that I do, I don't think that any of us could have imagined that I would end up as Sir Steven Redgrave.

If my children achieve anything, it won't be a surprise because their father has already done that. The window of opportunity is there for them. But, when I grew up, there was nothing – apart, maybe, from Sir Michael Redgrave to whom, as I have said before, we are related – to suggest that I could achieve what I have done. It was like a different world to us. I really enjoyed meeting one of his daughters, Vanessa, who was a guest on ITV's tribute programme to me, *Stars and Their Lives*.

Since Sydney, I've set up the Sir Steven Redgrave Charitable Trust. I'm trying to raise five million pounds in five years, with all the proceeds going to children's charities. It's a pretty big target, but I think it's achievable.

I have been asked by journalists whether I'm doing the charity work because I've received a knighthood. The answer is: not at all,

I'm doing it because I feel I can make a difference. In a boat I always felt I could make a difference to the crew I was involved with; now, in fund raising, I also feel I can make a difference and help other people. Not many people can say that. My principal fund-raising event was competing in the Flora London Marathon.

The whole of 2000 was amazing, not least because of the good-will. When the Germans had a really strong eight, everybody wanted to see them beaten. Maybe it was because of the manner in which they conducted themselves. Maybe I've been sucked into the euphoria of it all, but everybody seems so genuine that they wanted us to win.

One survey found that our race was the second most memorable TV moment of all time, only behind Neil Armstrong's moon landing. Proud though I am of that, I'm realistic enough to accept that in 30 years' time those grainy images of man's greatest achievement will probably still be at number one. I don't think we'll be number two.

People have come to regard me as some kind of superman. I don't think I'm any different than I was before that six minutes of racing and four years of build-up. But, yes, in contrast to all those millionaire pools winners, I have to say that it is going to change my life. Indeed, it already has. At this moment, it's still hard to quantify it, to take it all in.

Invitations flooded in. Among the most memorable events were receiving an ovation at Wembley during half-time of the England–Germany game. Standing in the centre circle and having nearly 76,000 people cheering you felt really good. I had a similar response at the National TV Awards. I was really quite shocked by that: when your peers, people in the entertainment world, some of whom I know quite well, stand in your honour, that's something quite special. I was also invited to present the trophy and medals at the final of Rugby League's World Cup at Old Trafford.

After the Olympics, it was time to re-evaluate myself and think about me as an individual, not as part of a team being organized by a coach. People have suggested that I will become a sporting celebrity, like Henry Cooper, say, or Trevor Brooking. That is prob-ably how I'll end up, although you never see yourself in that light.

Finally, I have no financial worries. Even before the Sydney Olympics, I had a lot of offers to give lucrative motivational speeches as far afield as the USA, the south of France and Dubai, but I had to turn a lot down because of the training. Now I have been able to accept them. I also hope to be able to do some ambas-sadorial work in the fields of sport and health.

I can't say that all of this has not changed my life, or my lifestyle, but I doubt if it will alter me as a person. I think I have kept my feet firmly on the ground because it's all happened to me gradually. If I had got all this attention from my first Olympics I might have been floating all the time.

It sounds obvious, but I want to enjoy the time I have left. You put yourself under great pressure, going down to Leander on a seven-day-a-week basis and doing the work that must be done to achieve your aim. At times, you do feel like a hamster on a treadmill.

People ask me, 'Will you ever go into coaching?' The answer is, 'Yes, I wouldn't mind doing a bit, but I don't want to go down to Leander every day, cycling up and down the bank.' Retirement is getting away from that, not doing exactly the same kind of thing.

I've hardly been up to the Leander Club since retiring. But when I did, I saw the others training and thought, 'God, they must be mad.' I had some photos taken in the gym and noticed that there was a new cycling machine. I asked Matthew and James as they walked out to go training, 'Where's the old one?' 'Oh, things don't just stand still, you know,' Matthew replied. 'Things have to move on.' And so do I, to the rest of my life.

My health will play an important part in that life. I will continue to keep fit because I have to. As a long-term athlete, especially an endurance-based one, you're always told that it's not good for you to stop completely. You've got to wind down and train down carefully. You've built up your heart to such a size and capacity that if suddenly you don't utilize it any more, it becomes like any muscle that you don't exercise – it goes all flabby. A flabby heart is definitely not good for you.

I may find it physiologically difficult to retire. Medical people say that being an elite sportsman is like being on heroin. Hard physical exercise releases morphine-like substances called endorphins, which create a sense of well-being. Athletes who stop exercising suffer from a cold turkey-like condition because they're no longer getting their fix.

Over the years, your attitude towards your health changes. At the time I was diagnosed with colitis, my future health was not a great concern. Even when I got diabetes, I thought it was something that would only possibly become a problem in what – 30 years' time? After all, I was a fit sportsman.

The effects of those conditions were worrying up to a point, but not foremost in my mind. But that's changed. Coming to the end of my career and going into a 'normal' life I've started thinking about my own mortality. On the day I was 38, in Olympic year, I started thinking, possibly for the first time, about how long I had left.

I know that being a diabetic means I will be slower to recover from illnesses. I would like to live to a healthy old age, but being a diabetic and having colitis, you think that's probably not going to be the case. That's quite depressing, particularly when you've got young children and want to see them grow up. But I'm told that modern treatments for diabetes are very effective and that the quality of life for diabetics is much better than it was.

The doctors say that people who have diabetic problems now tend to be older people who were not diagnosed early enough, those who did not control their blood sugar levels correctly from the start because there was not that much known about it.

They say, 'Steve, there's no reason why you can't live a long, healthy life if you make sure you control your blood sugar.' Yet you still have doubts in the back of your mind. I'm sorry, but I want to be the way I was before I had these problems.

Enough of the gloom. On the positive side, I hope that I will leave a lasting legacy. In many ways, I have been a pioneer, not just in achieving the results I have, but in my approach to training back in the eighties. I hope that I have also been an inspiration. I don't think my exploits have actually encouraged youngsters to come into the sport. They don't see me on TV and think, 'Oh, I'm going to take up rowing now.' That happens in football with people like Michael Owen, but not in my sport. But once they find the sport and start doing it, then they look up to the top people like myself. At the national trials, I quite often give talks to the junior rowers, as do Matthew, Tim and James.

There is nothing like the same exposure for rowing as some other sports. I understand that. The nature of the sport makes it less interesting to watch than a team contact sport, although we have attempted to create a more spectator- and TV-friendly version with the Supersprints, which began in September 2000. It is hoped to make them a series of annual events.

Supersprint is a Formula One concept translated to water, involving tough sprint and relay races over 350 metres. I developed the idea with Michael Davis, a rower turned telecommunications mogul. We sold the TV pictures to 100 countries.

The University Boat Race between Oxford and Cambridge creates an interest of sorts, and feature films, such as Dan Topolski's *True Blue*, have been made about it. The Olympic Games, particularly the Sydney ones, will also have stimulated interest, but that's only once every four years. It will have captured the imagination, but it's relatively short-lived interest.

In practical terms, I'd like to be involved in the development of sport, but in specific ways, particularly in regard to coaching. A top athlete in a certain sport has a good idea about what it takes to be a good coach, and much of it's down to temperament and the ability to communicate. Just because you've excelled in your field doesn't mean that you're a good communicator or motivator.

Hopefully, because you've been well coached yourself, you can put the message across. You've got to be a good man-manager, technically aware and have a good knowledge of the psychology of sport. People don't acquire those qualities without being taught properly.

I am a great believer in the old East German way of preparing coaches. Quite simply, there's got to be a university course. Students would study all aspects of coaching – the mental, the physical and the management side – then they would specialize. It's an obvious development and the biggest step forward we can make in this country. Sport is such an enormous industry today there's no reason why it shouldn't happen.

I have already been spoken to by Sport England about possible involvement. Its chairman, Trevor Brooking, has spoken to me and, hopefully, I could be instrumental in setting up a pilot scheme. I don't know whether it will happen, but that's what I'd like to do – go into universities and initiate a university qualification in basic coaching. It's the only way of moving sport on. In this country coaches tend to originate among those who do not quite make it as top-class performers, but just fancy the idea of coaching. There needs to be a lot more training of those people so they gain the necessary expertise.

In rowing, our coaches learn quite quickly. At training camps there'll be meetings on a daily basis. Jurgen, as head coach, gets everyone to talk about their session, and how their athletes have improved by what methods. That's not happened before. Even in the squad system, it was you and your crew versus the other coaches and crew within the country.

There's still a tendency for coaches not to share information. That's one thing that Jurgen has changed by giving people the opportunity to share his knowledge. Some coaches have benefited from that, combining it with their own natural acumen, and have gone on to work in other countries. One notable example is Steve

Gunn, who coached Jonny and Greg Searle from their schooldays to Olympic gold. He's now coaching in New Zealand.

But generally, we're starting from scratch all the time, and that's frustrating. When Mike Spracklen left, and before Jurgen arrived, I was the most experienced person on the team. That's an odd situation to be in. It was difficult to get anybody to coach me because they felt intimidated by my success. We'd have different people come out with us at the time Mike was departing. I valued the fact that they might have a fresh pair of eyes and new opinions, but instead of doing the job, they'd say nothing and let you get on with it.

With those who did voice opinions, I was always fair. I'd listen to what everyone had to say, analyse it, then probably decide it was wrong. But at least I listened. The trouble was that in those days it was all very amateur, in the worst sense of that word. People were just doing it for the love of it. Even now, there are only about six or seven paid coaches in this country. East Germany, in its prime, had 200 full-time rowing coaches.

But that leads me to another point. The East Germans concentrated far more on selecting people at a young age for certain sports. Here that's considered to be manipulatory, but I don't agree. Most young people like doing things they're good at; they avoid things they're bad at. Most schools do two or three sports, including one at a reasonable level – usually football, cricket or rugby – at the whim of the PE master.

The pupils who aren't, say, very good footballers go off sport. Perhaps they are better suited to more explosive sports or strength-orientated sports, such as discus or shot-put. If they were given the same encouragement as footballers, I'm sure they would enjoy a sport and get something out of it. Most people can do a sport of some sort to a good level.

When I was a teenager, I was extremely fortunate to stumble across a sport that suited my physique. I found a sport in which I could perform well, so that encouraged me to carry on doing it. Yet rowing is not all about powerhouses – or incredible hulks, as some of the media have described us. Even at our level, the four of us all brought something different to the boat. It would be quite easy for Tim, for instance, to have got depressed about the whole situation because he was a weaker athlete than the rest of us.

Yet, as I have explained, he brought a technical excellence to the crew and it was important for his confidence and self-esteem that he thought he brought more of that quality than anybody else.

It was the same for the rest of us. We all made different contributions. I always considered myself superior to everyone else when it came to producing power. Matthew had phenomenal strength and endurance and was a good stroke-man. James was a driving force in his own way. We harnessed all those elements, just as a coachman assembles a fine team of horses.

However, when you go to an Olympics and look at all the athletes, they could well be outstanding specimens, but may not actually be in the right discipline. In rowing, there's been an improvement in recent years. In the British eight, for example, they are all powerful and the right size for the sport. Some are slightly on the small size, but they are good athletes and have worked their way in.

In years past, I've watched a successful foreign eight and noticed that they were all around 1.9 metres (6 ft 4 in) tall and sturdily built, like me. If you looked at British crews, they'd be all shapes and sizes. They'd done well to get there, considering that disadvantage, but didn't actually go on to win medals. Or not often. It was all down to luck, and not much judgement. It has to be horses for courses; rowers for boats.

We've got to direct our youngsters into the right sports. There'll still be drop-outs, but at least the ones that remain will be of the right calibre. I don't think that such 'screening', for want of a better word, is a bad thing. In that respect, we don't do enough talent-detecting. In his own slightly idiosyncratic way, that's what Francis Smith used to do back at Great Marlow School when he surveyed the size of our hands and feet. Francis picked out 12 people when I was there and three of us made it to the 1988 Olympic Games and came fourth or better. That's from a school of 450 boys. Some record, when you compare it with Eton, where most of the pupils row at some stage.

In fact, Matthew was one of Eton's great successes as an oarsman. But even that can be partly attributed to the fact that he did not enjoy rugby there because he was being taught how to hurt the opposition, and not how to play the game. Rowing suited him far better.

I don't really want to get involved in the politics of sport because I like action, not sitting in meetings. However, I already have, in a sense. I was the sports minister's nominee in my own area, and used to attend a lot of meetings. I was particularly concerned with pursuing the interests of the elite athlete. I was also involved in trying to set up an initiative called 'Ambassadors for Sport' for the Sports Council, which meant going along to schools and talking about coaching and motivation.

Since Atlanta in particular, I've been invited to do a lot of charity work. I receive many letters saying, 'Please attend our dinner, please be our patron.' My attitude has been to select two or three that I want to work with, then do a reasonable amount of work for them, although I'm patron of several groups. They include the Royal Berks Diabetes Centre, which Matthew and I opened in November 1998.

My main interest, however, is SPARKS, the sportsmen's and women's charity which Jimmy Hill and others started in the sixties. The idea is to have fun raising money. It's successful because they do things that celebrities enjoy doing. We have a lot of golf days as fund-raising events, and it's linked with the Variety Club of Great Britain. We compete in their golf days and they come to ours.

That suits me ideally because golf is a passion and I get to play with some major names. My partners have included Darren Clark, Mark James and Sam Torrance. I do enjoy golf, and I'd like to play more than I do. My handicap is currently 16. I'll go round and get the occasional birdie and a few pars, but I'll also have some nightmarish holes.

You meet some entertaining and, in some cases, genuinely nice people. I think that Jasper Carrott and Russ Abbott, who are both on the golf circuit, are good fun, and so is the former judo man, Brian Jacks. Every time I see him, he's over the top. 'Haven't you been knighted by now?' is his favourite greeting to me.

Jimmy Tarbuck is another great character. At the time I was diagnosed as having diabetes he read in the newspaper about how I was going through quite a low point. He rang me at home and said that he had a small apartment in San Lorenzo, Portugal, and invited me to go out and play golf for a couple of weeks. I thought that was a decent gesture from a guy I'd spoken to only once before, although I couldn't actually take him up on it.

Over the last decade I've often been portrayed as a national hero. I'm humbled by that. Yet in truth, I'd rather be regarded as an inspiration to young people that you can make it, whatever your background, whatever your impediments. I've never really had heroes of my own, except for perhaps, in rowing, Perti Karppinen. When I was younger I used to look up to Steve Ovett, maybe because he was also a bit of a loner and used to get on with his own thing. He was also an awkward type, as I can be on an off day!

I am not what might be called a natural celebrity. I'm quite happy at, say, charity events to talk to strangers, but I am not at ease surrounded by a lot of people I don't know. A newspaper once asked me who I'd most want to be with on a desert island. My reply was that I'd be quite happy to be by myself.

I've never modelled myself on anybody, either. I was guided a lot by Mike Spracklen. He has always been the key to my philosophy. Although my ideas have changed a lot over the years with Jurgen, much of what Mike taught me in those early days has still stayed with me.

While I have never hero-worshipped those with talent, I have great respect for anybody who has a particular gift and uses it to the best of their ability. Those you would not put into that category would be people like George Best, who had a tremendous talent, but wasted it. He thrilled millions of people with his skill, but not to the degree that he could have done. That is unforgivable.

Not everybody can rise to the top within their sport, but if they've got a reasonable amount of talent and get the best out of it, I respect that. What I don't like is the peculiar British trait for supporting the underdog. We see it every time a lesser team meets a big-name club in the FA Cup final.

Admittedly, I was very much like that, too, when I was young. But that soon changes when you're in the position of being favourite yourself and you appreciate the pressure that's on you to perform. When Seb Coe was racing, I remember thinking at 1500 metres that he *was* going to win. There was no question about it. The pressure he would have felt was the same that I experienced, particularly at Atlanta. In that situation, I wanted *him* to win, not an inferior competitor who might get lucky on the day. If the underdogs play well and win, that's fair enough. But generally I will support class rather than plucky losers.

Most people's last day at work means party time. For me, the events at Penrith Lakes were the culmination of four years' work, or to look at it another way, 24 years' hard labour, punctuated by moments of glory and desperate periods of uncertainty and desolation, since Francis Smith first took me down to the River Thames one afternoon and introduced me to a fascinating sport called rowing.

Thanks, Francis. That was some skive...

CHAPTER 28

A NEW BEGINNING

I wrote those final words after Sydney nearly four years ago. Since then, life has been frenetic. Immediately after the 2000 Games everybody wanted a piece of me, and I received many requests to appear on TV and in advertisements, as well as numerous invitations to give motivational talks.

But the most important date in my diary was my investiture as a knight on 1 May 2001. I understand that the British Olympic Association proposed that I should be knighted immediately I returned to the country from Sydney. The answer apparently came back that, although I was an excellent candidate, to do that would be contrary to normal protocol. In fact, I believe that's not strictly true. Apparently, Sir Francis Drake was knighted as he arrived back in port...

I can't say a knighthood hadn't crossed my mind. However, I was aware that generally you've had to achieve something in more than one field and it is bestowed on you very much later in life. All the same, there was so much talk about it in the media that there probably would have been a public outcry if it hadn't happened.

Three years on, I still don't see myself as Sir Steven Redgrave and it feels odd when someone calls me that. I have to remind myself, 'Of course, yes, I'm knighted, aren't I?' I'm still the same person. I just see myself as someone who's enjoyed sport, got a lot of fun out of it and received a lot of plaudits along the way. I don't look at my honour as an award from the Queen, or from the government.

I see it as recognition by the British public.

It means a lot to me and my family and is a reward for all the years of hard work and dedication, ploughing up and down that river. People often ask, 'What means more to you, your knighthood or your Olympic medals?' My response is that they're very different. Your Olympic medals are special; you've actually achieved them on your own merits. Without them, you would not have been considered for a knighthood.

I imagine Clive Woodward would say the same about his knighthood if asked to compare it with his England team winning the rugby World Cup. As I have written previously I did go along and have a chat with his men before the 1999 World Cup. I had no direct involvement in 2003, but I gather from meeting some of the players that they still talk about the motivational ideas I raised, which is very gratifying.

I spoke to Clive at the 2003 BBC Sports Personality of the Year awards, at which I was presented with the most prestigious of my accolades since Sydney, the gold award, having been voted top of the viewers' poll of all 50 winners since the programme began. Clive told me that all the England rugby boys had been texting their votes for me, some actually during the programme! I was honoured to win, although I have to confess I did find it rather bizarre. How can you judge someone who was the winner in one year against those who have won over the other 49 years? And what about those who haven't won over that period, but should have?

Fortunately, for me, in programmes about the best sporting moment and the best sportsman, I've tended to come out very highly. In one poll I was even voted among the 'top 100 Great Britons'. David Beckham was around thirtieth, and I was a couple of places behind him. Bobby Moore was also there.

There were others on the list, of course, who had made significant contributions to society as a whole: people who had been responsible for important inventions or great medical advances. And yet, here we were, mere entertainers – which is how people in sport can be categorized – who should not have even be anywhere near that list. I'm quite certain that, if the process is repeated in 50 years, I will not be there. Nor will Beckham. It's all about timing. Still, I'm extremely honoured to have won the BBC award, particularly as it was revealed that my vote was double that of anyone else.

In the back of your mind, though, you do wonder quite how long the public appreciation is all going to last. Would it all dwindle by the build-up to Athens 2004? Thankfully, it hasn't so far.

I've been fortunate. Because of my knighthood, my achievements at Olympic level and a combination of the accolades I've received, I seem to have been propelled into an elite category. I suppose if there's a comparison it would be with someone like Henry Cooper. The British people still admire and look up to him even though he never won a world title. Bobby Moore is obviously another character who transcended sport to become a national icon.

I've become known a well-known figure through my work with the 2012 Olympic bid, through television appearances and through being regarded as 'an achiever'. It's rather like Gary Lineker being recognized by today's children as the guy who does the crisp adverts and presents football programmes, rather than because he was once an outstanding England striker. Neither of us is thought of simply as an ex-sportsman.

Speaking of which, I have to admit that there was a period when I did reconsider my decision to retire. Let me explain by taking you back to the 1 September 2003, just before the third anniversary of the day I won my fifth Olympic gold medal at Sydney.

I was out for a run, something I still enjoy doing in my retirement from rowing, after a lifetime of maintaining myself in top condition. It also allows me to get some clarity into my thinking. During this particular run I was contemplating a conversation I'd had recently with James.

It was just after the rowing World Championships in Milan. I had been out there as part of the BBC team, and had watched Matthew and James get well beaten in the pairs. Afterwards James planted an idea that got me thinking when he admitted they were considering making the switch to a four. If that was their plan, I thought, as I ran along, I may as well get myself back in condition and join the boat too. Initially it was just an idle thought. Then I began to think about it more seriously.

When I concluded my original story, I was absolutely determined that would be the end of my career on the water. But here I was, once again, considering a return to it. I know it sounds crazy, but it was not unfeasible. I had attended World Championships and seen medals being won by oarsmen that I used to be able to beat very easily. And I thought to myself: 'Well, it's three years from Sydney, but I'm still reasonably fit.'

I knew I was not good enough to be in the pair, but I believed I could still be an asset in the four. If I didn't make the four, then there was always the eight, which also had a chance of an Olympic medal. If necessary, I could travel as the 'spare' man for the Olympic team. Even if I failed to make the Athens squad, there was always the World Championships, in which I could row for Britain in the coxed pair or coxed four.

The ideal, of course, would have been to win an Olympic gold, but it was more about a personal challenge. I would be in a similar situation to that of Ed Moses. When I first thought about the comeback he was contemplating, I thought: 'Why the hell's he doing this at the age of 48?' But now I understood his motivation.

If I did return it would be some achievement at 42, the same age as Guy Nickalls had been when he had come back to win a gold in the British eight – even though that was in 1908!

I might not have been the best physical athlete in the squad. I wouldn't have been able to get back to my personal best performances, but experience can sometimes help other people achieve their aspirations. There were times even before the 2000 Games when I really felt I was struggling with the diabetes and that I was holding back the four, and Jurgen would tell me: 'The unit needs you.' What would his reaction be now to my suggestion?

If I'd had no health problems, I would have been confident about making a comeback. But could I do it as a diabetic? I'd certainly pushed myself through the Olympic build-up, but I recalled how hard it had been. The mental strength I had needed to grind out the training during the first two years of diabetes paid off within that boat. After I had been diagnosed with diabetes and, earlier, colitis, I was never the same athlete, but I was able to stay at the top of the sport, albeit hanging on by my fingernails by the time of the Sydney final.

I remember James observing in the BBC's *Gold Fever*, 'I never realized you were that ill'. I was still training, still performing. Occasionally, of course, they'd seen me struggle and seen me fail. I hadn't tried to disguise the problems I faced, but it was my own battle, not theirs. I had to deal with that and get through it. The human body is quite peculiar in how it gets performances out of itself.

But what about the time lapse? The assumption is that three years of not doing much would take its toll. Maybe I could prove that theory wrong. I'd been training and keeping fit for nearly thirty years; it doesn't just go away. How many people can go out and run quite hard for 45 minutes, as I still can?

And so the arguments raged within my mind.

There were financial reasons for not attempting a comeback. Everybody assumes that, having won five Olympic golds, I'm a multi-millionaire. The income since has allowed me to rebuild our house, but I'm certainly not financially secure. I knew that if I went back into training for the next 12 months it would be really tough.

From a more positive point of view, it would be back to the old routine of two or three training sessions at Henley and back home by mid-afternoon. I wouldn't have to worry about chasing around the country, or the world, to carry out speaking engagements. In some ways that was quite appealing.

In the end I let it drift until it was too late to do anything about it. If there had been 18 months, I could have made it. But ten months? That just wasn't possible. I knew that I'd never get back to my best by the time of the Olympics with the medical conditions I've got. I could have regained maybe 95 per cent of my fitness. It might have been enough, but probably not.

I did actually speak to Jurgen, who was quite intrigued to start with but, after some reflection on it, advised me not to go ahead. He was right, of course, but it was fun thinking about it. Everybody dreams, and even a five times Olympic gold medallist dreams of doing it again.

The Olympics have remained at the forefront of my mind, however. The 2012 Games and the possibility that they may come to London, that is. I was involved in the bid from the start when the British Olympic Association asked me to be involved as a member of what was called the Stakeholders Group.

Initially, it was a matter of persuading the government; the Mayor of London, Ken Livingstone; and the City to back us.

It was a long process, convincing everybody. I thought Ken Livingstone would be a very difficult 'sell', as he's not known as a great sports fan. But he appreciated the potential benefits to London immediately, was very supportive of the idea, and, with the BOA, tried to convince the government it was the right thing to do. I was extremely impressed by his reaction. Many people simply regard him as 'Red Ken', the left-wing politician. When you actually work with him, you appreciate that he is totally committed to improving London in whatever way he can. He recognized straight away that a successful bid would also produce benefits such as the regeneration of that area of east London and improved transport.

The government was much more difficult to convince, which in 2003 was not altogether surprising. The Iraq War had started at that time. Nobody knew how long that would go on or the expense it would involve. A bid for the Olympics in nine years' time could have been regarded as somewhat irrelevant. Inevitably, it was slow process, but that was understandable considering the problems the government had experienced over the Dome and the new Wembley. Instead of thinking about where they could cut corners, however, they were actually looking at it from the opposite point of view. How much was this going to cost if we actually won? They didn't want to proceed down the road and find it would cost far more than predicted.

The important thing was that all parties had to be 100 per cent committed. Initially, it looked unlikely that the government would back the bid. There was a feeling that the expense of it outweighed the benefits. But they were swayed by public opinion that we should be bidding. The government left it late, but in the end came out 100 per cent behind the bid, with Tony Blair helping to launch it.

I assumed that the South East in general, and particularly sporting bodies around the London area, would be very supportive of a London bid, with maybe some opposition, and that the rest of the country would approve far less. In fact, I was pleasurably surprised to discover how much goodwill there was towards the bid, not only in England but also in the other home countries.

I've no doubt myself that we should be bidding to host the Games. It's been a long time since we last did, in 1948, and the only previous time was in 1908. On both occasions we took the Games at quite short notice. The most recent was just after the Second World War. Originally, it was intended to go back to Athens, but the Greeks couldn't organize it in time, so we stepped in.

The sporting infrastructure will be immense. I don't mean just the main stadium and the venues that will be used for the Games itself. There will also be the training bases created around the country for use by the athletes of the many nations who will want to come here on a regular basis to prepare for the Olympics, just as we did when we went to the Gold Coast in Australia before Sydney 2000. That will provide a great legacy to British sport.

Once the bid had gone in, Barbara Cassani, who is chairing the project, invited me on to the board of London 2012. I am chairing two groups in the bid process. One is the Athletes Advisory Group, a collection of very experienced Olympians – some still current – whose remit is to make the Games as athlete-friendly as we possibly can.

The other group I'm chairing is the Ambassadors Programme. The aim is to encourage everyone who's been on the Olympic team in the past to be ambassadors for the bid, together with current athletes. We've also approached other sports to help support us in our bid. We've had a lot of enthusiasm from rugby, cricket and football. Then we thought, why stop at sport? Why not bring in entertainment, the arts, music, and business as well? Basically we'd like anyone of any stature to be an ambassador and help spread the word.

People ask me all the time: 'Can we actually succeed with our bid?' Of course, there are some excellent cities in contention, but my answer is: yes, if I have anything to do with it. We have a very strong chance when the decision is made, in July 2005, in Singapore.

When it comes to the Olympic Games, I'm not used to being defeated.

INDEX